contemporary jewelry

second edition

philip morton

HOLT, RINEHART AND WINSTON
New York   Chicago   San Francisco   Atlanta
Dallas   Montreal   Toronto   London   Sydney

Editor   Rita Gilbert
Picture Editor   Joan Curtis
Project Editor   James Hoekema
Manuscript Editor   Brenda Gardner
Project Assistant   Polly Myhrum
Production Supervisor   Sandra Baker
Design Assistant   James Hoekema
Designer   Marlene Rothkin Vine

Library of Congress Cataloging in Publication Data

Morton, Philip.
Contemporary jewelry.

1. Jewelry.
2. Jewelry making.
I. Title.
TS740.M67   1976   739.27   75-25851

College ISBN: 0-03-089644-4
Trade ISBN: 0-03-089924-9

Composition and camera work by York Graphic Services, Inc., Pennsylvania
Color separations by Offset Separations Corp., New York
Color printing by Lehigh Press Lithographers, New Jersey
Printing and binding by Capital City Press, Vermont
6 7 8 9   138   9 8 7 6 5 4 3 2 1

I have prepared this revised and expanded edition of CONTEMPORARY JEWELRY in order to provide craftsmen, students, and the generally interested reader with the most up-to-date information about jewelry making and metalwork. As in the previous edition, my aim has been to integrate an awareness of the glorious tradition of historical jewelry, a familiarity with current work and its practitioners, as well as an understanding of design concepts with the most thorough treatment possible for basic jewelry making techniques. The artist-jeweler today does not work in a vacuum but rather enjoys a strong bond with the metalworker who served the pharaohs of ancient Egypt, the jade artisans of dynastic China, and the master goldsmiths of Renaissance Europe. Moreover, despite the diversity of styles practiced today, contemporary jewelers share a common attitude toward their work and toward craftsmanship in general—an attitude of integrity and commitment to creative expression. Underlying all the jewelry and metalwork of past and present are certain fundamental design elements and principles that are applicable to the work of any craftsman.

So far-reaching have been the developments in this rapidly changing field that a thorough revision of CONTEMPORARY JEWELRY has been necessary. The present edition includes new material on electroplating, electroforming, casting, granulation, gem setting, surface embellishment, and work in plastics. An entire chapter on enameling for jewelry has been added, and virtually every section has been expanded and refined. The chapter dealing with jewelry of the past now offers an outline history, arranged chronologically, of jewelry from the ancient world to the 20th century, with more than 60 beautiful illustrations. In addition, I have devoted two chapters to a survey of contemporary jewelry in North America and in Europe, again with a full complement of handsome illustrations. Finally, the appendices at the back of the book have been enlarged, and a glossary of terms has been added.

Considerable work and thought went into the selection of illustrations for this revised edition. It was my intention to show the most sumptuous examples from the past and the most up-to-date and exciting work of the present, then to reproduce all as faithfully as possible. There are now more than 600 black-and-white illustrations—over 80 percent of them new to this edition—plus 18 full-color plates. All of the technical line drawings have been redone in order to make them clear, readable, and easy to follow.

CONTEMPORARY JEWELRY is divided into three broad parts. Part I, called "History," includes an introductory chapter on the functions of jewelry, the historical survey, a chapter that traces the emergence of contemporary styles, and then individual chapters dealing with current work in North America and in Europe.

Part II, entitled "Design," begins with a general introduction to the universal elements and principles of design, continues with a chapter that applies these elements and principles to specific jewelry-making techniques, and concludes with guidelines for the design of particular types of jewelry, such as rings, earrings, and bracelets.

Part III, called "Technique," treats in a step-by-step progression all the fundamental materials and processes of jewelry-making. It is this part that comprises the major portion of the book. Individual chapters discuss basic metal procedures, fusing and soldering, forming, cutting, hammering, casting, fastenings, and electroplating and electroforming. Because the "finish" of a piece may be as vital to its success as the underlying design, separate chapters are devoted to surface treatment, enameling, and general finishing. Others dealing with gems and their settings, plus an introduction to simple toolmaking, conclude this part. Beginning with Chapter 8 and continuing through Part III, topics and procedures are organized in brief numbered sections to permit easy cross reference.

In a technical book such as this, supplementary reference materials may be just as important as the text proper. Five appendices follow the text, and I have tried to organize them in such a manner that they can serve as convenient source material for any jeweler, from the novice to the experienced practitioner. Appendix A describes geometrical constructions as well as practical procedures that can facilitate the layout of jewelry designs. Appendix B lists sources of findings, materials, tools, and supplies, along with an illustrated description of the findings most commonly available. Appendix C provides technical information about the composition and characteristics of the metals used for jewelry, the different types of solder and flux, cleaning and protecting metals, and other metal treatments. It also includes a number of tables on sizes, weights, and measures. A list and description of gemstones and other materials for setting comprises Appendix D. Appendix E offers practical information about studio production, marketing, pricing, and financial planning for the jeweler who is ready to set up a profitable working shop. The book terminates with a glossary of terms, a bibliography, and an index.

It is my hope that the reader of CONTEMPORARY JEWELRY will use it as a full and accurate source book of basic information. No set formulas or patterns are given, because a rigid outlook is anathema to the free expression of contemporary jewelry. Instead, I have tried to put at the reader's disposal, and to organize in the most expedient way, all the fundamental "tools" of this most dynamic craft. Their application is up to the jeweler.

Acknowledgments

Many people have contributed their ideas and talents to this new edition. Above all I must thank the many craftsmen, throughout the United States and abroad, who responded so generously to my request for illustrations of their work. The limitations of the text made it impossible to include many examples that I would like to have shown, but the cooperation of so many jewelers did permit me to sketch the range of creative work being done today. Many of the same people also gave me the benefit of their expertise in special techniques they have mastered. For this advice I am indebted especially to Chuck Evans, Ed Lund, Stanley Lechtzin, John Marshall, Paul Mergen, Harold O'Connor, Alvin Pine, Heikki Seppa, Ronald Pearson, and the late Olaf Skoogfors. Stanley Lechtzin further tendered his critical advice in reviewing an early draft of the manuscript, as did Eugene Bahling and Max Weaver. To all of these and to the many other people who participated in the second edition of CONTEMPORARY JEWELRY, I express my warmest gratitude.

Bowling Green, Ohio   P.M.
March 1976

Contents

part one
History

The Functions of Jewelry

Most people think of jewelry as having none other than an aesthetic role: to adorn the body or to be beautiful in and of itself. Yet this analysis says very little about the functions that jewelry has performed throughout history and continues to perform in today's world. Some kinds of jewelry, such as pins and belt buckles, fulfill a specifically utilitarian purpose. Beyond this, nearly everyone relates to jewelry in terms of certain associative values, that is, values not intrinsic to the objects themselves but arising from social factors such as status, cost, commemoration, fashion, or even magic. Contemporary jewelers have learned to exploit many of these associative values, but increasingly they have emphasized the expressive role of jewelry—jewelry as a vehicle for the creative fantasy of the maker, and as a statement of self-image by the wearer.

In this chapter we will explore the various functions—utilitarian, associative, and expressive—that jewelry serves. A brief discussion such as this can only touch upon them, but it may open avenues of discovery for the contemporary jeweler.

Utilitarian Functions

At different points in history many kinds of jewelry have served eminently practical purposes. We might assign to this category the very first piece of jewelry any of us are likely to have worn: the safety pin that holds the baby's diaper. It may seem to be stretching the point to call safety pins jewelry, but the Scots, who made enormous and very handsome ones to hold their heavy

kilts together, considered them as such, and so did the ancient Romans. The safety pin is a direct descendant of the fibula (Figs. 1, 47), the "fastener" that kept people covered in the long period of time between the thorn and the button. Nor can buttons be excluded from the class of jewelry, for early ones were shanks or studs of metal added to garments for ornament, often quite independent of utility. Jeweled buttons, for example, appear in the hoards of Central Asian tribes as readily as in the wardrobes of 18th-century dandies.

Another practical piece of jewelry was the signet, worn either as a pin or as a pendant, later as a ring. Fashioned in various forms, the signet's basic property was that it made a unique mark, as a fingerprint does. An image or a bit of writing was hollowed out of the smooth surface of the ring or cylinder, so that after rolling it over a softer surface like wax or clay, one could leave an impression exactly the reverse of that carved into the signet. Thus, the seal could serve to indicate personal ownership of property or the certification of documents. Great quantities of tiny cylinder signets—from 1 to 3 inches long and often showing fine, delicate workmanship—have been found in the ruins of ancient Babylon. Their use was widespread, and signets remained common for more than two thousand years. Indeed, the use of seals was not at all an upper-class privilege. Ordinary businessmen sealed their bales of goods with signets before loading them onto camels or ships, and Roman wine merchants used them to seal great jars of wine. Until the very recent advent of the self-stick envelope, sealing wax, impressed with a signet, acted as a closure for all sorts of correspondence.

Fashions of 18th-century Europe popularized a particularly charming article of useful jewelry in the *chatelaine* (Fig. 2). Worn by both men and women, the chatelaine was a multicomponent piece usually developed around a decorated plaque and perhaps set with mother-of-pearl or semiprecious stones. The upper end was hung from one's belt, while the lower was equipped with a hook or hooks for holding keys, a watch, a prayer book, a sewing case, scissors, pencils, and any number of small useful objects.

Among the most fascinating of jewelry objects with a practical purpose are those that have a secret compartment. Rings with hinged openings were popular in Renaissance Italy (Fig. 3), and they often served as reliquaries— that is, containers for relics of the saints. Legend, however, ascribes to these rings a far more sinister and delightful role as hidden caches for poison to dispatch one's rivals (or oneself, should an emergency arise). We can easily imagine a 16th-century intriguer casually passing a hand over the goblet of his or her companion and releasing the lethal substance within.

A final purpose traditionally served by jewelry is the storage of wealth. In the days before banks or vaults, the safest place to deposit one's fortune was on one's body or the bodies of family members. And, for the well-to-do nomad, jewelry represented the only practical way to accumulate capital. Possibly more pertinent to our own times is the fact that jewelry, unlike money, tends to appreciate in value. Gold jewelry and gems remain an almost foolproof defense against inflation.

Precious jewelry is, of course, one of the most tangible forms of material wealth. Traditionally, refugees from all kinds of justice or oppression have fled with only their jewelry and the clothing on their backs. While jewelry is not as easy to liquidate as, say, stocks and bonds, we could cite a long history of instances in which gold or gems were translated into cash. The most notorious example of this was perpetrated by the Spanish *conquistadores*. When Cortez arrived in Mexico in 1521, he found an unbelievable treasure of precious

objects—all in gold and all of the most exquisite workmanship. As an agent of the Spanish crown, he dutifully pillaged the country, sending his finds back to the mother country. Without exception every piece shipped to Spain was melted down, and today little Mexican goldwork remains beyond the few pieces Cortez overlooked. All told, the *conquistadores* managed to remove from the New World more than *thirty tons* of gold jewelry within a single century.

Three hundred years later political conditions in Europe precipitated another liquidation of precious jewels, but this time a voluntary one. Under constant threat of attack by Napoleon's armies, the German government between 1813 and 1815 persuaded patriotic citizens to surrender their gems and gold to be converted into currency in support of the defense. As compensation, Germans who turned over their jewelry received pieces of Berlin ironwork (Fig. 4), whose delicate tracery and meticulous workmanship belies the crude nature of its material.

The association of women with jewelry, so often attributed to feminine vanity and greed, might also be related to the fact that women themselves have in many instances been considered transferrable property. The jewelry they wore attached to their bodies or clothing was manifestly an extension of their personal worth, and it went with them. In some places unmarried girls still wear their dowries, and if a woman is divorced, her personal jewelry may be all the property she can take with her. Under some laws, she can keep her jewelry, while her children and household goods belong to the man who married her. This leads us directly to a consideration of the next function of jewelry, that of a status indicator.

above left: 2. James Rowe. Gold repoussé watch and chatelaine, 1758. Fitzwilliam Museum, Cambridge.

top: 3. Enameled gold ring with pearls; Italian, 16th century. The hinged box bezel opens to reveal a secret compartment. Museo Poldi-Pezzoli, Milan.

above right: 4. Black cast-iron pin, a typical example of mass-produced Berlin ironwork, c. 1840. Österreichisches Museum für angewandte Kunst, Vienna.

below: 5. Tzu Hsi (1861–1908), the dowager empress of China, shown wearing silver fingernail cases.

right: 6. *Potence of the Herald of the Order of the Golden Fleece,* Chain of Arms of gold and enamel, made in the Netherlands after 1517. The piece consists of a neck-chain (not shown) and a collar bearing 51 coats of arms. Kunsthistorisches Museum, Vienna.

above: 7. Ship pendant of gold and enamel, with crystal, pearls, and rubies; German or Spanish, late 16th century. Metropolitan Museum of Art, New York (Michael Friedsam Collection, 1931).

Jewelry as Status

In the Aztec Empire the wearing of turquoise as a nose ornament was restricted to one individual—the King himself. Lesser officials wore other designated jewels, in a strict hierarchical order. This is only a single example of hundreds we could mention in which jewelry indicates the social position or associations of the wearer. Of course, the possession and display of precious jewelry automatically indicates great wealth (and therefore status) on the part of the owner. But some cultures have carried this principle even further. Chinese Mandarins, for instance, often wore highly elaborate fingernail cases, which rendered them incapable of even the simplest manual task (Fig. 5). By demonstrating that they had to be waited on literally hand and foot every minute of the day, these noble creatures flaunted their status. This practice is related to foot-binding, which made walking any distance impossible.

European royalty, kings and queens alike, have always bedecked themselves with jewelry, although in recent times this custom has been increasingly restricted to ceremonial functions. A special class of ornaments indicating elevated status were the emblems of various chivalric orders, of which the Order of the Golden Fleece offers the most lavish example (Fig. 6). Beginning in the 16th century, monarchs conferred orders on knights who were especially favored. The emblems of these orders, to be worn on state occasions, were magnificent products of the jeweler's art, studded with diamonds, rubies, and other precious gems. Besides showing high social rank, orders also were evidence of membership in a particular select group.

Numerous humbler associations have adopted special ornaments to identify their members. Fraternity pins, military insignia, lodge pins, regimental symbols—all proclaim the wearer to be an initiate in a certain group. The largest such group of all, of course, is that of married people, whose symbol is the wedding ring. A wedding ring asserts that its wearer is bound to a particular social group with specialized rights and privileges. It manifests one's status as "married person." Rings of betrothal convey a similar kind of information. In some tribes of equatorial Africa the message of the bride's being bound to her husband was made all the more explicit by marriage *neck*-rings of brass and copper, which were worn permanently.

Wedding and engagement rings, in Western society normally given by men to women, raise the entire question of gifts in relation to jewelry. For centuries jewelry has stood as the consummate gift from one person to a favored other. This, in turn, has psychological implications. Many behavioral scientists feel that gift-giving, in general, is an aggressive act, because it places the receiver in the giver's debt and thus enhances the status of the giver. The ultimate extension of this is the *potlatch,* a ritual feast once practiced by tribes in northwestern North America, in which each chieftan tried to outdo the others in giving away or destroying his worldly goods. The one who disposed of the most wealth had the highest status. In any event, a gift of jewelry is almost always thought to elevate the giver.

Symbolic Values

We have already touched upon one aspect of jewelry as symbol—the wedding ring as a symbol of the marital bond. Religious symbols worn as jewelry—the cross or star of David, for example—probably constitute the next largest category. Images of this sort convey a plethora of associations and ideas. From time to time more specialized symbols have appeared. The *nef brooch,* or ship brooch (Fig. 7), developed by the seafaring nations along the Mediterranean coast during the 16th century, was bestowed by sailors as a token of love and fidelity before their voyages or in gratitude for a safe return.

A particular kind of symbol is the commemorative or memorial one. In 18th-century England the guests at funerals were often given funeral rings of an appropriately mournful design to commemorate the event. And in many eras articles of jewelry provided space for a portrait of the dead beloved. During the rather macabre medieval period memorial jewelry sometimes featured a tiny skull or even a miniature three-dimensional skeleton in a "coffin" pendant. The most institutionalized mourning period in recent history occurred in Europe and the United States during the seemingly interminable mourning of Queen Victoria for her consort, Prince Albert. Death and its aftereffects were dwelt upon; widow's weeds were chic. Memorial jewelry of all sorts flourished. A very popular item in the mid-19th

8. Bracelet of woven hair, bone, and gold; American or English, mid-19th century. The clasp is a covered locket with a cornucopia of hair mounted on bone. Cooper-Hewitt Museum of Design, Smithsonian Institution, New York.

century was the hair brooch (Fig. 8) containing a lock of hair from the deceased arranged behind glass and set in gold or jet. Occasionally the romantic practice was carried even farther, and quantities of plaited hair were worked into filigree-type jewelry. Mercifully, this vogue ended along with the reign of Victoria.

We could not conclude our discussion of memorial symbols without reference to death masks—facial masks in the image of the deceased either to be buried with the body or to serve as an historical record. Among the most splendid of all such masks is that of King Tutankhamen of Egypt, discovered when his tomb was opened in 1922 (Fig. 9). This mummy mask, which covered the face of the king, was hammered of solid gold and embellished with lapis lazuli, turquoise, carnelian, feldspar, and glass paste. The molding of the facial contours is particularly fine, and we can probably consider it to be a good likeness.

below left: 9. Mask of King Tutankhamen, of gold inlaid with lapis lazuli, turquoise, carnelian, feldspar, and glass. Egyptian, from Thebes; c. 1350 B.C. (18th Dynasty). Egyptian Museum, Cairo.

below right: 10. Ceremonial tribal necklace, of gold alloy, with a large smokey topaz; from Simleul-Silvaniei, Romania, c. A.D. 400 Kunsthistorisches Museum, Vienna.

Magical Values

The very earliest jewelry objects no doubt had magical connotations, for the view of the world held by primitive peoples is a magical one. They find in nature powerful and fearful demons, spirits, and gods. All these figures are

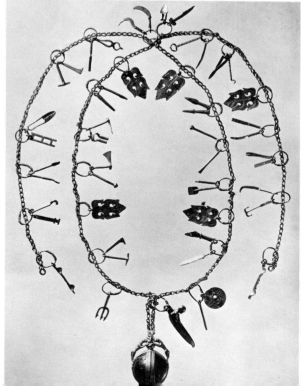

threatening and must be placated in one way or another. Animal hair, claws, and teeth are thought to endow the possessor with whatever characteristics the vanquished animal possessed—strength, ferocity, cunning, or fleetness. The needs of early peoples were elementary but quite pressing—moderation in weather, victory over prey, success of crops, defense against predators, and fertility—and their jewelry often incorporated symbols of these goals (Fig. 10). Throughout the history of mankind magical connotations have been attached to particular gems, metals, or types of jewelry, and some of these beliefs are very much alive today.

The fear of powerful unseen forces has generated millions of protective images and devices, including amulets, talismans, charms, and containers for magical emblems. The famous *Talisman of Charlemagne* (Fig. 11), actually worn by the Emperor and buried with him, has two enormous sapphires encasing a piece of the True Cross. Originally it is said to have contained relics of the Virgin's hair as well.

Followers of religions of the Book, like the Koran or the Bible, developed tiny wearable cases hollowed out to hold written prayers. Jewelry related to the "evil eye" is very widespread, and it is often worn by valued animals as well as by people. Cosmological systems that link human fate with forces above and below the earth draw precious stones and metals into the orbits of the stars. Birthstones, related to the signs of the Zodiac, participate in this kind of astrological system.

Oftentimes it is the form of the jewelry that is supposed to possess magical powers. The knot of Hercules (Fig. 12), a design dating from ancient Greece, was believed to have the power of healing wounds. Much more complicated systems, however, related particular gems or metals to magical powers. Gold was considered to possess the power of the Sun, amethyst would protect against drunkenness, toadstone was a sure cure for cramps, zircon prevented insomnia, amber would banish a toothache, and sapphires protected the wearer against poison. The Chinese believed that jade slowed down decomposition of the body, so they buried their dead with pieces of jade covering each of the body's nine orifices, or sometimes clad in whole suits of jade (Fig. 13). Today thousands of people wear bracelets of copper in the belief that they will cure all sorts of diseases, from arthritis to cancer.

Certain individual gems, always of fabulous size and beauty, have accumulated legends based on magical powers. Unquestionably the best known of these is the famed *Hope diamond*, which has left a trail of catastrophe behind it for the three centuries of its aboveground existence. Financial ruin, dishonor, death, suicide, and horrible illness have touched nearly everyone who owned

above: 11. *Talisman of Charlemagne,* pendant of chased gold with filigree, set with precious stones, pearls, and two back-to-back cabachon sapphires containing wood believed to come from the True Cross, c. A.D. 800. Cathedral, Reims.

left: 12. *Knot of Hercules,* diadem of gold and enamel, with garnets. Greek, from Thessaly; 2nd century B.C. (Hellenistic period). Benaki Museum, Athens.

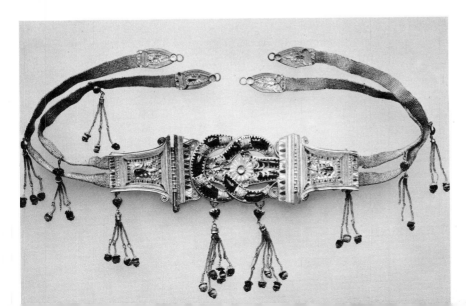

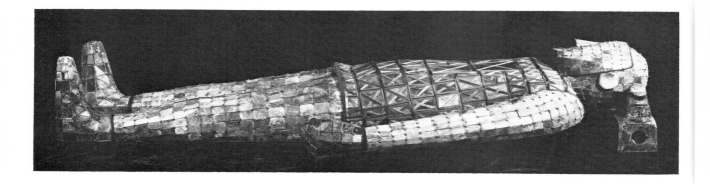

above: 13.

above: 13. *Burial Shroud of Princess Tou Wan,* constructed of 2160 jade plates, sewn together by gold wire. Chinese, from Mancheng, Hopei Province; c. 113 B.C. (Western Han Dynasty). People's Republic of China.

below: 14. **Douglas Wagstaff.** Collar and earrings of hammered and burned stainless steel, 1970. The stainless-steel head ornament is by **Georgina Thomas.**

the gem, including Queen Marie Antoinette of France. The Hope diamond now resides in the Smithsonian Institution in Washington, which to date has escaped calamity.

The interesting thing about the Hope diamond and similar gems with a checkered past is that people continue to covet and acquire them. Certain individuals seem obsessed with the need to own jewels that are the biggest, brightest, rarest, or most extraordinary in the world. This brings us to the question of self-image and expression, which is a major concern in regard to contemporary jewelry.

Jewelry as Expression

The jewelry a person chooses makes a statement about personality, and it is this value that contemporary jewelry has emphasized through its involvement in creative expression. Expression acts as a humanizing force, linking the unique fantasies and perceptions of the jeweler with the equally distinctive tastes and personality of the individual who chooses to buy and wear a particular piece of jewelry.

As the illustrations in this book will demonstrate, contemporary jewelers work in a very broad range of styles, which offer the "consumer" myriad choices in aesthetic form to express and differentiate personality. For one person a barbaric chunk of amber clutched by a primitive silver claw evidences a dramatic nature. Baroque forms allow a rich expression for the romantic, while the subtle flow of delicate gold around austere emeralds may indicate a serene, highly civilized disposition. Wearing a quite distinctive piece of jewelry (Fig. 14) is just as revealing of temperament as the selection of works of art to be displayed in the home or of music to be listened to. In a world replete with standardized artifacts, such options offer a personal means to augment and even create a self-image, to provide those subtle indications of self that enable us to communicate with others. The role of the contemporary jeweler thus becomes very important.

The psychological and social aspects of jewelry are a fascinating subject for study. To a large extent contemporary jewelers have concentrated on the last function we have discussed—jewelry as self-image. However, all the other roles—magic, symbolism, status, and even utility—can afford possibilities for interpretation in new, contemporary ways. The "magic" we seek today is different from that which engrossed our ancestors thousands of years ago, and our symbols, too, are different. Moreover, in an age when the rock star receives more adulation than the monarch, we must reevaluate our definition of status. All these ramifications of jewelry can legitimately be the concern of the contemporary craftsman.

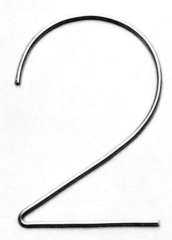

Only a very small fraction of all the jewelry produced through the ages has survived. In the absence of technology or the scarcity of metal itself, ancient jewelry was made of softer materials that rarely endure the ravages of time (Fig. 15). This is particularly important in relation to the jewelry of early and primitive civilizations. From archaeological excavations we know that items we would classify as jewelry can be dated at least to the Paleolithic era (c. 20,000–10,000 B.C.). But our knowledge of this work comes mainly from incidental evidence. Even in relatively recent times the jewelry of less-developed cultures has taken ephemeral form. In the South Pacific, in Africa, among many American Indian groups, and in the far north, jewelry appears in extremely varied, often fragile substances (Fig. 16). For us, gemstones and precious metals are the normal jewelry.materials, but shell, ivory, wood, bone, and nonprecious stones were used first (Fig. 17). Engraved and polished shell and ivory were combined with metal and gems (Fig. 18) and continue to be used in our own day. The wide range of substances employed by "primitive" jewelry-makers has often been an inspiration to modern designers.

Even when jewelry has been made from durable and intrinsically valuable materials, its preciousness has not saved it from destruction. Metal, particularly gold, can resist the force of time and weather, but it is all the more vulnerable to the actions of people. Metal jewelry is readily melted down and returned to the status of material. In times of scarcity, jewelry is destroyed to make utilitarian objects, weapons, and coinage. Chapter 1 gave two examples of this: the removal of Mexican gold by Cortez and the contribution of gold jewelry to the war effort in 19th-century Germany (Fig. 4). An intermittent scarcity of metal probably accounts for many gaps in the history of jewelry.

above left: **15.** Necklace of alabaster beads shaped as clubs and double axes; from a Megalithic barrow at Graese, Denmark. Danish National Museum, Copenhagen.

above right: **16.** Necklace of woven fiber with carved bone ornaments; Tlingit culture, from Alaska, 19th century. Museum of Primitive Art, New York (gift of Mr. and Mrs. Robert W. Campbell).

below left: **17.** Pectoral ornament of tridacna and pierced turtle shell; collected 1912 from Moklin, Admiralty Islands, Melanesia. Ubersee Museum, Bremen.

below right: **18.** Armlet of carved ivory, inlaid with copper; Benin, from Nigeria, A.D. 16th century. Museum of Primitive Art, New York.

Robbery is another source of loss. Thieves, uncertain of being able to dispose safely of their loot, obscure the evidence of their crime and still profit from it by selling the precious materials. When the tomb of Egyptian king Tutankhamen was uncovered in 1922 (Fig. 9), the discovery was considered phenomenal and received worldwide headlines—not because Tut was such an important pharaoh, but because nearly every other Egyptian tomb had been pillaged by grave robbers over the centuries.

Other problems confront us in our attempt to construct a logical history of jewelry. Because jewelry is wealth in portable form, the place where it is found is not necessarily the place where it was made. A great deal of jewelry has appeared in unlikely places, having been dispersed by looters or traders. The custom of trade beads—jewelry elements used for barter with ornament-loving peoples—is a very old one. The beads found in the Philippines, for example, were usually made in China and brought to the islands by European traders.

Besides the diffusion of finished jewelry, the traffic in jewelry materials, like the traffic in salt, is very ancient. This trade has resulted in the wide dispersal of rarely found materials. All the ancient amber discovered in the Eastern Mediterranean region was imported from the Baltic. For two thousand years, the southern leg of the difficult and dangerous Silk Route, from southern Russia to Peking, could have been called the "Jade Route," since jade from Turkestan supplied the jewelers of China.

An ideal history of jewelry would tell us what kinds of things were made, and when, all over the world. We would know how the work was produced, and why its owners prized it. Yet even when we have the jewelry itself, these questions often remain unanswered. The essay that follows can only suggest the fascinating variety of jewelry through the ages.

The Ancient World

Mesopotamia

In the area of the present Syrian-Persian border, surrounded by generally desertlike regions, two great rivers meet: the Tigris and the Euphrates. The land between them was called Mesopotamia, and its first known inhabitants were the Sumerians. In 1922 the Sumerian city of Ur was excavated, revealing, among other things, the amazing refinement and beauty of jewelry that had been made more than four thousand years ago (Fig. 19).

19. Sumerian jewelry of hammered gold, with lapis lazuli and carnelian; from the Tomb of Queen Shubad at Ur, c. 2500 B.C. University Museum, Philadelphia.

20. Necklace, earrings, and seal caps of repoussé and granulated gold; from Dilbat, near Babylon, c. 1700–1500 B.C. (Late Mesopotamian). Metropolitan Museum of Art, New York (Fletcher Fund, 1947).

The Sumerians produced virtually every type of jewelry worn today. Both sexes wore earrings, rings, necklaces, and bracelets; there were also pectorals (breast-plates) for the men and elaborate headdresses for the women. The variety of the Sumerians' jewelry was matched by the range of their techniques. Mesopotamian goldsmiths could produce sheets of planished gold and could draw wire—the basic skills that allowed them such elaborations as soldering, chain-making, engraving, chasing, filigree, and repoussé. They could cast and forge silver and gold, and they mastered a primitive type of granulation—tiny beads of metal attached to a metal base (Fig. 20). A decided taste for color was satisfied by scooping out hollows in the metal to hold colored stones that were cut and polished to fit their receptacles—an early form of cloisonné. The stones they used were carnelian, lapis, agate, and chalcedony, supplemented by substances of colored, claylike materials, chiefly faience in a clear turquoise color that was often combined with gold.

Most Sumerian jewelry types appeared in a variety of styles. Very naturalistic leaves are set side-by-side with more abstract flowers in Queen Shubad's headdress (Fig. 19). On the whole, Sumerian work shows an attentive respect for nature and reproduces natural forms in a regularized way. Mesopotamia was ruled by priest-kings, and the many gods took human form, although often with animal attributes. Many visual images we find elsewhere seem to appear first in Mesopotamia. The Ruler of the Animals, flanked by two facing horned beasts, was found, with variations, in Crete and Persia; the Tree of Life reappeared both in India and in the Christian West. The Sumerians also produced the first known images of the Zodiac, another set of symbols destined for a long history.

In addition to demonstrating the very early date at which the major techniques of jewelry making had been mastered, Sumerian work is important because its craft traditions and themes remained alive in the East through the many political changes that followed. The jewelry of Greece and Byzantium, in particular, was influenced by Sumerian production. Whenever we read of "Oriental" influence on European jewelry, it is usually carried by one of the long line of conquerors and inheritors of the Sumerian civilization.

below: 21. *Diadem of Queen Hetepheres,* of copper faced in gold leaf, with painted gesso; Egyptian, 4th Dynasty (2680–2258 B.C.). Museum of Fine Arts, Boston.

right: 22. *Pectoral Ornament of King Sesostris III,* of gold with cloisonné settings of carnelian, lapis lazuli, and turquoise. Egyptian, from Dashur; c. 1850 B.C. (12th Dynasty). Egyptian Museum, Cairo.

Egypt

Although Egyptian civilization is probably as old as the Mesopotamian, we have more jewelry and much fuller records from Egypt. Egypt is also closer to Western Europe—and the roots of our culture—lying directly across the Mediterranean. Yet Egyptian themes seem more alien and exotic to us; indeed the gorgeous strangeness of Egyptian jewelry is one of its charms.

The stability of Egyptian civilization, which lasted several thousand years, permitted a remarkable development of jewelry techniques. Repoussé, a process that seems to have occurred naturally among all metal-working people, was very important, and engraving and embossing were common. The Egyptians practiced stone setting, and their jewelry is especially prized for its semiprecious stones and "Egyptian paste." Forging and planishing, soldering and drawing wire, served as the foundation upon which all other techniques were based. Jewelry of remarkable quality came from the tombs of the Thinite Era, which dates to about 3000 B.C. Scholars divide the history of ancient Egypt into three periods: Old Kingdom, Middle Kingdom, and New Kingdom.

Most of the Old Kingdom (c. 2700–2135 B.C.) jewelry we have comes from the tomb of Queen Hetepheres, mother of Cheops, the pyramid builder. Large silver torques (necklaces made of a metal rod rather than joined plates or beads), inlaid with butterflies of turquoise, lapis, and carnelian, as well as large quantities of gold showing sophisticated workmanship, bear witness to the range of techniques the Egyptians mastered at a very early date. The diadem illustrated in Figure 21 was probably made when metal was rarer. It consists of a strip of copper faced with a layer of gold leaf. Fastened to this base are rosettes made of a form of papyrus (not unlike papier-mâché), representations of the crested *ibis* (a marsh bird), and papyrus-blossoms surrounding the hieroglyph for "life."

In the Middle Kingdom (c. 2040–1650 B.C.) the expansion of Egypt to include the gold mines of Nubia furnished increased quantities of this precious metal, and by the middle of the second millenium jewelry had reached its artistic peak in Egypt. The pectoral of King Sesostris III (Fig. 22), found at Dashur, is an example of harmonious design, movement, and color. Like much

23. Reversible scarab rings of glazed steatite. Egyptian, from Dier el Bahri, Thebes; 11th century B.C. (12th Dynasty). Metropolitan Museum of Art, New York (Museum Excavations, 1923–24; Rogers Fund, 1925).

Egyptian jewelry, the pectoral has semiprecious stones inlaid in gold. Little distinction was made among real gemstones, semiprecious stones, and glass or glasslike substances. Apparently, color was the most important consideration. Carnelian, lapis, and turquoise are often found in combination, while the less vivid amethyst was used alone or with garnets.

The repertoire of the Middle Kingdom jeweler included many types of ornaments, intended to be worn by both gods and humans. Pins were very rare, since the Egyptians fastened their clothing by knotting or draping the cloth, and finger rings were relatively uncommon. But bead bracelets, pectorals with elaborate pendants, and broad bead collars were widespread. Both collars and pendants were made with counterweights in the back —ornamental discs that kept the weight away from the wearer's neck. From the Middle Kingdom onward collars might be made from as many as twelve rows of beads, which were prevented from tangling by dividers or spacers, bars of gold pierced with holes to keep the strands properly aligned (Fig. 387). Earrings appeared late in the Middle Kingdom period.

Egyptian jewelry has a rich iconography of symbols. Representations of animal-headed gods and goddesses are common, especially Isis the moon goddess and Horus, her son-lover, the falcon-headed sun god. Egyptian writing—hieroglyphs—played an important decorative role, and characteristic Egyptian themes included the eye, the ankh, the papyrus blossom, and the scarab—symbol of rebirth (Fig. 23). New ideas arrived from foreign sources. Minoan Crete was the probable transmitter to Egypt of granulation, which has no early forms in Egypt. Foreign motifs like the winged griffin and the flying gallop, both Western Asian themes, appeared through commercial contact with Syria. Such borrowings were quickly absorbed into the strong traditions of Egyptian design.

The 18th Dynasty (1555–1085 B.C.) marked the beginning of the Egyptian Empire, also known as the New Kingdom. The incomparable craftsmanship of New Kingdom goldwork is evident in the remarkable death-mask of Tutankhamen (Fig. 9), discovered when his tomb was opened in 1922.

New Kingdom jewelry often utilizes the so-called "Egyptian paste." No idea of deception was attached to paste or imitation gems until late Roman times. Good paste was highly valued, and the "stones" were called by the same names as the real gemstones. The exact composition of Egyptian paste is still unknown, but it certainly contains silica, an alkali in the form of nitrate or carbonate of potash, and an oxide of lead in varying proportions, with small amounts of various metallic oxides added to color the mixture. The Egyptians did not have true enamel; their inlay was achieved by the tight joining of inset and metal by hand. After they had hardened, segments of glass, paste, or faience would be filed and polished to fit the metal cells.

Although New Kingdom jewelry presents few novelties of style or type, the work of the 18th Dynasty has given us great quantities of jewelry from this most luxurious period of Egyptian history. Egypt then received tribute from Syria and Palestine, and exchanged gifts with the rulers of Babylon and other Eastern kingdoms. The influence of her wealth and power was felt throughout the civilized world.

Crete and Mycenae

The Minoan civilization of Crete, which reached its height around 2000 B.C., barely affected the slowly waning creative activity of Egypt. Yet a brief account must be given of the Minoans and Mycenaeans, for they were major contributors to the yet unborn Greek civilization. Most of the island of Crete and all of the mainland territory of the Mycenaeans are still a part of Greece.

Early jewelry from Crete is technically elementary. It relied heavily on sheet gold, cut and decorated with dot repoussé, on gold wire and simple chains. There is no trace of Egyptian influence; the sources of this jewelry apparently lie in Sumerian Ur. Thin, simple diadems for everyday wear, beads, and leaf pendants are the most common jewelry types found, and gold was by far the principal material. About 1700 B.C. filigree and granulation made their appearance, along with the art of inlaying colored stones and the introduction of glass beads—the latter techniques probably learned from new contacts with Egypt. By about 1500 B.C. an integrated Minoan-Mycenaean style was regularly found throughout the Aegean area.

The great contribution of the Minoans was artistic rather than technical, and lay in their gaily intelligent emphasis on movement and lightness. A seafaring people, they stressed in their decoration motifs such as fish, marine plants, and octopi, as well as the ritual game of bull-vaulting. While the hornet pendant shown in Figure 24 does not illustrate physical action, it does show the Cretan talent for expressing visual movement. The vitality of the paired hornets comes from the gold pendant's open silhouette, the variety of its textures, and the play of circular forms in an apparently simple, naturalistic image. The circular honeycomb held by the insects, with its rather coarse granulation, is varied by the ovals of their bodies and the outward thrust of their wings.

Minoan civilization came to an abrupt end, for reasons unknown, around 1400 B.C. The next three hundred years also saw a decline in the power and wealth of Mycenae. The limited communications and material scarcity of the Aegean "dark ages" ended only with the birth of Classical Greece.

24. *Two Hornets Feeding at a Honeycomb,* gold pendant with repoussé and coarse granulation; from Mallia, Chrysolakkos, 17th century B.C. (Middle Minoan). Heraklion Museum, Crete.

Greece

In its earliest stages Greek jewelry was very simple, consisting chiefly of bronze wire, often composed in plain spirals. Between 800 and 675 B.C., however, jewelry of gold, silver, and electrum (a natural alloy of gold and silver) appeared in quantity. Many techniques were practiced, including gold-casting, repoussé, chain-making, filigree, and granulation.

The era known as the Archaic period (675–475 B.C.) brought great achievement in the arts, yet jewelry from this age is rarely found, although it is amply represented in sculpture and vase painting of the time. This dearth of examples probably resulted from the lack of gold, for much jewelry is available from later periods when gold became more abundant. The earrings shown in Figure 25, which date from the 6th or 5th century, have both granulation and filigree; they can thus be considered transitional, for the granulation that typified the Archaic period was largely abandoned in favor of filigree in the later Classical style. Earrings remained among the most popular items of jewelry throughout the Greek period. Animal heads (Fig. 25) and, later, human and mythological figures, were very common themes.

Gold evidenty became more plentiful in Greece after the Persian wars, for gold jewelry of the Classical period (475–330 B.C.) is plentiful. In the 5th century B.C. naturalistic wreaths featuring leaves of oak, laurel, olive, or ivy (Fig. 26) were developed—those of gold apparently meant for tombs. Buried with a dead hero, the wreath would indicate victories in life, just as a wreath would be presented to the winner of an athletic contest.

left: 25. Gold earrings with granulation and filigree; Greek, 6th–5th century B.C. Metropolitan Museum of Art, New York (purchase, 1898).

below: 26. Victory wreath of gold repoussé and wire; Greek, 5th century B.C. Metropolitan Museum of Art, New York (gift of C. Ruxton Love, Jr., 1964).

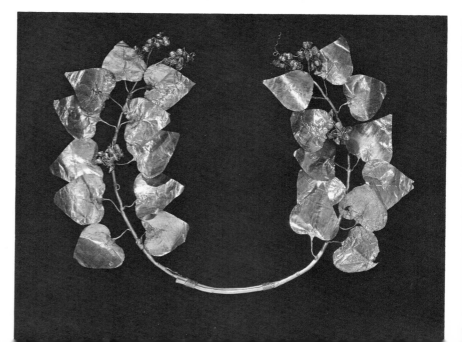

27. *Alexander the Great in the guise of Hercules,* gold signet ring with engraved face (*left*), and its impression (*below*); Hellenistic, 3rd–2nd century B.C. Metropolitan Museum of Art, New York (purchase, 1910).

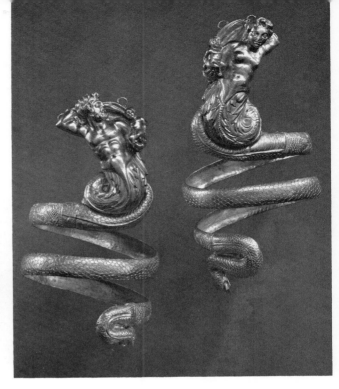

28. *Triton* and *Tritoness,* spiral armbands in repoussé and chased gold; Greek, 3rd century B.C. Metropolitan Museum of Art, New York (Rogers Fund, 1956).

Earrings continued to be popular in the Classical period, as were pendants, bracelets, diadems, and fibulae. As mentioned earlier, filigree replaced granulation, and enamel was introduced. The use of stones and inlay remained quite rare until the end of the period, when engraved stones for rings began to appear.

The period of Greek art termed "Hellenistic" is loosely related to the conquests of Alexander the Great (Fig. 27) and the spread of Greek influence. Oriental goods were sent back to Greece as booty, while Greek wares found new markets in the East. The weakening of the distinction between East and West gave birth to a new unity throughout the classical world, including Egypt and the newly conquered territories in Mesopotamia.

The first important fact about Hellenistic jewelry is that there is a great deal of it. The release and dispersion of the Persian treasures (Figs. 32, 34) made gold readily available in Greece for the first time since the Bronze Age. Second is the appearance of a new range of motifs and techniques. The Heracles knot (Fig. 12) with its two intersecting loops had mystical connotations and became a favorite theme. The crescent, the animal- or human-headed hoop earring, and the Greek motif of Eros were popular throughout the Hellenistic world. A new lavishness marked the use of colored stones, both plain and engraved. Generally speaking, earrings, pins, pendants, bracelets, buckles, anklets, and rings were highly complex in decoration. Dipped enamel, primarily used for earring pendants, offered a new way for adding color to jewelry. The fully developed theme of the figure in jewelry can be seen in a pair of gold armbands (Fig. 28), whose sinuous curves emerge from the half human, half piscine bodies of a Triton and Tritoness. Such pieces were meant to be worn on the upper arm. A tiny hook for attachment to the wearer's dress prevented the bracelets from slipping down.

While Alexander's empire did not long outlive him, the mighty empire of the Romans arose to absorb and sustain the internationalized imperial culture the Greeks had begun. We turn now to a consideration of the peoples who successively inhabited the Italian peninsula.

left: 29. Gold box earring with filigree and granulation; Etruscan, 6th century B.C. Victoria & Albert Museum, London.

below: 30. Gold bracelet inlaid with sapphire, plasma, and pearls; Roman, from Tunisia, A.D. 3rd century. British Museum, London.

right: 31. Gold bracelet with *opus interassile.* Roman, from Syria; A.D. 4th century. Staatliche Museen, Berlin.

Rome

Before the Romans came, a sophisticated people known as the Etruscans lived on the Italian peninsula. They are still mysterious to us, for we cannot read their writing, and their culture was long buried beneath that of the conquering Romans.

Except in its earliest examples, Etruscan jewelry was deeply influenced by the Greeks. Figure 29 shows an intricate gold earring with both filigree and granulation. The rosettes, flowers, palmette, and other motifs in the goldwork are all borrowed from Greek themes. The fibula in Figure 1 shows even more clearly the remarkable quality of Etruscan granulation, finer than that of any earlier or later practitioners of that technique.

It would be difficult to identify a uniquely "Roman" style of jewelry. Until about 250 B.C. Roman jewelry was essentially Etruscan, and soon afterwards the Roman world became suffused with the international Hellenistic style, partly because so many of the goldsmiths were Greek. Most of the major jewelry pieces remained in favor—bracelets, pins, fibulae, earrings, and finger rings. Diadems were less common, and wreaths became more stylized than the naturalistic examples of the Greeks (Fig. 26). Roman taste admired colorful polychrome effects. While enamel was almost unknown, rich stones set closely together and almost obscuring the goldwork offered vivid color (Fig. 30). The Romans also perfected *niello,* a technique in which engraved or chiseled lines are filled with a black mixture of lead, silver, and sulphur. Both filigree and granulation declined in favor of unbroken areas of gold. However, later in the Roman period a new technique called *opus interassile*—in which portions of sheet gold were cut out with a chisel—brought the opportunity for embellishing plain gold (Fig. 31).

Many of these tendencies in Roman jewelry were preserved in the eastern empire of Byzantium, from which they passed to medieval culture in Europe. Before discussing this evolution, however, we must turn to a region of the world in which quite different traditions were developing.

The Near East and Central Asia

The Nomads

Eastward from the Mediterranean, stretching across the colossal distance between Istanbul and China, lies a chain of great deserts, interrupted only by mountains and scattered areas of grassland. These territories are generally too dry to support settled life. A horseman can travel for weeks between one town and the next. As the classical world was creating and consolidating a Mediterranean civilization, the tribesmen of central Asia, scattered as far as Siberia, began to move westward toward Europe. They arrived in waves—Scythians, Samartians, Goths, Vandals, Huns, and others. They were not a single people and shared neither race nor language, but they were all nomads, warriors, horsemen, and breeders of cattle. Traveling in carts, they had no homes and built no cities; they wore their wealth in the form of jewelry and weapons, and the trappings of their horses might be made of gold.

The royal tombs of the nomads have been found scattered over southern Russia. Buried with the kings were horses, household goods, and jewelry —sometimes of silver or bronze, but chiefly of gold. The Oxus Treasure, found far to the East in southern Russia, was a repository of the Achaemenid Persians. The Achaemenids, a seminomadic people, assumed control in the 6th century B.C. of the lands previously under dominion of the Sumerians. At its height their empire extended from the boundaries of Greece nearly to India. A hair ornament from the Oxus hoard (Fig. 32), made of gold in the form of a lion-griffin, is delightful in its energetic sense of movement. This ornament is typically Persian in its stylization of the animal form.

The jewelry of the nomad barbarians is distinctive without being a unified style. Much of it shows various influences—ancient Eastern, Persian, and Hellenistic Greek—all mixed together. Besides horse-trappings, chariot-fittings, and weapons, jewelry types are few; they consist chiefly of small gold plates in repoussé sewn into clothing (Fig. 33), and elaborate buckles and belts.

Some of the nomad tombs, such as the Ziwiye Treasure found in Iran, contain jewelry for women (Fig. 34). The pieces from this treasure show greater complexity in technique, including granulation, inset gems, and cloisonné. In complicated works the separate elements are likely to have been

above: 32. *Lion Griffin,* hair ornament of gold repoussé; part of the Oxus Treasure, found near Samarkand in Uzbek, U.S.S.R. Persian, c. 450 B.C. (Achaemenid period). British Museum, London.

below left: 33. Decorative plaques in gold repoussé, for attachment to clothing or larger pieces of jewelry; Scythian, from Maikop, c. 450 B.C. University Museum, Philadelphia.

below right: 34. Bracelet of gold repoussé, from Ziwiye in northwestern Iran, 8th–7th century B.C. Guennol Collection, New York.

Jewelry of the Past   21

individually cast and soldered. What is distinctive about this jewelry is its motifs, particularly the so-called "Animal Style." Stags, felines, sheep, and fantastic birds of prey are often shown fighting each other, and men are depicted in action—wrestling, riding, and hunting. The nomad's strong sense of decorative design encouraged abstraction, and many examples show disjointed body parts, one animal superimposed on another, or a modulation of animal into geometric form.

The fierce beauty of this jewelry often commands respect, but the importance of the nomad work lies in the duration and amazing extent of its influence. These armed horsemen overthrew Rome in A.D. 410 and posed a constant threat to Constantinople. They deeply affected European jewelry of the Middle Ages, especially in Spain and northern Europe, even to the art of the Vikings. Their influence was also felt in the Far East, and it is to that part of the world that we now turn.

below: 35. Mongolian headdress of cotton and gold-plated silver with filigree and enamel, constructed with beads and settings of coral, silver, and turquoise; from Ordos, late 19th or early 20th century. Danish National Museum, Copenhagen.

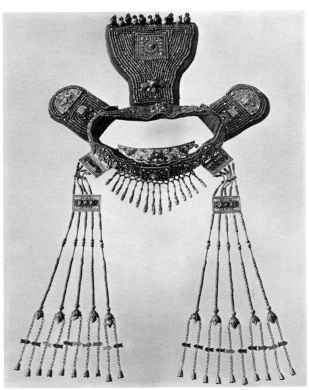

below left: 36. Tibetan silver headdress ornament with coral and turquoise, worn by Chiarong women of the Mantzu tribe; 19th century. The amulet, representing Garuda, the sun-bird vehicle of Vishnu, was thought to bring fruitfulness and protection from diseases. Newark Museum, N.J. (Carter D. Holton Collection).

below: 37. Korean crown of gold-plated bronze; A.D. 6th century (Old Silla Period). Museum of Fine Arts, Boston (Keith McLeod Fund, 1947).

The Far East

The Mongols

Although they now live in a large area north of the Gobi Desert between Siberia and China, the Mongols were nomads until relatively recently. They made up the armies of Kublai and Ghengis Khan in the 13th century, ruling in China as the Yuan Dynasty and marching to the gates of Vienna in 1525. Under Mongol control, travel between East and West was frequent and generally safe; Marco Polo's account is only one of the many medieval travel stories that have come down to us. Such records often express amazement at the elaborate jeweled coiffures of Mongol women (Fig. 35), who rode and fought beside their men. When representatives of the Danish National Museum went to Mongolia in 1938, they found that a wide variety of extravagant structures of hair and jewelry were still being worn. These structures represent the major type of jewelry in Mongolia.

Mongol jewelry is usually very heavy and very colorful. Turquoise, coral, and amber are the preferred gems, but semiprecious stones lie freely on the high plains of Mongolia, and many other stones were used. Pasted into the hollowed-out silver, the stones increase the bulk and weight of Mongolian as well as Tibetan jewelry. The massiveness of gem-encrusted earrings undoubtedly encouraged the development of headpieces to distribute weight. The many amulets required against the legions of Tibetan evil spirits also generated distinctive forms (Fig. 36). We find ring ornaments made to be attached to clothing and designed to support a number of small pouches. Similarly, chatelaines were suspended from buttons to carry such necessities as nail-cleaners, tweezers, earpicks, tinder bags for fire-making, chopsticks, and so forth. These carrying devices were worn by both men and women; sometimes a knife sheath was constructed to allow for the suspension of a chatelaine. It is interesting to compare the 18th-century version of the chatelaine, and the list of items that were typically carried by it (Fig. 2).

Today Mongol jewelry shows the influence of India, but the neighboring Koreans were famous jewelry makers in ancient times, and the crown of a Korean princess from the 6th century A.D. (Fig. 37) is perhaps a purer example of the original jewelry traditions of East Asia. The crown derives from the headgear of the Siberian *shamans,* the once-powerful pagan priests. It is made of gilt bronze, and its complexity lies in its structure rather than in the use of individually elaborate elements. The treelike forms are probably stylized Trees of Life. When the princess walked, a sound of tinkling pendants must have accompanied her.

China

Most of the Chinese jewelry that we know is from the Ch'ing Dynasty (1644–1912), which is Manchurian in origin and regarded as foreign and slightly uncivilized by the Chinese. To find the true character of Chinese jewelry, we must look at older periods. The famous ritual bronzes of early China are proof that, by 1000 B.C., the Chinese were masters of metal-casting and welding. A few pieces of old cast silver and gold have been found, but precious metals have always been in short supply in China; the history of Chinese jewelry is conditioned by their scarcity. Figure 38 shows an early type of belt-hook made of cast bronze and inlaid with gold, silver, and turquoise. Made in the 2nd century B.C., the belt-hook illustrates both the persistence of the old techniques and the stylistic influence of the Scythian nomads. During the Han Dynasty (206 B.C.–A.D. 220) granulation and the plating of bronze with gold and silver became common, but we find no special techniques of gold and silverwork.

38. Belt hook of cast bronze, inlaid with gold, silver, and turquoise; Chinese, 2nd century B.C. (Han Dynasty). Brooklyn Museum (gift of the Guennol Collection).

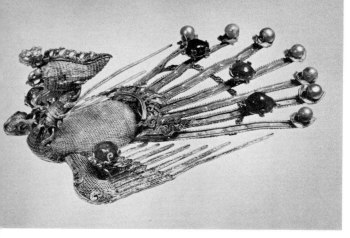

above: 39. *Phoenix,* hair ornament in gold filigree with pearls and cabochon rubies; Chinese, Sung Dynasty (A.D. 960–1279). Royal Ontario Museum, Toronto (Lee of Fareham Collection, on permanent loan from the Massey Foundation.

right: 40. Empress' gold burial crown, with pearls, rubies, and cat's eyes; Chinese, A.D. c. 10th century (Sung Dynasty). Metropolitan Museum of Art, New York (Fletcher Fund, 1934).

The few jewelry types that were made—hair ornaments (especially combs and pins), finger rings, and bracelets—show no particular advances until the 7th century, when many new techniques suddenly appeared. Precious metals were formed by hammering and decorated with chasing or tracing. Both soldering and filigree were used with great expertise. Compared to Persian work, Chinese technique seems rather light and delicate. Since little silver and gold were available, jewelers worked with very thin sheets of beaten metal. Engraving would have cut easily through the surface and was rarely used.

The Sung Dynasty (A.D. 960–1279) was the great period of Chinese art, and jewelry is no exception. Hair- and head-ornaments remained the major jewelry forms (Fig. 39). Elaborate gold and silver versions of an ancient type of hairpin, the *pu-yao,* became common. *Pu-yao* means "the hair ornament that quivers in walking," and Chinese jewelry is unique in its emphasis on physical movement. This interest is clearly visible in a Sung crown (Fig. 40), which developed from the fashion of setting pins around a delicate central diadem to which floral motifs were attached. Despite their size, these ornaments seem airy, because of their execution in gilt openwork. Attached to a light iron framework were thirty or forty separate ornaments set on long, flexible pins. Pearls, uncut rubies, and cat's eyes, often with free-hanging pendants, quiver from tiny springs to enhance the sense of movement. Frequently, gems and pearls were drilled through and attached by pins and wires to stand free of the metal work. Silver, usually gilded to prevent tarnishing, was preferred to gold.

In general, Chinese jewelry places great importance on invention and workmanship, with relatively little interest in intrinsically valuable materials. Delicacy, asymmetry, and a taste for fanciful irregularity accompany an emphasis on movement and sound. The emperor wore jades of specifically matched resonance—one set of tones on the right, another on the left of his belt—so that he might move to his own music.

above: 41. Nepalese gold brooch with filigree, set with carved turquoise, coral, and other semiprecious stones, A.D. 17th–18th century. Metropolitan Museum of Art, New York (Kennedy Fund, 1915).

right: 42. Turban pin of enameled gold; Indian, A.D. 17th–18th century. Victoria & Albert Museum, London.

below: 43. Indian woman wearing elaborate nose ornament and other jewelry.

Jade was always an exception to the general indifference to materials in China. The ancient Chinese jade girdle consisted of seven individual articles, each with its own form and title, linked together by chains or beads. As a complex it undoubtedly had a symbolic meaning, for the Chinese have often attached great importance to the *number* of emblems, while permitting a certain freedom in the choice of separate members of the set. The long tradition of jade included items of personal adornment and the better-known ritual jades, as well as the recently discovered burial suits (Fig. 13).

India

Chinese influence on jewelry making is marked to the south, in Burma and Siam. India, however, preserved her own ancient traditions, as we know by comparing modern work with ancient carvings. Unfortunately, Indian jewelry older than the 18th century is very rare.

The outstanding characteristic of Indian jewelry is the sheer amount of it, for in India the wearing of jewelry has never been confined to a single class. In a traditional Indian marriage, the woman's dowry was conveyed as jewelry. All local traditions include work in glass and base metals as well as silver. Superstitions attached to jewelry have discouraged novelty of design; indeed many jewelry forms have gone unchanged for hundreds of years. Gems, real or imitation, are more important than the metalwork, which is usually gold in ambitious pieces. The importance of gems is confirmed by the habit of leaving supporting metalwork unpolished, to dramatize the flashing light of the precious stones.

In northern India jewelry reflects the styles of Tibet and Central Asia (Fig. 41), while in the south it shows strong affinities with the jewelry of pre-historic Europe. Filigree is quite important in Indian jewelry, and granulation never disappeared as it did in the West. Floral motifs predominate in Indian work (Fig. 42), and Buddhism contributed its own repertoire of subjects. One of the most fascinating aspects of Indian jewelry, for the Westerner, is the variation in ornaments. In addition to the usual necklaces, bracelets, and earrings, Indian women at different times have worn nose ornaments (Fig. 43), anklets, and toe rings—items rarely seen in the West.

Europe

Byzantium, the Dark Ages, and Medieval Europe

In A.D. 326 the Roman emperor Constantine decided to move his capital to the Greek city of Byzantium in Turkey, which was to be renamed Constantinople. This act shifted the focus of the empire from West to East, a tendency that increased as the barbarian invasions gradually eroded the stability of the western provinces. By the end of the 6th century the western empire had, in effect, "fallen," while the eastern empire centered at Constantinople grew stronger and more prosperous than ever. This empire, which we call Byzantium, thus inherited the rich artistic traditions of Greece and Rome, preserving and developing them to be handed down to European culture of the Middle Ages.

Byzantine jewelry was distinguished by the fact that Constantinople remained a sophisticated, cosmopolitan center while urban life everywhere else had become a shambles. High standards of workmanship, wealthy patrons with luxurious tastes, and a more formal, abstract sense of design affected Byzantine production. Byzantine jewelry stressed regular outlines, keeping the overall shape clear and the interior zones distinct and separate. The result is that Byzantine jewelry often has an architectural look, even in the absence of architectural themes (although forms like the arch were popular).

Byzantine craftsmen continued the Roman technique of *opus interassile*. Pendants often were hung from elaborate gold chains (Fig. 44). The Roman love of color in jewelry also persisted in Byzantium, but to the repertoire of colored stones was added a mastery of cloisonné and champlevé enameling (Fig. 45). As in Rome, earrings were among the most popular jewelry items.

below: 44. Gold necklace with granulation and filigree, set with garnets; Byzantine, A.D. 6th century. Cleveland Museum of Art (Dudley P. Allen Fund and Elisabeth Severance Prentiss Fund).

bottom: 45. Gold earring with cloisonné and champlevé enamel; Russo-Byzantine, A.D. 11th–12th century. Metropolitan Museum of Art, New York (gift of J. Pierpont Morgan, 1917).

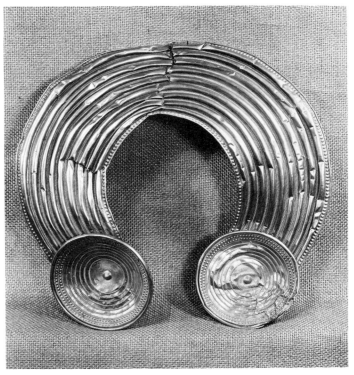

46. Gorget of repoussé and punched gold; Irish, 7th century B.C. Victoria & Albert Museum, London.

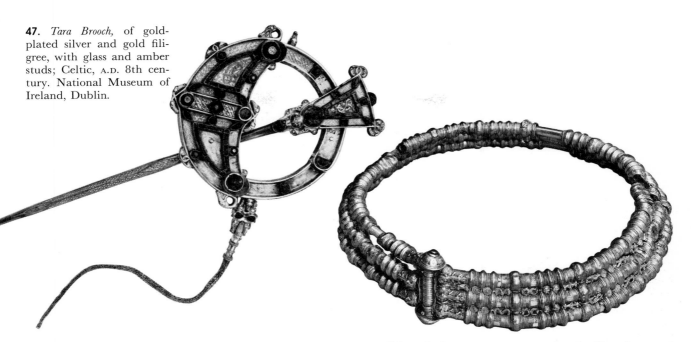

47. *Tara Brooch,* of gold-plated silver and gold filigree, with glass and amber studs; Celtic, A.D. 8th century. National Museum of Ireland, Dublin.

Jewelry in northern and western Europe has a very long tradition, dating back to the Celts, the Vikings, and far beyond to prehistoric ages. The *gorget,* or neckpiece, shown in Figure 46 was made by craftmen of a Bronze Age culture in Ireland about which we know very little. Its 7th-century B.C. date makes it contemporary with the earliest Etruscan work and with Archaic jewelry in Greece. The gorget is of gold with intricate banded repoussé and decorated with disks soldered at each end.

The oldest documented cultures in Western Europe are the Celts and the Vikings, from whom we have magnificent examples of jewelry. The Celts contributed cloisonné enamelwork and ribbon interlace to European jewelry. A fragmentary Celtic fibula (Fig. 47) shows amazingly intricate work. Viking goldsmiths of this period were capable of even more elaborate designs. Certainly the most splendid example of Viking jewelry is the necklace found at Ålleberg in Sweden, dating from the 6th century A.D. (Fig. 48). Made in two sections, the necklace consists of three tubes of gold embellished with ornate filigree. Spaces between the tubes are filled with animal profiles and tiny faces in gold.

With the dissolution of the Roman empire, between the 4th and 8th centuries, seminomadic barbarian tribes moved through Western Europe, gradually becoming integrated with the native populations. Our best example of the jewelry from this period is the Sutton Hoo Treasure, the burial hoard of a 7th century Anglo-Saxon ruler found in England. Jewelry from this treasure is mainly in the form of brooches—simple in outline but extraordinary in decorative complexity (Fig. 49).

Throughout the centuries we refer to as the "Dark Ages," contacts were maintained with Byzantium. In particular, the Vikings, famed sailors and traders, ranged as far East as the Byzantine Empire. And by the year 800, when Charlemagne was crowned Emperor and Europe was solidly Christian, ties with the Christian East were especially close. The ornate setting of Charlemagne's talisman (Fig. 11) is decidedly Byzantine in style.

Little jewelry remains from the early Middle Ages or the Romanesque period. Earrings dwindled in popularity, but fibulae, crowns, and disk brooches, either of openwork or inset with colored stones, continued to be

above: 48. Hinged collar of repoussé and granulated gold; from Ålleberg, Sweden, A.D. 6th century. Statens Sjöhistoriska Museum, Stockholm.

below: 49. Anglo-Saxon brooch of gold and niello; from Sutton Hoo, Suffolk, A.D. c. 700. British Museum, London.

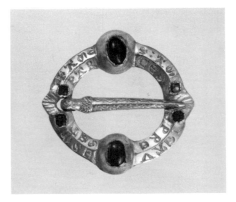

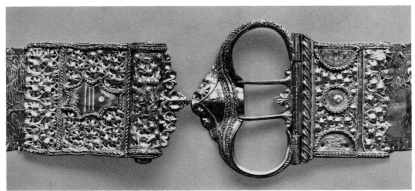

above left: 50. *Crown of Empress Kunigunde,* of gold with precious stones and pearls; from western Germany, perhaps Fulda, A.D. early 11th century. Schatzkammer der Residenz, Munich.

above: 51. Gold brooch with rubies and emeralds; found at Eniscorthy Abbey, Ireland; A.D. c. 1250. A typical medieval lovers' brooch. British Museum, London.

left: 52. Belt buckle of gold-plated copper and silver, with enamel and niello; Italian, 15th century. Victoria & Albert Museum, London.

made (Fig. 50). Until about 1200 precious metals and gemstones were scarce in Western Europe; indeed, they were among the items most eagerly sought by the Crusaders. If the travelers returned home safely, their trophies usually ended up serving the ceremonial requirements of the church or the courts. At first, the manufacture of such pieces took place in monastic workshops, but with increasing trade and patronage, professional craftsmen appeared. Sometimes we even know their names, a situation that became increasingly common with the establishment of the goldsmiths' guilds, which took over the production of jewelry and the training of jewelers.

During the 13th and 14th centuries, Italian traders from Genoa and Venice set up regular trade with the Orient, providing, among other things, a steady supply of jewelry materials. Brooches and rings were made in increasing numbers and grew in size and elaborateness (Fig. 51). Ornate belts and belt buckles became popular (Fig. 52); some were jeweled, others decorated with niello, a technique that had been preserved from Roman craftsmen through the Byzantine Empire. Gems were applied directly to the sleeves and necklines of garments. Gold, silver, and gilt bronze provided settings for enamels and pearls, for rubies, sapphires, and diamonds from India. Elaborate coiffures and jeweled headdresses made earrings unnecessary, but in the 15th century a new fashion for low-cut gowns revived the popularity of necklaces and pendants. Men wore jeweled metalwork collars set well below the neck over the tunic.

The Black Death, the plague that terrorized Europe in the 14th century, stimulated a macabre form of religious jewelry: the *momento mori,* in which images of skeletons were juxtaposed against youthful figures as a warning of life's brevity. This theme became more widespread in later centuries, particularly the 16th and 17th, when the plague reappeared.

The Renaissance

The skills and capital that had been accumulating during the later Middle Ages prepared the way for Renaissance jewelry by developing ever more elaborate versions of crosses, reliquaries, and pendants illustrating Biblical themes. Two of the major types of Renaissance jewelry, the *enseigne* and the emblematic pendant, were basically nonreligious forms of Christian jewelry. The *ensigne* was a hat ornament, usually circular, attached to the turned-back brim of a man's hat. In the Middle Ages such pins were pilgrim's signs made of lead; by the middle of the 15th century they had become purely ornamental. Gold, enamel, and precious stones replaced the base metals by degrees; portraits and moral allegories were introduced as supplements to religious subjects. The gold and enamel *enseigne* shown in Figure 53 features an elaborate border of diamonds and pearls in enameled settings.

Renaissance pendants assumed a great variety of forms as the new interest in classical mythology inspired highly imaginative designs (Fig. 54). The 15th and 16th centuries marked the relaxation of Christian antagonism to the "pagan" world of classicism, the beginning of the modern belief that a human-centered world is not necessarily an alternative to religious salvation but may be honorably reconciled with it. The implied acceptance of nature, reason, and the senses encouraged a new and open concern with the pleasures and lessons of human experience. The arts were believed to mirror life, and the central fact of Renaissance jewelry is its figural emphasis. Jewelry exploited pictorial and sculptural subjects in rich compositions, and the old classical figures were used to express literary and moral ideas.

top: 53. *St. John the Baptist in the Wilderness,* hat medallion of gold and enamel, with a border of pearls and diamonds in enameled settings; Italian, 15th century. Metropolitan Museum of Art, New York (gift of J. Pierpont Morgan).

left: 54. Simonetta Vespucci, wearing a pendant inspired by classical mythology, in a portrait by Sandro Botticelli (1445–1510). Städelsches Kunstinstitut, Frankfurt-am-Main.

above: 55. Design for a pendant by Hans Holbein the Younger (1497–1543). British Museum, London.

below: 56. Pendant of enameled gold, with gemstones and pearls; Italian, late 16th century. National Gallery of Art, Washington, D.C. (Widener Collection).

As artists began to claim a status above that of craftsmen and guild members, jewelers aspired to the new status of artists. The little figures —animal and human—that adorn many *enseignes,* pendants, and brooches, are often triumphs of the sculptor's art. They might be carved or cast, or beaten into high relief—a method described by Benvenuto Cellini. The brilliant enamels so often combined with gems and gold called on the painter's art, and the elaborate structures of pierced and modeled forms required the constructive talent of the engineer or architect. Many painters, sculptors, and architects had been trained as goldsmiths and continued to make jewelry even though their main practice lay in other fields of expression. A list of those who made or designed jewelry but were better known as "fine" artists includes Botticelli, Pollaiuolo, Michelozzo, Ghirlandaio, and Hans Holbein the Younger (Fig. 55).

Rarely can we attach the name of a definite maker to a piece of Renaissance jewelry, although there has been a popular tendency to attribute every fine piece of 15th-century work to Benvenuto Cellini, the most famed goldsmith of his day. Actually, much jewelry was made in Cellini's style (Fig. 56). Not only did jewelers move freely among the countries and courts of Europe, but engraved patterns for jewelry—executed by master designers in Germany, Flanders, and Italy—reached workshops everywhere. Such designs were adapted or freely copied, often making it impossible to trace a jewelry idea to its source.

Renaissance jewelry is marked by its imaginative treatment of a variety of subjects, each piece showing a wide range of materials and techniques. Intaglios based on classical modes were produced by the highly skilled lapidaries of Italy. Even portraits of rulers and popes were executed in this taxing technique. A new method of decoration, called *verre églomisé,* involved engraving and coloring a design in gold or silver foil, which was then applied to the underside of crystal or glass.

The Baroque Period

The Baroque style that dominated Western Europe during the 17th century influenced all aspects of the arts. Above all a grand, monumental style, the Baroque taste emphasized large-scale, flowing curves—often held within an overall symmetrical format—strong contrasts, and deep colors. The elements of surprise and drama are intrinsic to Baroque art. All these carried over into the design of jewelry (Fig. 57).

A profound change slowly overtook the tradition of jewelry. On the surface there was merely a shift in fashionable subject matter: a preference for purely decorative floral themes replaced the wider range and more symbolic images of the Renaissance. The pearls and enamel that had lightened the effect of Renaissance jewelry gave way to a denser, more dignified mood. Religious jewelry took on new significance as the Christian community divided into Protestants and Catholics. But the change went deeper than that and related to the increased role of wealth and economic power. Queen Elizabeth's adoration of jewels led her to wear enormous numbers of them all at once, as her portraits show (Fig. 58). Spain, fantastically enriched by gold, silver, and emeralds yielded by her American conquests, became the wealthiest country in the world. The prestige of jewelry lay increasingly in its monetary value. Earlier jewelers and their patrons had chosen their gemstones primarily for the beauty of their color rather than for flawlessness. But in 1640 and 1670 two developments combined to shift the focus of jewelry onto faceted gems set close together in glittering masses.

The first was a technical invention known as the Mazarin cut, a method of faceting gemstones to increase their brilliance. In 1670 the pace of this

left 57. *Cock,* brooch of enameled gold with rubies and diamonds; South German, 16th century. Rijksmuseum, Amsterdam.

right: 58. "Armada Portrait" of Queen Elizabeth I, attributed to Marcus Gheeraerts, c. 1588–1603. Woburn Abbey Collection (by kind permission of the Marquess of Tavistock and the Trustees of the Bedford Estates).

advance quickened as important diamond deposits were discovered in Brazil. Toward the end of the century the "brilliant" cut was developed, which caused the light entering the stone to be refracted back to the surface. The result was a dominance of diamonds over metalwork and design elements (Fig. 59)—a dominance that in "fine" jewelry has lasted, essentially unchanged, to our own day. It was further confirmed in the late 19th century when the diamond mines of South Africa were consolidated and exploited by de Beers. Great wealth and "good taste" in jewelry came to mean wearing a few matched pieces containing flawless, large, well-cut diamonds. These sets, called *parures,* appeared during the Baroque period and became important during the 18th and 19th centuries.

For the jeweler, the overwhelming emphasis on diamonds has been unfortunate. Frozen into an embodiment of wealth, jewelry design of the 18th and 19th centuries often seemed a mere exercise in historical ingenuity, as a sequence of style revivals took the place of a full reexamination of the artistic and expressive possibilities of jewelry materials and forms. The development was also damaging in historical terms, for ambitious jewelry came to mean big stones, which could always be salvaged from old or unfashionable pieces. Thus relatively few jewels of the 17th and 18th centuries have survived in their original form.

The Rococo Style

The first major style of the 18th century was the Rococo, which overruled the Baroque taste for heavy and impressive pieces. Under the leadership of French taste, Rococo artists produced light, asymmetrical, whimsical designs, using shapes such as scrolls and shells. Colors were predominantly pastel. Two brooches from the 18th century—one in the Baroque style, one Rococo—will

59. Gold and silver aigrette with diamonds; Italian, late 17th century. Museo Poldi-Pezzoli, Milan.

right: 60. Gold bodice ornament set with rose-cut diamonds; Spanish, from Saragossa, early 18th century. Victoria & Albert Museum, London.

below: 61. Floral brooch of enameled gold, with diamonds and precious stones; Spanish, late 18th century. Victoria & Albert Museum, London.

help to illustrate the difference between the two modes (Figs. 60, 61). While both employ naturalistic forms and flowing curves, the Baroque piece (Fig. 60), which is rigidly symmetrical, seems static and contained, its curves always directed back *into* the brooch. By contrast, the later Rococo pin (Fig. 61) is more dynamic in its asymmetry, with the curves leading the eye outward in all directions.

Although light in mood and form, Rococo jewelry was elaborate; the chatelaine became popular partly because it permitted ingenious and individual expression. Like the charm bracelet, the medieval belt-hook, or the nomad's belt-ring, the chatelaine was fastened to the clothes or body by chains and acted as carrier of small practical or symbolic objects—keys, scissors, snuff-boxes, watches, or tiny prayer-books (Fig. 2). During the early 1700s, chatelaines were worn by men as well as women. Large gems were out of place on such pieces, intended for daytime wear. They therefore provided an opportunity for ambitious metalwork and the use of semiprecious materials. While the chatelaine later disappeared, another 18th-century innovation, the *rivière* necklace composed a row of large single stones, usually diamonds bordered by small rubies or emeralds, remained popular.

In the course of the 18th century, men came to wear less jewelry. Shoe and belt buckles were important, and finger rings remained common, although fewer of them were worn at a time.

Neoclassicism

The discovery of Pompeii in 1755 brought an end to the Rococo by inaugurating a new enthusiasm for classicism (Fig. 62). During the French Revolution this meant a preference for simple forms, like the oval cameo, set with "classical" restraint. Although Neoclassicism, as this revival was called, lasted through Napoleonic times, it was associated with middle-class morality and sentiment, the artistic ideals of the English rather than the French. At first it discouraged an ostentatious display of gems in fancy settings, but favored pearls, wreaths, and small tiaras to ornament the simplicity of coiffures.

Under Napoleon the Neoclassic themes were executed with 18th-century extravagance (Fig. 63), for Josephine's passion for jewelry made rich jewels, often designed in sets, acceptable. France set the standards of European taste, but the more innovative jewelry of the 19th century appeared in England and Germany. England had begun producing jewelry made of cut steel in the last

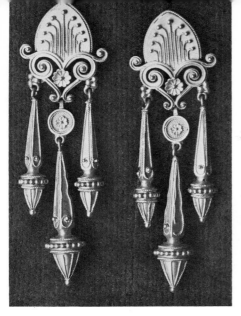

above: **62.** Gold earrings in the Neo-Greek style; French, c. 1878–1900. Musée des Arts Decoratifs, Paris.

quarter of the 18th century, and the Royal Prussian Foundry began manufacturing ironwork jewelry in 1804. Although we associate these materials with industrial products, these early forms of mass-produced jewelry were neither cheap nor clumsy (Fig. 4). On the contrary, Berlin ironwork specialized in flexible pieces of very fine wire.

The Victorian Age

Victorian England took the lead in applying new technological inventions to the production of jewelry. *Pinchbeck,* a new alloy of zinc and copper, had been developed in 1820 as a substitute for gold and was widely used in a cheap jewelry. By 1850 the technique of electroplating base metals with a film of real gold or silver was in commercial use, and the quality of imitation gems and ivory had greatly improved. The 19th century showed a general preference for monochrome jewelry or a combination of gold and black. Jet, which is found in England, came into wide use as jewelry material for the first time (Fig. 64). With the death of Prince Albert in 1861 these novelties of taste, material, and technique merged with England's eager adoption of mourning jewelry.

Popular in the same period and serving the same commemorative purpose was jewelry incorporating human hair (Fig. 8). Lockets and brooches made of gold, jet, pinchbeck, or enamel were made to hold locks of a loved-one's hair, held in place by small panels of glass. Woven or braided hair was also used as a construction material in bracelets, necklaces, and watch-chains, with fastenings of real or imitation gold. Even when Victoria's period of official mourning was finally over in 1887, the orgy of sentimental jewelry continued. The theme simply shifted from death to love, so that hearts, clasped hands, or photographs were incorporated in popular jewelry. The crudeness of much late-19th-century jewelry, in materials and finish as well as in conception, corresponds to a shift in patronage. This work was mass-produced for a new market, middle- and lower-class customers for whom jewelry was an unfamiliar luxury (Fig. 82).

above: **63.** Parure of gold and enamel, partially machine-made: necklace, two bracelets, earrings, and a belt buckle (shown in a specially designed case); French, c. 1830–40. Musée des Arts Decoratifs, Paris.

below: **64.** Jet hair ornament; Bohemian, c. 1898. Jablonec Museum, Czechoslovakia.

65. A. W. N. Pugin. Neckband of enameled gold, with half-pearl borders, diamonds, turquoises, and a ruby; English, c. 1848–50. Exhibited at the Great Exhibition of 1851. Victoria & Albert Museum, London.

66. Firm of Carl Fabergé. Easter egg of carved lapis lazuli, mounted on hinged gold rims set with half pearls, ruby, and rose-cut diamond. White and yellow enameled interior simulates an egg, of which the yolk opens to reveal (originally rising by spring mechanism) a miniature replica of the Crown of Catherine, in diamonds with a small ruby. The removable crown opens on tiny hinges to release an egg-shape ruby on a gold strand. Russian, from St. Petersburg, c. 1900. Cleveland Museum of Art (India Early Minshall Collection).

Neoclassicism was not the only revival to flourish during the post-Rococo period. In fact, the 19th century could be considered the grand era of revivals. Egyptian revival, Gothic revival, Elizabethan revival, Renaissance revival, Chinese style, Islamic style—all followed one upon another in a dizzying progression. Often, two or more styles were mixed! This spirit of eclecticism characterized an age that created no style of its own. A 19th-century bracelet in the "Gothic revival" style (Fig. 65) is decorated in enamel with half pearls.

With all the jewelry made during this imitative age, one name stands out—the most famous jeweler of modern times: Carl Fabergé. Fabergé's family owned a prosperous jewelry firm in St. Petersburg, the Russian capital, and the young Fabergé traveled extensively in Europe before returning to take over direction of the business. Artistically sophisticated and ambitious, Fabergé specialized in the production of exquisite figures and objects made of precious materials, especially the famed "surprise" Easter eggs (Fig. 66). His output of personal jewelry was low. Fabergé had at his disposal hundreds of skilled craftsmen and the most rare and obscure gems of Europe and Asia. His products were brilliantly inventive and meticulously crafted, stressing the artistic possibilities of the materials more than their monetary value. International society in Europe was enchanted with his beautiful objects until 1914, when the Russian Revolution and the First World War shattered the only kind of world in which Fabergé's tradition could survive.

The 20th Century

Art Nouveau

Art Nouveau reached its peak between 1895 and 1900, but it can be considered a 20th-century style on the basis of its dynamism and its conscious rejection of historical precedents. Art Nouveau appeared in the context of a broad artistic movement that embraced architecture, furniture design, painting, sculpture, and the graphic arts. Everywhere in Europe and even in the United States the style cut across national traditions, appearing under a variety of names—the Whiplash style, Jugendstil, Sezession. Art Nouveau jewelry was usually inspired by natural forms, but only of a certain type: lillies, water themes, butterflies, peacocks, insects, serpents, and slender women with flowing hair (Figs. 67, 83). The ideal Art Nouveau theme was graceful, showy, and exotic. Because it was a highly linear style and a fully original one (not simply reinterpreted), Art Nouveau called forth the best efforts of first-rate jewelers, among them René Lalique, Henri Vever, Georges Fouquet, and Georg Jensen (Fig. 68).

Although industrial, low-cost versions of Art Nouveau jewelry were produced, the style was fundamentally extravagant, requiring a wide range of skills and materials. Enameling, for example, was carried to a new height of technical expertise. Art Nouveau also signaled a new collaboration between the fine and applied arts, a tendency that was elevated to a principle in the years following World War I.

right: 67. **Georges Fouquet** (from a design by C. Posroziers). Gold pendant with plique-à-jour and translucent enamel, set with diamonds and moonstones; French, 1890. Victoria & Albert Museum, London.

below: 68. **Georg Jensen.** *Butterfly,* silver buckle with stones; Danish, c. 1905. Kunstindustrimuseum, Copenhagen.

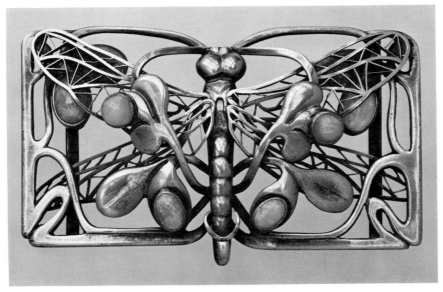

69. Art Deco jewelry (*counterclockwise from upper left*): sterling and ivory brooch; necklace of Bakelite, aluminum, and enamel; necklace of chrome and plastic; sterling and enamel ring (designed by Jean Desprès); and a silver and gold pendant with mother-of-pearl (also by Desprès); c. 1925. Collection Holly Solomon, New York.

Art Deco

It is usually said that the Art Deco style was influenced by the Bauhaus, the radical German art school that presented students with the first real alternative to the Renaissance tradition of arts and crafts (see p. 44). But one could equally claim that Art Deco and the Bauhaus represented simultaneous and related solutions to problems faced by all artists in the postwar world. The old artistic methods and goals were gone, along with the old forms of patronage. Industrial production, novel materials, and, above all, a new society demanded new forms and new ideas of art. In jewelry, Art Deco met the challenge with a firm rejection of "nature" and the craftsman's hand in favor of a machine-made look (Fig. 69). It aimed at precision without atmosphere, a harsh metallic sheen, and strict geometric shapes (Fig. 84). In pins, necklaces, and bracelets, an initial rigidity of form soon yielded to elegance. The best examples of Art Deco jewelry have a startling purity. "Rich" and "poor" materials were ruthlessly juxtaposed; sleek black plastic might be paired with a slab of polished platinum or diamonds in paved settings.

Art Deco jewelry flourished for only a brief period, the years between 1920 and 1935, and it was never as popular as Art Nouveau had been. It was a designer's style more than a craftsman's, but it represented an authentic and sometimes powerful response to the energies of its time.

Native Jewelry in Africa and the Americas

Africa

As noted at the beginning of this chapter, a large portion of the jewelry made by native craftsmen in Africa consists of impermanent materials. However, there are rich lodes of metal, including gold, on the African continent, and several tribes have practiced metalworking. Two of them—the Ashanti and the Benin—have raised it to the level of an art.

The Ashanti inhabit the nation of Ghana, once known as the Gold Coast. Abundant deposits of gold are to be found in Ashanti territories, and during the 18th and 19th centuries the tribe attained great wealth and power through trade with Europe. The entire Ashanti culture centered around gold, with gold dust serving as the medium of exchange. Small cast or repoussé weights

left: 70. *Goldfish,* Ashanti gold-weight of cast brass; from Ghana, 18–19th century. Museum of Primitive Art, New York.

below: 71. Ashanti dress ornaments of repoussé and chased gold; from Ghana, 19th century. British Museum, London.

made of brass were used for measuring the gold (Fig. 70), and fairly elaborate brass boxes were fabricated to hold the gold dust. The Ashanti also worked directly in gold, which was either cast by the lost-wax method or hammered as sheet gold (Fig. 71). Ornaments in the form of decorated disks, masks, animals, and human heads adorned members of the ruling class.

The neighboring Baule tribe had a metal tradition similar to that of the Ashanti. The Baule also used small figurative brass weights, and these often are difficult to distinguish from the Ashanti versions. Especially fine examples of Baule metalwork are tiny masks cast in gold (Fig. 72), with stylized human features. Apparently, these masks were meant to be attached to the swords of warriors to indicate success against the enemy.

The Benin tribe of Nigeria is best known for extraordinary sculptures cast in bronze. However, the Benin also worked in copper, sometimes combining it with carved ivory, which was a major component of their jewelry (Fig. 18). Other tribes have developed intricate patterns by chasing or chiseling in metal (Figs. 73, 74), a craft tradition that has carried over into the modern period.

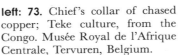

above: 72. Gold mask cast from lost wax; Baule culture, from the Ivory coast, 19th century. Museum of Primitive Art, New York.

left: 73. Chief's collar of chased copper; Teke culture, from the Congo. Musée Royal de l'Afrique Centrale, Tervuren, Belgium.

right: 74. Ahmed ould Moilid. Anklet of hammered and chiseled silver; Boutilimet culture, from Mauritania, collected in 1951. Musée d'Ethnographie, Neuchatel, Switzerland.

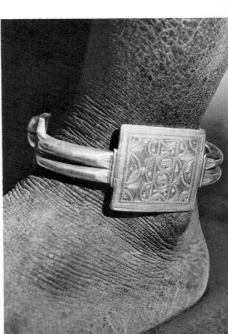

right: 75. Mask in gold repoussé, with embossed ear spools; from northern Peru, after 1000. Private Collection, Lima, Peru.

below: 76. Head band or sash, of pierced sheet gold originally backed by cloth and feathers; Inca, from southern Peru, c. 1500. Museum of Primitive Art, New York.

Pre-Columbian America

In South America the metal-bearing Andes mountains provide silver, tin, copper, lead, and a great deal of gold. One of the most splendid developments of goldsmithing the world has ever known was accomplished by the Inca of Peru. Although masses of pre-Columbian gold jewelry were taken back to Spain by the *conquistadores* in the 16th century, much still remained.

To understand the metal art of the Inca, we must look to their predecessors in the Andean region—the Mochica, the Naxca, and the Chimu. These groups all submitted to Inca imperialism and offered their conquerors skills developed over a period of eight or nine hundred years. Goldworkers in Peru, by and large, showed a preference for hammering; the pieces have broad planar areas with some patterned detail. The repoussé mummy mask in Figure 75, dating from after A.D. 1000, is interesting in and of itself, but it also shows how jewelry was worn in that ancient culture. The ear spools shown on the mummy were also worn by living humans of the ruling classes.

The Inca empire prevailed in Peru in the hundred-year period between about 1438 and 1532. The Inca independently developed most of the techniques known to European and Asian goldsmiths: casting, hammering and repoussé, wire making, gilding, tracing, and engraving (Fig. 76). Men wore splendid headpieces, earrings, breastplates, necklaces, and disk-shaped nose ornaments hooked into their nostrils. Women wore earrings, necklaces, and bracelets on their arms and ankles. Since gold was believed to hold the power of the Sun, it had also been used in the Inca sacrifices and burial customs practiced for two hundred years, and these applications put some of the treasure beyond the reach of the Spanish plunderers.

right: **77.** Necklaces of cast tumbago; Quimbaya culture, Colombia, before 1500. The small ornaments represent fantastic insects. Museo de América, Madrid.

below: **78.** *Figure with Crocodile Head,* pendant of gold and pyrite; from Costa Rica, c. 1000–1500. Museum of Primitive Art, New York.

79. Mixtec ring, cast in gold from lost wax. From a tomb at Monte Alban, Oaxaca, Mexico; 14th–15th century. Museum of the American Indian, New York (Heye Foundation).

Most historians believe that metalworking techniques moved from Peru to Colombia, then north into Panama and Costa Rica, finally reaching Mexico. While Colombian goldworkers used a hammering technique similar to that of Peru, they also cast the metal, often in highly naturalistic figurative forms. In addition to pure gold, much work was done in *tumbago,* a gold-copper alloy that gives a rosy warmth to the jewelry (Fig. 77). Central American work generally is cast, with a preference for "grotesque" animal, bird, and human forms that are richly decorated (Fig. 78). Gold jewelry from Mexico (Fig. 79) is more often cast (though sometimes hammered), and it displays a wealth of symbolic images related to the complex religious systems of the pre-Columbian period.

Native Jewelry of North America

In North America there exists no pre-Columbian metalworking tradition as there does to the south. None of the jewelry-producing tribes mined their own metal, and the few tribes that do produce metal jewelry—notably the Zuni and the Navajo of the Southwest—learned their craft from Mexican smiths sometime around 1860.

Each of the tribes developed its own style. Navajo jewelers show a strong concern with the metal itself and use stones only for accents in cast and hammered jewelry (Fig. 80). The Zuni jeweler, on the other hand, is chiefly fascinated by turquoise; stones are massed closely in conventional patterns, and the silver is little more than a support (Fig. 81).

The decade of the seventies has witnessed a revival of interest in historical jewelry. This is, of course, a positive impulse, as long as it generates new ideas rather than stimulating mere imitation. Today's jeweler can learn much from the work produced by colleagues hundreds or thousands of years ago. A practical understanding of the historical roots that led to today's styles can provide the beginning jeweler with a standpoint for evaluating current experimental tendencies.

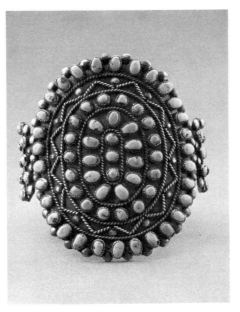

left: 80. Navajo squash-blossom necklace, of coin silver with turquoise; c. 1890. Collection the author.

right: 81. Silver bracelet with turquoise; Zuni, c. 1910. Collection the author.

The Emergence of Contemporary Styles

At the turn of the 20th century the traditional handcrafts and their practitioners had virtually disappeared from the United States, England, and parts of western Europe. In the short space of a hundred years the Industrial Revolution, launched in the mid-18th century, all but destroyed a craft economy whose roots lay in the Early Middle Ages and beyond.

The Craftsman in the Machine Age

Industrialization reached the United States in the early 1900s, and within a short time skilled craftsmen had become scarce. And, with diminished need for the services of trained workers, educational and apprenticeship programs declined. The few areas of specialization that continued to demand craftsmen imported them from Europe. By 1930 architects were no longer specifying wrought-ironwork for their buildings, so the profession of ironworker became obsolete. Silversmiths gradually disappeared during the forties, with smaller shops either closing down or adapting their businesses to plating or repair work. Blacksmiths had vanished by the thirties or had survived by converting to torch welding or horse shoeing. In most jewelry shops the repairman and benchworker could no longer be found; all but the largest jewelers were sending their repair work and ring sizing to central outlets in the big cities.

In one sense jewelry making suffered less than did the other crafts, for jewelry continued to be made by hand, while textiles, ceramic wares, glass objects, and furniture had fallen almost entirely into the province of the machines. Nevertheless, jewelry became standardized and mechanical, wedded to conventionalized forms. Factories in England spewed out thousands of identical "jewelry" items for the mass market—often machine-stamped metal pieces featuring sentimental themes that today we can only describe as vulgar. In both England and the United States, such dubious types of mass-produced jewelry could be purchased from large mail-order firms at extremely low prices (Fig. 82).

Paralleling the disappearance of the handmade object was a decline in workmanship and in the quality of form and design often referred to as "taste." Previously, the craftsman serving one patron or a small clientele had been forced to maintain high standards of workmanship in order to remain in business. The machines, however, were not accountable to their customers. The buyer of an inferior product could scarcely complain to a giant entrepreneur, and if he took his business elsewhere, he was likely to be confronted with the same shoddy standards.

Mass production, moreover, had by its very nature to appeal to the lowest common denominator of taste—the style that was least offensive to the largest number of people. In many or most cases this tendency stimulated the fashion for "historicism"—a clinging to historical styles and designs in the face of completely new methods of fabrication. To a great extent we still see this phenomenon today, in "period" furnishings and "Colonial" houses, for example. Certain styles are "safe" or "official," and such legitimacy was very important to the 19th-century consumer. The poorer classes, for the first time able to purchase quantities of consumer goods, wanted those goods to look as much as possible like the precious handmade objects that graced the homes and persons of the wealthy. Historicism carried over into all areas: steel-frame buildings sported classical moldings, mass-produced furniture mimicked the elaborate turnings and carvings of the wood-craftsman. Indeed, the machines had proved so competent at piling on decorative effects that many of the goods produced in the late 19th and early 20th centuries seemed overwhelmed with embellishment.

Reaction to the machine's dominance and the prevalent fashions took many forms, but its leaders fell generally into two camps: those who sought to abolish the machine altogether, and those who tried to master it. The first group embraced the 19th-century romantics John Ruskin and William Morris, from whose teachings grew the English Arts and Crafts Movement. Morris, founder of his own design studio, loathed the machine and its products. The only hope for design reform, he felt, lay in the reestablishment of the handcraft tradition. Unfortunately, Morris' hand methods and high standards resulted in goods that were so expensive as to put them out of the reach of the clientele he hoped to serve.

The Art Nouveau style of the late 19th and early 20th centuries, discussed in Chapter 2, owed much to the writings of Ruskin and Morris. Art Nouveau sought a complete break with the past and the creation of a new style free of

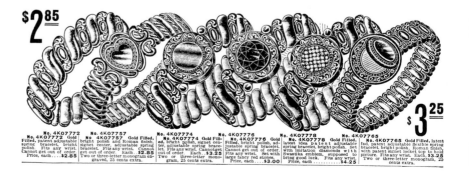

82. Mass-produced bracelets of gold-filled metal, with patented springs and joints, set with imitation diamonds and other stones; from the Sears, Roebuck catalogue for 1908.

83. René Lalique. *Dragonfly,* corsage ornament of gold and plique-à-jour enamel, with chrysoprase and moonstone, c. 1900. Gulbenkian Foundation, Lisbon.

historical precedent (Fig. 83). It took its forms from nature, from the curving, sinuous patterns of plant and animal life as well as from the human body. The fashion for Art Nouveau, however, was short-lived, for just as it admitted no antecedents it proved difficult to build upon. Far more durable effects developed from movements that set out to channel the machine's production, to devise new forms, materials, and methods that would be compatible with industrialization. Preeminent among these were the *De Stijl* movement in Holland and especially the German Bauhaus.

De Stijl and the Bauhaus

In direct opposition to Art Nouveau, *De Stijl* (the style) took as its objectives order, clarity, mathematical precision, and above all the straight line. Its proponents, notably the Dutch artists Piet Mondrian and Theo van Doesburg, hoped to abolish all sentiment, romanticism, and historicism in art. To replace 19th-century historicism, members of the *De Stijl* group were searching for an aesthetic based on pure, abstract relationships of shape, form, and color implicit in the new technological world. Beyond painting and to some extent architecture, the concrete results of *De Stijl* were few, but the movement paved the way for later initiatives, most notably that of the famed Bauhaus.

The Bauhaus was founded as a school of design in Weimar, Germany, in 1919, and later moved to Dessau. Under the leadership of the architect Walter Gropius, the school drew its faculty from among the preeminent painters, architects, craftsmen, and industrial designers throughout Europe. The essential goal of the Bauhaus was to wed art and technology, to harness the machine in a way that would serve aesthetic expression. Whereas previously designers and the leaders of industry had been antagonistic, Gropius encouraged his industrial design students to go out into the factories and learn to understand their methods; conversely, managers from the plants were invited to the school so that they could become familiar with the design process. Students were trained to be artists *and* craftsmen, skilled not only in visual expression but in the use of tools and the direct experience of materials.

Geared as it was to mass production, Bauhaus design eliminated all nonessential details and ornament. Clean lines, honest use of materials, and solid construction were among its tenets. The influence of such Bauhaus principles manifested itself most clearly in architecture; the International Style of Ludwig Miës van der Rohe, Philip Johnson, and Marcel Breuer is a direct outgrowth. Too, many items of furniture designed by Bauhaus masters became, and have remained, classics. Jewelry designs inspired by the Bauhaus aesthetic tend to be rather stark and geometric (Fig. 84).

In 1933 the Nazis forced the closing of the Bauhaus, and the great experiment came to an end. However, a large portion of the students and faculty emigrated to the United States—Gropius and Breuer to Harvard, László Moholy-Nagy to the Chicago Institute of Design, several others to Black Mountain College in North Carolina. The influence of the Bauhaus thus was perpetuated to the present day.

Art Styles of the Early 20th Century

At much the same time that Bauhaus designers were expounding principles of order and precision, artists in France and other parts of Europe were building a style based on illogic, fantasy, Freudian psychology, automatism, dreams, and unreality. Shocked by the brutalities of World War I, the Dadaists—who took their name from a nonsense word—maintained that the old order, all the old rules, should be abolished. In other words, if this carnage was *sense,* then *non-sense* should be the new goal. Similar ideas motivated the Surrealists, of whom Salvador Dali is the best known example. Surrealism postulated the superiority of dreams to waking reality, of imagination to analytical thought, of the subconscious to the conscious. It was a direct challenge to the harsh "reality" of a mechanized, violent world.

Dali's painting of "melted watches"—formally titled *The Persistence of Memory*—is well known. A design for an actual watch (Fig. 85), in enameled

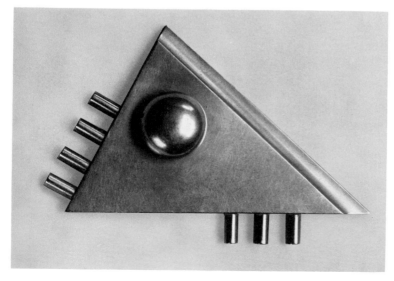

84. Georges Fouquet. Yellow-gold brooch, 1925. Musée des arts décoratifs, Paris.

platinum set with diamonds and a ruby, creates the same mysterious effect. Of this piece Dali said: "Man cannot escape or change his time. The eye sees the present and the future. . . ."

Dada and Surrealism are not the only nonrational styles to come to prominence during the 20th century, but they are possibly the most dramatic. In our discussion of contemporary jewelry from the thirties to the present, we will continually see the coexistence of the two modes—rational as typified by the Bauhaus, and nonrational as exemplified by Dada and Surrealism.

Pioneers of Contemporary Jewelry

The close of World War II brought an explosive development in architecture, industrial design, and the handcrafts. Indeed, the traditional crafts have, over the last few decades, enjoyed a renaissance of almost unbelievable proportions. The reasons for this are complex and the subject for hot debate. However, it seems clear that a reaction to modern industrialization, standardization, and depersonalization has expressed itself in the desire for one-of-a-kind hand-made objects.

By 1950 a number of people were making contemporary jewelry on a professional scale in the United States. No list of these craftsmen would be exhaustive, but we will briefly discuss a few who could be considered "pioneers" in the development of contemporary jewelry. Others are mentioned and their work illustrated throughout this text.

Sam Kramer acknowledged his debt to the imagery of Salvador Dali. As early as 1936 he was making "surrealist" jewelry, and in 1939 he established a shop in New York's Greenwich Village where he worked until his death in 1964. Kramer was well known for his consistently sincere and expressive jewelry (Fig. 86). His designs combined fused and forged forms made of sheets of heavy-gauge metal. Kramer exhibited widely and was included in all three Walker Art Center Exhibitions (see pp. 49–50), as well as many other important shows.

Italian-born Harry Bertoia studied at the Cranbrook Academy of Art and began his work in California. His contribution to the development of contemporary jewelry lay in exploration of the expressive means of fusing combined with forging. Bertoia was also interested in devising fastenings suitable to particular forms. For the most part his designs are light, delicate, and fanciful (Fig. 87). Since 1950 Bertoia has concentrated on sculpture, but the sheer creative vigor of his jewelry has left a mark on that medium.

Ronald Hayes Pearson attended the School for American Craftsmen at Alfred, New York, and in 1948 opened his own workshop in Alfred. During the next five years he produced spun-bronze hollowware. In 1952 he moved to Rochester, New York, where with three other craftsmen he organized Shop One, an outstanding retail craft outlet. During the 1950s Pearson participated in many exhibitions and later taught at the School for American Craftsmen at Rochester. Pearson has concentrated on forged and cast forms (Fig. 88). His forged designs demonstrate the ultimate refinement to which a process can be subjected by a master craftsman. With Shop One he proved that a high-quality crafts outlet can survive and prosper in modern society.

Ward Bennett was art director for Hattie Carnegie for several years. He exhibited at the Museum of Modern Art in 1946 and at the Walker Art Center exhibition of 1948. Bennett worked in plate-shape forms, achieving very sensitive shape-configurations (Fig. 89).

Danish-born Adda Husted-Andersen completed her studies in Copenhagen. She served as president of the New York Society of Craftsmen for several years and maintained her own shop in New York. An active exhibitor, Husted-Andersen displayed her work in the Museum of Modern Art exhibition of 1946 and in all three Walker Art Center exhibitions (see pp. 49–50), as well as many other national shows. Her work is essentially in plate-shape and

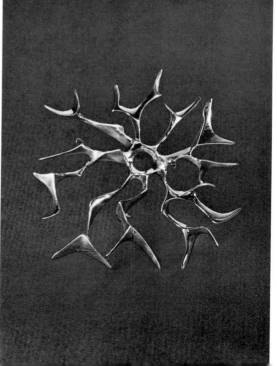

left: 87. Harry Bertoia. Jewelry in hammered silver, including a fused piece (*lower right*) and two pins constructed with brightly colored thread; c. 1940–50.

below 88. Ronald Hayes Pearson. Pin cast in 14k gold, 1966.

left: **89. Ward Bennett.** Hammered silver pendant, c. 1946.

right: **90. Adda Husted-Andersen.** Pin of yellow gold, rutiliated quartz, and tourmaline, c. 1959.

below right: **91. Paul A. Lobel.** Sterling-silver pin, c. 1946.

constructed forms (Fig. 90) and owes more to the influence of European formal traditions than is true for most contemporary jewelers working in North America.

Paul A. Lobel was born in Romania but came to the United States as an infant. He studied at the Art Students League in New York, working in many media—sculpture, design, silversmithing, painting, drawing, etching, metalwork, and glass. During World War II Lobel opened a jewelry shop in Greenwich Village, which he operated until 1964. He exhibited widely in national and regional shows, including the 1946 exhibition at the Museum of Modern Art and in the 1948 Walker exhibition (see p. 49). In 1949 the American Museum of Natural History in New York mounted an exhibition of his hand-wrought jewelry and silver sculpture under the title "Shining Birds and Silver Beasts." Lobel's jewelry reflects an imaginative skill in designing three-dimensional forms from flat sheet metal (Fig. 91). These designs were often lyrical formalizations of such natural images as flowers and fish, and they always expressed a respect for the integrity of the material.

Margaret De Patta studied at the San Diego Academy of Fine Arts, the California School of Fine Arts in San Francisco, and the Art Students League in New York, where she was twice winner of national scholarships. De Patta began making jewelry in 1930, under the tutelage of an Armenian craftsman. Her contemporary work began after study with László Moholy-Nagy and Eugene Bielawski at the Chicago Institute of Design. De Patta established a studio in the San Francisco area, where she remained throughout her life. De Patta's development of strip-plate forms and her exploration of faceted stones (Fig. 92) contributed much to the development of contemporary jewelry. Rejecting the traditional lines of faceting because of their narrow formal limitations, she carried out a study of reflection, refraction, magnification, and distortion, then designed facet forms to exploit these qualities. The integration of setting with total form was also an important creative problem for this artist. De Patta exhibited widely; her work was included in the "First International Exhibition of Modern Jewellery, 1890–1961," held at the Victoria & Albert Museum in London in 1961.

Although far better known as a sculptor, Alexander Calder was among the first modern artists to utilize jewelry as a means of serious artistic expression in the United States. Many of Calder's forms resemble those of primitive jewelry, but it cannot be assumed that they are copied. Wire is a medium that suggests its own possible relationships, and any artist who naïvely explores the formal capacities of wire will independently arrive at similar forms. Calder's contribution to contemporary jewelry has been his recognition of the aesthetic

92. Margaret De Patta. Pendant of white gold and faceted crystal, c. 1960.

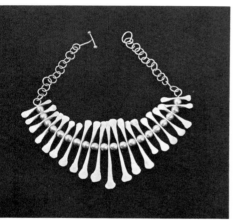

top: 93. Alexander Calder. Hammered-wire necklace, c. 1946.

above: 94. Fred Farr. Hammered sterling necklace, c. 1946.

principle inherent in a fresh, untrammeled treatment of his material (Fig. 93). He pioneered wire-linear forms, having his first exhibition of wire jewelry at the Willard Gallery in New York in 1940.

Fred Farr studied at the University of Oregon, the Portland Art Museum, and the American Artists School. He has exhibited widely in the various media in which he works—painting, sculpture, design, and jewelry. Farr's work, mainly in plate shapes and constructed forms (Fig. 94), was included in the 1946 Museum of Modern Art exhibition, as well as the Walker show of 1948.

Major Exhibitions Before 1960

An indication of the health of the contemporary jewelry movement, as evidenced by the work of pioneers such as those discussed above, was the surge of important exhibitions during the forties and fifties. It may seem difficult to understand now, but the mere fact that contemporary jewelry was deemed worthy of such attention constituted an unusual step in the 1940s. The Museum of Modern Art in New York took the initiative in promoting modern styles in all the arts after World War II and held the first major exhibition of contemporary jewelry in 1946. The Walker Art Center's *Design Quarterly,* then edited by Bauhaus-trained architect Hilde Reis, was one of the earliest museum publications to focus on contemporary design as applied to furniture, decorative accessories, architecture, and the crafts. Many other influences also helped to foster the spread of contemporary styles, including new training programs and university-level courses.

The Museum of Modern Art, 1946   The era of contemporary jewelry in the United States can be said to have begun with the first national exhibition, mounted by the Museum of Modern Art in 1946. That show displayed 135 pieces of jewelry by 26 artists. Not all the exhibitors were professional working jewelers, but they all participated in an important historical event.

Nearly all the jewelry reflected the influence of modern art, being about equally divided between the "rational" Bauhaus-inspired style and the "nonrational" Surrealist-inspired design. Among the professional jewelers appearing in the show, Ward Bennett, Paul A. Lobel, and Fred Farr exhibited plate forms (Figs. 89, 91, 94); linear forms characterized the work of Julio de Diego (Fig. 95); Fannie Hillsmith and Adda Husted-Andersen showed constructed forms (Fig. 90); strip-plate forms appeared in the work of Margaret De Patta and Hurst & Kingsbury (Fig. 96); Harry Bertoia, in the pieces submitted for this show, employed fused forms (Fig. 87). Artists known primarily for their work in other media, but who exhibited jewelry in the show, included Alexander Calder, José de Rivera, and Richard Pousette-Dart (Figs. 93, 97, 98).

far left: 95. Julio de Diego. Necklace of forged sterling, c. 1946.

left: 96. Hurst & Kingsbury. Necklace assembled from sterling strip and plate shapes, c. 1946.

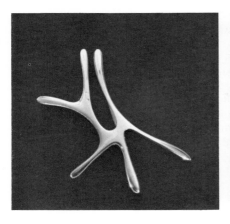 

far left: 97. José de Rivera. Stainless-steel pin, c. 1946.

left: 98. Richard Pousette-Dart. Pierced brass pendant, c. 1946.

Walker Art Center, 1948 The second national exhibition of contemporary jewelry was organized by the Walker Art Center in Minneapolis in the spring of 1948. The show was sponsored by the Everyday Art Gallery, directed by Hilde Reis, and packaged as a traveling exhibit by Bill Friedman, assistant director of the Walker. It toured for two years, stimulating interest in contemporary jewelry throughout the United States.

The first Walker exhibit included 282 pieces by thirty artists. It is interesting to note that only seven of these had been represented in the Modern Museum's 1946 show: Bennett, Bertoia, De Patta, Hurst & Kingsbury, Farr, Husted-Andersen, and Lobel. Except for electroforms, all the major techniques were in evidence. Four jewelers showed cast jewelry; eleven, plate-shape forms; two, strip-plate forms; two, forged forms; one, repoussé pieces; and two, jewelry in plastic.

Walker Art Center, 1955 The Walker Art Center followed up its first effort with another exhibition of contemporary jewelry in 1955. This show was sponsored by *Design Quarterly,* newly reorganized and edited by Meg Torbert, and featured the work of five jewelers: Harry Bertoia, Margaret De Patta, Sam Kramer, Philip Morton, and Bob Winston. It also exhibited 115 pieces of jewelry by 84 artists. Although much of this work derived from that done by the "pioneers," all of it was well executed, and some pieces were seen to be outstanding in terms of freshness of concept and expressive means. The niello cuff links of Philip Fike (Fig. 99) transcended the ordinary conception of this item, and its utilization of the traditional technique of niello in a contemporary manner encouraged experimentation. Jerome Gates' open-ended ring (Fig. 100) represented an important new direction that was to be explored further.

above: 99. Philip Fike. Cuff link of silver and niello, c. 1955.

below 100. Jerome Gates. Cast silver ring, c. 1955.

Walker Center, 1959 By the time of the third Walker Art Center exhibition, held in 1959, a new roster of names had appeared. In all, 88 artists exhibited 155 pieces of jewelry. Of these, only two had been included in the Museum of Modern Art show, seven in the first Walker exhibit, and 44 in the 1955 Walker. These figures reveal the increasing interest in contemporary jewelry and give some indication of the number of young people newly at work in the field. The show was extremely important because it forecast many tendencies that were to become dominant in the sixties. The general level of originality in design and craftsmanship was high, and the major techniques were clearly illustrated.

Only three jewelers showed an interest in what might be called "primitive" references—the inclusion of such materials as polished bone and quartz (Fig.

above: **101. Philip Morton.** Silver pendant with found quartz pebble, c. 1959.

below **102. Irena Brynner.** Ring set with black opal and freshwater pearl, c. 1959.

101) and the use of charcoal casting. The open-ended ring reappeared with Irena Brynner's stone-set entry (Fig. 102). Indeed, with this exhibition the ring emerged as a form of dominant interest in contemporary jewelry. The interlocking wedding-ring set, which has become so popular in recent years (Figs. 240, 241) was first exhibited in this show by Robert Engstrom.

A number of other pieces displayed much originality and refinement. A necklace by Ronald Hayes Pearson (Fig. 103), sculptural in concept, evidences unusually fine workmanship and finish. For the first time in a national exhibition, the rediscovered art of granulation was represented in the entry by John Paul Miller, who has continued to explore the technique (Fig. 473).

The 1959 Walker exhibition revealed the immense popularity of the casting process, which was soon almost to dominate the field of contemporary jewelry in the United States as well as Europe. Cast and constructed forms were significantly the two most popular expressions, followed by linear forms. Interest in fused forms, plate-shape forms, strip-plate forms, and forging clearly had waned, and no jeweler exhibited repoussé work.

The final exhibition of the Walker Art Center was of great importance in revealing the heights of contemporary jewelry in 1959 and in forecasting trends that would be developed in the following decade. Meanwhile, another noteworthy national exhibition program of contemporary crafts was being organized.

St. Paul Gallery, 1951   The St. Paul Gallery initiated its biennial exhibition, "Fiber, Clay, and Metal," in 1951. Until then there had been little sustained support for the contemporary crafts movement on the part of regional communities apart from the Eastern seaboard. The St. Paul Gallery committed itself to a sustained program for the encouragement and support of independent craftsmen working in the contemporary idiom. All during the fifties this program attracted outstanding craftsmen from all sections of the United States. Through purchase awards the St. Paul Gallery acquired a splendid collection of contemporary crafts (Fig. 104).

Craft Organizations

Another important stimulus to the growth of the contemporary crafts movement was the establishment of organizations that inform, support, and foster communication among craftsmen. By far the largest of these is the American Crafts Council; of particular interest to jewelers is the Society of North American Goldsmiths.

103. Ronald Hayes Pearson. Necklace forged in 14k gold, 1958.

American Crafts Council   Among the staunchest supporters of the contemporary crafts movement in general has been Aileen O. Webb. It was largely through her efforts that the American Craftsmen's Council (later renamed the American Crafts Council) was founded in 1943, with the stated aim of stimulating "interest in the work of handcraftsmen." The Council serves as a communications medium among craftsmen and concerns itself with all phases of the crafts movement—education, exhibition, marketing, and popularization of all crafts.

One of the first acts of the Crafts Council was the establishment of America House, a retail outlet, originally in New York and later in other cities, to market the work of producing craftsmen. From the outset America House tried to set high standards to justify the higher costs of hand production. During the 1950s it stood as a symbol of survival for many craftsmen, serving as a concrete manifestation of the principle that useful products, made by hand, could be sold to people willing to pay a premium for imaginative design and individual craftsmanship. Lamentably, America House was closed in 1971, a victim of real-estate taxes.

In 1944 the American Crafts Council founded the School for American Craftsmen at Alfred, New York. Another notable offshoot of the Council is the Museum of Contemporary Crafts in New York, which maintains a lively program of exhibitions. In 1960 the Council initiated a program for the regional craft centers throughout the United States, which groups initiate fairs, exhibitions, seminars, and teaching programs. A special Department of Research and Education was formed in 1960. This section keeps folios and slides of the work of American craftsmen; provides architectural and design services for those requiring access to custom arts and crafts; offers educational films, filmstrips, and slide kits to schools and other groups; and maintains directories of craftsmen, craft courses, and craft outlets.

The First World Congress of Craftsmen, assembled in 1964 by the American Crafts Council, formed a World Crafts Council, which now meets biennially, each time in a different country. The first World Crafts Exhibition was held in Hamburg in 1973. Regional organizations have been founded for Africa, Asia, Europe, Latin America, and North America. The contemporary crafts movement is unquestionably an international phenomenon.

Society of North American Goldsmiths   In 1968 an exchange of letters among a small group of jewelers led to a meeting to plan the organization of an international guild of contemporary jewelers and metalworkers. The ultimate result of this meeting was the Society of North American Goldsmiths (SNAG), which first met at the Minnesota Museum of Art in 1970. Charter members of SNAG were: Bob Ebendorf, Fred Fenster, Philip Fike, Michael Jerry, Hero Kielman, Orland Larson, Stanley Lechtzin, Kurt J. Matzdorf, Philip Morton, Ronald Hayes Pearson, Alvin Pine, John Prip, Heikki Seppa, and Olaf Skoogfors.

The formation of SNAG was an important step toward international communication among contemporary jewelers and metalworkers. It expressed a growing sense of unity and a concern for defining and maintaining standards of performance and education. SNAG's basic goals were and are: recognizing excellence in design and craftsmanship; establishing professional standards for exhibitions, competitions, and private workshops; setting guidelines for the training of young goldsmiths and silversmiths.

During the first years of its existence, SNAG concentrated on education. Its first two major exhibitions, "Goldsmith '70" and "Goldsmith '74" are discussed on pages 64–68. A series of stimulating workshop-conferences have been initiated, and the society has also established a research library with slide and film resources.

104. Svetozar Radakovich. Cross set with stone, c. 1958.

Contemporary Jewelry in the Sixties

By the 1960s contemporary jewelry in the United States had matured. Jewelers had mastered their techniques and attained a level of sophistication that enabled them to explore new realms of design and expression. Systematic training programs, almost nonexistent twenty years earlier, had become commonplace. A number of major exhibitions were mounted during this decade, but the St. Paul Gallery's 1964 show is perhaps one of the most interesting.

The 1964 edition of "Fiber, Clay, and Metal," mounted by the St. Paul Gallery, attracted nearly four thousand entries, of which only 101 pieces were chosen for exhibition by the jury. This show marked a change in the state of contemporary crafts and confirmed that the so-called "minor arts" are indeed a rich means of expression.

Only eight jewelers were included in the 1964 St. Paul show, and none had participated in the exhibit ten years earlier. The entry under the name of "Abraham" marked the appearance of "pop" jewelry (Fig. 105). Actually, the piece was submitted by Christian Schmidt, one of the jurors, as a satirical protest against the lack of a consistent criterion for judging the entries in the various crafts. To Schmidt's consternation the pendant was accepted enthusiastically; its presence in the exhibition underscores the persistent influence of Dadaism in contemporary art (Fig. 85).

The 1964 St. Paul exhibition raised the question of whether contemporary jewelry had reached a plateau of expression. Its jury found the majority of entries "repetitious or imitative, or contrived with the obvious effort to be different." As increasing numbers of people become involved in any art activity, the level of quality may be lowered. Nevertheless, current explorations are moving both forward into new forms, and backward toward a reexamination of some traditional styles.

During the sixties contemporary jewelers turned increasingly to gold and precious stones. This trend was no doubt inevitable, since the contemporary idiom can more easily enter the larger jewelry market with the preciousness of materials the public demands. Early jewelers relied simply on silver and even valueless materials as a necessary part of the affirmation of expressive form over extrinsic values, but this almost defensive posture no longer seems necessary. There is little tendency among today's contemporary jewelers to sacrifice expressive means to extrinsic values.

Modes of Design in Contemporary Jewelry

It is difficult and dangerous to categorize jewelry, or indeed any art form, into discrete modes of expression. However, we can identify *tendencies* in the work of certain individuals and in specific pieces that would seem to divide them into two groups: those deriving from the Bauhaus credo and those based on the fantasy aesthetic of Dada and Surrealism. Of course, these two groups are loose and overlapping; both tendencies could be found in the work of a single jeweler and conceivably in a single piece. But in very general terms we can attempt to point out the dominant characteristics of the two modes, which for purposes of discussion we have labeled *rational* and *nonrational.*

The focus of the "rational" mode is simplicity—a direct corollary to honest use of materials and tools. Simplicity cannot be thought of as a quality of primitive or unskilled craftsmanship; rather, it is expressive of a rationalized milieu that always seeks the simplest, most direct, most effective, and most economical forms (Fig. 106). Rational design eliminates all nonfunctional elements, relying on clean form and pure structure. No doubt this approach is related to the nature of scientific technology, the machine, and the modern

105. "Abraham" (Christian Schmidt). *Medal of Honor,* pendant made from assorted gems, wire, and found pieces, 1964.

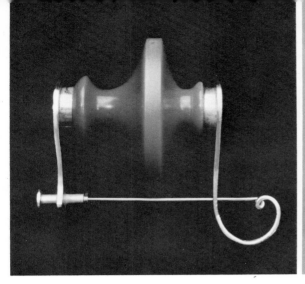

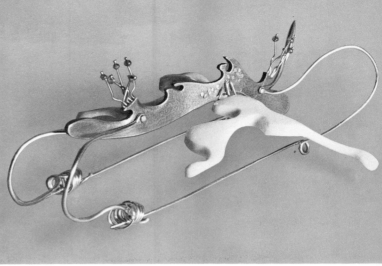

left: 106. Amy Buckingham. Brooch of
gold-plated bronze, and polyester
resin cast and turned on a lathe, 1973.

right: 107. Ccarol Phillips. *Double
Stemmed Fibula*, constructed of
14k gold, sterling silver, emerald
beads, and hand-carved ivory, 1974.

industrial process, all of which avoid the rationally superfluous; the mode has
earlier roots, however, in many historically evolved craft traditions. In the
"rational" mode tool textures and the natural textures of materials generally
displace all other surface decorations. Contemporary jewelers working in the
idiom strive to achieve the most direct expression of form arising from simple
processes, and the inherent qualities of materials.

The "nonrational" mode is the antithesis of scientific realism. Deriving
from the fantasies of Dada and Surrealism, it strives for wholeness not
perfection, symbol not concept, evocation not description. The mode can be
whimsically light-hearted or strangely saturnine in mood (Fig. 107). Particular forms celebrate the natural, the chance happening, or the organic, with its
strange alloy of patterned structure and unique occurence. In some instances
this type of expression has resulted in fantasy forms arbitrarily imposed upon
the material, rather than being a natural expression *of* the material. But when
fantasy is seen as an affirmation of the totality of human existence, it can
adapt itself to the appropriate treatment of materials.

Contemporary Crafts Today

One of the most important contributions that craftsmen have made over the
past fifty years has been in the preservation of standards in creative design and
workmanship. Moreover, they have made this contribution through the very
fact of their survival. When the masses of consumers allow their standards to
be eroded, high levels of quality can still be preserved among a small group of
working craftsmen. Historically, craftsmen have been dedicated to the principles of integrity; this is the essence of their way of life. True craftsmen want
to make real things that are useful, beautiful, original, and well-fabricated.
Their reputations rest on integrity of design and workmanship.

Unlike the "fine" artist, the craftsman is concerned with making objects
that are not only expressive but functional. A ring, for example, no matter
how inspired its design, must be considered a failure if it cannot be worn. The
creative problem of the jeweler is to integrate the aesthetic with the functional.

Contemporary jewelry is an important means of giving artistic expression
to the world of today. In order to achieve this expression, the jeweler calls into
play not only skill in mastering techniques but powers of observation and
aesthetic insight. The play of imagination is essential to any art. In the next
two chapters we will trace the development of contemporary jewelry in the
United States and Europe during the 1970s, and attempt to show how many
of today's craftsmen have attained a synthesis of function and expressive form.

Contemporary Jewelry in North America

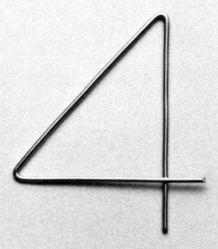

Throughout the early 1960s contemporary jewelry remained fairly imitative of earlier work. Designs tended to emphasize a pure use of materials, the direct impact of tools and techniques, and a quality of genuinely "worked" metal. Forms were basically simple and "classic." Many jewelers of the early sixties also continued to utilize traditional faceted gems, although some craftsmen in Europe and the United States experimented with form in gems as well as in metal.

Another characteristic of jewelry from this period was the relative flatness of many designs, which possibly can be traced to the influence of Art Nouveau (see Chap. 3). Art Nouveau had been a fundamental effort of the artist to create a style independent of historicism, free from pretension, and genuinely expressive. These same goals, taking quite different form, reappeared in the Pop Art movement of the sixties, to which some jewelers also responded.

During the decade between 1965 and 1975 a number of new tendencies emerged in contemporary jewelry. Craftsmen experimented with new techniques and materials, as well as modern applications for a number of ancient ones. The possibilities for content were broadened with symbolic, "message," and actually pictorial jewelry. Also, the range of jewelry objects was expanded beyond the traditional list of rings, earrings, bracelets, and necklaces to encompass a very wide range of items. New design ideas incorporated such elements as motion, thus adding time to the dimensions of form. Finally, there was a determined reinvestigation of historical forms, materials, and techniques to discover how these could be adapted for the 20th century.

This chapter, then, will outline these trends, as well as focus upon jewelers who came to prominence during the sixties and seventies. It concludes with a brief discussion of important jewelry exhibitions during the 1970s.

Current Trends

Materials

In terms of "acceptable" materials, the repertoire of the jeweler has broadened tremendously during the 1970s. For one thing, jewelers have turned increasingly to metals other than gold and silver, often combining them with precious metals in the same piece. But even more striking is the willingness among contemporary jewelers to incorporate materials not traditionally thought of as suitable for jewelry in Western culture. Frank Parkel often works with shells (Fig. 108), which he may set against metal, semiprecious gems, or leather. Gail Larson joins "found" objects with some fabricated elements to create jewelry of a pristine, machined elegance (Fig. 109). Others have explored the possibilities of materials that could be considered "primitive." A chased and etched silver brooch by Arline Fisch terminates in parrot feathers (Pl. 1, p. 149) to yield a fascinating contrast between rigid and resilient, no-color and color, shine and soft texture. Yet more exotic is a

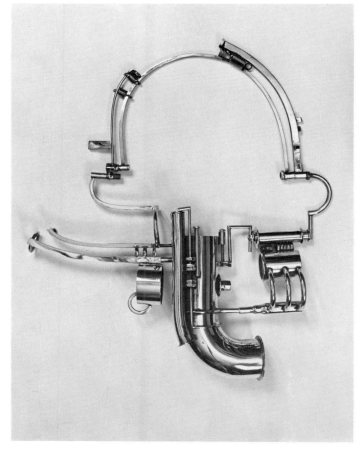

above: 108. Frank Parkel. Bronze and sterling pendant, cast by the lost-wax method, with leather, two sundial shells, and a reddish-brown onyx, 1975.

right: 109. Gail Larson. Neckpiece constructed of found objects and handmade brass parts, 1973.

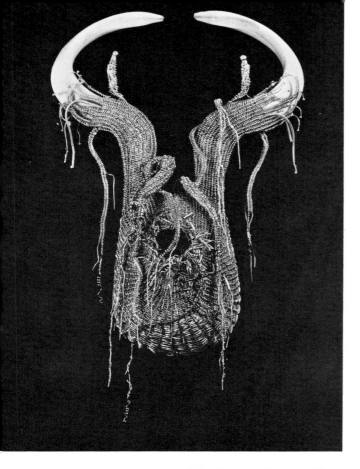

left: **110. Mary Lee Hu.** *Neckpiece #8,* wrapped, woven, and constructed of fine silver, gold-filled brass, and boar's tusks, 1973. The wire basketry (22-gauge warp, 26-gauge weft) was shaped as the work progressed, without the use of a frame.

below: **111. Amy Buckingham.** Pin constructed of gold-plated bronze and a Plexiglas block, 1975.

right: **112. Sandra Parmer Zilker.** *Armored Car Elbow Ornament,* neckpiece of fused sterling and flexible hollow plastic tubing, with moonstone, 1975.

neckpiece by Mary Lee Hu (Fig. 110) made from woven silver and brass wire worked upon a support of boar's tusks.

A number of jewelers have turned to plastic as the material most representative of the 20th century, often combining it with metals in a manner reminiscent of Art Deco jewelry (see p. 36). Amy Buckingham has worked in Plexiglas, which is drilled and filed to create the impression of distortion (Fig. 111). Gilt-bronze tubes provide a support for the pin illustrated. Sandra Zilker's neckpiece (Fig. 112) is of fused and fabricated sterling silver, with a moonstone set against flexible plastic tubing.

Jewelers of the seventies seem particularly fascinated with mixtures of materials, some precious and some crude, of varying textures and colors. A handbag by Eleanor Moty (Fig. 113) joins sterling silver, brass, inlay of various metals, agate, ivory, and leather to create an effect that is amazingly unified. Ed Lund merged leather with fused and forged copper in a heavy, organic pendant (Fig. 114). Lund has also worked with feathers (Fig. 143).

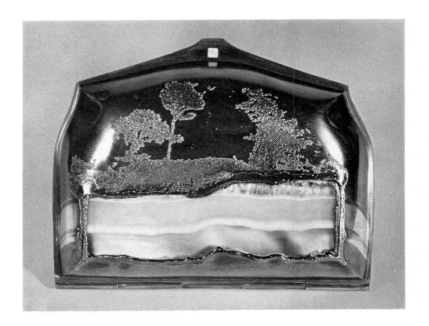

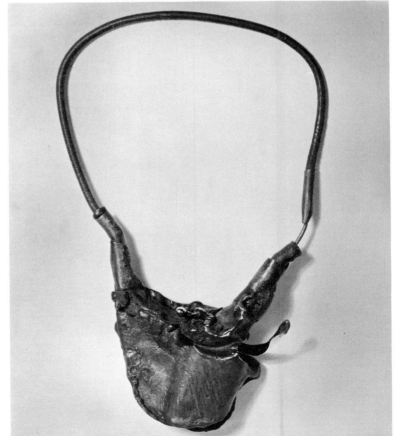

above: 113. Eleanor Moty. *Landscape Handbag,* of sterling silver with silver photo-electroplating, brass, assorted metal inlays, agate, ivory, and photoprinted leather, 1973.

right: 114. Ed Lund. Pendant of fused and forged copper, with leather, 1969.

Technique

Paralleling the wider range of materials in the seventies has been a much expanded repertoire of techniques and methods of working—some revivals of ancient processes, others made possible by the technology of the 20th century. In the first category is granulation, which was perfected by the ancient Etruscans more than two millenia ago. A thoroughly contemporary interpretation of the method appears in the work of John Marshall (Fig. 115), in which small gold chips substitute for the usual beads. In the brooches illustrated here Marshall has fused the gold chips to silver, so that the colors of the metals complement the irregular, organic shapes.

Another ancient technique involves the interlacing, knotting, and wrapping of flexible strands. As adapted by Mary Lee Hu, with strands of silver and gold-filled brass (Fig. 110), such weaving assumes a character that is bold, harsh, and evocative of 20th-century primitivism. In sharp contrast is the work of Thomas Gentille, who used strands of brass wire wrapped and knotted over ebony in a brooch of classic, elegant form (Fig. 116).

The ancient technique of forging has come into greater prominence in the development of fantasy forms and in the exploration of the rich textures—rather than the plain surfaces—of metals. As a further expression of interest in textural contrasts, the ancient Japanese art of *mokume* has been investigated. A pendant by Chuck Evans (Fig. 496) successfully exemplifies both of these techniques.

Electroforming and electroplating are, of course, techniques very much of our own age. The acknowledged master of electroforming is Stanley Lechtzin, who has developed the process over many years of experimentation. In the brooch shown in Figure 117 he has set tourmaline crystals and a mobe pearl into a free-form electroformed shape. Very different in character is *False Façade* (Fig. 118), a copper-electroformed belt buckle by Stephen Albair. Here the electroforming technique served the artist's fantasy in mimicking the outlines of a building. Found objects, Plexiglas, and silver tubing complete the effect. The process of photo-electroplating decorated a handbag by Eleanor Moty (Fig. 113), which also includes photo-printed leather.

left: 115. John Marshall. Silver brooches, repoussé and chased, with gold chips granulated to the surface, 1971.

right: 116. Thomas Gentille. Pin of pierced ebony wrapped with brass wire, set in a bezel of cast and pierced 10k yellow gold.

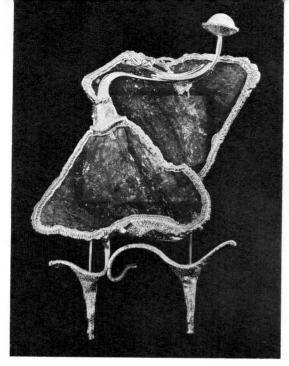

Content

As the distinction between artist and craftsman has become increasingly blurred, craftsmen have begun to introduce more and more explicit "content" into their work, and jewelers are no exception. It is not uncommon today to find pieces of jewelry that make a definite statement—political, social, cultural, or simply nostalgic. Works of this kind are typically titled; often they incorporate words, found objects, or photographs (Fig. 119). Nilda Getty's *In Faith . . . Deceived,* a pin-medal of gold and silver with semiprecious gems, is part of a series the artist calls *Proud American* (Fig. 120).

left: 121. J. Fred Woell. *Family Icon/Mother,* medal of silver, brass, glass, steel, and copper, constructed from found objects including a den-mother badge, camera lens, and a faceted glass bead, 1967.

right: 122. Bob Ebendorf. *Color Smoke Machine,* pin of copper, silver, Plexiglas, and pearls, 1974.

Found objects are an integral part of much "message" jewelry. For example, J. Fred Woell describes *Family Icon/Mother* (Fig. 121) as being "fabricated out of parts and pieces of things I had found or collected." The photograph (stained to "age" the image), came from a magazine advertisement for salt, the glass covering the picture was an old camera lens, and the emblem at top is an actual den-mother badge. Conversely, jewelry objects that resemble machines or other nonjewelry items are sometimes totally fabricated. Bob Ebendorf's *Color Smoke Machine* (Fig. 122) is made of copper and silver with Plexiglas and pearls.

Since painters and sculptors have long been incorporating messages and symbols into their art, it is not surprising that jewelers should adopt the tradition. This tendency refers back to Dada and Surrealism (see pp. 44–45), as well as to the Pop Art of the 1960s. And, of course, jewelry featuring portraiture has a long history, even though modern interpretations may be satirical or nostalgic.

Historical References

In contrast to the sentimental, imitative historicism of the 19th century, historical references in the work of many contemporary jewelers have a fresh and imaginative quality. Such references may be in the form of design characteristics, techniques, or actual objects made or otherwise associated with another era.

In the pin shown in Figure 302, Philip Fike set out deliberately to experiment with the wire-coiling techniques of the ancient Etruscans. The artist considers it a challenge to duplicate with faithful exactitude the painstaking methods of the early jewelers—in this case, to get a complex design from a single piece of wire. However, the form to which this old process is applied is wholly contemporary, as is the contrast between gold and black wood.

The historical references in Figures 123 and 124 are visual rather than actual; they both suggest historical forms reinterpreted in a modern idiom. A necklace by William Fuhrmann (Fig. 123) recalls Berlin ironwork of the 19th century (Fig. 4), yet it includes contemporary and even Pop elements. Similarly, a mirror by Richard Mafong and Jon Eric Riis (Fig. 124), which at first glance seems reminiscent of Victorian prototypes, is actually quite contemporary in its flat, stylized design and the use of metallic threads.

The only historical element in Joseph Gatto's ring (Fig. 125) is the borrowing of an ancient symbol as decoration—the Egyptian scarab. This usage continues a tradition that has prevailed for thousands of years—that is, the incorporation of ancient symbols, such as the key, the acanthus leaf, and the cross, as pure design elements. When used in Egyptian jewelry (Fig. 23), the scarab acted as a symbol of rebirth; in Gatto's ring it pays tribute to a culture far removed from our own and yet full of meaning for us. On the back of the ring, Gatto has signed his name in hieroglyphs.

Objects

One of the most interesting aspects of jewelry in the seventies is the freedom with which craftsmen have enlarged the traditional roster of acceptable jewelry objects. Our society is perhaps among the most staid in the kinds of pieces it permits for adornment; jewelry is essentially limited to rings, earrings, bracelets, cuff links, and necklaces. But, as Chapters 1 and 2 show, other cultures have accepted a much wider range of items, and the contemporary jeweler is now beginning to experiment with them.

A number of craftsmen today are fabricating belt buckles (Figs. 118, 204) or even whole belts from metal (Fig. 126). Such objects offer the potential of elaborate or innovative decoration, particularly because they present a broad, flat surface. Nonwestern cultures provide a number of jewelry objects that are new to us. Glenda Arentzen has worked with fingertip cases (Fig. 127), which recall those of the Chinese nobility (Fig. 5). Jonathan Parry's mask (Fig. 128) shows the influence of African prototypes in its exotic ferocity, though certainly not in design or materials.

Bracelets are very common in our jewelry repertoire, but they are much less usual on men than on women. David Laplantz' man's bracelet (Fig. 129), with its heavy iron links, seems specifically designed to be worn on the thicker, hairier male wrist. A different kind of bracelet, the large, hinged cuff, has been worn in many parts of the world. Anne Echelman's pair of bracelets (Fig. 433) echoes historical styles but in the modern idiom.

Several jewelers have branched out even further into items not worn on the body. Barbara Becker's picture frame of bronze, silver, and Plexiglas provides the setting for an old tintype (Fig. 130). Frames and mirrors have also become popular, no doubt because the combination of reflective material with metal and gems holds such fascination (Fig. 124; Pl. 2, p. 149).

Design

Part II of this book deals with questions of design for contemporary jewelry and points out the trends that seem to characterize the 1970s. However, we might mention briefly here some of the concerns that are of special importance for the present decade.

A number of jewelers have explored the concept of motion in jewelry (Fig. 131). Albert Paley, for one, designs many of his brooches in such a way that

left: **126. Nilda C. Getty.** *Shan,* belt cast and constructed in sterling silver, with moonstones and jades, 1974.

right: **127. Glenda Arentzen.** Fingertip cases of vermeil with pearls, enamel, and gems, 1973.

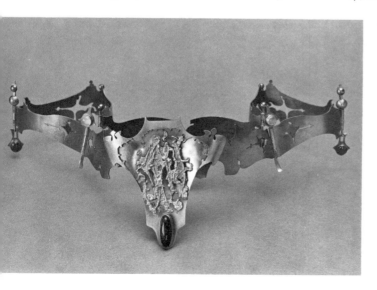

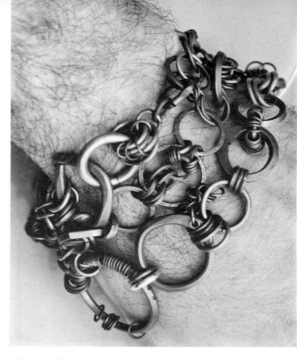

above left: 128. Jonathan Parry. Mask of gold-plated silver, forged and constructed with stone and feathers, c. 1974. Minnesota Museum of Art, Saint Paul.

above: 129. David Laplantz. Man's bracelet, constructed from copper, silver, brass, and iron links of various sizes and shapes, 1971.

above: 130. Barbara Becker. *Sojourn,* picture frame of pierced and cast bronze, sterling silver, tintype photograph (c. 1860), and Plexiglas, 1972. Back leg swivels to allow the frame to be either hung on the wall or placed on a table.

right: 131. Philip Morton. Slide-catch brooch, cast in 14k gold, with moonstone, tourmaline, sapphire, and zircon, 1969. The moonstone is set on a movable catch that slides to the right to release the pin.

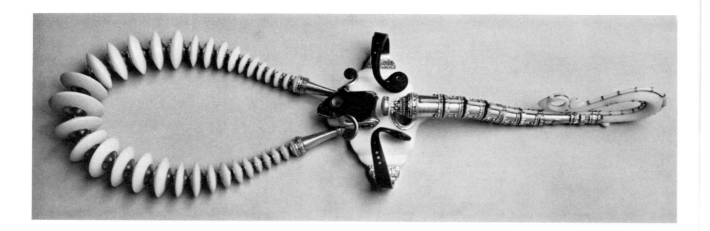

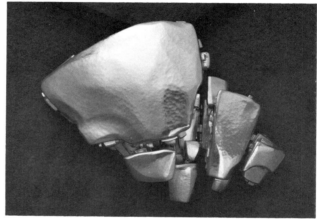

top: **132. Albert Paley.** *Pendant 142,* constructed from silver, copper, 14k gold, and Delrin, with tourmaline and glass lens, c. 1974.

above left: **133. Helen Shirk.** Hinged bracelet of forged silver, copper, and red brass, with oxidized finish and agate setting, 1975.

above right: **134. John Paul Miller.** Pendant/brooch forged in 18k yellow gold, 1973.

they conform to every movement of the body (Fig. 132). Another tendency is the development of highly complex forms, often with mixed materials and techniques (Fig. 133). But existing side by side with this complexity is a design aesthetic that exploits the intrinsic characteristics of materials (Fig. 134). All of these trends, and others as well, have been represented in the important jewelry shows of the 1970s.

Major Exhibitions of the Seventies

Goldsmith '70   The seventies opened dramatically for contemporary jewelry with "Goldsmith '70," an exhibition sponsored jointly by the newly formed Society of North American Goldsmiths and the Minnesota Museum of Art in Saint Paul. "Goldsmith '70" summarized the most advanced jewelry and metalwork being done in the United States and Canada through the sixties and included work by the leading practitioners in the field. The show demonstrated how a major art institution and an independent craft guild could achieve perfect cooperation without loss of identity. For the museum, successor to the old Saint Paul Gallery, it represented a continuation of the "Fiber, Clay, and Metal" shows (see pp. 50, 52); for SNAG it marked the initial step toward a modern integration of an ancient craft.

"Goldsmith '70" included 127 works by 72 North American jewelers. Both metalwork and jewelry were represented. As a whole the show was substantial, mature, and in the highest order of craftsmanship and design. There seemed an effort to transcend traditional, regular, hollowware forms with irregularity, asymmetry, and the development of volume. Of special interest was the revival of crease-raised forms and spatially exploded forms.

Several entries reflected the Pop Art movement of the sixties. Among the more successful was David Laplantz' *Real American Male Pendant* (Fig. 135), which, by virtue of its hard-edge arrow, directs our attention to the fact that both zip codes and cheese spreads are inescapable. John Prip's entry (Fig. 136) celebrates the rational and geometric, in a masterful display of virtuosity. J. Fred Woell's *Family Icon/Mother* (Fig. 121) is more in the Dada idiom, an area of nostalgia that Woell has consistently explored. We also see in the 1970s a minor trend of fascination for 19th-century decoration.

A sterling necklace by Alma Eikerman (Fig. 137) provides a beautiful example of the contemporary handling of pure metal, speaking of and for itself. Here the metal contrasts marvelously with the pellucid moonstone.

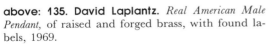

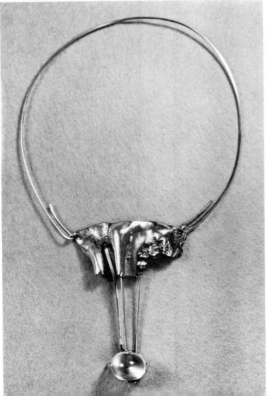

above: 135. David Laplantz. *Real American Male Pendant,* of raised and forged brass, with found labels, 1969.

above right: 136. John Prip. Gold-plated sterling pin, set with mother-of-pearl, lapis lazuli, and glass, c. 1970.

right: 137. Alma Eikerman. Neckpiece of repoussé sterling, with moonstone, 1970.

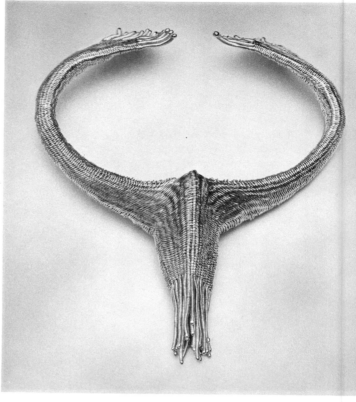

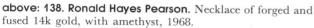

above: **138. Ronald Hayes Pearson.** Necklace of forged and fused 14k gold, with amethyst, 1968.

right: **139. Mary Lee Hu.** *Neckpiece #5,* wrapped and woven of fine and sterling silver, 1969. The wire basketry (22-gauge warp, 26-gauge weft) was shaped as the work progressed, without the use of a frame.

below: **140. Olli Peter Valanne.** *Ju-Ju Ring,* cast and constructed of gold-plated bronze and plastic, 1969.

Ronald Hayes Pearson's entry (Fig. 138) illustrates conventional forging carried to flawless execution.

Mary Lee Hu's neckpiece (Fig. 139) established the trend toward mixed media—in this instance fiber techniques applied to metal. Weaving, of course, is an ancient device, but its application to jewelry in the 20th century represents a real exploration to controvert post-Renaissance conservatism. A ring by Olli Peter Valanne (Fig. 140) asserts the suitability of plastics for jewelry, the material here being combined with bronze. This usage calls into question some of the traditional aspects of jewelry: durability, rarity, and preciousness. It remains to be seen whether the underlying identity of jewelry can be expanded to embrace new industrial materials for the sake of their intrinsic qualities.

Both Miye Matsukata and Richard Mawdsley exhibited works that suggest historical reference. Matsukata's pin (Fig. 141) seems to combine antiquity with a modern approach in its mixture of gold, Chinese pi, Mayan beads, tourmaline, and ruby. Rich textures and simple forms integrate the exotic artifacts with metal and gems. Mawdsley's *Calliope* (Fig. 142), a necklace of silver, pearls, lapis, and enamel, seems cast in the image of medieval symbolism. The piece both intrigues and baffles us, in the manner of a slightly demonic toy.

All told, the "Goldsmith '70" exhibition represented all the new trends we have touched upon—materials, technique, content, historical reference, and design. After closing in Saint Paul, the show traveled in its entirety to fourteen other museums, and an auxiliary invitational show reached an even greater audience. Such demand indicates the interest that contemporary jewelry generates.

National Student Metal Invitational Another exhibition of contemporary jewelry and metalwork that has been important for the seventies is the "National Student Metal Invitational." Initiated by Bob Ebendorf while he was at the University of Georgia, the recurring show is now sponsored by the Society of North American Goldsmiths. Its third edition was held at the Tyler School of Art, Temple University, in Philadelphia.

The major purpose of the "National Student Metal Invitational" is to give stimulus and encouragement to advanced students, as well as to provide a public showing of current work. Invitations have been offered only to students of jewelry working under the tutelage of SNAG members, but in the future this may be broadened to make the show a truly national one.

Metal + 72 The "Metal + 72" exhibition, organized by Thomas Markusen, was sponsored by the State University of New York, College at Brockport. This show invited ten established metal craftsmen to exhibit, and each was to select two additional craftsmen of outstanding talent. In all, 25 craftsmen were represented by 123 works, offering a wide range of techniques, materials, and designs. In terms of craftsmanship, the exhibition offered an outstanding display.

Jewelry Invitational: American Goldsmiths and Silversmiths Held at the Fairtree Gallery in New York and then at Washington's Corcoran Gallery of Art in the fall of 1972, "American Goldsmiths and Silversmiths" brought together a group of avant-garde jewelers, primarily from the East Coast (Pl. 3, p. 149; Fig. 116). Works that embody fantasy made a very strong appearance, and the heritage of both Art Nouveau and Dada were evident. In terms of technique a very broad range was represented, including electroforms, photo-engraving, enameling, plastic processes, and work in ferrous metals.

above: **141. Miye Matsukata.** Pin of 18k and 24k gold, set with Chinese pi, Mayan beads, tourmaline, and ruby, c. 1970.

left: **142. Richard Mawdsley.** *Calliope,* sterling pendant with pearls, lapis lazuli, and enamel, 1967.

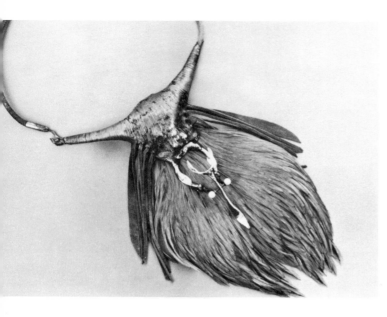

above left: **143. Ed Lund,** *Ritual Pendant* of copper and leather, with rooster feathers and pearls, c. 1970.

above right: **144. Lee Barnes Peck.** Ring of cast silver, plated in fine gold and copper, with hematite and glass, 1972. Minnesota Museum of Art, Saint Paul.

below left: **145. Richard Mawdsley.** *Wine and Roses,* ring cast and constructed in 14k gold, with garnet, 1974. Minnesota Museum of Art, Saint Paul.

Profiles in Jewelry An interesting national competition, "Profiles in Jewelry," was held at Texas Tech University in Lubbock during the spring of 1973. For the most part this show drew young jewelers concerned with attracting recognition, and it included some really outstanding work (Figs. 143, 125, 476). It is a healthy sign for contemporary jewelry that a national exhibition should be held beyond the major craft concentration areas—that is, the East and Far West.

The Goldsmith The great demand for jewelry on the part of museums and galleries around the United States led to a joint decision of the Renwick Gallery in Washington and the Minnesota Museum of Art to sponsor "The Goldsmith" in 1974. The Society of North American Goldsmiths cooperated in assembling the show; after its initial stay in the two museums, the exhibition toured the country extensively.

Included were 164 pieces from 128 metalworkers—51 invitational works and 113 chosen from more than seven hundred entries. "The Goldsmith" illustrated the tremendous vitality and energy that enlivens contemporary jewelry of the seventies. Exhibiting craftsmen showed a vastly increased interest in fantasy and the "baroque" style (Figs. 144, 145). There was also a marked tendency to explore a wide range of materials, including iron, leather, fiber, copper, brass, bronze, and feathers (Figs. 110, 128). Traditional jewelry pieces—rings, bracelets, earrings, and so forth—declined in favor of the pendant (Fig. 132), which allows the maximum freedom of expressive virtuosity. Taken all together, the entries in "The Goldsmith" displayed a broad cross-section of contemporary metalwork at its best.

The history of modern art begins in Europe, with the experimental work of Impressionism, Cubism, Dada and Surrealism. However, the expression of this movement in jewelry appears to have originated, or at least manifested itself most clearly, in the United States during the 1930s. The explanation of this must lie partly in the fact that European craftsmen, to a far greater extent than their American counterparts, are immersed in their own rich traditions —traditions not only of aesthetic styles but also of habits of craftsmanship. Moreover, certain venerable jewelry firms catering to a conservative market have long dominated the European jewelry scene. The contemporary styles in jewelry may have found a more responsive audience in the United States simply because there existed no long indigenous traditions in jewelry.

By the 1960s, however, tendencies already established in the United States were beginning to appear in European work. The "First International Exhibition of Modern Jewellery," held in London in 1961, took note of jewelers' interest in uncut stones, in machine fabrication of chains, and especially in casting—all signals of a turning toward contemporary modes. During that decade great advances were made, and a large number of exhibitions gave support to the movement of contemporary jewelry. We will briefly discuss this formative decade before moving to a consideration of work in individual countries during the 1970s.

European Jewelry of the Sixties

Several interesting tendencies were to be found in the work of European jewelers during the sixties. In Germany, Friedrich Becker explored gem forms

(Fig. 146) and showed a special interest in movement as an aspect of design, developing a number of changeable or kinetic designs (Fig. 147). Gunter Wyss, working in Switzerland, displayed a lyrical mastery of sheet-metal forms (Fig. 148). The Spaniards Joaquin and Manuel Capdevilla worked in a style that was delicate yet commanding (Fig. 149). In England, John Donald explored the beauties of crystalline natural forms (Fig. 150), and Andrew Grima utilized rich textural effects in combination with strong, simple shapes (Fig. 151). Textural richness, as found in the subtle art of reticulation, was an important goal for many European jewelers in the sixties. A pin by Reinhold Reiling of Germany (Fig. 152) shows a delight in chanced-upon qualities of form. Conversely, many jewelers, including the Italian Mario Pinton, re-affirmed the ideal of absolute simplicity (Fig. 153).

left: 146. Friedrich Becker. White-gold ring with light-blue topaz, 1967.

below left: 147. Friedrich Becker. Kinetic brooch in white gold, with diamonds, 1967. Eight adjustable levers bear on hinge points to allow changes in the shape of the brooch.

below right: 148. Gunter Wyss. Gold pin shaped as a double mobius strip, 1966.

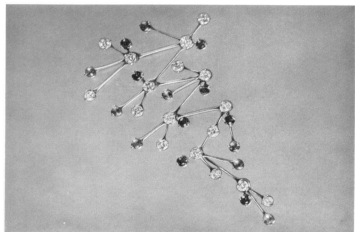

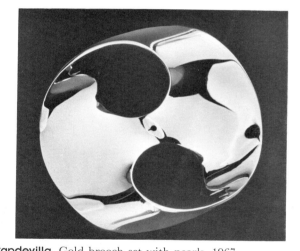

below left: 149. Joaquin Capdevilla. Gold brooch set with pearls, 1967.

below right: 150. John Donald. Gold watch bracelet and matching pin with diamonds, 1967.

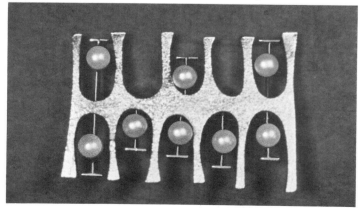

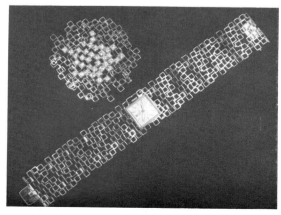

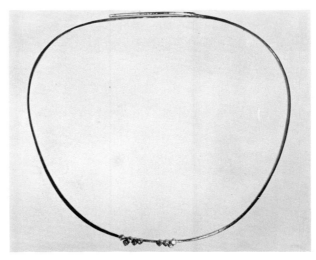

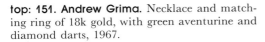

top: **151. Andrew Grima.** Necklace and matching ring of 18k gold, with green aventurine and diamond darts, 1967.

above: **152. Reinhold Reiling.** Reticulated gold brooch, with moonstone, yellow sapphire, green and blue sapphire, diamond, quartz, and pearls, 1967.

right: **153. Mario Pinton.** Gold necklace, 1967.

Contemporary Jewelry in Europe **71**

154. Andrew Grima. White-gold necklace, with pendant of carved black agate and a diamond, on a stem of white gold, platinum, and channel-set diamonds, 1973.

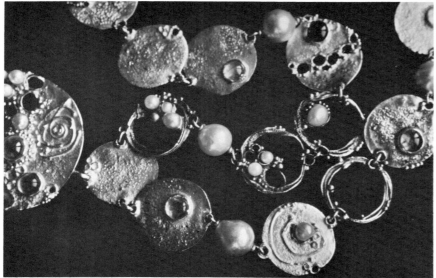

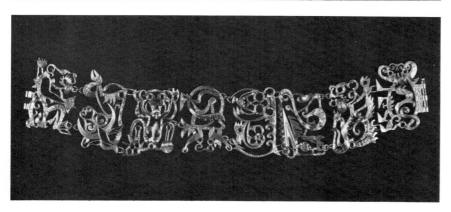

above left: **155. Gerda Flockinger.** Necklace fused and constructed of 18k gold and oxidized silver, with gray cultured pearls, natural Lake Biwa pearls, green and pink tourmalines, quartz, and orange garnet, 1973.

left: **156. Malcolm Appleby.** *Bulls and Bears,* link bracelet made from different-colored golds, with deeply engraved surface decoration, 1973. Links form stylized representations of bulls and bears.

European Jewelry of the Seventies

In the 1970s one can identify certain trends that are paralleled in Europe and the United States—a shift toward fantasy in style, a greater curiosity about plastics and other industrial innovations in technique. While it is possible to make generalizations about the jewelers throughout Europe, it is perhaps more interesting to discuss the work of individuals in relation to their compatriots, especially within the context of educational and industrial programs existing in the different countries.

England   Most English jewelers take their training in one of the large art schools, among the foremost of which is the Sir John Cass School of Art in London. At this institution a four-year program instructs students in design and the techniques of metalwork—including engraving, which is virtually a lost art in the United States. The program emphasizes mastery of conventional diamond mounting and the design of forms appropriate to such mounts. Graphic design and rendering form the basis for creation of jewelry meant for industrial production.

Only in recent years has contemporary design begun to penetrate the programs of English craft schools, but it is rapidly becoming the dominant direction. Under the leadership of Graham Hughes and Peter Gainsbury, organizations such as the Worshipful Company of Goldsmiths are taking an active role in promoting contemporary metalwork and in bringing new jewelry styles to industry. At the same time, jewelry training courses in England are providing students with the technical background to support original design. A number of creative jewelers have attained the enviable position of gaining a degree of acceptance in industry while at the same time preserving their strong identities as experimental craftsmen. These include John Donald (Fig. 150), Andrew Grima (Figs. 151, 154), and Gerda Flockinger (Fig. 155). Jewelry of the seventies in England is well represented by the work of Anthony Hawksley (Fig. 388), Douglas Wagstaff (Figs. 14, 233), Malcolm Appleby (Fig. 156), and Gunilla Treen (Fig. 157), as well as Wendy Ramshaw (Pl. 4, p. 150).

157. Gunilla Treen. Acrylic brooch with anodized titanium background and silver birds and rivets, 1974.

France   Two aspects of contemporary jewelry in France are illustrated by the work of Gilles Jonemann and Arlette Baron (Figs. 158, 159). Jonemann is primarily a sculptor, and his jewelry is highly sculptural in conception. A two-finger ring of gold (Fig. 158) is capped by a free-form organic shape of polished ebony. For other works by Jonemann, see Figures 197, 236, and 535.

Baron works exclusively in silver but using the techniques of goldworking, which she learned during her apprenticeship under the Swedish goldsmith Torun Bülow Hübe. Figure 159 shows a unique silver collar made from hammered wire soldered to vertical bars of silver. A hammered-silver necklace by Baron appears in Figure 544.

left: 158. Gilles Jonemann. Two-finger ring of ebony and 18k yellow gold, 1973.

right: 159. Arlette Baron. Collar formed and constructed of silver wire soldered to connecting silver strips, 1970.

Denmark   Although Denmark today is almost synonymous with modern design, her jewelers have been relatively slow—compared to those in the United States—in adopting contemporary styles, no doubt because of the solidly entrenched conservative tradition championed by the firm of Georg Jensen. A positive side effect of this dominance, however, is the emphasis on impeccable craftsmanship, which is supported by an arduous educational and apprenticeship system. Students receive thorough grounding in gold- and silversmithing techniques, followed by a period of practice in the shop of a master metalsmith. Advanced programs include training in enameling, stone setting, metallurgy, and casting, as well as special studies in design. The Danish government and the Goldsmiths' Union jointly support this educational process. Graduates of the training program are now beginning to be welcomed by industry.

Not surprisingly in light of Danish design generally, there is a tendency among Danish jewelers toward simplicity of form and directness of technique. This is evident in the work reproduced here, by Agnete Dinesen, Helga and Bent Exner, Ole Kjaer Jensen, Poul Sørresiig, and Willy Palden (Figs. 160–164).

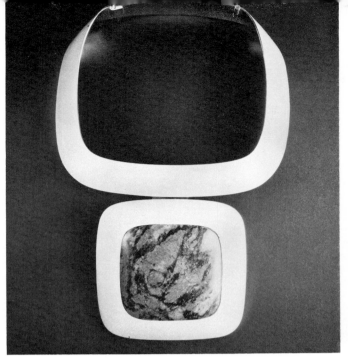

above: 160. **Agnete Dinesen.** Sandblasted silver necklace with a red and black gneiss, c. 1974.

above right: 161. **Helga and Bent Exner.** Brooch in white gold and cubes of tugtupite, created for H. R. H. Queen Ingrid of Denmark, c. 1972.

right: 162. **Ole Kjaer Jensen.** Chased gold ring, c. 1974.

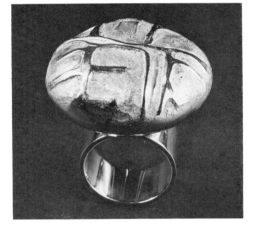

below: 163. **Poul Sørresiig.** Seven rings of sterling silver and individually cut lapis lazuli, 1972.

below: 164. **Willy Palden.** Cast silver ring, 1970.

Sweden   Like the Danes, Swedish jewelers have by and large eschewed extreme innovations in design, but their craftsmanship is superior. The overriding goals are technical purity and enduring design quality, rather than avant-garde sensationalism. There is a tendency for individual jewelers to work in depth rather than in breadth, and thus to achieve an impressive mastery over specific techniques.

Ohl Ohlsson has experimented with etching silver since the early 1960s; his metalwork and jewelry reflect the skill in depth that results from such concentration (Figs. 165, 480). Ohlsson achieves unusual but controlled biting effects—textural dots and parallel ridgings—by means of sulphuric acid in a strong solution, stopped out by an asphalt ground. He has also experimented with fusing a low-melting-point silver (840/1000 alloy) on regular sterling, directing gas to the torch through a liquid fluxing tank. This gives absolutely

166. Ann-Christine Hultberg. Forged sterling bracelet, c. 1973.

clean fusing with no oxidation. For further carving and texturing of the surfaces, Ohlsson uses a flexible-shaft drill with very fine burs.

The work of Ann-Christine Hultberg is not unusual in the technical sense, but her designs reflect a special sense of rhythm and a complete mastery of the basic processes (Fig. 166). Other Swedish jewelers—including Kerstin Öhlin Lejonklou, Theresia Hvorslev, and Eric Robbert—have mastered the art of stone setting in fresh and inventive ways (Figs. 167–169). Sigurd Persson works in plastic (Pl. 5, p. 150), combining it with precious metals and occasionally with gems. Persson has also experimented with unusual forms, such as the collar-necklace shown in Figure 170. Other works by Persson are reproduced in Figures 198, 211, 213, 248, and 252, and on the cover.

above left: 167. Kerstin Öhlin Lejonklou. Brooch in 18k gold, with diamonds, 1963.

above: 168. Theresia Hvorslev. Bridal crown of sterling silver, with 18k-gold spheres and white pearls, c. 1972.

above: 169. Eric Robbert. Silver brooch with tourmaline and pearls, c. 1973.

right: 170. Sigurd Persson. Silver necklace, 1965.

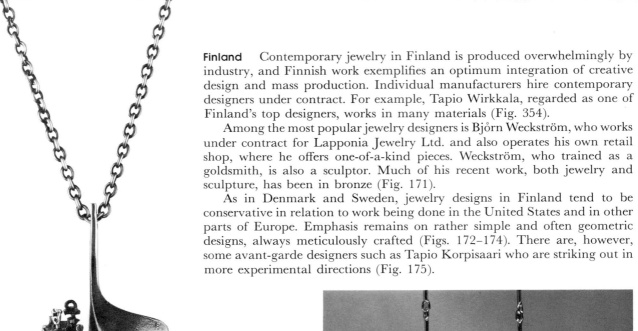

Finland   Contemporary jewelry in Finland is produced overwhelmingly by industry, and Finnish work exemplifies an optimum integration of creative design and mass production. Individual manufacturers hire contemporary designers under contract. For example, Tapio Wirkkala, regarded as one of Finland's top designers, works in many materials (Fig. 354).

Among the most popular jewelry designers is Björn Weckström, who works under contract for Lapponia Jewelry Ltd. and also operates his own retail shop, where he offers one-of-a-kind pieces. Weckström, who trained as a goldsmith, is also a sculptor. Much of his recent work, both jewelry and sculpture, has been in bronze (Fig. 171).

As in Denmark and Sweden, jewelry designs in Finland tend to be conservative in relation to work being done in the United States and in other parts of Europe. Emphasis remains on rather simple and often geometric designs, always meticulously crafted (Figs. 172–174). There are, however, some avant-garde designers such as Tapio Korpisaari who are striking out in more experimental directions (Fig. 175).

top: 171. Björn Weckström. *Springfield,* pendant cast in bronze, c. 1972.

above: 172. Reino Saastamoinen. Hinged bracelet, cast and constructed with rose quartz, c. 1974.

above right: 173. Juhani Linnovaara. *Notturno,* white-gold pendant with diamonds, c. 1973.

right: 174. Mirjam Salminen. Gold ring with natural garnet crystal, c. 1973.

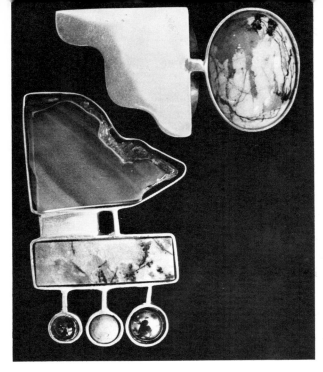

left: **175. Tapio Korpisaari.** Silver pins set with natural stones, c. 1974.

below: **176. Emmy van Leersum.** Stainless-steel bracelet, 1968.

bottom left: **177. Gijs Bakker.** Aluminum bracelet, the two parts cut and formed without soldering, 1972.

bottom right: **178. Gijs Bakker.** *Profile,* stainless-steel face ornament (modeled by Emmy van Leersum), 1974.

The Netherlands Two Dutch jewelers of international reputation, Emmy van Leersum and Gijs Bakker, can be considered representative of the most innovative designers working today in the Netherlands. Although they maintain separate studios, Van Leersum and Bakker share an underlying concept and design aesthetic in their pristine, utterly simple jewelry. Their materials are stainless steel and aluminum, the most common pieces starkly simple bracelets and collars.

A bracelet by Van Leersum (Fig. 176) illustrates the drastic simplification of technique that both jewelers have sought. Here form is created by bending alone, leaving the industrial sheen of the metal and pure geometry of shape to carry the design. Similarly, an aluminum bracelet by Bakker (Fig. 177) was formed purely by cutting, with no soldering or other joining techniques. In a more frivolous but equally stark vein is a stainless-steel "profile" (Fig. 178) created by Bakker and modeled by Van Leersum. With this recent work the craftsman was attempting to "make the shape less important and let the body make the shape."

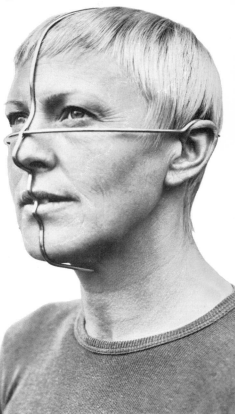

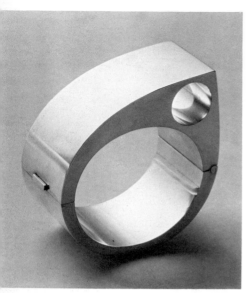

Another Dutch jeweler, Chris Steenbergen, works in silver and with less elemental forming and joining techniques. Still, the bracelet shown in Figure 179 demonstrates the same cool, precise, geometric quality as the work of Van Leersum and Bakker. All of these pieces could be described as the ultimate extension of the "rational" mode of design discussed in Chapter 3 (see pp. 52–53), in that they exemplify pure form, pure use of materials, and absolute clarity of technique.

Germany In West Germany, the contemporary style has only begun to penetrate the jewelry industry, which is large, technically oriented, and extremely energetic. With the possible exception of Finland, however, West Germany is probably moving more completely toward contemporary expression than any other European country.

A number of schools exist for the training of metalsmiths, and there is some opportunity for cooperation with industry for trained designers. In general, however, goldsmiths must find their own way in individual workshops or through teaching.

Design trends parallel those being followed elsewhere on the Continent, with a great curiosity about new materials and techniques, as well as an interest in fantasy forms (Figs. 180, 181). Many of the most interesting new designs seem to be graphic in quality (Fig. 182), while there is a continuation of the strongly mechanical, industrial, and "minimal" type of form—not surprising in a nation that holds the legacy of the Bauhaus.

179. Chris Steenbergen. Hinged bracelet in sterling silver, 1970.

above: **180. Herman Junger.** Still-life brooches of various gold alloys and silver, c. 1972.

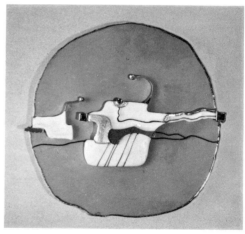

below: **181. Uwe Böttinger.** Brooch of gold and ivory, with green copper patina, 1973.

left: **182. Klaus Ullrich.** Brooch of gold and stainless steel, with emerald, c. 1973.

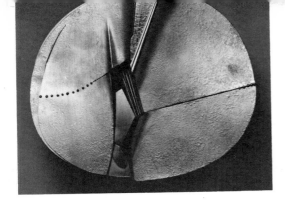

left: **183. Othmar Zschaler.** Reticulated gold brooch, 1972.

right: **184. Elisabeth Kodre.** Pendant of yellow and white gold, with tourmalines and brilliants, c. 1973.

below right: **185. Helfried Kodre.** Pin of gold and silver, with tourmaline and brilliants, c. 1974.

Switzerland   In terms of jewelry, Switzerland almost inevitably calls to mind Swiss watches, but this is by no means the beginning and end. The fact that Switzerland is a vacation mecca for the rest of Europe opens an almost inexhaustible market for fine handmade goods, including jewelry. While the established jewelry trade serves most of this market, there are independent craftsmen who are carrying on the development of advanced design (Figs. 183, 228). The cause of contemporary design in general has been greatly fostered by the ambitious exhibition program of the Musée des Arts Decoratifs in Lausanne.

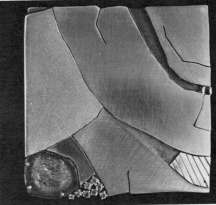

Austria   Among the more prominent Austrian jewelers are Elisabeth and Helfried Kodre, who have participated in important European exhibitions. A pendant by Elisabeth Kodre (Fig. 184) is organic in form and shows an interesting use of gems. Helfried Kodre's pin (Fig. 185) exemplifies a two-dimensional aesthetic that stresses textures and space divisions—a preoccupation very important to European jewelers of the seventies.

Poland   The work of Joachim Sokòlski and of Jadwiga and Jerzy Zaremscy of Poland reflects a continuing interest in contemporary design. Sokòlski's rings (Fig. 186) have a machined, industrial quality and exhibit a unique use of gems—amethyst in one, topaz in the other. The Zaremscy necklace (Fig. 187), cool and precise in form, has a classic elegance.

186. Joachim Sokòlski. Silver rings, with amethyst (*left*) and topaz (*right*), 1973.

187. Jadwiga and Jerzy Zaremscy. Formed silver necklace, c. 1974.

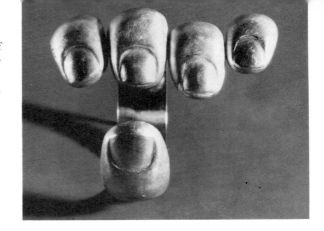

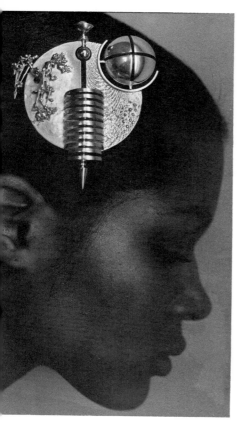

below: **188. Arnaldo Pomodoro.** Brooch or hair ornament of white and red gold, constructed from hammered sheet and cuttle-bone-cast portions, 1969.

right: **189. Bruno Martinazzi.** *Goldfinger,* bracelet chiseled and embossed in yellow and white gold, 1973.

Italy   Three sculptors, Bruno Martinazzi and the brothers Arnaldo and Gio Pomodoro, have dominated contemporary jewelry in Italy for decades. A brooch/hair ornament (Fig. 188) and a belt buckle (Fig. 204) by Arnaldo reveal the Pomodoro brothers' concern with textural contrasts and their interest in geometric forms. We tend to think of contemporary Italian design as being purely industrial, absolutely clean-lined, and committed to plastic and steel. Jewelry design, however, does not necessarily follow this pattern. Bruno Martinazzi's bracelet *Goldfinger* (Fig. 189) demonstrates a fascination with playful, whimsical designs developed from Surrealism.

Spain   Sergi Aguilar of Spain reveals an absorption with technological form and construction in his current work, such as the silver-plated brooch in Figure 190. Even more specifically industrial in its reference is a pin by the Capdevilla brothers (Fig. 191). Jewelry of this kind stands as an honest search for aesthetic relevance in the forms and processes of 20th-century life.

It should be apparent from this very brief survey that contemporary jewelry has made enormous strides throughout western and central Europe during the past two decades. While many different types of expression are represented, all the pieces illustrated in this chapter share one common characteristic: a freedom and lack of inhibition in exploring contemporary form, materials, and techniques.

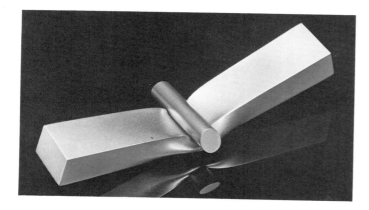

above: **190. Sergi Aguilar.** *Cop,* gold- and silver-plated brooch, c. 1973.

right: **191. Joaquin and Manuel Capdevilla.** Silver brooch sprayed with enamels, c. 1973.

part two
Design

Elements
and Principles
of Design

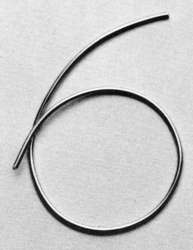

Design is the organization of materials and forms in such a way as to fulfill particular human needs. This definition presents four basic concepts: *organization, materials, forms,* and *needs. Organization,* of course, is a process of selection and arrangement. *Materials* are the basic ingredients of any product—in the case of jewelry beginning with, but not restricted to, precious substances. *Form* is in part the shape of the designed object, but it is more than that; we will discuss form in more detail under the elements of design. Finally, human *needs,* the great moving forces in human behavior, may be biological, psychological, social, or spiritual. All play a part in the process of design.

Many ideas and concepts are required to explain the process of design. The student who wishes to delve more deeply into the field should consult texts in basic design, some of which are listed in the Bibliography (see p. 339). However, the material presented here will provide a description and an application of the ideas and terms referring particularly to jewelry design. The most common system is to isolate for analysis the basic *elements* of design: line, form, space, texture, color, and movement. Next we will consider the *principles* governing these elements: equilibrium, emphasis, and proportion.

Elements of Design

Line

Attributes of Line The attributes of line are *direction, width, implied area,* and *intensity* or *value.* This definition, like all definitions pertaining to art and

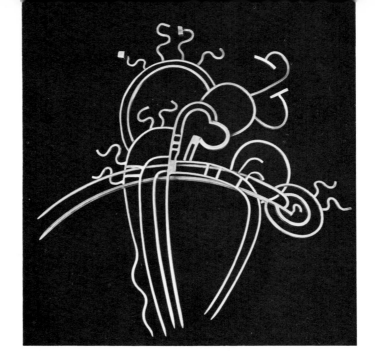

192. Marjorie Schick. Sterling-silver hairpiece, 1975.

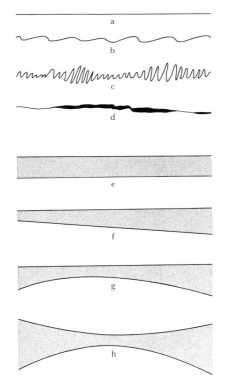

193. Varieties of line: straight (*a*), undulating (*b*), agitated (*c*), of varying thickness (*d*); pairs of straight lines in parallel (*e*) and diverging (*f*) relationships; straight and curving lines in opposition (*g*); curving lines opposing each other (*h*).

design, can serve only as a sort of clue to guide you until you begin to develop your own feeling for aesthetic qualities. You can give these attributes specific attention, but they are only partial ideas of what line really is. A line may have an independent life and vitality of its own. In jewelry, it may be the overriding aspect of a particular design (Fig. 192).

A line is significant or interesting to the extent that it demands continued visual inspection in order to be comprehended (Fig. 193). A geometrically straight line usually lacks emotional quality and interest, because it can be understood instantly in all its relations. A *straight line* (Fig. 193*a*) may be compared to a single musical tone sounded continuously—and monotonously. A *moving line* (Fig. 193*b*) seems more interesting, a line that varies in its movement (Fig. 193*c*) still more interesting. The line that varies in width (Fig. 193*d*) introduces another compelling element. It should be noted that, while some of these lines vary in movement, all have the same direction as the straight line.

Parallel straight lines (Fig. 193*e*) exist in a static relationship, because the direction of the lines is identical. In addition, they delineate an implied area that is also static, since the relationship of the boundary lines is constant and unchanging. (Compare the discussion of form and space, p. 88) *Straight lines that diverge* in direction (Fig. 193*f*) create dramatic conflict and, therefore, offer more visual interest because of the opposition in line direction. The implied area is also more interesting, because the relationships of the area are changing constantly. This visual activity can be called *area transition* or *area modulation;* it imparts movement to shape.

A moving or *curved line* works more dramatically against a straight line (Fig. 193*g*) or against another moving line in opposition (Fig. 193*h*) because of the conflict of directions as well as the area transition that takes place. A single curved line creates implied areas by itself (Fig. 194), and such areas become an important design consideration.

The Study of Line   A line can be viewed as a sort of track that records the movement of the arm and hand. In order to draw different lines, you must think of different ways of moving your hand. In jewelry, silver wire is a linear material. Chasing and engraving techniques produce lines, and the edge of a metal sheet is a line. Lines can be sawed into a sheet of metal. All these lines, like the pencil line, depend for their movement on the movements you make with your hands.

A good exercise is to explore with a pencil all the movements the arm and hand can make: zigzags, wiggling lines, curves, cross-hatchings, overlaps—the possibilities are endless (Fig. 195). You should search every part of your environment for line movements, not only in nature but also in industrial plants, grain elevators, machines, industrial equipment, laboratories, and any other field that is available. One reason for working your line drawings over one another in the sketchbook is that it will strengthen your graphic sensitivity. You will find many fascinating relationships of line, value, contrast, and shape. The pressure of the pencil can be varied in order to achieve variations of line width and intensity. Many of these graphic line relationships will serve as a point of departure for jewelry ideas. After you have explored the potential of line thoroughly, you can try out these line movements with actual materials.

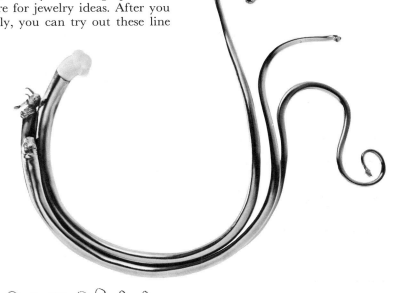

right: 194. Barbara Becker. *Menagerie,* neckpiece constructed of hollow tubes of gold-plated copper, with animal heads cast in bronze from plastic, and carved and filed Delrin, 1975.

below: 195. Line variations sketched freehand.

The Geometric Line Since the pencil line drawn freely with the hand is a record of subtle organic tensions of the hand and arm, it can be considered an *organic* line. Its sensitivity and variation arise from the delicately balanced functioning of muscles and nerves. By contrast, the line drawn with a straight edge derives from nothing other than geometric precision.

This difference is important, for the two kinds of lines evoke different feelings and aesthetic responses. The geometric line has an impersonal quality that is strong in direction and conviction but lacking in expressive sensitivity. The response to geometric lines is more intellectual than emotional. Geometric lines resulting in a square, rectangle, triangle, or circle are very static in comparison to the dynamism of freely drawn lines. They convey a sense of equilibrium, repose, and resolution. In combination, however, geometric lines—the straight line, the square, and the arc that is part of a circle—can make a powerful statement (Fig. 196).

The characteristic line movements of modern technology retain the precision and strength of basic geometric lines, but they are sometimes more subtle. A study of industrial forms may offer insight into the complexities and developments of geometric line.

left: **196. Helen Shirk.** Copper neckpiece constructed from 14-, 11-, and 10-gauge sheet, with oxidized finish, jasper settings, 1974.

right: **197. Gilles Jonemann.** Ring of 18k yellow gold and carved wood, 1973.

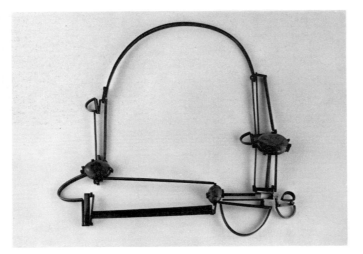

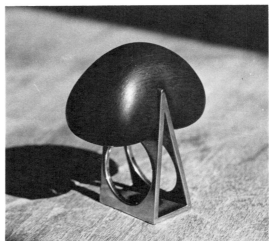

Form, Shape, and Space

Three elements of design—form, shape, and space, are so closely related that it is almost impossible to isolate them for discussion. The first two, form and shape, are similar but not absolutely synonymous concepts. Throughout this text we have used them interchangeably, but to consider them as elements of design we really should make a distinction. Shape, the simpler of the two, is the overall configuration of something, in this instance a piece of jewelry. Shape encompasses both outline and area or volume. Form means shape, but it may also refer to the nature of the object, the method of fabrication, and several other associations. For example, the object in Figure 197 is in the *form* of a ring; it consists of two interlocking *forms;* one of these is geometric, the other organic in form. Moreover, the ring was *formed* from gold and wood, and the result is a highly sculptural *form.*

Space is the negative counterpart of form. Rather than thinking of space as a void—as the layman tends to do—the designer should consider space as a malleable element to be carved and delineated by form. The illustrations in Figures 198 and 199 should make this clear. Sigurd Persson's ring (Fig. 198)

above: **198. Sigurd Persson.** Silver ring, 1973.

right: **199. Marilyn Ravanal.** *Upper Arm Bracelet,* forged and constructed of sterling silver and silver-plated copper, with moonstones, shell, and glass beads, 1972.

makes dramatic use of negative form, or space. To say that this ring form, with its open slash down the center, could not take this shape unless space were interjected in the slash seems absurdly elementary, but few people stop to think in these terms. The space establishes limits for the form, just as the form demarcates the space.

Marilyn Ravanal's upper-arm bracelet (Fig. 199) carries out this idea in a somewhat more complicated way. Here the projections into space carve out *implied* areas for the piece, and these can be just as important to the designer as the actual area. The drawings in Figure 200 will help to illustrate the concept of implied area. This must be taken into account by the designer in working through relationships such as the balance of visual weights.

One attribute of shape that we have not touched upon is thrust (Fig. 201). The thrust of a shape can be considered to be a line capable of being set in opposition to other lines or movements in the design organization. Every shape, with the exception of the perfect circle—and even this could be argued—exhibits thrust. Thrust will be an important factor in the development of such principles as balance, rhythm, and emphasis.

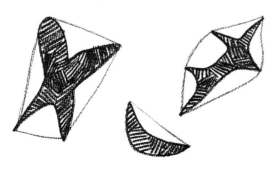

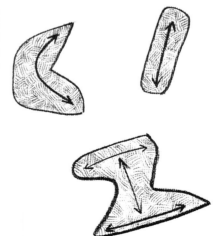

left: **200.** The actual and implied areas of a given shape seldom coincide.

right: **201.** Almost every shape includes an implied directional thrust.

Kinds of Shapes   Needless to say, the possibilities for shape are unlimited. Any attempt at classification can only be aimed at furthering an understanding of how shapes operate. For this purpose, we might divide shapes into two broad categories: geometric and organic.

Geometric shapes, of course, are based on the circle, the square, and the triangle. A projection of these basic forms includes all kinds of regular, machined shapes. Organic shapes are more or less amorphous or undefined, but they are always characterized by a nongeometeric flowing movement of line. They may relate directly to some identifiable form in nature or be more generalized "natural" forms. The pendant in Figure 202 would probably fall into the latter category. Its motifs suggest earth striations or some other geological formation, but we cannot relate it to anything specific. (The neckpiece, by contrast, takes the geometric form of the circle.)

The Study of Shape   One method of exploring shape is to begin with a simple outline and develop it into a family of related shapes by applying one or more deviations (Fig. 203).

left: 202. Olaf Skoogfors. Pendant of gold-plated sterling, with ivory, 1973.

below: 203. Three simple shapes, each developed into a family of shapes by one or more deviations.

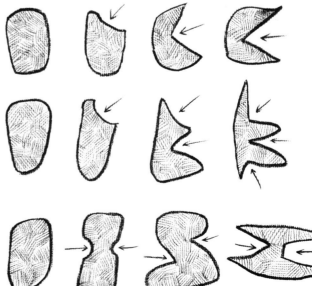

above: **204. John Paul Miller.** Belt clasp of fine and 18k gold, 1970.

right: **205. Arnaldo Pomodoro.** Fused silver pendant, 1969.

below right: **206.** Pencil textures suitable for chased patterns in metal.

For purposes of design a shape does not exist until it has been drawn. Every shape you draw increases your stock of ideas for design use. Your knowledge of shapes could come from any number of sources, including direct experience in tools and materials, observations of the environment, an interest in machined forms, the study of nature, and graphic experiments in drawing.

Shapes will emerge from all sorts of experimentation. They can be sawed out of brass, bronze, or copper sheet, which will often give a better idea of the dynamics of shape than a drawn line. The nature of metalwork is such that the craftsman often is confronted with an undefined area of sheet metal. The problem then becomes one of working a shape out of both the surface area and the modulation of that surface. A shape may emerge from the process of working the metal or from assembling separate pieces. The craftsman will unconsciously apply design principles outlined in the second half of this chapter, shaping the material until it seems "right."

Texture

Texture is the visual result of massing detailed elements closely enough together over an area to create an appearance that differs from the appearance of a single visual element. Texture is equivalent to tone or color value and can be used in the same way to differentiate areas by contrast and to achieve an emphasis of space. Natural textures proliferate from the surface appearance of materials. These textures have always been recognized and used in various types of design, but they are of special importance to the contemporary jeweler (Fig. 204).

In designing jewelry, the craftsman may differentiate areas by texture (Fig. 205), especially when complicated textures are offset by smoothly polished metal. The techniques for surface finishing described in Chapter 19 all give their own kinds of texture.

The Study of Texture   One direct method of understanding the infinite variety and subtlety of texture is to make pencil rubbings of materials. This is done by taking a sheet of thin paper, laying it against the material, and rubbing a light or dark value on the paper with the side of a pencil or conté crayon. The variety of graphic textures you acquire will depend on your initiative in finding materials of varying surfaces. You can also explore the textural variations you can devise with a pencil (Fig. 206) for later reproduction with chasing tools.

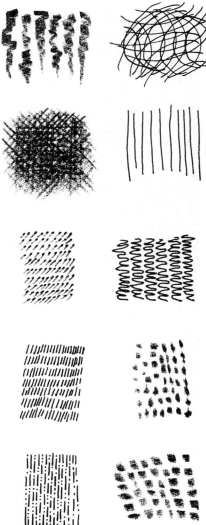

above: **207. Philip Morton.** Reversible sterling pendant, with agate and black onyx, 1974.

top: **208.** Pendant of Figure 207 in open position, shown from the rear.

Color

It is easy to forget the element of color in jewelry, because the classic precious metals, gold and silver, do not seem to have much color interest of their own. In fact, however, silver has a subtle, cool color all its own, and the warm sheen of yellow gold contrasts richly with many stones. Thus, color can become a very significant factor in jewelry—even in the absence of colored stones, as a glance at the color plates in this book will show (pp. 149–156). The contrast of two metals, for example gold and silver, may provide a subtle interest in itself. And of course the introduction of stones, found objects, feathers, chunks of wood, and all the other objects that are in the repertoire of the contemporary jeweler makes the palette as broad as that of the painter.

Motion

The concept of motion in jewelry involves us in the realm of time, since we perceive an object differently as it moves through space. This is similar to the experience of walking around or through a work of sculpture, or of passing slowly through a large building, gradually understanding its forms and spaces.

Motion has always played a role in certain types of jewelry, such as the swinging pendant or dangle earring—both ancient forms. But the jeweler who deliberately incorporates motion—and change through motion—into a piece is calling into play the fourth dimension, with all its problems and its exciting challenge (Figs. 207, 208).

Principles of Design

Equilibrium

Equilibrium, or balance, refers to the relationship of visual elements in terms of *visual weights*—the direction and position of elements in a field. Visual weight is determined by the size of a visual area or element and by its value in terms of color or texture. *Area transition* refers to the disposition of the area of a shape in terms of visual weight. Equilibrium can be achieved by redistributing the area of any given shape.

far left: 209. Nilda C. Getty. *Aunt Nani,* sterling pin with jade log, coral bead, old photograph, and plastic mirror, 1973.

left: 210. Nilda C. Getty. *Moonscape,* neckpiece forged and fused of sterling silver and 14k gold, with moonstone, 1972.

Most of our experience with the idea of balance refers to our physical relationship to the force of gravity and hence to the center of the earth as an external point of reference. In design, however, equilibrium or balance refers to the internal relationships of a designed form. There are two types of equilibrium.

Symmetrical equilibrium, traditionally referred to as "formal," results when equal visual weights or movements are placed or operate at equal distances or with equal force across a center of equilibrium. In other words, that which is on one side of an imaginary center line mirrors that on the other side (Fig. 209). Symmetrical equilibrium is the easiest to achieve, but unless it is handled sensitively, as in this illustration, it can be somewhat boring.

Asymmetrical equilibrium, sometimes known as "informal" or "occult," results when unequal visual weights or movements are placed or operate at proportionately unequal distances across the center of equilibrium in the field. This type of balance tends to be more dynamic. In the pendant illustrated in Figure 210, the three lower appendages are all of different lengths and different visual weights. However, the two at left balance the longest one at right, both actually and visually.

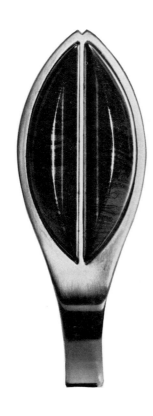

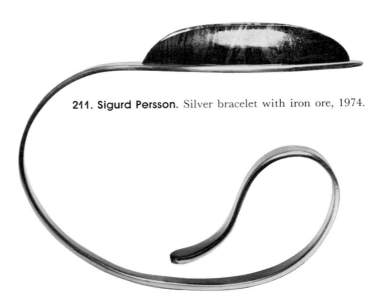

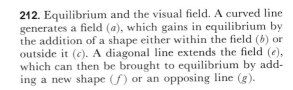

211. Sigurd Persson. Silver bracelet with iron ore, 1974.

The bracelet in Figure 211 shows an interesting aspect of equilibrium, since it encompasses both symmetry and asymmetry. Viewed from above, the bracelet is absolutely symmetrical, with equal distribution on either side of the center line. But from the side the bracelet is discovered to be dynamically asymmetrical, preserving through the meticulous distribution of weight—both actual and visual—a delicate balance.

One simple example will perhaps illustrate the way in which a designer can work with equilibrium on paper (Fig. 212). The implied area of a line (*a*) is the approximate field of that line. The center of equilibrium is the approximate center of this field. An additional shape can organize the empty space of the field by establishing equal weight or movement across the center of equilibrium (*b*). In this case the added shape works against the line movement. The field is enlarged by the placement of another shape outside the existing field (*c*). Thus, the two elements establish equilibrium across the center of the field.

212. Equilibrium and the visual field. A curved line generates a field (*a*), which gains in equilibrium by the addition of a shape either within the field (*b*) or outside it (*c*). A diagonal line extends the field (*e*), which can then be brought to equilibrium by adding a new shape (*f*) or an opposing line (*g*).

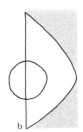

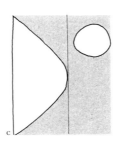

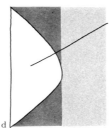

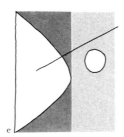

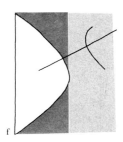

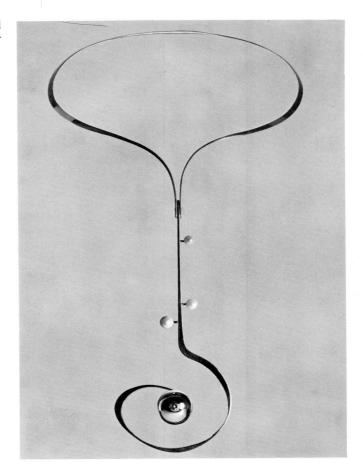

213. Sigurd Persson. *Backafall,* gold necklace with diamond and freshwater pearls, 1973.

In drawing *d,* lines generate a rectangular field. These lines work strongly in opposition, but there is not sufficient visual weight on the right side. Equilibrium can be achieved by adding another shape. A linear organization or shape like this can be placed in equilibrium in at least two ways: by placing an additional shape in the empty space to balance the visual elements across the center of equilibrium (*e*); or by setting another curved line in opposition to the first curved line, thus organizing the field (*f*).

Focal Point

In design a center of emphasis, a *focal point,* is often necessary or desirable in order to pull the design together. Without a focal point, interest would be dissipated; there would be no resting place for the viewer's eye as it moves about the composition and explores it gradually. The focal point of the necklace in Figure 213 is, of course, the gold ball at bottom—not only because it has the heaviest visual weight and is centrally located, but because the curve of the necklace leads the eye to this point over and over again.

The focal point serves as a place of entry into a design. It also acts as a point of rest or of final attention for the eye. The designer can activate an empty or unorganized area of a design by the sensitive placement of a focal point. The focal point provides the jeweler with an opportunity to achieve maximum contrast of materials and color through the use of stones, bone, wood, or special colored or textured metal shapes or forms.

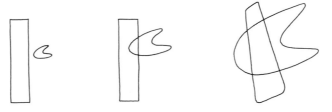

214. Scale variations in the relationship between two shapes.

Proportion and Scale

Proportion and scale are two closely related terms, both dealing with size relationships. In terms of design, when a distinction is made between them, *proportion* is usually taken to mean the size relationships between various parts of a design, such as two sections of a necklace. *Scale* tends to be considered in terms of some absolute standard, such as the human body or even some traditional conception of size. For example, the ring in Figure 246 could be considered to be of large scale in relation to the finger as well as in relation to what most people consider "ring-size." Both proportion and scale are extremely important to the jewelry designer.

Figure 214 illustrates the drastically different effects that changes of proportional relationships can produce. In the first sketch, the size of the organic shape is insignificant in relation to the geometric shape, and the composition seems incoherent. In the second sketch, the organic shape acts as an accent to the geometric shape. The third sketch modifies the geometric and enlarges the organic to bring the two shapes into a more satisfying proportional relationship.

Jewelry falls within the sculptural range of the small and subtle, and personality exercises an individual choice in scale, both physical and aesthetic (Fig. 237). Scale in jewelry is also determined by the functional requirements of neck, arm, finger, and so forth. Appropriate scale relationships between the shapes chosen for jewelry are extremely important.

In summary, as we have tried to point out, design principles are really *relationships* of visual elements. The reason some relationships are "good" or effective and others are not arises from the capacities and limitations of our own physical and psychological equipment for perceiving and understanding what we see.

Design ideas sketched freely serve as a starting point for the design process (Fig. 215). The sketches should be examined in light of the aesthetic responses they evoke: which ones embody dramatic graphic qualities; which seem dead or uninteresting; which are trite and stereotyped? This evaluation is perhaps the most difficult for the beginner. There are no rules or formulas. The experienced designer learns to know instinctively when a design "works" and, if it does not, why not. A consistent study of paintings, sculpture, and the work of other jewelers will help to develop an understanding of formal relationships and provides a basis for aesthetic judgments.

Jewelry that is worn always becomes an integral part of the visual appearance of the wearer. It is seen as part of the person and as a dimension of the personality. As a part of the person, jewelry may become a focal point, a visual accent in the design of personal appearance or in the organization of a costume, a visual movement at the neck or on the ear—an *element* of design emphasis and contrast. The definition of jewelry as purely "decorative" fails to clarify this specific demand to serve as a design element for the whole person. Thus we see that the design of a piece of jewelry is only one small segment of a broader design continuum.

215. Design ideas sketched in charcoal.

Design for Jewelry

The elements and principles of design considered in Chapter 6 are guidelines that apply to the design of anything—from the smallest piece of jewelry to whole cities. In this chapter, we will begin to show how design elements and principles apply specifically to jewelry. The first part of the chapter analyzes two broad categories of shapes: linear and plate. The second half discusses some design factors related to various jewelry techniques, as well as some of the ways by which the jeweler can search for forms appropriate to these particular techniques.

Linear and Plate Shapes

Linear Shapes

Metal in wire form evokes unique and consistent aesthetic responses in the designer and in the observer (Fig. 216). Linear organizations are a reflection of basic capacities and limitations of the human mind. The exact aesthetic effects particularly characteristic of line can be described in terms of clarity, sharpness, and precision.

The emotions generated by line seem to be related to the delicacy and sensitivity of a pure relationship between spaces and borders or edges. Abstractions from life, rather than life itself, seem to be portrayed by line. Delicacy, not depth, is achieved by line. Bear in mind that *line,* not lines, is being discussed. When lines are massed, we begin to get value, which is quite a different visual element.

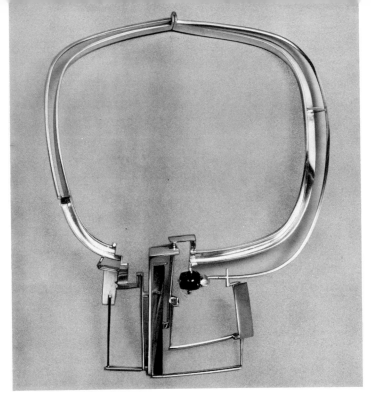

216. Helen Shirk. Neckpiece constructed from 14-, 16-, and 18-gauge sheet sterling, with amethyst, 1972.

Graphic Experimentation with Line   Drawing closed linear organizations is a good exercise in learning to develop design ideas for jewelry (Fig. 217). Such drawings should be done freely and rapidly, without too much regard for control until you begin to understand the design relationships involved. Try to preserve a free and flowing quality of line, even as you attempt to guide the line in terms of the principles discussed in Chapter 6.

The discussion and illustrations that follow will show how simple linear organizations can be evaluated, modified, and adapted to achieve maximum effectiveness, even before the craftsman begins to work in an actual material. These sketches are not, of course, presented as dogmatic or absolute design solutions. The purpose of the illustrations is merely to indicate how the questions of space division and space relationships can be dealt with in order to increase unity and dramatic impact.

Figure 218 shows an example of how a linear organization can be worked out through gradual modifications of the initial configuration. In this case

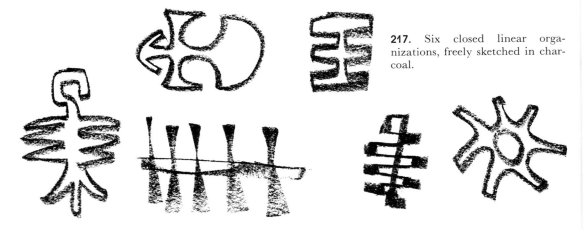

217. Six closed linear organizations, freely sketched in charcoal.

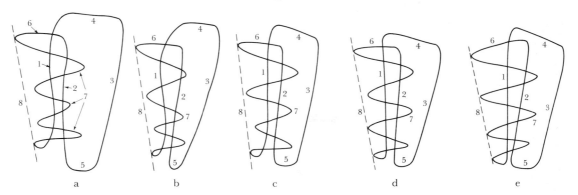

218. Progressive modifications of a linear organization.

the starting point is a single intertwined line, as shown in sketch *a*. The final design should consist of the best possible placement of the elements that make up this starting configuration.

One of the first things to be observed about a linear organization is that, although it consists only of pure line, it inevitably involves two-dimensional space, or area. In this sketch there is both *actual* area and *implied* area. The implied area, indicated by dotted lines, is just as important as that actually enclosed by line. Together these areas constitute the visual *field*.

In sketch *a*, lines 1 and 2 are two verticals that work with maximum dramatic contrast against 7, the entire zigzag movement. Within this movement, line 6 works with maximum contrast against 1; lines 4 and 5, though parallel, work against 1, 2, and 3. Line 3 also works against 7, restating the direction of 1 and 2. In short, the general line relationships work fairly well. The area relationships, however, are poor. The areas between 1 and 2 and between 8 and 2 are too small in relation to the area between 2 and 3, where there is a feeling of emptiness. How can these weaknesses be corrected?

One way of considering modifications to a design is to lay tracing paper over the original sketch and on it make changes among the unsatisfactory relationships while retracing the lines that are good. By using tracing paper over successive sketches you can gradually bring the design into complete control without losing anything good. However, unless you consciously strive for freedom, this process will almost always give rise to a tightness of line.

In sketch *b*, the large area between lines 2 and 3 has been reduced. However, the lower end is now too narrow in relation to the top. The organization is out of balance, because too much of the implied area has been excluded from the design. The loop of the zigzag line at 7 comes too close to 3 and pinches off the area between 2 and 3. Lines 1 and 2 come too close together at the bottom, thus pinching the space too tightly.

In the next sketch (*c*) a correction of the mistakes noted has been attempted. Space at the bottom has been increased. The direction of 4 has been altered to avoid duplicating the direction of 6. Now, however, line 4 is too short to provide a sufficient space at the top between lines 2 and 3, which in turn seem to lose something for being parallel. Finally, zigzag line 7 is rhythmically too irregular.

In sketch *d*, many of the errors have been corrected, but the loops of 7 do not come across line 2 far enough to create significant areas. These loops must be lengthened.

Sketch *e* is a final solution to the design problem. Compare it with the original sketch. It has been transformed into a much tighter line organization. The spaces between 8 and 1, between 1 and 2, and between 2 and 3 all vary interestingly in width. Maximum line opposition has been developed, the area distributions are well balanced, and the design "works." Notice how the terminations of loops in the zigzag create implied space divisions, as indicated by dotted lines.

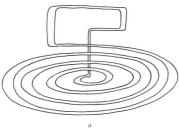

a

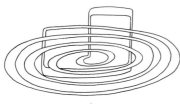

b

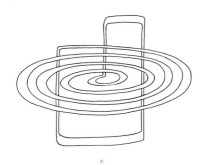

c

219. Modifications of a linear organization in wire.

below left: 220. Bending a zigzag pattern in sterling-silver wire.

below right: 221. Philip Morton. Sterling wire bracelet, 1956.

Experimentation in Metal   When you reach the stage of design at which it is necessary to work with the thickness of a wire line, do not spend too much time on graphic rendering, because your ideas must ultimately by worked out in terms of what the tools and materials can do. Therefore, go right to work with silver wire (Fig. 219). Never give a thought to the amount of material you are spoiling in unsuccessful experiments. You will acquire freedom and courage only by working directly and experimentally. Eventually your design ideas should emerge in the form of expressive sketches, which you will work out in detail in the material itself. You will find that many a design idea improves as possible modifications or new relationships arise during the actual construction.

If you were working directly in material with the design idea shown in version *a* of Figure 219, it might occur to you to fold the rectangle at the top of the spiral directly underneath, as in version *b*. Such an idea might never occur while you were working graphically, except as you recall other experiences of working with wire.

Such experiences lead to a useful technique in the exploration of design ideas. The technique is always to try out every possible relationship that occurs to you in terms of opposite possibilities. If the direction is up, try it down. If it is moving left, try it moving right. If it seems to project forward, try it receding backward.

If you were to try folding the rectangle directly underneath, you might decide that the scale of the rectangle needed changing in order to work well against the spiral, as in version *c*. You would also find that this wire design cannot be completely bent to shape before hammering. It must be bent and hammered step by step. Rather extensive experiment and planning is necessary to execute this type of design, but you have to start at the beginning in any case.

For the serious research of linear wire forms, the student will need coils of 24-, 20-, 18-, 16-, 14-, and 12-gauge sterling wire. It is true that 12-gauge wire can be drawn down to finer gauges if a drawplate and drawtongs are at hand. However, 24-gauge is somewhat difficult for the beginner to draw out. The drawplate for square, triangular, and half-round wire should be available, and each of these forms should be explored (**11.1, 11.2**).

Exploration in wire must start with improvisation. Begin with any tool. Take a pair of round-nose pliers, for example, and try out the patterns of bending that can be achieved. Remember that it is the way you see your tools that leads to variations of form. The beginning of experimentation requires a special attitude toward materials and tools. They should be tried

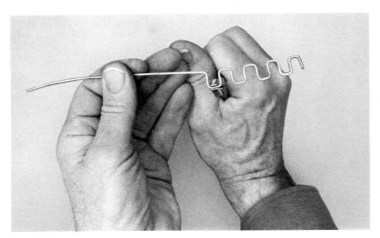

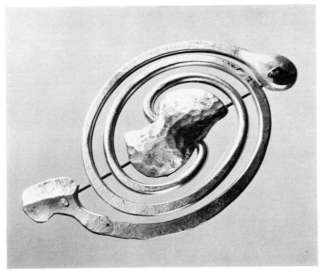

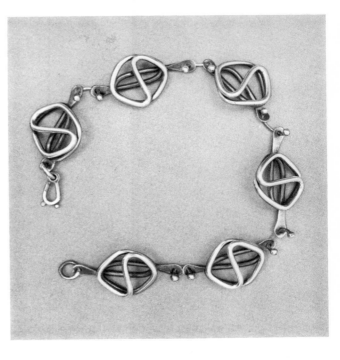

above: **222. Harry Bertoia.** Pin of hammered sterling, c. 1940–50.

right: **223. Philip Morton.** Bracelet constructed from sterling wire, 1956.

out in every possible way and position—backward, forward, upside down, down-side up, inside out, outside in. In no case can the student be stingy with materials. A reluctance to use up materials in experimenting because of cost will lead to an immediate tightness. This should be avoided, since the beginner is already inclined to be tight in approaching design. Often students expect each trial to lead to a finished work. Actually, each trial must be seen as a preliminary step toward the final form. Several trials may be necessary in order to arrive at correct relationships or dimensions. The seeking artist must spend time, energy and materials lavishly in order to advance creative development. Carrying out direct experiments in material is the best way of discovering what is possible. Designs should emerge from the process.

A line motif made with two pairs of pliers of different jaw widths is shown in Figure 220. One set of bends was made around the jaws of a wider pair of pliers, and the other set around the jaws of the narrower pair of pliers. The problem of this type of line movement is to keep the zigzag elements uniform, and the use of pliers here to establish the intervals between the bends reveals an important principle of designing in terms of what the tools can do. After the necessary length of this zigzag line was bent up, the horizontal flanges were hammered flat. This created a variation of line width. This particular line motif lent itself to use for both a bracelet (Fig. 221) and a necklace.

The discovery of the possibility of hammering facets on a length of wire emerges rather quickly from a little experimentation with the hammer (Fig. 222). This motif can be applied to a variety of designs. A spiral bracelet and a loop necklace are obvious but effective designs. The ends of the bracelet can be finished off by fusing. Nothing seems simpler than hammering the end of a wire flat, yet the result may depend entirely on how the hammered parts relate to the design as a whole. Bracelets of varying designs can be made by taking short lengths of wire and hammering each end flat, drilling holes, and joining the links with short wires with beaded ends (Fig. 223). In each case, the gauge of the wire is important in determining the aesthetic effects.

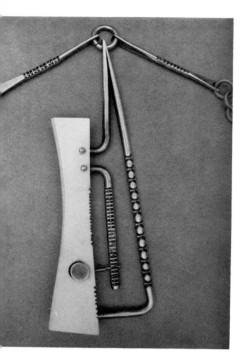

Twisted wire (**11.21**) might be called a form of textured wire. Experimentation with twisting wires of different sizes together will lead to interesting possibilities, although results must be carefully evaluated to avoid triteness. Another form of texture in wire can be achieved by stamping it with punches and chasing tools (Fig. 224). Rich surfaces for rings or structural members can be made in this way (**13.11**). Again, experimentation is the fundamental step toward discovery.

Linear Strip Forms   A strip shape (Fig. 225) must be designed so that its upper and lower edges lie in two parallel planes. Narrow metal strips cut with hand shears or with squaring shears will invariably be curved and twisted. Therefore, it is necessary to straighten out all twists in a cut strip before doing any bending. Straightening can be done by taking each end of the strip in a pair of square-nose pliers and twisting the ends in opposite directions while pulling on both ends. When bending a strip to the desired shape with the pliers, be sure that bends are perpendicular to the length of the strip. After each bend, check to see that each section of the strip is still straight, and adjust the bend if necessary.

Strip forms are seldom successful if the ends do not come together in a closed, straight line (Fig. 225). Leaving the ends open is not satisfactory for the simple reason that, visually, a line always leads the eye to its ending. If there is no significant focal point at the end, the line is better closed on itself to form a continuous movement between the joined parts.

When designing such a closed strip form, start with one end at a point on the outside of the organization, rather than at a point within it, so that soldering can be done on the periphery of the form (**11.14**). Avoid placing solder joints on a flat section. Always put the solder joint in the center of a sharp bend.

After a strip form has been soldered and trued up, it can be placed on a flat anvil and tapped lightly along the top edge to ensure that the edges lie in a single plane. To finish such a form, take a large, flat hand file and file across the top and bottom surfaces until the edges of the strip are of uniform width and lying in parallel planes. In order to avoid filing slots in the surface, always slide the file across the piece, sideways, as you file forward and back. Rotate the pieces every few strokes to ensure that an even surface is attained (**19.3**).

If the strip has been bent correctly, there should be no kinks in the sides that require filing. The jewellike quality of every form will depend on the perfection of the surfaces, unless the design requires a rough finish.

Chased Linear Forms   Everything that has been said about the visual aspects of line holds true for any means of achieving line, though the technical processes vary and each one must be mastered. Nevertheless, the expressive form of chasing does differ from that of wire, for the chased line must be carried on a metal surface (**13.8**). The design problem is that of relating an inner linear organization within a shape to the boundary line of that shape. If the inner linear design is complex, the outer shape is best kept fairly simple. The designer should avoid letting such simplicity lead to dullness, however, and the outer shape should not be made too large in scale.

Pierced Linear Forms   Piercing, which is the technique of sawing lines and other openings in sheet metal according to a designed pattern (**12.6**), is a technique that deserves more attention from the contemporary jeweler. Designs of extreme delicacy can be achieved. Small holes are drilled at the beginning and end of the line movement before sawing, and the line is designed so that the metal is not cut apart entirely from the support of

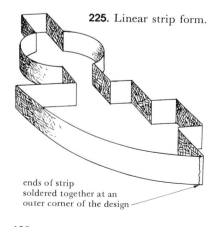

225. Linear strip form.

ends of strip
soldered together at an
outer corner of the design

226. Harry Bertoia. Hammered silver necklace, forged thin from heavy sheets, and torch-textured, c. 1940–50.

adjacent metal. Piercing requires a relaxed and quiet approach on the part of the jeweler. The results can be quite exciting (Pl. 6, p. 151).

Etched Linear Forms   The very complex process of etching must be considered in relation to linear forms, since the graphic quality of the hand-drawn line can be impressed onto metal by the etching bath (**17.12–18**). This line is, of course, purely graphic, unless etching is carried out so deeply as to create a three-dimensional quality. All of the graphic resources of etching, including texture and value in addition to pure line, can be applied to the surface.

Plate Shapes

Simple shapes cut from sheet metal are the easiest form to achieve and can be the most banal of jewelry forms. It is for just this reason that an especially careful study of shape is necessary, if meaningful, contemporary, and expressive shapes are to be achieved. When sensitively designed, the simple shape can be almost as dramatic as the most complex piece. In dealing with simple shapes, every stereotype that comes to mind must be rejected. This is why the constant drawing of shapes is necessary for the contemporary jeweler. Every acquired image must be explored so that the designer will have a range of possibilities, while at the same time every dull image must be discarded. The search for unique configurations can follow a systematic procedure, once the given mode of expression has been selected. Shapes fall within almost every category of aesthetic feeling.

Plate shapes preserve an intellectual delicacy and symbolic purity comparable to line, unless the edges of the surface are modulated in some way. The thinness or thickness of a metal also modifies its quality in a range from delicacy to massiveness. A shape cut from heavy-gauge metal can be transformed aesthetically if the edges are fused, thinned, or rounded, or the surface curved (Fig. 226).

With the exception of certain geometric shapes—such as the perfect circle, the square, and the rectangle—it is almost a rule that the boundary-line configuration of a simple plate shape must be active in its movements and area disposition in order to achieve dramatic interest. Other exceptions to this rule might be simple shapes that are given interest by textural treatment of the surface. Even so simple a texture as that resulting from forging or planishing can be effective, especially if the hammering modulates the thickness of the sheet (**13.2, 13.5**).

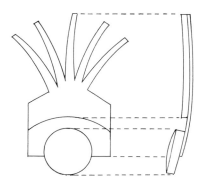

227. A complex plate shape using partially laminated plates.

Complex Plate-Shape Forms   As soon as other visual elements are added to a simple shape, the complexity is increased and the form moves out of the category of the simple plate-shape forms. For example, the addition of a single line to divide a simple shape can be effected in two ways. One is to solder a wire or strip across the shape. When this is done, it is practical to lay the wire across the plate with the ends projecting beyond the edges. Binding wire can be used to hold the wire in position. After the wire has been soldered, the projecting ends are sawed off flush with the edges of the plate and filed smooth. The other way of creating a space division on a simple shape is to utilize the boundary line of another plate, which is soldered on top of the first plate. In effect, this is a partial lamination of two plates (Fig. 227). The simplest way to do this is by sweat soldering (**10.19**). It is easier to get an exact fit if the additional plate is roughly cut to extend over the boundary line of the simple shape. After soldering, it can be sawed to the edge of the first plate and filed and finished.

A line creating a space division offers the opportunity to differentiate the two areas by means of texture (Fig. 228). The texture should always be applied before any other part is soldered to the surface. If one part is to be textured and the other polished, the jeweler will usually texture the under-plate, since the upper plate will be more accessible for polishing. While it would be possible to reverse this relationship, it is better to deal with materials in the simplest and most logical manner, and to incorporate the limitations of the medium as part of the design. Also remember that a textured or darkened area is visually stronger than a smooth, polished area. To achieve visual balance, therefore, keep the textured area smaller (Fig. 228). The final edges of a plate shape should be prepared only *after* texturing, because stamping the edge with punches will smash it down. After texturing, the final boundary line can be sawed, filed, and finished.

These guidelines for plate texturing apply with equal force to the design of strip-plate forms.

Strip-Plate Forms   Soldering one plate onto another often produces a certain impression of depth, especially if there is a textural contrast, but such complex plate forms nevertheless remain essentially two-dimensional. Designs of greater, fully three-dimensional depth can be achieved with *strip-plate* con-

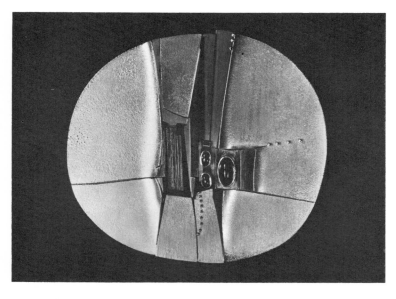

228. Othmar Zschaler. Textured gold brooch, with ruby and two sapphires, 1972.

structions, in which a forward plane is raised well above a background plane by a length of bent strip metal. Soldered between the two plates like a wall between two floors, the strip not only separates the plates but also keeps them in place. As shown in Figure 229, the strip can be soldered along the inner boundary line between the upper and lower plates (*a*), along the outer boundaries only (*b*), or just around the perimeter of the upper shape (*c*).

A sample design for a strip-plate form (Fig. 230) shows a forward plane of highly polished silver and a textured background plane, on which a gemstone cabachon is set as a focal point. The back plate, not only textured but also darkened by oxidation (**19.15**), thus serves as a field against which the primary shape and gemstone stand out and interact. Note that the cabachon is proportionately scaled to serve as the focal point of the design—it is neither so small as to be a mere accent, nor so large as to dwarf its surroundings.

For such strip-plate forms, the principal shapes can usually be made of 18-gauge plate, and the strip should be of this or greater thickness. The width of the strip, and thus the amount of separation between the plates, will depend on the height of the cabachon to be used. A strip about $\frac{1}{8}$ inch wide is ordinarily sufficient for a low cabachon, but greater widths may be appropriate for a higher cabachon, for creating a special deep-space effect, or if a low cabachon is to be lifted up on a high bezel (**21.1**). If a texture is desired on the strip, the texturing must be done first, so that the strip can be straightened if the stamping has distorted it.

Design in Specific Techniques

Fused Forms   Fused forms emerge as a natural result of heating metal with a hot flame until it melts (**10.4**). When the flame is applied to such metals as silver, brass, copper, and gold, the surface usually bubbles, oxidizes, and becomes darkly textured in patterns that are characteristic but variable from one time to another. The molecular forces within the molten metal pull it together into round forms, which are dependent partly on the original shape and partly on the accidental operation of the natural forces involved. It is from this operation that the unique aesthetic quality of the fused form emerges (Fig. 231).

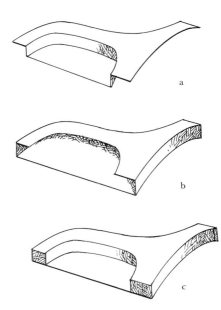

above: **229.** Designs for a strip-plate form. The two plates can be joined by a strip along an inner boundary (*a*), an outer border (*b*), or both (*c*).

below: **230.** Design sketch for a strip-plate form.

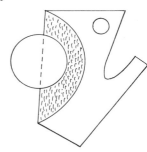

231. Mary A. Kretsinger. Brooch of (*clockwise from top left*) mica, fused brass, purpurite, and fossil trilobite, 1970.

The design of fused forms follows the usual procedure of either direct experiment or preliminary sketches. The beginning student should start with direct experimentation in order to acquire a basis for thinking about design in terms of the process. It is desirable to have a good supply of silver scraps on hand, so that new silver need not be wasted.

The design of fused forms begins with a study of what happens to silver when it is heated by the torch. Fused metal produces organic and accidental qualities, as well as rich textural effects. An interesting variety of effects is easy to get, but a specific result is hard to control. At a certain temperature, fused metal will roll up into a molten ball. Experiment is needed partly to establish judgment about this limitation. Practice in fusing develops an understanding of the capacities and limits of molten metal.

Pieces of scrap silver of various sizes and gauges can be assembled into simple compositions and fused together. Combinations of techniques—such as fusing and forging—offer infinite design possibilities. The design of fused forms is generally freer and more subject to chance effects than that in other techniques. Emotional fullness and visual richness may replace intellectual precision.

Fusing techniques can develop powerful forms that retain a free and unexpected quality. For best results in fusing, the metal should be pickled once or twice (**9.2**) and handled with copper tongs so that oil or grease will not interfere with the free flowing of the metal. Flux need not be used with this process if the metal is clean, unless it is desired to interfere with the natural movement of molten metal. Yellow ochre and possibly other materials can also be applied if the designer wishes to interfere with the free flow of metal. Pieces of sheet, wire, or tubing can be wired together in complex relationships and fused together, after which the piece can be shaped by filing.

Electroforms   Electroforming is a mode of electrodeposition (see Chap. 16). No matter what the material, the process creates a unique aesthetic quality (Pl. 7, p. 151). Electroforms are similar to cast forms in that they require a pattern to be duplicated in metal. The pattern, or *matrix,* can be made of any material capable of accepting a coating of metallic lacquer and of being removed after electrodeposition. The aesthetic qualities of electroforms depend somewhat on the matrix material used. Expanded polystyrene gives a characteristic rough or rippled surface that can be duplicated exactly, regardless of the particular form of the pattern.

One of the important characteristics of electroforming is that hollow forms can be made directly, thus opening up many possibilities not available in other techniques. For example, a wax pattern can be melted out of an electroform very readily, leaving the form hollow, thin, and relatively lightweight.

Not surprisingly, exploratory work in electroforming does not follow procedures readily adaptable to other techniques. An attractive possibility of electroforming is that stones and other materials can be embedded directly in the matrix, so that electrodeposition produces an automatic "setting" that fits the stone exactly. Such "settings," of course, must be designed in a manner appropriate to the technique. Porous materials to be set in metal by this method should be sealed to prevent the plating solution from soaking into them. If hollow forms are designed with the intention of removing the matrix material after electrodeposition, some hole must be provided in an inconspicuous place for the fumes, ashes, or the actual matrix to escape.

Hollow forms can be sawed apart, if necessary, for the installation of concealed hinges or fasteners. Furthermore, there is no limit to the possibilities of executing very light, hollow forms and delicate traceries by painting interrelated lines in metallic lacquer over the surface of a wax volume.

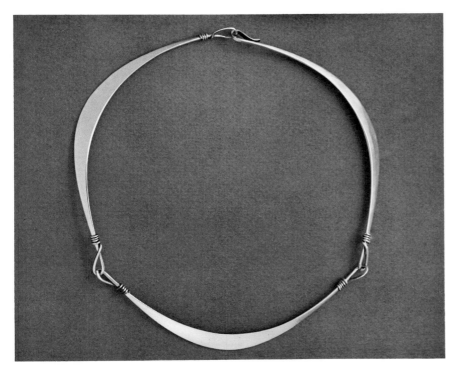

232. Ronald Hayes Pearson. Necklace of forged sterling, 1965.

Like casting, electroforming is likely to produce shapes that are organic rather than geometric, and that have a greater affinity with natural or found gem forms than with traditionally finished, mechanically or geometrically faceted gems.

Carved Forms   Carved forms tend to be sculptural in effect. They can be made by carving, grinding, filing, or casting. The category includes all simple shapes that are too thick to be classed as plate shapes and must be worked on all sides or edges. In other words, they are three-dimensional forms. A cuff link made of 8-gauge sheet, for example, is better treated as a carved form than as a plate shape. Thick shapes of ivory or ebony would probably best be treated as volumes to be carved.

Forged Forms   The design of forged forms must be based on experience in the process of forging (**13.1–4**) and on experiment, for shape cannot be arbitrarily imposed upon the material. The shape must be drawn out of the metal by the action of the forging hammer in displacing the metal, blow by blow. It is a good idea to begin forging experiments with a short length of 6- or 8-gauge wire and to see just how much variation in width you can make between the center and the end. In forging a tapered movement from thick to thin along a bar of metal, one soon learns to adjust the weight of the blows to the tapered thickness of the material. Ronald Pearson has employed the simple technique of forging in the design of exquisite bracelets and necklaces (Fig. 232).

Repoussé Forms   Repoussé forms are actually sculptural relief forms pressed out from the back of a sheet of metal (**11.16**). They may range in design from natural to geometric, technological, or abstract images. Because of the

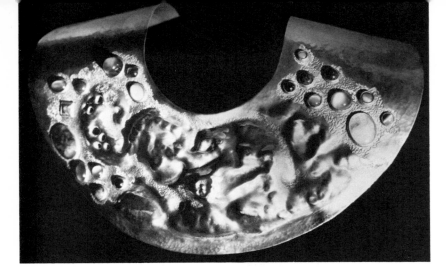

233. Douglas Wagstaff. Collar of repoussé, chased, and engraved alloy metal, electroplated in gold, with moss agates, turquoises, rose quartz, moonstones, tigereye, lapis lazuli, and garnets, 1971.

nature of the process, the forms most naturally emerge as organic (Fig. 233). Regardless of the image, it should be remembered that repoussé is most effective when restricted to a moderate depth. Shallow relief can be well controlled, and many problems can be avoided if the forms are not too deep. As revealed in ancient jewelry, one very effective way of making repoussé forms is to solder together two hollow halves of sheet metal. Embossing into a stone mold is another method of producing repoussé. Contemporary jewelers have yet to take full advantage of the possibilities of repoussé.

Although almost any image can be imposed in relief on sheet metal, the image must be carefully composed to avoid the problems of foreshortening, which cannot be handled effectively on the scale of jewelry. Therefore, figures derived from natural forms must be composed in a plane parallel to that of the sheet-metal surface, not perpendicular to it.

The technical process of repoussé is discussed elsewhere (**11.16–18**). There is no substitute for struggling out a first attempt. The process must be carried out freehand. The design is drawn in reverse on the back of the sheet, and the front surface is put against a pan or bowl of pitch, which supports the metal while allowing it to be pushed out with tools from the back. Only a generalized form can be pushed into the metal at the first stage. The design cannot be raised tightly or precisely from the back; deep and narrow forms must be pushed down quite broadly at first. When the sheet is turned over, the image can be somewhat more precisely defined as the general rounded areas are pushed inward along boundary lines. This is a plastic process, and the design must be formed in the process. It is not a question of accurately duplicating a predesigned form. It is a question of bringing the form into existence through successive stages of working the metal.

Cast Forms   Cast forms are not necessarily sculptural, insofar as almost any form can be cast—even a simple, flat shape that could better be sawed out of sheet. But casting is the means by which sculptural forms can be fully realized (Fig. 234). There are two distinct and legitimate uses for casting. One is for the duplication of production pieces. The other is for the realization of forms that can be achieved in no other way. The process is extremely complex—perhaps the most complex of all—and involves a great deal of equipment, especially if emphasis is placed upon controlled production (see Chap. 14). Yet in many ways it requires less skill to develop cast forms by modeling in wax than through the use of other jewelry means, such as chasing, repoussé, forging, or simple construction. It is for this reason that casting is often reserved for an advanced course in jewelry making. Even though casting is a most appealing means of jewelry production, every jeweler needs to master the direct, basic processes of working with metal. Wax modeling, in itself, is not the most important of metal processes.

Cast forms depend for their dramatic impact not only on the extension of the elements into three-dimensional space but also very much on the modulation of the elements themselves. A sculptural form will always show a transition from thin to thick, from narrow to wide, and back again.

Plastic Forms   During the seventies an interest in new materials has led to considerable experimentation with forms both carved and cast in plastic. Contemporary jewelers have utilized hard plastics, such as Plexiglas, Delrin, and Lexan, which can be filed, carved, and turned on a small machine or wood-turning lathe to achieve distinctive forms (Fig. 235). Also of great interest to the jeweler are the epoxy and polyester resins (**14.21–24**), which can be cast or laminated into a variety of expressive shapes (Fig. 236). These plastics can also be mixed with interesting materials such as metal powders, sand, glass, and almost any other inert material. They can be colored with pigments and dyes, thus offering an interesting extension to the traditional source of color through enameling. Finally, cast resin surfaces can be textured or finished to a high polish.

below left: 234. David Laplantz. Wedding rings of cast 14k yellow gold and engraved sterling, with opal set in woman's ring (*left*), 1974.

bottom left: 235. Amy Buckingham. *Brooch #6,* of gold-plated bronze with three lathe-turned Lexan pieces, riveted together to move separately, 1973–74. Collection Helen Drutt.

below right: 236. Gilles Jonemann. Pendant of brushed silver and white Altuglas, 1974.

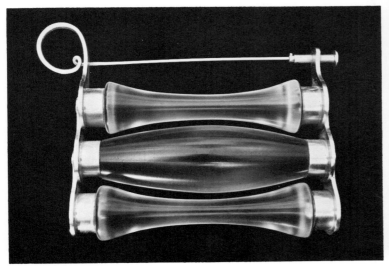

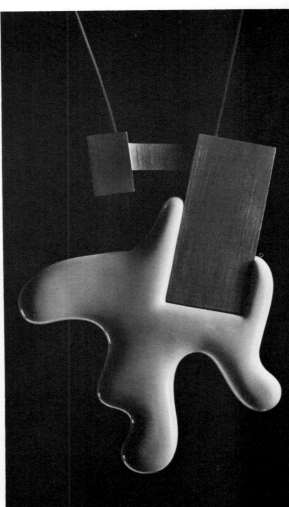

Functional
Design

Traditionally, a distinction has been made between the "applied" or "minor" arts, that is to say the crafts, and the "fine" arts. This distinction is based generally on the question of function. A craft object serves some readily identifiable purpose, such as holding food or liquids, covering furnishings or the body, or fastening together parts of clothing. The fine arts, according to this line of reasoning, have no other function except to *be*. Their aesthetic statement alone is sufficient reason for existence. In particular, the craft of jewelry making seems wedded to the functional role. We are familiar with handcraft ceramic, glass, and fiber objects that serve no useful purpose, that are purely *objects d'art*. But rarely until contemporary times has jewelry been made except to be worn.

In recent years the division between "fine" and "applied" arts has become increasingly blurred. We have come to understand that function extends to intangible psychological and spiritual aspects of existence. Art can no longer be regarded as nonfunctional in the light of its role as an integrative process in human personality, bringing together thought, feeling, intuition, and sensation. In spite of this broader interpretation, however, the question of actual function remains integral to the fabrication of jewelry. To be sure, some jewelers have pushed the limits of function to great extremes, allowing themselves considerable freedom of expression (Fig. 237). But from a practical point of view, function in jewelry must be considered in relation to the special requirements of wearability. Each type of jewelry presents certain limitations and demands. The ring must be designed to fit comfortably on the finger, the

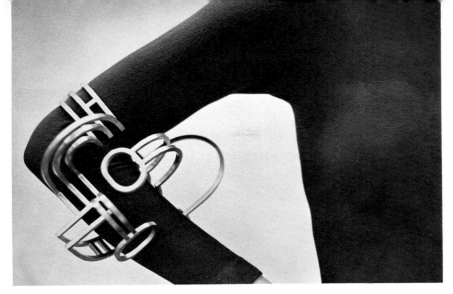

above: **237. Gail Larson.** Four-piece armlet of brass rod, 1975.

left: **238. Philip Morton.** Man's wedding ring in 14k yellow gold, 1971.

right: **239. Philip Morton.** Wedding ring of stamped sterling silver, 1968.

bracelet must adapt to the arm, and so forth. This chapter, then, outlines some of the functional problems in the design of particular jewelry pieces.

8.1

The Wedding Band   Rings are perhaps the most common and popular items of jewelry. The functional parts of a ring are the ring band and the table, or setting, if any. One contemporary tendency is to merge these two parts into a single form (Figs. 238, 239). The design of a ring always raises first the question of size and width. It is obvious that the band must be of the right size to fit the finger. The ring must also be designed so that it fits between adjacent fingers without being cumbersome or uncomfortable.

In taking an order for a wedding ring set, the jeweler uses the ring-size set (Fig. 322) to find out the required sizes—but size also depends upon the desired width. A $\frac{1}{2}$-inch-wide ring band has to be made about half a size larger than the measurement if it is to fit comfortably. In determining the width of the band, the jeweler should examine the client's hand. Seldom can a person comfortably wear a band that is much wider than $\frac{1}{2}$ inch. This width will normally be for a man's ring. A band meant for a woman should usually not be wider than $\frac{3}{8}$ inch. If the ring size is 7 or under (**C.19**), the band should probably be somewhat less than $\frac{3}{8}$ inch wide. Each jeweler will form independent judgments about these limitations, and even these may sometimes be overruled by the client. The designer, however, is reluctant to make a ring that will not be comfortable to wear over a whole lifetime.

Aside from the size and width, the jeweler will be interested in the kind of design expression the client desires. As a part of this question the size and width of the client's hands will be discussed, as well as the expressive style.

From a functional point of view it is probably unwise to make a wedding band any thinner than 14-gauge for the woman's ring and 12-gauge for the man's. A 16-gauge ring is generally too thin for long-term wear, as well as being too slight visually; 16-gauge should be used only for very small sizes or for children's rings. Here, again, ring size is correlated with thickness as well as width. For a size 5 ring, 12-gauge may be too heavy; for a size 12 ring, 10-gauge might be suitable.

The thickness of a ring band is also determined by the kind of processing that is to be done. Bands that are to be stamped with a punch (Fig. 239) require a thick gauge—probably at least 14—in order to take a sufficiently deep impression.

After the wedding band has been properly sized, it is important to remove the sharp edge on the inside of the band. This can be done by hand with a half-round file, although such rounding can be done more rapidly by using a cone on the spindle of a lathe or flexible shaft. When this beveling must be done by hand, it is best accomplished by taking a counted number of strokes in one position and then rotating the ring band and repeating the same number of strokes in other positions. This ensures even rounding all around. Care must be taken, also, that the rounded bevel on the edge maintains the same width evenly all around. Depending on the ring, the inner edge can be filed to a fairly wide roll (even up to the top edge of the ring in some designs) or merely enough to eliminate the sharp edge. In either case the edge must be emeried and then polished with tripoli to remove the file marks.

8.2

The Engagement Ring   For contemporary jewelers the traditional concept of the engagement ring has undergone considerable modification. Social conditioning has led to the general acceptance of the diamond set in platinum or gold as the appropriate symbolic form of the engagement ring. People who reject this conventional form become the clients of the contemporary jeweler, who is usually less interested in the restrictions of conventional form than in the opportunity to exercise personal creativeness within a relatively unrestricted range of design possibilities. Even though a diamond or other

left: 240. Stanley Lechtzin. Interlocking wedding rings of cast 14k gold, with peridot, 1967.

right: 241. Rings of Figure 240 in interlocked position.

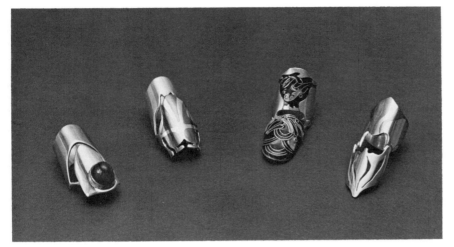

left: **242. Nilda C. Getty.** *Knuckle Rings,* of sterling silver, with jade, copper inlay, and cloisonné enamel, 1975.

below left: **243. Friedrich Becker.** White-gold ring, 1967.

below: **244. Vada Beetler.** Sterling-silver ring, constructed with beaded wire on fold-over shank, set with lime-green chrysoprase, 1975.

conventionally faceted gem may be used, the contemporary jeweler will try to create an expressive form consistent with the client's aesthetic orientation and interesting in form and color. It will become a "conversation piece," though on a somewhat more restrained level than the so-called "dinner ring." Mated or fitted wedding and engagement rings are becoming increasingly popular (Figs. 240, 241).

8.3

The Dinner or Cocktail Ring   The ring as a "conversation piece" gives an opportunity to employ a full range of design resources. Combinations of stones and unique direct methods of setting stones are a part of the contemporary design trend (Figs. 246, 537). Rings of this type can be large, provided they are designed functionally for comfortable wearing. Many women collect rings for wear on special occasions, and, while they may prefer a ring of modest size for everyday wear, perhaps because they wear gloves, they do not object to a larger size for the occasionally worn conversation piece (Figs. 242–244). In the past large rings have often been in fashion, and the tendency of contemporary jewelry toward larger rings has found a good response among clients.

If you happen to be wearing a ring, you will notice that the ring band fits into the crease between the palm and the inner finger joint. The crease usually determines the width of the ring band at that location. If the band is too wide there, the ring is likely to be uncomfortable to wear. If it is made quite narrow, however, it must be thick (up to 14-gauge for silver) in order to provide sufficient strength.

You will probably find from your own experiments that it is often preferable to taper the band, making it narrow at the bottom and wider on top, rather than have a band of uniform width. If the setting is long, the band should be wide at the point where it joins the setting, or table. For example, if you were using an oval cabochon 3 inches long and $\frac{3}{8}$ inch wide, it would be advisable to widen the band at the top by about 1 inch in order to hold the setting along the finger. A narrow band would allow the long stone to twist sideways on the finger. Ideally, such a ring should pass over the knuckle but not twist or turn when being worn. Usually, if a narrow band is used with a large, heavy setting, the ring will be sliding constantly to one side. Two solutions to this problem are a nonround ring shape and an open shape with some kind of spring tension.

Obviously, the corners and edges of a large ring must be smoothed to avoid discomfort to the wearer. In designing a ring, too, it is essential to avoid sharp projections that will be a danger to the wearer's hand or clothing, or to the well-being of others!

8.4

The Man's Ring   The functional design of a man's ring involves few aspects not already discussed in relation to other rings. Because a man's hand typically is larger than a woman's, the ring can be designed more massively (Figs. 245, 246). Delicacy is normally not a design quality sought in the man's ring; simplicity rather than extravagance and complexity will tend to predominate in the design.

below: 245. John Marshall. Man's diamond ring, with band of granulated silver and gold, 1970.

right: 246. Alvin Pine. Man's ring cast in 18k gold, with rubilite, jade, and pearl, c. 1968.

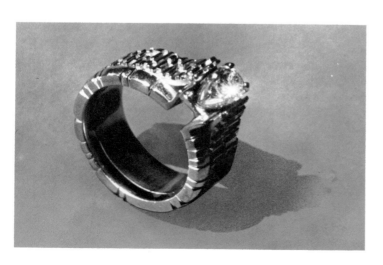

below: **247. Miye Matsukata.** Pair of earrings in 18k and 24k gold, with brilliant-cut diamonds in prong settings, 1975.

right: **248. Sigurd Persson.** Silver dangle earring, 1967.

8.5

The Dangle Earring Weight and comfort are two overriding functional considerations in the design of an earring. As with all forms of jewelry, the personality of the client is the point of departure for aesthetic design. The client will no doubt express preferences about size, weight, and simplicity or ornateness of design. But, regardless of size, excessive weight should be avoided (Fig. 247).

The problems of weight and comfort are bound up with the type of ear back employed. The screw type (Fig. 607) tends to be less comfortable than the spring-clip type (Fig. 608), whose clip has a larger area than that of the disk on the screw type. For many people it is possible to use the wing-back type, which fits into the ear instead of attaching to the lobe (Fig. 611). By itself the wing-back may look a bit strange, but it can be made to fit perfectly and causes no pinching discomfort. Since it is unusual, many clients may need persuasion to accept this type. (For ear-back findings, see **B.2**).

In general, a clip with a large area is more comfortable to wear and less likely to fall off than the typical screw back. Whenever possible, it is desirable for the contemporary jeweler to design clips or other attachments as an integral part of the earring (Fig. 248, 249).

249. Philip Morton. Clip earring constructed of sterling silver, 1946.

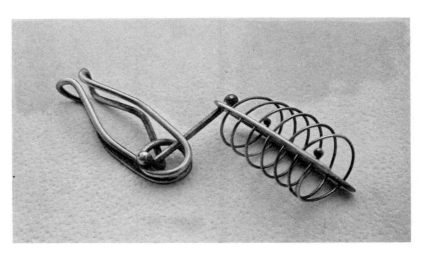

The dangle earring requires an ear back with a small ring on which to hang the dangle, and usually this type of ear back must have a button above the ring to cover the screw disk. Many jewelers incorporate this feature into the design. The length of the dangle will be determined by the client, but the jeweler must also relate the design to the length of the client's neck. Obviously, someone with a long neck can wear a long dangle more effectively.

8.6

The Button Earring   One of the functional problems of the button type of earring is to design it so that it does not tip over on the lobe of the ear (Fig. 250). This means that it must not be top-heavy, and the ear back must be placed somewhere above the center unless the button is quite small or light. The button type can be made for pierced ears by using the post-and-screw ear back. Otherwise, a clip or screw back is necessary.

8.7

The Pierced-Ear Earring   The pierced ear is very much in fashion, and a pierced-ear wire can be made easily by the contemporary jeweler. If made of silver wire, it should be hard-drawn, by beginning with at least 12-gauge wire and drawing it down to 22- or 24-gauge without annealing. This will stiffen the wire by work hardening (**9.1**).

Aside from considerations of weight and the type of ear back, the possibilities of size and shape are without restriction. However, observation of the client will reveal how long and how large the earring can be. A dangle hung on a small wire through the ear lobe should not be very heavy (Fig. 251).

251. **Heikki Seppa.** Pendant earrings for pierced ears, in 14k gold, with pearls, 1967.

The Bracelet The limitations of the bracelet are determined by the preferences of the client. There are three types: link, slip-on, and hinged.

The link type of bracelet must be sized to fit the wrist comfortably, but it should not be so large as to slip over the hand. Small links allow a piece to drape flexibly on the wrist. This type of bracelet can be fastened with a sister hook (Fig. 614), a spring ring, or a ring and hook devised by the jeweler.

The slip-on bracelet is normally fairly rigid and either open (Figs. 252, 253) or closed (Fig. 176). A closed bracelet must be just large enough to fit over the wrist without slipping off when the hand is relaxed. The open type must be made so that the gap will go over the side of the wrist, which is quite narrow. The metal of a slip-on bracelet should be work-hardened for stiffness, unless it is very heavy, because a certain amount of spring is necessary. Even with a closed bracelet, some spring tension is desirable.

The hinged type of bracelet requires a hinge and locking catch that allow it to be opened and closed snugly on the wrist (Pl. 8, p. 151). This type offers the jeweler an opportunity to devise a concealed hinge and a special catch, which might be made an integral part of the bracelet (Fig. 254).

Like a ring, a bracelet is likely to be bumped against hard objects. Stones used in the bracelet should be hard—at least 5 or 6 on the Mohs' scale (**20.4**).

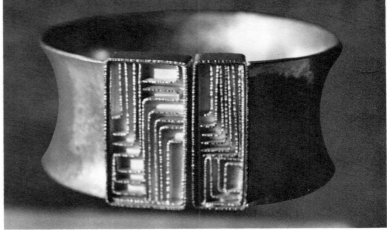

above: 252. Sigurd Persson. *Bubblegum,* silver bracelet, 1973.

above right: 253. Mary A. Kretsinger. Bracelet of hammered 18k gold, 1974. Collection Mrs. Dwight Wallace, Wichita, Kan.

right: 254. Helen Shirk. Hinged bracelet of formed and forged sterling, 1970.

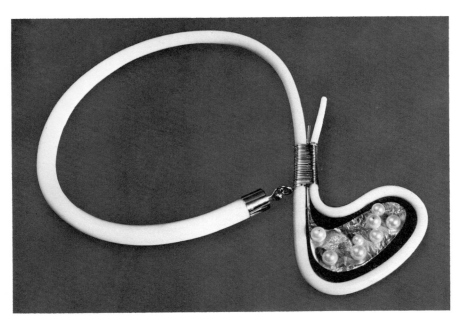

255. Heikki Seppa. Neckpiece of Teflon and 14k gold, with pearls, 1973.

8.9

The Necklace   Limitations on the design of a necklace hardly go beyond the question of comfort and the security of the fastener. Obviously, dangerous or uncomfortable points must be avoided on both the top and bottom surfaces of the necklace. Corners, edges, and surfaces should be smooth. Size and weight are essentially questions of personal preference (Figs. 255, 256).

A choker made by forging heavy wire or rod must be fitted carefully to the individual neck (Fig. 232). Pendant necklaces with large attachments hung in series from a chain or cord must not extend too far onto the shoulders. As a rule of thumb, such attachments should be hung from no more than one-quarter of the chain. Pendant forms tend to hang straight down rather than fan out. They therefore assume parallel positions unless some kind of anchoring arrangement is devised to hold them in a fan position (**A.8**).

As a fastener, an ordinary wire hook passed through a jump ring may often fall open. One solution to this problem is to give the wire hook some spring tension by flattening it slightly and setting it so that a small pressure is necessary to slide it over the ring. The conventional spring-ring (Fig. 615) is efficient and can always be used, but it is less interesting to the creative jeweler than a specially designed interlocking device.

8.10

The Pendant   There are virtually no limitations on the design of a pendant (Pl. 12, p. 153; Figs. 257, 258). Functional requirements are few and flexible, so that weight and size can be designed to suit the limitations and preferences of the client. Comfort and security are the major considerations. Beyond these, one might follow the rule that the heavier the pendant, the larger the diameter of the cord or chain. Rayon and silk cord of $\frac{1}{8}$- to $\frac{1}{4}$-inch diameter is universally popular. Both the necklace and the pendant offer an opportunity for unlimited expressive design. The contemporary jeweler generally designs a forged and modeled metal strap to carry a pendant or necklace array. This strap is usually open at the back, springing apart for putting on and taking off. Often the pendant is hung upon a swivel device so that it can hang in all positions as a three-dimensional form in the round.

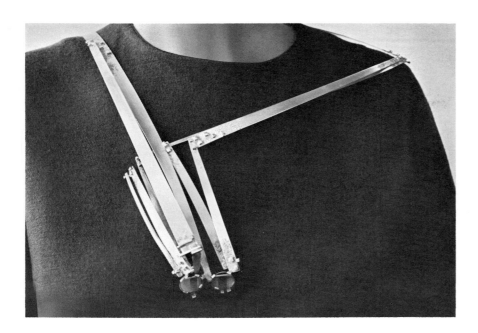

above: **256. Alma Eikerman.** Shoulder collar in sterling silver, partially textured, with two black onyxes, 1970.

below: **257. Richard Mawdsley.** *Camera,* sterling pendant constructed with cast eagle's head, set with amethyst, 1972.

right: **258. Olaf Skoogfors.** Pendant of gold-plated sterling and ivory, 1975.

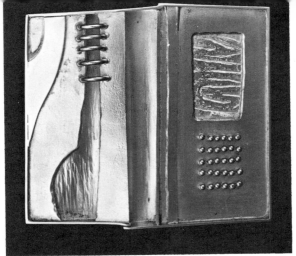

8.11

left: 259. Olli Peter Valanne. Pin of
electroformed and reticulated 14k
gold, c. 1972.

right: 260. Olaf Skoogfors. Pin of
gold-plated sterling, etched and textured, with buckshot, 1974.

The Brooch   Beyond the functional limits of comfort and security, the weight
of a brooch must be related to the type of fabric it is to be worn on. The client
will give this information. A pin to be worn on the lapel of a firm wool suit can
be heavy, if the client is willing. However, a pin meant for a thin blouse must
not pull heavily on a weave of delicate material. Having satisfied these
criteria, the jeweler can give free rein to the imagination in designing a brooch
(Figs. 259–261).

Once the weight problem has been solved, the position in which the pin
will hang must be determined, so that the joint and catch location can be
planned. In most cases the pin tong must be placed above the center of gravity
of the pin so that it does not tip forward to expose only its upper edge.
Sometimes a three-dimensional projection at the back of the lower edge will
help to maintain the pin in a vertical position. Otherwise, the pin must be
designed for its natural wearing position.

There has not been a great effort to find alternate solutions for fastening
the brooch beyond the traditional means of pin, joint, and catch. Spring claws
work well as a substitute for the pin on loosely woven materials. Considerable
opportunity awaits the experimenter in the direction of integral catches and
perhaps other alternatives to the pin tong.

below: 261. Mary A. Kretsinger. Pin
of fused 18k gold with aquamarine,
1970. Hinges and spring catches allow
for change of positions; the large
aquamarine can be removed and
worn separately as a pendant. Collection Mr. and Mrs. Donald Lewis,
Dallas.

right: 262. Philip Morton. Cuff links of
cast sterling, with green jade, 1950.

8.12

The Cuff Link   The functional problem of the cuff link is to design a back that
can be readily attached or removed and yet not fall off. A compromise must
be made about the size and shape of the cuff back. A double cuff link, each

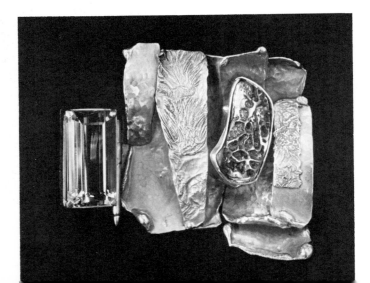

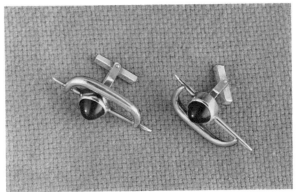

side of which fastens to a side of the cuff and then snaps and unsnaps, is an attractive idea that has not been exploited sufficiently in recent times. All designers value the idea of the cuff back that is an integral, if not equal, part of the design.

The typical commercial cuff backs are relatively unattractive in design. They are strictly functional (Fig. 612), and, with the hinged bar that swings out, they are easy to attach and remove. The type that bends off at an angle (Fig. 262) probably provides a better fit than the straight type.

A chain between a cuff-link front and its smaller back can be used as a design element. The back as well then becomes an aesthetic factor in the design. In planning this type of cuff link, be sure to allow at least $\frac{5}{8}$ inch between the front and the back, or the user will have difficulty in fastening it to the cuff. It is convenient to use a circular jump ring on each of the two parts of the cuff link and three oval jump rings, all soldered, between them.

The size and weight of cuff links should be set by the client (Fig. 99).

8.13

The Tie Clip   Comfort and security are basic limitations for the tie clip, but two additional requirements must be fulfilled. The space at the hinge or spring side must be great enough to accommodate about a $\frac{1}{4}$-inch thickness of material—usually two thicknesses of tie (which may be wool and quite thick) and one thickness of shirt. The jaws of the clip must be designed in such a way as to grasp the material without causing snags or holes in it. The commercial tie-clip backs satisfy both of these requirements (Fig. 617).

If the clip back is to be custom designed, it must be work-hardened sufficiently to provide a durable spring tension. The double curve in the tie clips illustrated in Figures 376–378 is necessary to provide both space and length for sufficient spring tension. In finishing the custom clip, all parts must be smoothed, so that no snags will occur. Also in finishing, all grease and dirt must be removed, so that the clip will not soil the tie or shirt.

top: 263. Barrette with integral pin and catch.

above: 264. Philip Morton. Barrette, in ebony and sterling silver, 1949.

below: 265. Marilyn Ravanal. Hair ornament of forged and chased sterling, with natural shells, 1973.

8.14

The Tie Tack   The main problems of the tie tack (Fig. 616) are to use a pin that is strong and stiff enough to resist bending without being much thicker than 18-gauge, and to devise a simple spring clip that can be applied or removed by squeezing. Silver wire can for this purpose be somewhat stiffened by twisting (**11.20**). The use of nickel-silver wire is probably desirable if the tie tack is in sterling. Gold wire, of course, possesses adequate stiffness.

8.15

Hair Ornaments   The function of the barrette is to hold hair (Fig. 263). This usually calls for a slotted clip that extends about halfway around a circle 2 inches in diameter and a pin of metal, wood, or other material, which is passed through the hair and held in the slot. An older style of barrette is flatter and utilizes a double spring clip and double pin hinged opposite the clip. Regardless of the form, a barrette must hold the hair and be held firmly by the hair, but a great deal of design freedom is possible (Fig. 264).

There has always been a certain amount of interest in the comb, but particularly so during periods when long hair has been popular. The decorative comb (Figs. 39, 192, 265) has a number of teeth ranging from two on up, which are usually curved transversely to fit the shape of the head. The teeth should be not less than 3 inches long and may need to be as much as 4 inches long for increased security in fastening the hair. The teeth, or pins, can be sawed from plate or assembled and soldered. They may be given a parallel or opposing movement to enhance the visual pattern and increase fastening security.

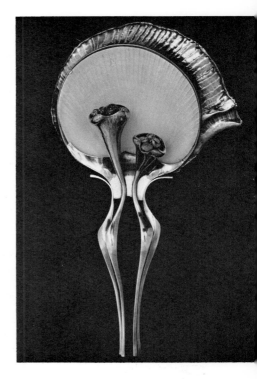

Tiaras are seldom worn today, but in the past they were objects of sumptuous and complex design (Figs. 19, 21, 40). Contemporary jewelers are reexploring the attraction of elaborate ornaments (Fig. 266).

8.16

The Buckle   The function of the buckle is to hold fast a cloth or leather belt. Since belt buckles are subjected to the action of opening and closing more than any other piece of jewelry, they should be constructed strongly, if not massively. Many interesting variations have been made of the device that locks the belt in place (Fig. 267). The most common is a small pin or hook that penetrates a centered hole in the belt. Interesting functional solutions that are an integral part of the design are possible. In sterling, the loop that holds the belt end should be made of at least 10-gauge wire. The pin should also be about 10-gauge wire. Otherwise, the strain on the belt will cause these parts to bend out of shape. It is desirable to thread the belt loop through a piece of tubing in order to allow this loop to lie flat against the belt rather than stand out from the back of the buckle (Fig. 268).

In recent years, jewelers have shown a greatly revived interest in the design potential of belt buckles and even whole belts (Figs. 126, 204, 269).

266. Arline M. Fisch. Hat, woven in fine silver wire, with white turkey feathers, 1974.

above: 267. Fastening device on a belt buckle.

below left: 268. Hinged loop on a belt buckle.

below right: 269. Ccarol Phillips. *Black Swan*, belt buckle electroformed and constructed in 14k and 18k gold and fine silver, with enamel and black moonstone, 1973.

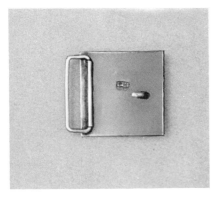

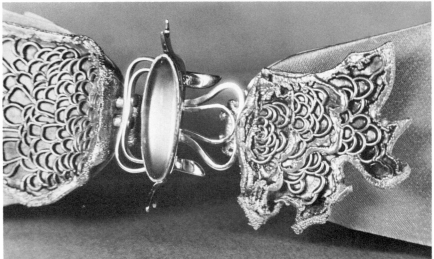

part three
Technique

In a basic text the fundamental processes of a craft must be described as simply and clearly as possible. Such a concise presentation will seldom do justice to the many alternative methods that arise out of experience and may be equally effective. No two jewelers work in precisely the same way. However, the procedures outlined in the following chapters will be a point of departure for the student, who, with increased practice, will gradually acquire a personal "style" of craftsmanship.

Similarly, there exists no uniform system for classifying processes. For the sake of clarity, and to allow presentation of the material in a systematic way, the chapters in this section have been broken down as follows: basic procedures, fusing and soldering, forming, cutting, hammering, fastenings, casting, electroforming and electroplating, surface treatment, enameling, finishing, stone setting, and toolmaking. In practice, of course, the creation of a piece of jewelry is a creative continuum that may involve any number of techniques in any order or sequence of interchange.

Topics in this section have been numbered to permit easy cross-referencing. Technical details related to some of the processes are explained more fully in Appendix C, and for this reason references to specific sections of the Appendix also occur from time to time throughout the text.

Basic Metal Procedures

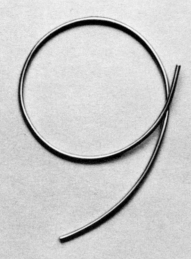

Certain operations are fundamental to most kinds of jewelry making, and a knowledge of these underlies even the most elementary types of work. In this chapter several of these operations—and the equipment necessary to carry them out—will be described. *Annealing* and *pickling* are two terms that will recur during subsequent descriptions of jewelry making; removal of *fire scale* is a basic corrective measure that the beginning metalworker should be familiar with.

The most standard piece of equipment is the jeweler's bench (Fig. 270), often equipped with a tray to catch *lemel* or filings, a V-block for sawing, a bench pin in the center of the slot for filing, as well as drawers and racks for tools. It should be obvious that a good source of light must be provided, since jewelry making requires a close and accurate use of the eyes. A plan for an ideal studio appears in Figure 271. Other portions of the studio will be illustrated as they relate to specific techniques.

9.1

Annealing　To understand why the process known as annealing becomes necessary from time to time, one must first visualize how metal is structured. All metals consist of aggregates composed of large numbers of crystalline grains (Fig. 272). Although the internal structure of a grain shows an orderly arrangement of atoms in a definite pattern (which depends on the metal in question), the grain's external shape is determined by the manner and number of contacts with other grains. Therefore, the crystalline planes of the grains run haphazardly in all directions.

above: **270.** Jeweler's bench.

right: **271.** Plan of a convenient studio for an independent jeweler.

below: **272.** Photomicrograph (×1000) of sterling silver, showing its irregular granular structure.

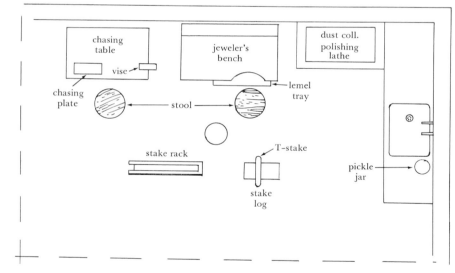

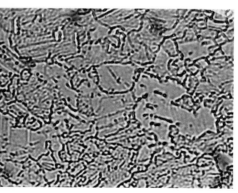

When *nonferrous metals*—metals that contain no iron—are subjected to certain forms of work at normal temperatures (bending, hammering, twisting, drawing, and so forth), the external force causes a distortion of the metallic crystals along slip planes. This plastic deformation of the metal produces a condition known as *work hardening,* in which the metal becomes brittle because its crystals are too closely packed to allow further shifting. Nonferrous metals that are important for jewelry making include gold, silver, copper, brass, and bronze—all of them subject to work hardening. When the jeweler notices that the metal being worked has begun to lose its soft, malleable quality, work should be stopped until the metal can be softened, or *annealed.* If work-hardened metal is not annealed, it will eventually crack. A good experiment for the beginner would be to take some scrap pieces of metal and work on them to discover the limits of malleability.

In annealing, the work-hardened metal is heated to the appropriate temperature at which the grains assume their normal relationships, thus eliminating the strain and restoring the metal to its malleable state. The jeweler quite often needs to anneal metal that has been rolled or hammered or drawn in order to prevent it from cracking. Repoussé (**11.16**), in particular, work-hardens metal and therefore must be accompanied by systematic annealing.

Metal to be annealed should be placed in an annealing pan (Fig. 273), a deep circular, rotating tray usually filled with pumice pebbles graded to about $\frac{1}{4}$-inch diameter. A reducing flame (one slightly yellowish at the tip, **10.2**) is then played over the entire surface of the metal as the annealing tray is rotated to distribute the heat evenly. A large piece of metal requires a large, bushy flame, but a small flame will suffice for delicate work. Yellow, red, or green gold, as well as sterling silver, should be heated until a *low red* color is visible, or to about 1100°F. for the gold alloys and 1200° F. for the silver. Copper, bronze, and white gold require heating until they are *cherry red*, or to about 1400° F. When wire finer than about 16-gauge is being annealed, it should be coiled compactly in order to increase the volume, for otherwise the wire may melt.

Because the low red color will be hardly visible in a brightly lighted room, it is necessary at least to turn down the room lights. Most jewelers, however, prefer to work in an annealing booth (Fig. 273), which has sides all around to protect the work from cooling by air drafts and to shield the work from room light. It is important that the metal not be heated past the required temperature, since overheating increases the fire scale (**9.3**) that forms on the surface of alloys, particularly silver. When the proper color has been reached, the metal is ready for pickling and cleaning.

Always keep lead and lead solder away from the annealing pan and the soldering blocks on which you work with silver or gold. Lead will soak into any silver or gold that has been heated to annealing or soldering temperature and cause holes to be eaten into the metal. To remove lead that has gotten onto your metal, first scrape the surface carefully and thoroughly with a scraper (Fig. 361). Appendix C gives a formula that will dissolve and remove any remaining amount of lead (**C.15**).

273. Annealing booth, the annealing pan filled with pumice pebbles.

9.2

Pickling   When metals are heated, the surfaces become oxidized and dirty, so that during the various processes that require heating—such as soldering—a piece of jewelry may have to be cleaned several times. The usual method of removing oxides, old flux, fingerprints, dirt, and other stains is to drop the heated metal into a *pickle solution*, generally made of water and sulphuric or nitric acid (**C.11**). If the hot metal is dropped in, the pickle will react immediately to clean the surface, but this may prevent a uniform annealing of the metal. Another objection is that the hot metal will vaporize some of the pickle acid. The resultant fumes could present a hazard to the respiratory tract even if the room is well ventilated. When pickling is repeated throughout the day in a small, poorly ventilated workshop, the room will become filled with acid fumes. For these reasons, it is better either to quench the work in water or to allow the metal to cool gradually before immersing it in the pickle solution. The one metal that should never be quenched is brass, for quenching will make brass harder and more brittle than it was before annealing. Brass can be pickled only after it has cooled completely. Silver, too, may become brittle and crack unless it is air cooled before pickling. (For more details and pickle solutions for gold, silver, and brass, see **C.11**.)

When mixing the pickle solution, *always add the acid to the water* rather than the other way around. If water is poured into acid, an explosion will

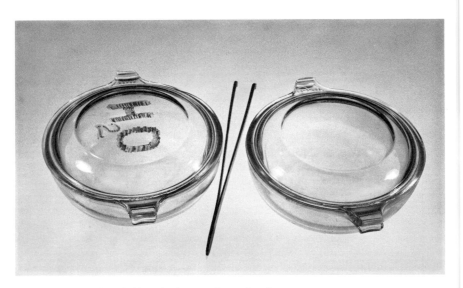

274. Pyrex jars for pickle solution, and a pair of tweezers.

occur. The pickle solution can be kept in one of several types of containers: a lead pan, a porcelain crock, a Pyrex jar (Fig. 274) that rests on a hot plate, or a crock with a thermostatically controlled heating element. The last of these is available at some supply houses. Because the fumes are corrosive and the solution tends to evaporate, the container should be covered when not in use. (If the solution does evaporate, water can be added.) The pickle crock is kept near a sink where the work can be washed off easily.

Pickle solution can be irritating to the skin, and you should take care that it does not splash on clothing. Stand away from the pickling crock, and drop the pieces in on the near side, so that splashes will move away from you. The cover of the crock can serve as a shield to prevent you from being splashed. If you use tongs, be sure they are made of copper, brass, or stainless steel. Iron tools—tweezers, annealing tongs, or binding wire—should never be put into the pickle, for iron will cause a copper deposition on your work.

A cold pickle solution reacts slowly on cold metal. In most instances jewelers will prefer to go on with other projects while the pickle does its work. However, for quick cleaning of metal, a small quantity of pickle can be heated on a hot plate in a copper pickle pan. The jewelry is placed in the pan and heated until the pickle begins to steam. By this time the work should be clean, and the pickle can be poured carefully back into the crock. This process will release acid fumes into the air and should be done only under a ventilating hood or in a well-ventilated room. Properly pickled silver turns a pure, flat white from the deposit of pure silver left on a surface when the alloy crust is dissolved by the pickle. Copper turns a flat, powdery, red. Sometimes jewelry—traditional filigree work, for example—is left with the pickled color.

After the piece has been pickled, it can be neutralized by boiling in a solution of water and sodium bicarbonate (baking soda). This is often done with a piece that has crevices and hollows where the pickle may lodge and continue to eat away at the work. However, for most work ordinary washing will suffice to wash away the pickle. It is common practice to keep a pan of boiling soapy water on a burner, with a strainer in the pan; all pickled work is dropped in the pan after polishing to wash away the surface coating.

The soapy water will also neutralize the acid. When the work has been pickled and washed, it should be dried with a towel, after which it is ready for further processing.

9.3

Fire Scale   When gold or silver is heated to a low red color or hotter, the base metal of the alloy separates on the surface and forms a dark film. This is called *fire scale* or *firecoat,* and it is difficult to remove. On a piece of silver that has been polished lightly, it will appear as a dark shadow, against which the polished edges shine in contrast. Fire scale can be seen most plainly if the back of the hand is held just below the piece of silver, so that it becomes visible as a reflection in the surface of the metal.

Fire scale is caused by the cuprous oxide and cupric oxide that both result from the oxidation of the metal surface. One of the oxides can be removed easily by pickle solution, but the other can be eliminated only by buffing, stripping, or filing and emerying.

Sometimes fire scale is used as a color for design purposes, but more often it will be considered undesirable. You will never be able to get a high polish on silver until it is removed. Silver on which the fire scale is allowed to remain tarnishes very rapidly.

The buildup of fire scale can be reduced, though not completely eliminated, by covering the work to be heated with Prip's Flux or with a yellow ochre preparation (**C.12**) mixed with dissolved boric-acid crystals. The trade jeweler uses a solution of borax dissolved in alcohol, which evaporates quickly to leave a coating of borax on the work.

There are several ways of dealing with fire scale:

■ A quick silver plating will cover the fire scale. This is probably the most common and practical method.

■ Polishing with tripoli or Lea compound on a muslin buff is the usual system for removing fire scale. This works well if the surfaces are easily accessible, but there is some danger of grinding off the edges or putting grooves in the silver if you overpolish the work.

■ Burnishing with a scratch brush will remove the thick white coat of free silver on the surface that results from repeated annealing and pickling.

■ The fire scale can be stripped by immersing the piece for a short time in a boiling solution of nitric acid and water (**C.13**). This requires a special blower installation to carry off the corrosive fumes and is not a safe process for inexperienced workers. Few jewelers follow this old practice today. In any event, nitric acid should not be used on a piece of jewelry that has nickel-silver findings, since there is no way of protecting the findings from corrosion.

■ The work can be stripped in an electroplating tank by reversing the direction of the current. The electroplating equipment usually has a stripping as well as a cleaning and a plating tank (**16.4**).

Fusing
and
Soldering

In ancient times work meant to be fused and soldered was heated in a small open-hearth furnace built of firebrick. The craftsman would build up a charcoal fire and then place the work inside the furnace. A hollow reed, covered with clay to prevent its burning, was used as a blowpipe to increase the heat for soldering or fusing.

The means of heating and soldering metal advanced little until fairly recent times, and many of the older procedures are still in use. Variations of these methods were employed until the discovery of illuminating gas.

Torches

10.1

Torch Equipment   There are many kinds of soldering torches available on the market and in use in jewelry and metal workshops. The kind of work you will be able to do depends upon the kind of torch equipment you have. An alcohol or gas lamp was used with a small mouth blowpipe (Fig. 275) in Europe and America until the end of the 19th century, and this equipment is still found in many old workshops. Foot bellows often replaced lung power in the use of the blowpipe. Though these old methods may seem clumsy in relation to modern equipment, extremely delicate soldering operations have been done with them. The use of the mouth blowpipe is still a superior method for soldering pewter. If other equipment is lacking, work can be placed upon a heating frame over a gas plate and heated to a low red color.

The final soldering is then done with a mouth blowpipe and the flame of a bunsen burner. Soldering is often better accomplished with the blowpipe and bunsen burner than with a modern torch clumsily handled.

The alcohol torch, the blowpipe, the prestone tank, and the propane or butane tank limit the range of work that can be done, because higher temperatures cannot be reached.

The prestone tank was almost the only torch available for the jewelry workshop until the development of the small, hand-held propane and butane torches. The standard prestone tank contains acetylene gas and features a single hose and a single valve at the torch. At the tank there is a tank valve and an air regulator that can be opened or closed to adjust the flame. The air regulator should be turned so that enough air flows through the torch to consume the carbon of the gas completely. A reddish-colored flame indicates insufficient air; add more air until the flame burns clean and bright.

The small portable propane or butane torch with a replaceable tank is handy for the beginner, or for someone who is going to do only a limited amount of work (Fig. 276). The tank and the torch come as one inexpensive unit that is discarded when the fuel is used up. The air adjustment on these torches is set at the factory. The torch is lighted simply by turning on the valve slightly and igniting the gas. More often, the modern workshop is equipped with the air-gas torch, utilizing natural gas or propane gas and air from a compressor, or the oxygen-gas torch.

The serious jeweler should invest in an oxygen-gas or air-gas torch (Fig. 277); the initial expenditure for one of these units is quite high, because acetylene-gas and oxygen tanks must be purchased. However, empty tanks can be exchanged for full ones at a low cost, and the versatility of these torches makes them worth the money. The torches are provided with various tips. Small hand torches with large flame tips give a flame that is large and soft, ideal for annealing or soldering large work.

The air-gas torches are generally preferred for most nonferrous metal-work and silversmithing, because the flame is softer but still hot enough for annealing and soldering purposes. Air is supplied by either a small air compressor or a foot bellows. Air-gas torches are usually installed in an annealing booth. Most jewelry shops, however, use an oxygen-gas torch that gives a flame with a wide range of temperatures. Such torches are necessary for gold and platinum work and can readily be used to heat or fuse nonferrous metals. The oxygen-gas torch requires an oxygen tank, a tank regulator to adjust the pressure of the oxygen, and a torch with hoses.

275. The mouth blowpipe in use, as illustrated in Diderot's *Encyclopedia* (1751–65).

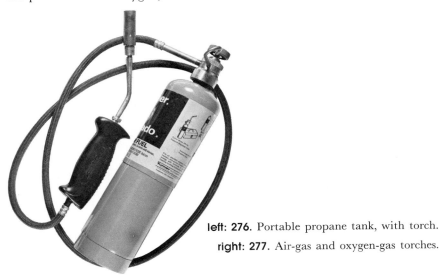

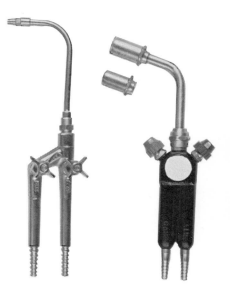

left: 276. Portable propane tank, with torch.

right: 277. Air-gas and oxygen-gas torches.

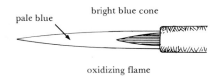

pale blue — bright blue cone

oxidizing flame

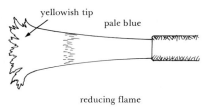

yellowish tip

pale blue

reducing flame

278. Reducing and oxidizing flames, fed by an air-gas torch.

Oxygen-gas torches are generally designed for low-pressure gas. In most cities, low-pressure city gas (LPCG) is maintained at a pressure of about 8 pounds. If you use such a torch with propane or butane, you will need a regulator to reduce the tank pressure. There are two kinds: the *automatic* regulator, which is preset for appropriate pressure, and the *adjustable* regulator. If you have the adjustable regulator, it should be set at from 7 to 10 pounds (3.17 to 4.53 kilos). The oxygen tank will always require a regulator, and this should be set to about 15 pounds (6.79 kilos) pressure unless you are forging or hardening tool steel, in which case it can be set at up to 25 pounds (11.32 kilos). Tank valves should be turned off at the end of the working period. The line valves, too, should be closed, and the torch valves opened to relieve the pressure on the regulator diaphragms.

10.2

Flame Adjustment Proper flame adjustment is essential to the efficient use of the torch. There are two kinds of flame: oxidizing and reducing (Fig. 278). In the oxidizing flame, more compressed air or oxygen is fed to the flame than the flame actually burns, and the excess oxides appear like a dark film on the surface of the metal. This flame is all blue in color, hotter than the reducing flame, and it usually makes a hissing sound. It is useful for some kinds of work. For heating gold and silver, a reducing flame is to be preferred because, even though it takes longer to do the job, it will leave the work relatively clean (unless you allow the metal to become overheated). A reducing flame consumes all of the air or oxygen that is fed into it through the valve and leaves the metal with a mirrorlike surface. This flame should have a slightly yellowish tip.

10.3

The Use of Torches You can learn more from actually experimenting with the torch than you can from reading about it. Nevertheless, there are a number of hints that will help you carry out initial experiments:

- A large flame should be used to heat a large piece of metal.
- The size of the flame can be varied by changing the tip on the torch or by increasing or decreasing the amount of gas.
- The heat intensity of the flame can be increased by mixing more oxygen or air with the gas.
- The hottest part of the flame is at the tip of the blue cone of gas inside the flame where it leaves the torch tip (Fig. 279).
- Light an oxygen-gas or air-gas torch by first igniting the gas and then turning on the air or oxygen. Turn off the torch by closing first the oxygen and then the gas.
- If the oxygen-gas torch pops and goes out, it is because the oxygen is blowing the flame off the torch tip. If the gas will not light, it is probably because too much gas has been turned on. In order to avoid a possible burn, *be careful to turn on only a small amount of gas* when lighting the torch.
- To solder a particular place on your work, heat up the entire work to a point just below the melting point of the solder, using a medium-hot flame. Then apply a small but hotter flame to the local area to be soldered.
- Always keep your flame aimed directly at the work and always *keep your flame moving* around and around over the work. If the flame remains in one place, the metal may melt.
- To fuse pieces of metal together without solder, first flux the pieces at the joint (**10.10**).
- A striker, or sparker, is usually used to ignite a torch in preference to matches.

279. Reducing flame, showing the blue cone of concentrated heat in the center.

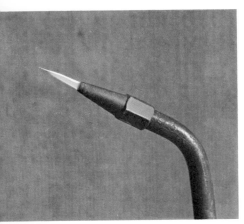

Fusing

Fusing is the liquefying of metal under an extremely hot flame. Two pieces of metal can be fused in order to join them without soldering, or a single piece of metal can be fused into a new form. All nonferrous metals can be fused with the torches described above. To investigate the possibilities of this process, the beginning jeweler may want to experiment. First, try fusing several small pieces of metal together into a ball; this does not require much skill. The metal must first be prepared by thorough cleaning and pickling (9.2). The use of flux (10.10) will also ensure good fusing. Then, place the metal on a level charcoal or asbestos block (fused metal will roll off an inclined surface). Heat the metal slowly and evenly, using a rotating motion of the oxygen-gas torch. As the metal becomes molten, it will undergo changes in texture and color that you should learn to recognize. It will take some practice to control the fusing within desired limits. If the force of the torch tends to roll the metal off the block, carve an indentation in the charcoal deep enough to prevent the metal from moving away from you. The particles of metal, when molten, will form a ball.

10.4

Controlled Fusing   As a second experiment, try fusing two larger pieces of silver together by melting the edges and then joining them. Under controlled conditions it is quite possible to fuse *fine silver* (pure, unalloyed silver) and *sterling silver* (925 parts silver to 75 parts copper) without first coating them with flux and obtain clean and perfect fusion. The secret of controlled fusion is a large, soft flame such as that of the air-gas torch. Take the two pieces of metal that you want to join and clean them thoroughly. Set them together on a good insulating material such as bismuth or charcoal (not asbestos or brick). Adjust the torch so you have a soft, bushy, and slightly reducing flame—one with a yellowish color at the bushy end. Heat the two pieces until they are molten, and then move them together with a poker until they are joined.

It would be difficult to fuse particles of fine silver onto a larger base of fine silver, because the small pieces would melt into the surface of the base. Sterling silver will hold its form on fine silver much better. When sterling is fused onto copper or brass, there is a tendency for the sterling to melt into the other metals. However, it is possible to fuse the two successfully if you use a soft, easy flame. After you have had some experience with fusing broad pieces of metal, try fusing preshaped wire or metal scraps onto a flat surface (Figs. 280–283). First, heat the base until it is beginning to melt; then position

280–283. A technique for controlled fusing, demonstrated by John Dickerhoff.

top: 280. Hammered wires are placed on the background metal.

center: 281. All parts in position, ready for fusing.

above: 282. Detail showing all parts fused in place.

left: 283. The finished brooch.

the wire or small pieces of metal that have been simultaneously heated to a similar degree. You can fuse the same metals or experiment with combinations. Experience and patience will help you to gain control of your torch and materials.

10.5

Fusing Beads from Wire   Small beads can be made very easily by fusing the ends of wire. First, cover the end of the wire with flux (which will help the metal flow smoothly; **10.10**). Then hold the wire, end down, in the tweezers, and hit the end quickly with a tight, hot flame. When the end begins to melt, it will draw up into a bead (Fig. 284). This bead will drop off after attaining a certain maximum size. Large beads can be made by supporting the end of the wire on an asbestos block and fusing to the desired size. To keep the bead smooth, turn off the air or oxygen after the sphere has formed on the end of the wire, allowing only the gas flame to play on it. Then gradually extinguish the flame, hitting the bead until it drops off the wire.

10.6

Fusing Granules and Beads   You can make granules or beads of silver and gold from pieces of wire cut into equal lengths. To get exactly matched granules without measuring each bit of wire, coil a length of wire tightly around a mandrel of the correct size—a thick one for larger beads, a thinner one for finer beads. Slide the rings off the mandrel, and saw through all the rounds of the coil (Fig. 327). Layer these rings in powdered charcoal inside a tall, narrow crucible, and heat the crucible in a furnace to the appropriate melting temperature. Be sure to cover the bottom of the crucible with a thick layer of charcoal before beginning the layering. After firing, empty the contents into a pan of water and rinse the charcoal away. Finally, pickle the beads (**9.2**). If there are only a few beads to be made, you can fuse one at a time on the asbestos block. Tiny beads, called granules, are prepared in this way as a first step in the intricate process of *granulation* (**17.3–8**).

Large beads can be made separately on a charcoal block by the following method. Drill a small hole of appropriate size a little way into the block. Then press and rotate a dapping punch of the right size into this hole until a perfect hemispherical hollow is formed. Carefully place a small scrap of silver over this depression and melt with the torch. The lower half of the molten metal is supported as a perfect sphere. The upper half is pulled into shape by molecular attraction of the molten metal. If this bead is to be

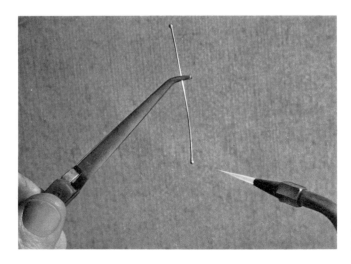

284. A hot reducing flame fuses beads on the ends of silver wire, held with soldering tweezers.

285. Mary Lee Hu. *Neckpiece #22,* wrapped and fused of fine and sterling silver, 1975.

finished perfectly and polished, it is best to solder it to a wire. Then place the wire in a pin vise (Fig. 304) where the bead can be filed, finished, and polished quite readily everywhere except at the point of attachment. Afterwards, saw the wire away from the bead. For some design purposes, the bead may be left on the wire (Fig. 285).

Torch Texturing   Fusing or melting the surface of metal, if carried out properly, will create a textured surface that offers rich visual qualities. This process, known as *reticulation,* is fully discussed elsewhere (**17.2**).

Soldering

Soldering is the process of fusing two pieces of metal together with another metal of lower melting point. The soldering metal must be of the same color and have a composition similar to that of the base metal for the completed join to be strong and undetectable when finished. In nature, metals are usually found combined with other elements in the form of ores, although some deposits of free and relatively pure metals exist everywhere. From such deposits came the first metal objects. Long before anything was known about the extraction of metals from ores, the Egyptians were making jewelry of free gold and a natural alloy of gold and silver, *electrum.* Through centuries of experience it was found that certain alloys of gold melted at a lower temperature than other alloys. This discovery made it possible to solder pieces of metal together.

286. Soldering equipment (*left to right*): charcoal block, binding wire, torch, tweezers, sheet and wire solder, sable brush, flux, and yellow ochre.

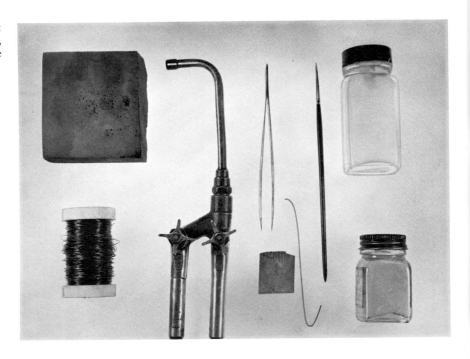

Soldering Equipment

For soldering you will need the following equipment (Fig. 286):
- hard or soft solder, depending on the job
- flux and a sable brush to apply it
- yellow ochre (anti-flux) to hold and prevent the flow of solder where necessary
- air-gas or oxygen-gas torch
- an annealing pan or an asbestos or charcoal block to support the work, or a heating frame and tripod
- soldering tweezers and/or a steel pick
- binding wire where necessary
- pickling equipment

10.7

Hard Solders   Soldering with silver-alloy or gold-alloy solder is called *hard-soldering*. The melting point of pure or "fine" silver is 1761° F. When a small amount of pure brass is melted with fine silver, the resulting alloy melts at a lower temperature. Five grades of solder are available on the market (**C.7**), and these will suffice for most soldering jobs:

1. I. T. solder melts at 1460° F. and is used primarily for soldering metal that requires a very strong bond or is to be enameled.
2. Hard-grade solder, which melts at 1410° F., serves for the first one or two solderings on a piece that requires multiple solderings.
3. Medium-grade solder—the grade most commonly used for general soldering—melts at 1360° F.
4. Easy-grade solder, which melts at 1310° F., is used at the second stage of soldering when some parts have already been soldered with medium solder.
5. Easy Flo solder melts at 1175° F. It serves for delicate and fine work when strength is not a factor, for repair work if stones cannot be removed, and for the third stage of a complex soldering project.

10.8

Soft Solders   The term *soft solder* refers to solder containing lead in an alloy with tin. One standard soft solder, called "fifty-fifty" and made with equal parts of lead and tin, melts at about 400° F. Soft soldering is used to join alloyed metals such as pewter, to solder silver and brass together, and to fasten ear wires and cuff-link backs to jewelry when the temperature of hard soldering might anneal the metal or burn up the steel spring in the clip. Soft solder is not used on gold or silver jewelry. Be careful not to overheat the metal if you are soft-soldering; use a small flame, and heat the work only to the melting point of the soft solder. The completed work should be air cooled, then pickled (**9.2**) and rinsed in clear water. Pickling is never done on lead solder. If it is necessary to remove soft solder from a piece, heat the deposit, then wipe and scrape away as much as possible (**C.13**). Small amounts of unwanted soft solder can be filed and polished away.

10.9

Cutting Paillons of Solder   When you receive a sheet of silver solder, take your scribe and mark one side of the sheet with lines or cross-hatching. If you are using three grades of solder, make a distinctive cross-hatching for each grade. One common system is single hatching for easy grade, cross-hatching for medium grade, and triple hatching for hard grade. Once cut, the different grades of solder should be stored in distinctive containers. If different grades get mixed together, or if you are not sure of the identity of a piece, discard it.

Place a sheet of white paper on your workbench and cut a small strip of solder, perhaps 1 inch wide, from the sheet. Fringe one end of it, holding the strip by the unfringed end. Then cut off a narrow strip of the fringe (Fig. 287), and you will have a group of little *paillons* on the white sheet of paper. Your forefinger should lie along the blade of the shears and on top of the fringe, to keep the paillons from flying away as they are cut off. The paillons should be oblong in shape so that they will lie closely along the solder seam. Square pieces project from the seam farther than necessary and may leave a trace when melted. It may be necessary to hammer the paillons flat either before or after cutting to ensure that they are much thinner than the metal being soldered.

287. Shears are used to cut solder paillons from sheet.

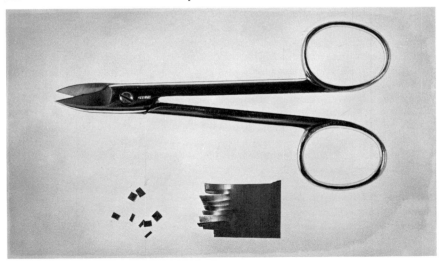

10.10

Flux   In order to solder one metal onto another, the surfaces must be clean and bright and must remain free of the oxides produced during the soldering process. To ensure cleanliness and to help the solder flow more easily, metal and solder surfaces are painted with a liquid or paste solution called *flux*. Different varieties of flux are used for various purposes. Descriptions of some commercial fluxes used for hard and soft soldering and a recipe for homemade flux are given in the Appendix (**C.10**). Acid-base fluxes are irritating to the skin, so they should be handled carefully; also, since they are corrosive, they should be tightly capped when not in use. An inexpensive sable brush should be used to apply the flux, and if an additional application is necessary during soldering, take care that the brush does not burn and leave particles on your work. This brush should be reserved for fluxing and for one kind of flux. Individual pieces of solder can be fluxed by setting them in place with a flux-moistened brush. Some types of flux act as temperature indicators: borax, for example, turns glassy at a temperature of about 1200° F. Flux is effective only with moderate amounts of heat. If it becomes overheated during the soldering process, it will start to bubble and pull away from the surface of the metal. Experience will show you how to heat your work quickly and evenly, and how to make the solder flow into place in the most efficient manner possible.

Jewelers who undertake fairly sophisticated types of soldering should be aware of certain industrial equipment that may be useful to the metal craftsman. The *fluxing tank,* marketed under the trade names Gasflux and Jet Flux, is designed to hold a liquid flux through which gas is bubbled before it is led into the torch. Fluxing tanks operate with standard air-gas or oxygen-gas torch equipment, but the gas is connected to the fluxing tank, rather than directly to the torch. In bubbling through the liquid flux, the gas carries sufficient flux to the torch so that the work being soldered comes under a constant application of flux. Thus, the work remains completely free of corrosion and flux residue. This process has proved to be especially useful for nonferrous metal sculpture and for copper and brass brazing. Its only disadvantage is that the flame burns with a greenish cast that demands the use of goggles. Fluxing tanks are available through welding supply companies.

10.11

Holding Soldered Seams with Yellow Ochre   When a piece of work requires more than one soldering job, there is some danger that previously soldered seams will melt when the work is reheated. A good way to hold these seams is to coat them with the same mixture of yellow ochre that is used to protect work from fire scale. Yellow ochre is a powdered earth material. When mixed with a supersaturated solution of boric acid and then heated to soldering or annealing temperatures, it bakes on hard and prevents existing solder seams from running. It will also hold small parts in place and prevent small elements, such as the prongs of a crown, from melting.

Yellow ochre must be used with care, for it will also prevent solder from flowing in the seam you wish to join. Therefore, it is wise to follow this procedure: assemble and position the pieces to be soldered, using binding wire if necessary (**10.15**). Clean the seams, and flux them thoroughly. Apply the solder paillons. Air dry the work or dry it with a torch. Paint the yellow ochre mixture over the entire work except for the solder seams that have just been prepared. Allow the yellow ochre mixture to air dry, for torch drying would cause it to flake off. Then heat the work to the temperature at which the solder melts and flows into the proper areas.

Yellow ochre solution bakes on quite solidly, but an extended pickling time will dissolve it completely.

10.12

Rules for Soldering   The observance of the following guidelines will help the beginning jeweler to solder successfully:

1. *The surfaces to be soldered must fit together perfectly and squarely* and therefore must be scraped and filed clean. If two ends of strip are to be soldered, the surfaces should be bent around to overlap and then sawed through at the same angle (Fig. 325). Seams for sterling silver need not be perfectly smooth but must be square and exact. Seams for gold must be filed more smoothly. Filed edges on silver will generally not require further finishing if the cut is true and even.

    Solder will not fill irregularities between joints. Therefore, there must be no warps, dents, or imperfections of any kind, no matter how small. Flat pieces can be hammered or filed even on a plane surface, and kinks can be removed from wire by bending. If you try to even out a surface after you have begun soldering, you may shatter the metal that has been made brittle by the heat of the torch, so do all evening-out beforehand. When you think that the surfaces are as smooth and even as they can be, hold them together against the light in order to check for a flush fit.

2. *The surfaces to be soldered, as well as the solder itself, must be absolutely clean and shiny.* Fingerprints, dirt, oils, oxides, and metal filings must be removed, or the solder will not flow over the surface of the metal. There are several methods for effective cleaning:

    ■ Annealing and pickling (**9.1, 9.2**). This chemical cleaning method takes more time than the other procedures, but it is the most thorough. The pickled work should be rinsed.

    ■ Rubbing with emery paper or emery cloth. A fresh piece must be used, or you will leave dirt on the work.

    ■ A carborundum stone will clean a piece with a sharp corner.

    ■ Cleaning with household ammonia diluted with water. Use an old, soft toothbrush and rinse the piece well.

    After the work is cleaned, it should be handled carefully to avoid further soiling.

3. *The metal and the solder must be properly fluxed.* Any surface to be soldered should be covered with flux. Be sure to use the right type of flux for the metal you are soldering: With high-melting-point metals, use a flux that liquefies at a high temperature, or it will flow long before your metal is hot enough to solder. When you are doing multiple solderings on the same piece, you will need to flux repeatedly.

4. *The solder must be properly positioned for the type of work you are doing.* It must touch both surfaces to be joined. The different types of joins include: flat surface to flat surface, wire to flat surface, wire to wire, ring joinings, edge to surface, and findings to piece. The soldering of *findings* (catches, clasps, earring and cuff-link backs, and other commercially available fastenings) presents several different problems, which will be treated in a separate section (**10.23–27**). If it is not properly placed, solder may flow in the wrong direction and have to be repositioned. The removal of the hardened solder leaves a scar that is difficult to eliminate. It is best to place solder on your work correctly at the outset and avoid having to undo mistakes.

5. *Heat should be applied in the proper amount* to melt the solder without overheating. Solder melts at a lower temperature than the base metal, so that when the metal is heated to the correct temperature, the solder will flow properly along the seam. Timing is important, for too much or too little heat causes problems.

10.13

General Procedures for Soldering

1. Prepare the piece by making sure the surfaces to be soldered are smooth and even. Clean it thoroughly. Select the right type of solder for the job, and be sure it is perfectly clean and unmixed with foreign matter. If you are soldering two or three joints on the same piece, plan to do the first with hard-grade solder, the second with medium-grade, the third with easy-grade. (A very experienced person who has good control of the torch may be able to solder all three joints with the same grade of solder by bringing only the seam to be soldered to soldering temperature).

2. Place the pieces to be joined on whatever support works best (**10.14–16**); secure them with binding wire if necessary. Some jewelers prefer to solder in the annealing booth (Fig. 273) so they can observe the subtle color changes that indicate the temperature of the metal.

3. All surfaces to be soldered should be covered with flux. Set the fluxed solder in place (**10.17**) or prepare solder wire if you are using the strip method (**10.18**). Give the flux a chance to set for a minute. Have a steel pick or tweezers on hand to adjust any section of work or piece of solder that may be moved out of place later by the liquefied flux or the capillary action of the solder.

4. Turn on the torch; the gas valve should be turned just enough to allow you to light the flame. When the flame is lit, turn on the oxygen or compressed-air valve. Adjust the flame so it is soft and slightly reducing.

5. Start rotating the torch over the entire piece, allowing just the outer, dark blue cone of the reducing flame to touch the surface. Then concentrate the torch on the area to be soldered, rotating it all the while so that the entire area is evenly heated. Do not apply the torch to the solder. If the solder melts before the metal surfaces are sufficiently hot, it will form a ball.

6. Use the flux as a temperature gauge: Borax flux will turn white during the first stage of heating, after which a crust will form on it. When the metal is almost hot enough to melt the solder, borax flux will turn brown and then glassy. Too much preheating causes the flux to lose its oxide-absorbing property, as does too little heat applied for too long a time. If any part of the metal or solder should move out of place during the heating, use the pick or tweezers to push it back without stopping the action of the torch.

7. As the solder begins to melt, it will flow toward the juncture of the surfaces to be joined. It will also be drawn toward the hottest part of the metal —hence the reason for heating all parts of the juncture evenly. Once the solder has begun to flow, be careful to keep the heat steady and even. The molten solder will "freeze" if the heat is removed for even a few seconds. If the heat has been correctly applied, the solder will flow into the joint, forming a thin seam that will be practically undetectable when the piece has been polished and buffed. Air cool, pickle, and rinse.

Beginners encounter two common difficulties when soldering. Either the solder fails to flow, or the piece is melted in the attempt to solder. A simple analogy may provide a practical guideline to prevent these problems. Think of each piece of metal as a volume that will soak up and hold a certain quantity of heat, depending upon its size. If you adjust a water tap to a certain constant flow of water, it will take twice as long to fill up a quart jar as it does to fill up a pint jar. This relationship applies to heating pieces of metal. Therefore, when soldering a small piece of silver to a large one, direct the flame to the larger piece first and for a longer period of time, in order to bring both pieces up to temperature at the same time. If you heat the small piece first, the solder will immediately fuse to it and then fail to fuse to the larger piece.

Needless to say, successful soldering requires plenty of practice and experience to develop the necessary coordination. Specific soldering methods are described below.

10.14

Holding Work for Soldering   The methods of holding work for soldering will be dealt with in relation to specific problems; however, certain basic methods should be understood.

If the work is self-supporting and need not be set on a flat or specially prepared surface, it is best placed in the annealing pan, on a bed of pumice-stone fragments. Pumice stone, a good nonconductor of heat, allows the flame of the torch to flow underneath as well as around the work, thus making it possible to heat the work evenly. All work should be annealed in this pan, which is particularly useful when you are soldering a large, flat sheet, because the flame can be thrown underneath the sheet rather than on top, where other small parts may be overheated before the large sheet is brought up to temperature.

A small charcoal block is excellent for supporting work to be soldered, since in addition to being a good nonconductor it actually helps to concentrate heat. It can be carved or shaped to fit irregularities of the work. Steel pins can be forced into it to hold work in place. It can also be held in the hand and moved as the work is being heated. The one disadvantage of the charcoal block is that it breaks apart easily. It will hold together better if binding wire is wrapped tightly around the sides of the block.

In the past many jewelers used blocks of asbestos sheet and asbestos strip, but in view of the danger to health that asbestos products present, it will be wise to find some alternative. A bismuth block is remarkably good because it is clean (unlike charcoal) and soft and can be carved; bismuth is also especially nonconducting.

A special soldering block should be kept for soft solder, in order to avoid getting soft-solder flux on your hard-soldering blocks. Fumes from soft-solder flux will interfere with hard soldering. Also, there is some danger of getting leftover lead solder onto your work from previous lead-soldering operations.

Many jewelers use for support a small tangle of fine iron wire (about 24 gauge) twisted into a little pad, which is fixed to a wire or wooden handle held underneath (Fig. 288). This is called a *mop*. The wire should not be too fine, since it will fuse and burn in a hot flame. It must be soft iron wire, rather than carbon steel wire. Work is placed on the mop, which is held in the left

288. Work can be held in a *soldering mop* of fine iron wire on a wooden handle.

hand and rotated while the flame is played on and around the work. The advantage of the mop is that the wire allows the flame to come up underneath the work.

A heavy wire screen for holding work is available from many suppliers. The screen is usually set on a ring tripod, and the flame is applied underneath the screen.

Small pieces can be held in the soldering tweezers, which lock the work rigidly in position. *Never place your work on heat-conducting materials such as transite, brick, firebrick, stone, or metal,* since these materials will draw heat away from your work as fast as it is applied. As a result, the upper surface is likely to burn, while the lower surfaces remain cold.

10.15

Holding Work with Binding Wire or Steel Pins If gravity will not hold parts together for soldering, or if they are likely to shift position when heated, soft iron binding wire can be used.

Never apply binding wire by wrapping it around and around. It should be applied precisely where it will hold the work together and in a manner that allows it to be removed easily after soldering is completed. Notice in Figure 289 how the ends of the wire are carefully bent around the edges of the sheet and then bent up, with the excess wire clipped off. The bent-up ends can be gripped easily with pliers after soldering and pulled off quickly for pickling the work while it is still hot.

Kinks in binding wire are made firmly with square-nose pliers in order to tighten the binding (Fig. 290). Silver expands as it is heated. The kinks allow the wire to expand with the silver. Otherwise the rigidly tight binding wire will distort the work.

Strips, shapes, and wires that require fixed alignment for soldering can be held in place by placing the work on a charcoal block and holding the parts in position with steel pins or small pieces of iron wire with sharpened points, which are pressed into the block (Fig. 291).

10.16

Holding Work in Position with Plaster When a number of small parts must be assembled in the air (that is, without any supporting structure) and soldered together, they can be set in plaster. First, clean the pieces by scrubbing with soap and water and then pickling and rinsing. Flux well. Assemble the pieces on a small cake of beeswax modeled to the correct shape. Press the pieces in about halfway. Then build a small wall around the wax, and pour plaster over it to a depth of about 1 inch. When the plaster sets, remove the wax carefully, leaving the pieces embedded in the plaster. The plaster can be scraped away around the pieces until they are clean and accessible for soldering.

10.17

The Paillon Method of Applying Solder The simplest method of solder application is by melting solder paillons (Fig. 287) along seams to be joined. When a piece requires only a minimum amount of solder, as in a ring joining, or when you are soldering wires or delicate pieces together, or beads to a flat surface, a few paillons of solder strategically placed will do the job effectively.

After fluxing the seam, place the paillons at intervals along the seam by picking each one up on the tip of the fluxbrush and setting it down in position (Fig. 292). When doing this, wipe the brush against the neck of the flux bottle to remove excess flux. If you have an excess of flux along the seam, squeeze the flux brush with your fingers and touch the brush to the excess material. The brush will soak it up. Only experience can tell you how much solder

right: 289. Binding wire holds metal in position for soldering.

far right: 290. Kinks in the binding wire allow it to expand during soldering.

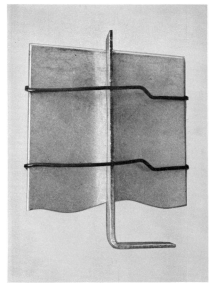

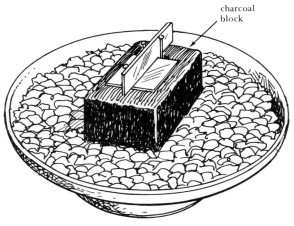

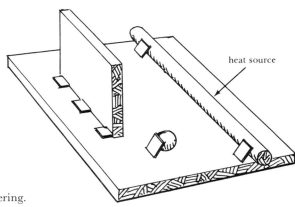

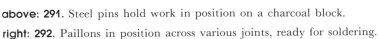

above: 291. Steel pins hold work in position on a charcoal block.

right: 292. Paillons in position across various joints, ready for soldering.

is enough for any given seam. Too little solder will leave open seams; too much builds up and must be removed with scraper or file.

Be sure that the paillon touches *both* surfaces that are to be joined. Place it where it will be most effective. If you want to attach a strip of sterling silver to a flat base, the paillon should be placed at the end of the strip and the molten solder allowed to run down the seam as far as it will go. When you are soldering beads to a surface, make a small depression with a dapping punch where you want to place the bead. Put the paillon in the depression and liquefy it. When it cools, reflux it and join the bead to the solder that is already in position. Soldering very fine work such as jump rings and ring shanks requires the use of paillons; the special problems involved are treated in a later section of this chapter (**10.26**).

293. A length of hard solder wire is held ready as the metal is brought to the proper temperature.

10.18

The Strip or Wire Method of Applying Hard Solder   The strip or wire method requires considerable skill and is especially useful for soldering two larger parts together or when it is difficult to place and hold little paillons in position. In this operation, the solder is held in one hand, ready to be dropped into position at just the right moment, while the torch in the other hand brings the metal juncture to the correct temperature (Fig. 293). Use a piece of wire solder or cut a narrow strip from sheet solder. Flux the end of the wire and all surfaces of the work to be heated. Heat the work while holding the wire ready, fluxed end out, in the soldering tweezers. At the moment the work reaches the proper temperature, apply the solder down the length of the seam, at the same time removing the torch.

This is by far the most flexible method of applying solder, and with practice it becomes possible to judge the heat of the metal and to apply quickly just the right amount of solder. The difficulty of this method lies in the need to coordinate both hands so that the torch is removed instantaneously, just as the solder strip is applied. Before mastering this particular bit of coordination, the beginner will either forget to move the flame away while concentrating on moving the solder strip into position (thus melting the solder into a bead) or will move the flame away too quickly, thus allowing the work to cool down too much.

10.19

Sweat Soldering   To solder two flat pieces of metal, surface to surface, you ordinarily use the sweat-soldering method, which results in a thin layer of solder sandwiched between the two metal layers, There are several ways to do sweat soldering. The first uses solder strips: Flux the surface of the underside of one piece, and, using thin strips, distribute over it half enough solder to cover the surface. Now flux the surface of the second piece of metal and place them together, surface to surface, in the correct position. Heat the entire work, as though you were annealing it, until the solder fuses the two pieces together. You will know this has occurred when you observe the bright flash of solder at the edges of the work.

Another method of applying solder is to place paillons uniformly over the surface. Depending upon the size of the piece, you can use paillons up to $\frac{1}{8}$-inch square distributed uniformly over the area (Fig. 294). A very small paillon should be placed at any narrow projections to ensure joining at those points. The work is assembled in the same manner as described above.

If a number of small pieces must be sweat-soldered to a base plate, it is best to fuse small paillons onto the underside of each piece and then assemble them in correct position on the well-fluxed base plate. The pieces can be secured with binding wire if placement must be accurate. Again, you will know when the fusing has taken place by observing the bright flash of solder at the edges of the small pieces.

When laminating together two sheets of the same size, it is simpler to cut and shape the exact size of the top plate and place it on an uncut lower plate. After soldering, the lower plate can be cut to the upper shape.

294. Small paillons evenly distributed for sweat-soldering two sheets of metal.

10.20

The Pick Method of Applying Hard Solder   A *pick* is made from a length of soft iron wire of about 10-gauge diameter, and perhaps 8 inches long. A piece of $\frac{1}{8}$-inch welding rod works well. A tapered point is filed at the end of the wire, where a tip about 1 inch long is bent down at right angles. The point is dipped in flux and used to pick up a ball of solder fused by the torch from a paillon of proper size. The work is heated to soldering temperature, and, at the strategic moment, the fused ball of solder is touched to the seam, which the solder runs to fill immediately. Favored by experienced craftsmen, this method allows for precise positioning and avoids the accumulation of excess solder around the seam, from which it might run elsewhere on the work.

10.21

Solder Filings   Another way of applying solder is in the form of fine solder filings. This is best done by filing a heavier section of solder than is usually at hand, though the standard 26-gauge solder sheet can be used. The filings can be collected on a clean sheet of paper and kept in a small bottle. A small portion can be placed in a shallow dish and Battern's or Prip's Flux added (**C.10**). The brush is then used to apply the flux and filings at the desired joints.

10.22

Solder Powder   Solder filings well mixed with powdered borax in about equal portions constitute solder powder. This powder is applied by taking a spatula (the flattened end of a piece of 16-gauge silver wire will serve) and dropping a small portion over the joint. Solder is applied in this way for filigree work (**11.23**), but this method may also be used in many other situations.

Procedure for Soldering Findings
10.23

Preparation for Soldering Joints and Catches   Joints and catches are manufactured commercially in various designs and are satisfactory for use with many brooch designs. They are available in nickel-silver, sterling, and gold. The findings come in two general types. Those for soft soldering have a small hollow disk attached at the base to provide greater surface contact for the softer lead solder. Those for hard solder need no such disk.

Catches are made with the slot opening either at the side or on the top (**15.9**). If the piece of jewelry requires a short pin tong, the top-opening catch is better, since the pin can swing directly into the slot. When ordering catches, always specify the type. If only one type is stocked, the top opening is probably best, although some jewelers regard the side-slot catch as safer.

Joints usually come with the flanges spread, and these should be squeezed parallel with the pliers. For a secure and permanent soldering job it is wise to hold each piece—the joint and the catch—with the pliers, and file the bottom lightly with a fine file. This ensures clean surfaces for soldering. It also flattens the joint, which will have become slightly curved from bending.

The spot that the joint is to occupy should be scraped clean and fluxed with a small drop of flux. The joint is then set into position and a small paillon of easy-grade solder placed on each side. The same procedure is followed with the catch. Do not place the paillons at the front or back of the safety catch, or the solder may run into the hinge. Always adjust the safety catch so that the two little knobs are on top.

10.24

Soldering Joints and Catches   Before soldering, carefully line up the joint and catch so that the pin tong will go directly through the catch (Fig. 295). Avoid directing the torch on the joint or catch. Heat the work slowly and completely, moving the torch around until the last moment, when the solder is ready to run.

The following is a useful and flexible method for soldering a joint and catch onto a piece of work:

1. Hold the catch or joint in self-locking tweezers in such a way that the tweezer ends run across the safety catch slot (Fig. 296). Lay the tweezers over the block so that the joint or catch extends over the edge, bottom up. The catch must be open, so that the solder will be less likely to flow into the opening and block it.
2. Flux the bottom of the catch or joint and heat it to a dull red color. Apply solder in strip or wire form, held in another pair of tweezers. Care must be taken not to apply too much solder.
3. Now take the work, scrape and flux the locations of the catch and joint on the base, and place the work on the soldering block.
4. Hold the catch in the tweezers so that when the heel of the hand is placed on the bench and the tweezers pivoted, the catch is lowered into exactly the right position on the piece of work (Figs. 297, 298). The hand should rest on the bench so comfortably that it swings naturally into the correct position.

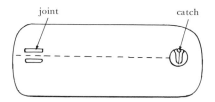

295. Catch and joint must align, and they should be positioned above the center of gravity of the pin or brooch.

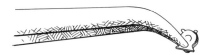

296. A safety catch held across the slot by soldering tweezers.

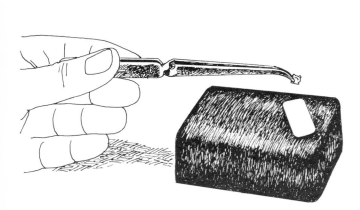

left: **297.** Hand in position to swing the catch down to its exact position for soldering.
right: **298.** Catch in position for soldering.

5. Swing the tweezers up out of the way of the torch, and heat the base.
6. When the base has been heated to the soldering temperature, swing the catch down into place, and hold it steadily in position until the solder melts again and adheres to the base.
7. Now take the joint with the tweezers. The ends of the tweezers should be across the open slot of the joint, or the pressure will squeeze the sides together. The joint should be turned in the tweezers so that, when the hand is positioned and swung down, it too will land on the work in exactly the correct position, aligned with the catch (Fig. 299). *The slots of the joint and catch must line up* (Fig. 295). Repeat the soldering process.

In description, all this may seem to be a laborious process, but when mastered it can save a great deal of time. Joints and catches often have to be placed on narrow or rounded edges where they cannot be made to stand. Fusing the solder in place on the work is not good craftsmanship, since it allows an unnecessary spread of solder, but this process permits quick and exact placement. The important thing is to set your hand on the bench in just the right position with respect to the work.

299. The joint, held across the slot, ready for positioning.

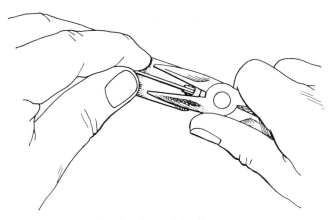

300. Fastening the pin tong by squeezing the rivet with pliers.

10.25

Fastening the Pin Tong to the Joint   The pin tong is not fastened by soldering, but it is the final step necessary in soldering the joint and catch. The tong has a small rivet pin at one end. This can be squeezed out with the square-nose pliers and set carefully to one side. Place the tong in position in the joint, and check the stop flange, which should point downward, to see whether it needs filing down in order to allow the pin to swing into the catch and be stopped at the correct "spring" position. The stop flange usually requires some filing. In case the stop flange should not extend down far enough to give slight spring tension when the pin is in the catch, planish the flange on the side with a cross-peen hammer to stretch its length. Then file it to finish and shape. Set the pin tong in the hinge of the joint, take the rivet in the square-nose pliers, and start it into the hinge hole. Then use pliers to squeeze the rivet all the way through the hinge holes (Fig. 300). To set this rivet, grasp the joint in the base of the pliers, where the leverage is greatest, and squeeze strongly. If the pin tong is found to point slightly out of line with the catch, take the hinge in the pliers and twist it gently until the pin is in line.

Never solder a joint onto the work with the pin in the joint, since this will anneal and soften the pin tong.

If the rivet pin is missing, it is easy to make one by filing a flat taper of nickel-silver or sterling wire in the pin vise. This tapered end should be inserted down into the hinge and the excess clipped off from both sides. File the snipped ends flat, leaving a small amount projecting beyond the hinge on each side, and then squeeze firmly with the pliers, as already described.

10.26

Soldering Jump Rings, Rings, and Ring Shanks   The section dealing with bending shows how to prepare and close jump rings (**11.15**). Soldering the jump ring closed is a delicate process, for the ends must touch each other, but it can be done easily if the correct technique is used:

1. Clamp the tweezers at the lower end of the jump ring, opposite the seam. If another ring is attached to the jump ring, or if it is part of a chain, the attached ring and tweezers must be held as far away from the seam as possible. Hold the tweezers in a vertical position, with the jump ring seam on top.
2. Flux the seam with a touch of the flux brush, and pick up a paillon of solder. This paillon should be very small, since a wire ring seam will require very little solder. Place the paillon on top of the seam so that it lies across the seam and touches both sides.
3. A small torch tip should be used for soldering. A tip with a hole about the size of a No. 57 drill is best for small jump rings. The flame must be small in order to heat the ring without heating a large section of chain.
4. Place the flame near the seam, not touching the solder or the jump ring but heating the air. The heat will evaporate the flux without blowing off the paillon.
5. Now hit the seam with the flame once or twice—on and away with a quick motion. With a little practice you will find that this can be done quickly the first time. If you allow the flame to linger, the ring will melt at both ends. The purpose of the hot flame is to heat the ring quickly and yet avoid heating or melting other attached rings. The flame should be directed onto the ring in such a way that it is also directed away from attached rings or other parts. This technique will require a little practice, but by the time you have made a foot of chain, you will be an expert.

Soldering ring shanks, jump rings, and circles of wire or strip can be done by the following method:

1. The two ends of the shank or circle must be brought squarely together in the curved line of the circle and under spring pressure, which holds them together (**11.15**). If this is not done, the ends may separate while being soldered.
2. Clamp the tweezers across the lower end, opposite the seam. Flux the seam and, for a ring band, place between the two ends a paillon of solder that is a little longer than the band is wide and a little wider than the band is thick. The solder paillon should project slightly all around. If the ring is of heavy strip, it is easy to spread the seam apart by sliding the ring up the ring mandrel until the seam opens far enough to allow the paillon to be inserted. When the solder is in position, the seam should be thoroughly fluxed. For a jump ring, place a small paillon on top of the seam (Fig. 301). When a ring is stamped or textured, solder can be kept from running into the depressions if the paillon is kept flush with the outside surface and the ring held so that the seam is horizontal, facing upward. Excess solder will then run downward to the inside of the ring, where it can be filed off.

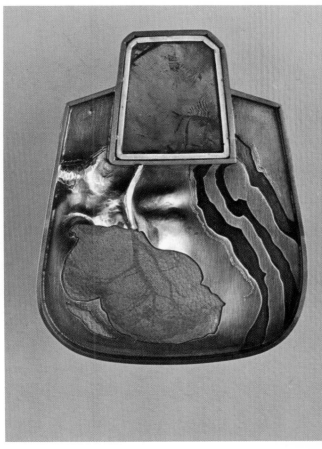

above: **Plate 1. Arline M. Fisch.** *Feather Lady,* brooch of chased and repoussé silver, etched and fire-gilt, with parrot feathers and transparent epoxy resin. 1971. *See page 55.*

right: **Plate 2. Eleanor Moty.** *Mirror Image,* hand mirror of sterling, brass, copper, and photo-printed leather, with amethyst, 1974. *See page 62.*

below: **Plate 3. Amy Buckingham.** *Tubular Brooch,* constructed of sterling, brass, and bronze, 1970. *See page 67.*

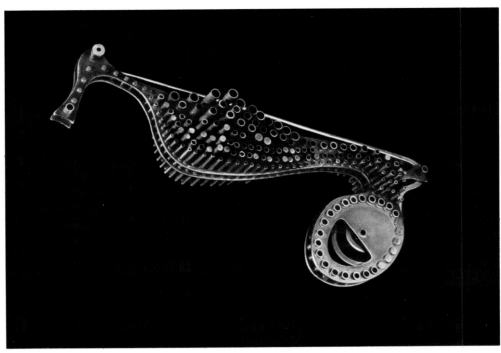

left: **Plate 4. Wendy Ramshaw.** *Pillar Ring* of turned silver, with enamel inlay and amethysts, 1970. The ring is mounted on a screw-on Perspex stand. *See page 73.*

below: **Plate 5. Sigurd Persson.** Bracelet of silver and cast plastic, 1974. *See pages 77, 218.*

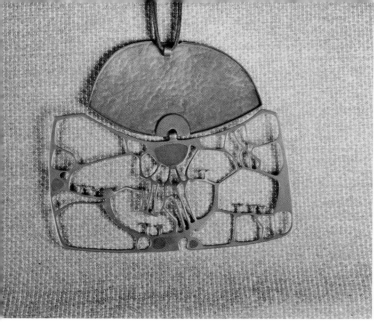

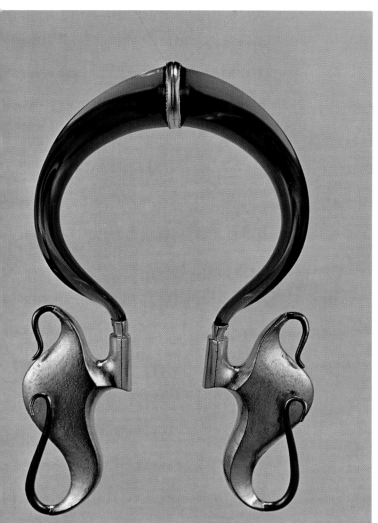

left: **Plate 6. Paul Mergen.** Pendant of forged and pierced bronze and copper, 1973. *See page 103.*

left: **Plate 7. Stanley Lechtzin.** *Torque,* neckpiece of electroformed, gold-plated silver and cast polyester resin, 1973. *See page 106.*

above: **Plate 8. Marjorie Schick.** Armlet forged and constructed of brass and silver, 1965. *See page 117.*

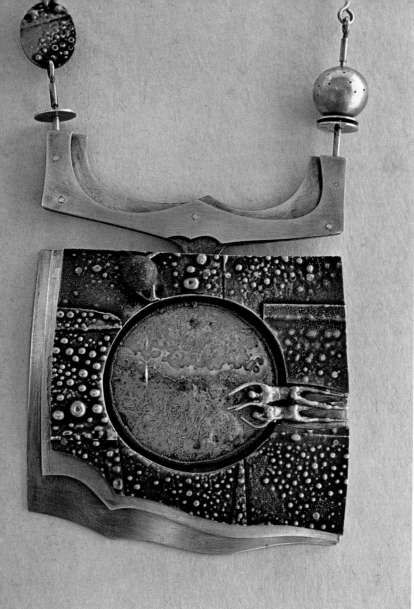

left: **Plate 9. Francis Stephen**. Pendant cast and constructed of sterling and brass, with crazy-lace agate, 1973. *See page 118.*

below: **Plate 10. Elliot Pujol.** *Rattle Ring*, of repoussé copper, 1974. *See pages 174–175, Figures 333–338.*

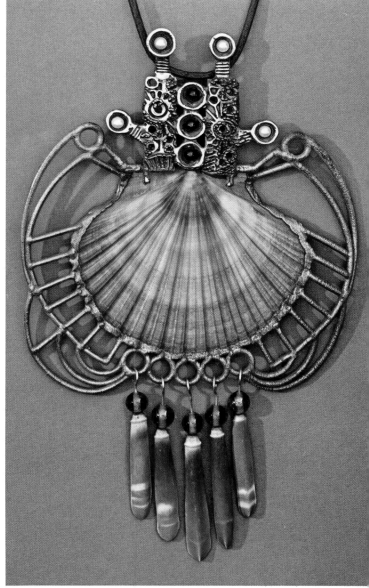

above: Plate 11. Harold O'Connor. *Transfusion,* brooch of sterling silver and cowbone embedded with rose resin, 1974. *See page 217.*

right: Plate 12. Lee Barnes Peck. Pendant of cast sterling, electroformed copper, and 24k-gold wash, with seashell, sea-urchin spines, amethyst spheres, and cultured pearls, 1975. *See page 239.*

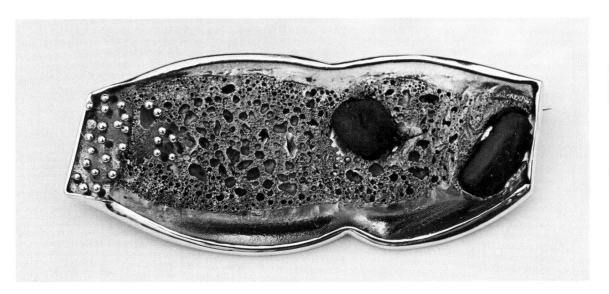

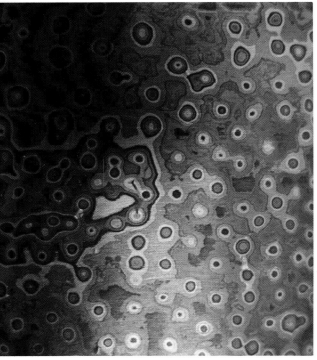

top: **Plate 13. Heikki Seppa.** Reticulated
pin of 14k gold and nickel-silver, with
azurite, 1973. *See page 242.*

above: **Plate 14. Chuck Evans.** Detail of a
mokume piece in progress. The surface
has been filed and finished smooth. *See
page 258.*

right: **Plate 15. John Paul Miller.** *Cephalopod,*
pendant of enameled and granulated
gold, 1974. *See page 262.*

above: **Plate 16. Mary A. Kretsinger.** Pendant/pin with tubular catch, of 18k gold, with cloisonné enamels laid between partitions of fused metal, 1974. The movable bottom section has stone settings and the owners' monogram on the back. Collection Dr. and Mrs. Walter Leudtke, Emporia, Kan. *See page 268.*

below: **Plate 17.** Unconventional stones and slabs of potential interest to the jeweler. *See page 282.*

green tourmaline   pink tourmaline   green tourmaline   blue topaz   yellow-green beryl   kunzite   green beryl

amethyst   aquamarine   amethyst   peridot   amethyst   fluorite   aquamarine

Madeira quartz   golden quartz   emerald   yellow quartz   star ruby plum   smoky quartz   garnet

malachite   precious topaz   aventurine   stone cameo   cabochon precious topaz   carnelian   blue zircon   tigereye   labradorite

Phillipine pearl   baroque pearls   amber   carnelian shell cameo   black opal   black star sapphire   treated opal   flash opal   opal doublet

oxblood coral   turquoise   matrix turquoise   emerald cabochon   cat's-eye quartz   Chinese jade   snowflake jade   nephrite jade

amethyst   citrine   chrysoprase   garnet   moonstone   hematite   lapis lazuli   bloodstone

sodalite   rhodonite   snowflake obsidian   rhodochrosite   eye agate   pink tourmaline   green tourmaline   eye agates

Plate 18. A selection of commonly available gems and semiprecious stones. *See page 282.*

301. Paillon on the seam of a jump ring, ready to solder.

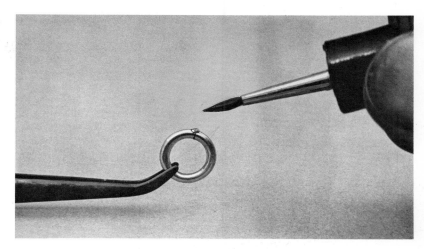

3. Holding the tweezers up, throw a medium-size, medium-hot flame over and around the entire ring. As the ring band comes up to the proper temperature, the solder will flow quickly. Remove the flame immediately and drop the ring into the pickle. For soldering a jump ring, use a very small, rather tight flame. You may have to switch to a smaller torch tip.

10.27

Special Soft-Soldering Problems   All sterling ear backs are soft-soldered to the earring. *They are never hard-soldered,* since the high temperature required by hard solder takes the temper out of the ear back itself and also out of any spring that may be used to hold the clip in place. Screw-back types often come apart when hard-soldered to the earring. For these reasons the low-melting-point soft solders are used.

Almost all ear backs are made with a small hollow cup to hold soft solder. The simplest way to solder these backs to the earring is to touch the hollow cup of the ear back first with the flux brush. Soft solder requires zinc chloride or soldering salts (**C.10**) as a flux. Clip off a small piece of lead solder and place it in the cup of the ear back. The ear back is held in the self-locking soldering tweezers so that the cup is facing upward. A small flame is now played under the cup until the solder flows and fills the cup. With a little practice you can judge the right amount of solder to just fill the cup. Another way to fill the little cup is to set the locked tweezers holding the ear back on the soldering block, with the ear back projecting over the edge, and apply the solder as the cup is heated. This is the strip method of applying solder (**10.18**). Solder should be fed into the cup so that it is just flush with the rim.

After solder has been put into each cup, place one ear back in position on the earring, and set the self-locking tweezers to hold it there. Flux the joint between the earring and the ear back; then apply a small flame to the underside of the earring, playing the flame at the cup. As soon as the solder runs, dip the earring into a cup of water. This will immediately chill the solder and cool the earring. (If stones have already been set in the earring, it should not be dipped in water, for this may crack the stone. Such an earring must be allowed to air cool.) If the soldering has been done properly, there should be no excess solder to clean off around the ear-back cup. Wash the earring very thoroughly after soldering, because the flux used for soft soldering is highly corrosive and will burn the wearer's ear if it is not completely removed.

The same soft-solder procedure is followed for cuff links. Cuff-link backs usually have a steel spring, which will become annealed if hard solder is used.

Industrial Welding Techniques

Two specialized welding techniques, employed in industry and often by sculptors, may have limited applications for the jeweler-metalsmith. Only the rudiments of the processes are presented here, so that craftsmen can get an idea of their potentialities.

10.28

Gas Tungsten-Arc Welding   Gas tungsten-arc welding, or GTAW, is a process in which the arc and the weld zone are shielded from the oxidizing atmosphere by a flood of inert gas—most often argon or helium. The shielding results in a welded joint that is stronger, more ductile, and characterized by less distortion than that produced by other welding processes. Also, the need for fluxes is eliminated—a great advantage in welding nonferrous metals, since fumes and sparks do not occur, and there is no contamination by flux residues in the subsequent cleaning processes.

In gas tungsten-arc welding, coalescence of the metal is achieved with an electric arc between the work and an essentially unconsumable tungsten electrode. Additional welding metal is supplied from a filler rod that is fed into the puddle in the same manner as used in the oxyacetylene process. GTAW was originally developed for use on metals that oxidize rapidly, such as aluminum and magnesium, but it is now applied to a wide range of special alloys and also serves to hard-surface dies and cutting tools. Gas tungsten-arc welding equipment is known under such trade names as Heliarc and Heliwelding. Equipment is available from welding supply companies. Metalworkers find the process especially useful for production-welding copper or brass, as well as for sculpture.

10.29

Plasma Arc Welding   The plasma arc welding process (PAW) depends on a central core of extremely high temperature, surrounded by a sheath of cool, inert gas—usually argon or helium. Heat is produced by an arc between the base metal and the tip of the electrode. However, the electrode is located in a constricting nozzle. Argon or helium gas, called *plasma gas,* is fed through this nozzle and accelerated to a sonic velocity of 4000 feet-per-second, reaching an intense heat of 30,000° F. Actually, the welding process takes its name from the fact that the gas is heated to a temperature high enough to change the state of the gas to plasma.

Plasma is regarded as a fourth state of matter, the other three being gas, liquid, and solid. When matter passes from one state to another, latent heat must be transferred in the process. For example, when ice (a solid) melts and changes to water (a liquid), considerable latent heat is absorbed. Similarly, when gas is transformed into plasma, considerable heat is absorbed. Conversely, when the plasma changes back into gas, that latent heat is released to create an intensification of heat at the welding zone.

As a result of this heat intensification, the arc gas strikes the metal and cuts a deep hole. The molten metal in front of the arc flows around the arc column and is drawn together behind the hole, forming a weld bead.

Plasma arc welding is effective and superior for welding stainless steels, carbon steels, monel, inconel, titanium, aluminum, copper, and brass alloys. One of its great advantages is that butt welds up to $\frac{1}{2}$ inch in thickness can be made in a single pass without a filler rod or edge beveling.

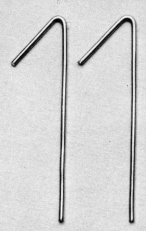

The various metal forming processes have one thing in common: they rely on mechanical means to change metal from its original shape into another. In drawing wire and tubing, metal is made longer and thinner; in rolling, it is compressed and elongated. Bending metal gives it new angles, or curves it, as in ringmaking. Repoussé sculptures metal into low relief. Twisting wire forms it into patterns, sometimes complex ones, and filigree solders fine wires into intricate designs. Each of these processes is treated in this chapter.

Drawing Wire and Tubing

Wire is an essential ingredient of many forms and styles of jewelry. To draw wire means to take heavy-gauge wire and reduce it to the gauge size wanted by passing it through a drawplate.

As you carry out the simple process of drawing wire, you might reflect on how the Egyptians prepared the wire for their exquisite jewelry. Having hammered out sheets of gold between polished stone boulders, they cut narrow strips with stone knives. The strips were then rolled into a tight spiral, just as paper drinking straws are made to form a tube. The spiral seams were soldered, and the tube was pulled through a stone drawplate to reduce it in size to a fine hollow wire. This long, tedious preliminary work may seem arduous to us, yet it undoubtedly gave the Egyptians a deep understanding of the nature of metal, its capacities, and its limitations.

You should make two observations about the process of wire drawing. First, metal is extremely malleable when dealt with properly, and it can be

302. Phillip Fike. Fibula of grenadilla wood and 14k yellow gold plate and wire, 1968. A single length of wire runs through the laminated plate and wood sections, winds around in a double reverse-coiled spring, and extends outward to form the pin tong. (See also cover photo.)

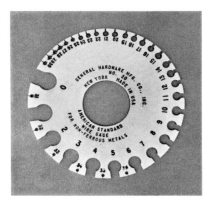

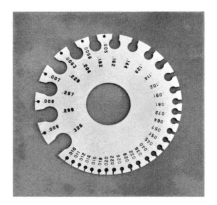

303. Front (*top*) and back (*above*) of the Brown & Sharpe standard gauge plate.

reduced in size merely by drawing it through a tapered hole. As you squeeze the metal in this way, you pack its crystals closer together and displace some of the metal, thus increasing the length. Second, whenever you work metal, by drawing it for instance, it becomes less malleable and more springy and brittle (**9.1**). Compare the tension in a piece of drawn wire with the relative plasticity of a piece of wire that has been annealed. This hardening characteristic can be utilized in jewelry (Fig. 302). For example, if you wish to make a sterling brooch or ear clip of wire, you will find it desirable to use drawn wire, since it is hardened and springy and will hold its shape better than a piece of annealed wire. To maintain this springiness, you should avoid heating or soldering the wire and devise some other means of fastening (see Chap. 15).

The size of wire, as well as of sheet, is measured by the Brown & Sharp standard gauge plate (Fig. 303), frequently referred to as the B&S. A variety of gauge sizes of wire are available on the market, but it is useful to know how to draw wire from large sizes down to small diameters. Also, in a well-equipped shop for production operations it is cheaper to buy large quantities of 6- or 8-gauge wire and draw down smaller sizes as required. You can also save sterling scrap and cast it into ingots of rod, which can be rolled down to a size suitable for drawing (**11.4**).

11.1

Preparing Wire for Drawing   To prepare wire for drawing, first take the wire (about 12-gauge, sterling) that is to be reduced and cut it into 12-inch sections. This length wire can be pulled easily through the drawplate in one continuous motion. You will need a pin vise and a hand file that is not too coarse. File a V-shape notch in the edge of your workbench or bench pin with the edge of a half-round file. Grasp the wire in the pin vise so that about 1 inch projects beyond the jaws of the vise (Fig. 304), and position the wire end in the V-shape

304. A taper being filed on the end of a wire, held and rotated in a pin vise.

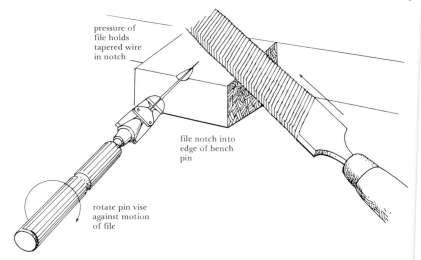

pressure of file holds tapered wire in notch

file notch into edge of bench pin

rotate pin vise against motion of file

notch. Place the hand file on the wire and, with a forward stroke of the file, rotate the pin vise against the direction of the file stroke. At the end of the file stroke, reverse both directions, keeping the pin vise rotating always against the direction of the file. Suitable pressure of the file will hold the wire in the slot as you rotate the pin vise. A fine-cut file will work better on fine wire. File a long, flat taper in the wire so that, as you reduce the size of the wire by drawing, the taper will remain long enough to go through the drawplate. You will probably have to refile the taper as the wire is reduced in size.

11.2

Drawing Wire To draw wire you will need a drawplate, drawtongs, beeswax, and, if the wire is to be considerably reduced, annealing and pickling equipment. Drawplates are generally made of hardened steel and have a series of round, half-round, square, and rectangular holes of graduated size (Fig. 305). These holes are larger in the back of the plate and taper to a smaller opening in the front. The numbers stamped near the holes do not correspond to gauge sizes but enable you to keep track of the hole you are drawing through. Before beginning the drawing, rub beeswax over either the holes you are going to use in the drawplate or the tapered point of your wire. This will melt as friction heats the wire and provide a lubricating film to make the pulling go smoothly and reduce wear on the drawplate.

Anchor the drawplate in a vertical position in the draw bench or bench vise, with enough clearance above the vise jaws to allow the drawtongs to be centered on the row of holes you are using (Fig. 306). Find the hole that just fits the size of wire you are using. Place the tapered end snugly into the next smaller hole. The wire goes into the tapered-cone side of the drawplate and is pulled out the numbered side. Grasp firmly with the drawtongs as much of the

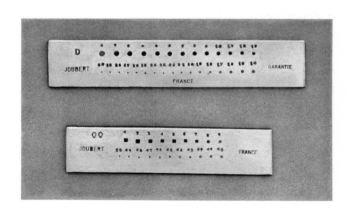

right: 305. Drawplates with round and square holes.

below: 306. Drawtongs pull a length of wire through the tapered hole of the drawplate, which is firmly held in the bench vise.

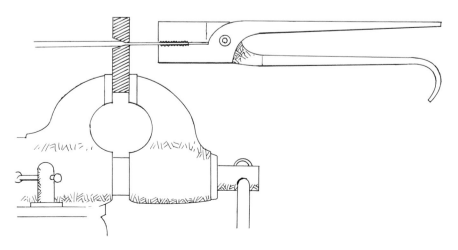

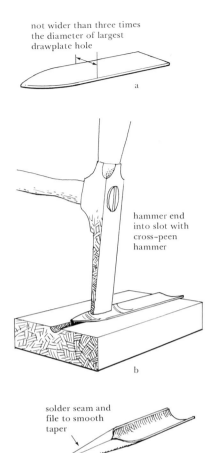

not wider than three times
the diameter of largest
drawplate hole

a

hammer end
into slot with
cross-peen
hammer

b

solder seam and
file to smooth
taper

c

307. A strip with tapered end (*a*) is hammered into a groove with the cross-peen hammer (*b*) until the edges of the taper can be hammered together, soldered, and filed smooth (*c*).

tapered end of the wire as you can get hold of, and, with both hands holding the tongs closed on the wire, draw it completely through the hole. Pull with your entire body, not just your arms. To avoid curling the wire, always draw straight away from the plate. Move to each smaller hole in succession, being careful not to skip any.

If you see that the wire is becoming brittle, you should anneal it (**9.1**). To do this, coil the wire and wind another piece of silver wire around it to hold the coil together. Place it on the wire screen on the tripod and anneal it, being careful to heat the coil evenly. Pickle it, rinse, unwind gently, and dry thoroughly. Then the drawing can be continued.

Half-round wire can also be drawn in the regular drawplate by soldering the ends of two wires together, filing the taper, and drawing them down together. In order to prevent their twisting, a burnisher or smooth mandrel must be held in a fixed position between the wires and against the back of the drawplate. Triangular wire can be made in a similar manner by drawing two wires through a square-hole drawplate.

11.3

Drawing Tubing   The drawplate can also be used for making tubing of a diameter slightly smaller than the largest hole. This is done by cutting a strip of sheet metal, 20 gauge or smaller, to a width slightly less than three times the diameter of the largest hole in your drawplate. You must be able to draw your tube through the largest hole and cannot make a tube of larger diameter, though one of smaller diameter can be made.

With the shears, cut a taper that runs back about $1\frac{1}{2}$ inches on each side of one end. Then, with a small cross-peen hammer, form the tapered end into a gutter-shape channel on the tin block or in a groove of the right size (Fig. 307). Part of the strip beyond the tapered end must also be curved into a channel. With a small hammer, close the channel from the tip to a short distance beyond the taper. Then solder this tapered end and file it into a smooth tapered point.

Now you are ready to rub the taper with beeswax and begin the drawing operation. Place the point of your burnisher in the channel and snugly into the tapered cone at the back of the drawplate, and hold it firmly in position as you draw the strip through (Fig. 308). At this first draw, the tube will begin to form. Draw the tube through successively smaller holes until the sides have closed and the tube is the desired size. The seam can then be soldered. You will note that as the tube size decreases, the wall thickness increases.

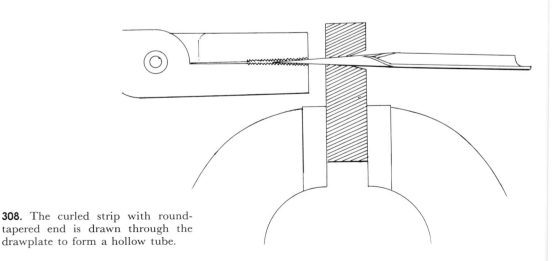

308. The curled strip with round-tapered end is drawn through the drawplate to form a hollow tube.

Rolling Metal

In earlier times, metal was formed into sheets by the laborious process of forging cast ingots down to size and planishing them smooth. This slow method undoubtedly taught metalworkers much about the qualities of metal. It would be desirable for all jewelers to try this as a learning experiment. Even though we can easily buy sheet metal of every gauge, it is convenient to be able to roll pieces of metal to special sizes by means of the rolling mill (Fig. 309). The mill is especially useful for forming gold and platinum.

11.4

Rolling Ingots into Sheet Metal   If you have at hand a silver ingot to be rolled, the first step is to forge the ingot once over on each side with the forging hammer. (**13.1**). This serves to pack the crystals more tightly together. Then smooth the surfaces by planishing evenly (**13.5**). Take the scraper and clean out any pits or imperfections that appear on the surface or along the edges. If these are not scraped out, they will spread as the metal is rolled. Finally, anneal the ingot (**9.1**).

309. A combination rolling mill rolls both square wire and sheet metal.

Place the ingot between the rollers, and screw down the rollers snugly upon the metal. Then remove the metal and give the mill a small additional turn until, by trial, you find that the ingot is being pulled into the rollers. Next roll the ingot through the mill. Be careful to note which end leads through the mill. Turn the ingot over end for end, so that the sides are in the same relative position to the mill. At the same time you should observe whether the ingot has begun to curve to the right or left. If one side of the rollers is tighter than the other, that side will squeeze the metal harder and lengthen it more. If this has happened, the screw on that side must be released a bit or the screw on the other side tightened slightly. As the ingot is rolled through, the screws are tightened a little after each pass. Do not try to take too big a bite at one time. After the ingot has been put through three of four times, it will have work-hardened and must be annealed. Soft metal will roll much more easily.

As you roll the ingot, watch for cracks along the sides. Cut them out at once, right up to the end of the crack. Watch also for blemishes on the surface, and scrape them out.

The purpose of rolling is to lengthen a metal strip; it will not make a strip appreciably wider. If you wish to widen the metal, feed it into the mill at a slight angle.

11.5

Rolling Wire   Special dies can be bought or made to fit the rolling mill so that it can be used to make many simple and complex shapes of wire. Such wire is called *gallery wire* (**13.12**).

If silver wire is to be made in the workshop, long rods of $\frac{1}{2}$-inch or $\frac{1}{4}$-inch diameter can be cast. These can be rolled down, between rollers with specially sized grooves, to smaller diameters that can be accommodated in the draw-plate.

Rolling Textures in Sheet Metal   Rolling textures into the surface of soft sheet metal with the rolling mill gives unique visual effects that can be obtained in no other way. This process, called *roll printing*, is discussed elsewhere (**17.22**).

Bending Metal

Bending is one of the fundamental processes of metalwork. Though it is a simple process, jewelry construction demands many special techniques, of which the most basic and typical are described below.

11.6

The Mechanics of Bending   A knowledge of the simple mechanics of bending will help you to think correctly about all bending problems. When a piece of metal bends, its internal structure is placed under tension on the outside of the bend and under compression on the inside. These inner strains are relieved because the crystals of the metal shift along slip planes and take up new positions, thus allowing the metal to stretch on one side and contract on the other. The thicker the metal, of course, the greater is the resistance to deformation, and also the greater is the radius of displacement. For this reason, a thick piece of metal, when bent sharply, will break. Bending hardens the metal and reduces its capacity for further bending. Repeated bending eventually results in failure or breakage of the metal. It is advisable to anneal metal when construction processes require successive bending at the same location.

When metal is rolled or bent in a curve, the true length of the metal around the curve must be calculated by a radius measured to the center line of the thickness of metal, or by a diameter measured from center to center of the material. Thus, if you wish to roll a piece of 12-gauge silver into a ring with an inner diameter of 2 inches, add one whole thickness of the 12-gauge material, or .0808 inches (**C.20**), to the inner diameter, and multiply the sum (2.0808 inches) by *pi* (3.1416) to calculate the length (6.537 inches) required (**A.7**).

11.7

General Bending Techniques   The following general guidelines are applicable to all types of bending:

1. Whenever possible, use your fingers to bend wire, strip, and sheet metal. You will thereby avoid putting unwanted kinks or nicks into the metal.
2. To make a right-angle bend in wire or strip, place the edge of your square-nose pliers exactly at the point of the bend, and push the metal against the side of the pliers with your thumb (Fig. 310). This will not yet give you a right angle. Therefore, place the pliers on the other side of the bend, with the edge of the pliers in the nick made by the first operation, and again push the metal against the side of the pliers. By working back and forth once or twice, you should get a perfect bend. You will not get a sharp corner, naturally, because of the curve around the corner. If you still fail to get a square bend, take your snipe-nose pliers, place the edge in the *single* nick you have made, and press the metal until you have brought it past square. Then with the square-nose pliers, squeeze the wire or strip close against the bend until it comes to a right angle.
3. Never try to bend a curve in wire or strip with a flat-faced pair of pliers. The sharp edges of the pliers will make unwanted nicks. Use half-round pliers, placing the curved face of the pliers on the inside of the curve you wish to make. For small-radius curves, use round-nose pliers. For bending wire or flat metal, use only pliers that are perfectly smooth. Dents or bumps in the surface of the pliers' face will flaw the metal.
4. Always estimate carefully the location of a sharp bend, place your pliers in the right place, and make the bend perpendicular to the wire or strip.
5. Kinky wire can be smoothed by drawing it through the next smaller hole in the drawplate. Kinky strip can be smoothed by annealing it and then tapping it all over on both sides with a rawhide mallet on a smooth, flat anvil.
6. Always approach your work experimentally. If you are trying a design idea for the first time, consider the work to be an experiment, which you can change and rework to discover the problems involved, so that you can execute the final version perfectly.

310. A square bend is made with square-nose pliers.

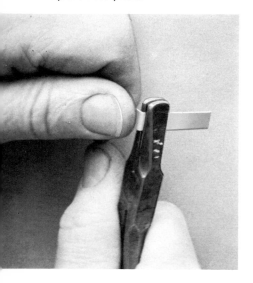

11.8

Bending a Wide Strip of Sheet Metal   Sheet-metal shops have a machine called a brake (Fig. 311) with which bends can be made in sheet metal. If a brake is not available, the jeweler must use hand tools, as follows:

1. Scribe a light, straight line at the bend point on the back of the sheet.
2. Place the sheet in the jaws of the vise with the bend line set to the top surface of the vise jaw. If your vise jaw is not smooth, you must bend small copper sheets over each jaw to protect the sheet metal.
3. Take a smooth hardwood block, set it with the edge on the inscribed line, and press the metal over against the vise jaw. Then take a mallet and pound the block in order to set the bend sharply (Fig. 312).

11.9

Bending a Strip to a Circular Radius   Techniques for making ring bands and other circular strips follow the same general pattern. From the required diameter, calculate or estimate the circumference **(11.6).** Always allow extra length, especially for sheet metal that is 14-gauge or heavier.

11.10

Bending a Thin Strip of Metal into a Circle   Follow this procedure when the metal to be worked is thin enough to be bent by hand:

1. A thin strip of metal can be rolled with the fingers around a *ring mandrel*—a tapering rod divided by grooves, each marked with a ring size—or an ordinary mandrel of suitable size. Hold one end in place on the mandrel at the desired size, and roll the strip around it until the strip overlaps (Fig. 313). With the rolled strip held snugly around the mandrel, make a small mark on the outer end of the strip at a point just beyond the desired inner end of the strip.
2. Set the circle of strip in a flat position on the V-block, and saw vertically straight through the outside strip toward the center of the circle (Fig. 314). The edges at both ends must be cut squarely. It is advisable to allow a bit of extra material on this first cut.
3. With round-nose pliers, adjust the edges until the ends come perfectly and squarely together in all planes.

311. Brake.

312. A wide sheet is bent in the bench vise with a mallet and a block of wood.

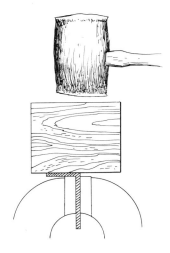

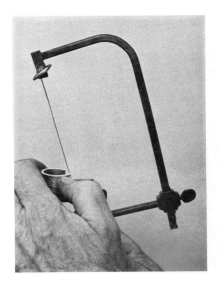

313–320. Bending a ring band.

left: 313. Thin strip can be bent by hand around a ring mandrel.

right: 314. The bent strip is then set on a V-block and sawed through vertically.

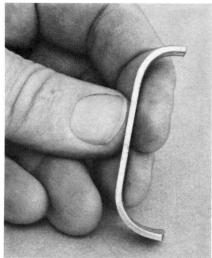

left: 315. Thicker strips must be hammered at each end around the ring mandrel.

center: 316. Ring band after each end has been hammered over the ring mandrel.

right: 317. Hammering the band into ring shape with the rawhide mallet.

11.11

Bending Heavy Strips of Metal into a Circle   Thick strips of metal, such as ring bands, need more elaborate treatment of the ends, and the bending must be done with a rawhide mallet.

1. Determine the necessary length of the metal strip. This can be done by measuring a ring mandrel at the groove marked with the proper ring size. Cut a piece of paper to the width of the ring and about 3 inches long. Wrap it around the mandrel at the ring size, and mark the overlap with a pencil. Cut a piece of metal to the proper width and to the length you have marked, allowing a little extra length to account for the thickness of the metal.

2. Hold each end of the strip over the mandrel and hammer first one end, then the other, down with the mallet (Figs. 315, 316).

3. Hold the strip on the bench or on an anvil, by one of the curved ends, and tap it into a circle with the mallet (Fig. 317). When the ends are brought nearly together, slide the ring on the mandrel and strike it all around to smooth out the irregularities. This process may need to be repeated several times.

4. The ends of the strip often become separated by this process and must be closed again. Place your left thumb on one end of the ring and press it against the mandrel (Fig. 318). The other end of the strip should now project above and to the right of the mandrel (Fig. 319). Strike the strip with the mallet at a point very close to the thumb. This will bring the end down to the mandrel. Now slip the ring off, turn it over, and repeat the process on the other end. Repeat this sequence until the ends are touching snugly.

5. Another method of bringing the ends together is to use a *ring-bending block*. (This can be made by sawing a series of V-cuts into a hardwood block. An even better block can be constructed as follows: Take a block about 3 inches wide, 3 inches thick, and perhaps 10 inches long (Fig. 320). Lay out a center line on the side with the grain-end, and drill a series of spaced holes of decreasing diameters: 1 inch, $\frac{3}{4}$ inch, $\frac{5}{8}$ inch, $\frac{1}{2}$ inch, $\frac{3}{8}$ inch, $\frac{1}{4}$ inch. Afterwards, saw the block down the center line and you will have two blocks.) The block is used by setting the ring band in the slot of appropriate size, with the ring band ends up. Place the small end of the ring

right: 318. The ring band is closed to its proper shape by hammering it around the mandrel.

far right: 319. Hammering displaces one side of the ring band.

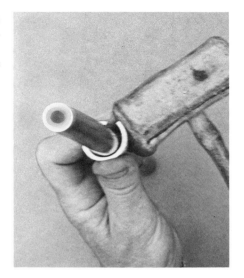

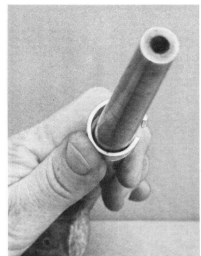

mandrel in the ring, and give it a sharp blow with the rawhide mallet. This will squeeze the ends together. The ends can be evened by shifting the position of the ring to one side or the other, as required, and tapping the mandrel so as to pull one end into line with the other.

6. If your ring appears to be *slightly larger* than you need, measure the exact size of the ring on the mandrel and estimate the amount of material that must be cut from the ends to reduce the ring to the size wanted. Experience will enable you to make this estimate. Meanwhile, figure about 2 millimeters of length to equal one ring size on the mandrel. You will approach the correct size by successive approximations.

7. Place the ring flat on the V-block, and saw one-half the reduction off each end. In sawing (12.2–4), line your jeweler's saw so that you saw in a plane that runs through the center of the ring circle.

8. Now carry out operation 4 again until the ends are brought into snug contact. If your cuts are square and true to the center of the ring, the ends should butt together perfectly. If they do not fit perfectly (Fig. 321), you must saw through the open wedge of the seam repeatedly until the excess material is removed and the ends butt snugly. After each sawcut, the ring must be closed again by the method described in step 4. You will not be able to fill a gap in the seam with solder.

left: 320. A ring-bending block can be used to bring the ends of a ring together.

right: 321. Ring band closed. The V-shape gap can be sawed out.

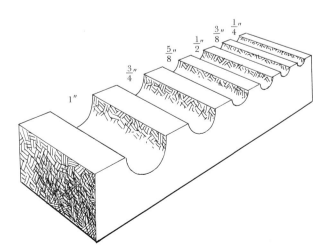

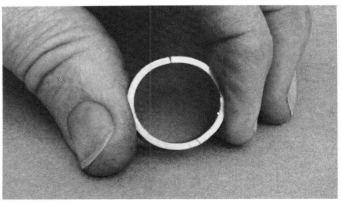

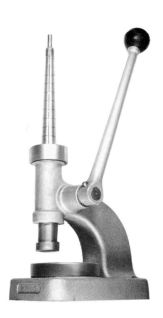

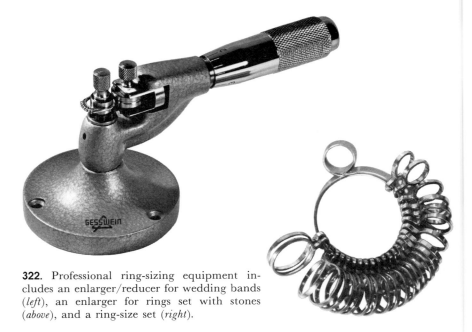

322. Professional ring-sizing equipment includes an enlarger/reducer for wedding bands (*left*), an enlarger for rings set with stones (*above*), and a ring-size set (*right*).

9. Measure the actual size of the ring again. If it is still too large, saw a little more off one end, as you did in step 7. Repeat this procedure until the correct size is reached. This is the only stage where the ring can easily be made smaller. A soldered ring that is too large can be adjusted only by removing a piece (including the soldered joint), realigning the edges, and resoldering to the proper size.

10. Now the ring must be soldered. Set it in the annealing pan (**9.1**), solidly supported with pumice pebbles, or brace it in self-locking tweezers. Hard or I.T. solder must be used for this join (and medium or easy solder for any subsequent joins on the ring). Use more solder than you would for an ordinary join. The rationale for the extra solder is that any additions to the ring, such as stone settings, will require further solderings, and some of the solder may run away. The excess should be on the outside of the band rather than the inside, so that it can be filed and polished away during the final stages. Be sure when you are heating the ring before soldering that both sides of the join are heated evenly. When the solder has melted, check the inside of the ring to make sure that the join is complete. Then pickle the ring to remove every trace of fire scale and flux. (**9.2**).

11. If the ring is *too small*, but not excessively, solder the seam and then place the ring in the ring enlarger, if one is available, or set the ring on the mandrel and planish to stretch it to the correct size. In planishing, strike light, even blows all around the ring, holding the planishing hammer loosely in the hand so that the hammer face will of its own accord find the flat plane of the strip surface. Begin by hammering directly on the seam. If too much solder has been applied and has collected on the inside of the seam, you must remove it with a half-round file before planishing.

   If a ring enlarger (Fig. 322) is available, sizing is much simpler. Merely solder the ring to a size somewhat smaller than that desired. After soldering and finishing the seam, stretch the ring to the correct size in the ring enlarger.

12. After the ring has been soldered, it can be trued, or rounded, on the ring mandrel by hammering it with the planishing hammer, rotating it slowly until it is the proper shape. To prevent the ring from becoming cone shaped, take it off the mandrel periodically and reverse its position.

323. Procedure for bending up a rectangular box.

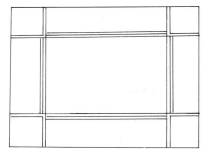

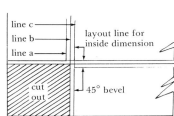

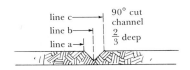

11.12

Bending Oval Rings of Strip or Wire   When it is possible to do so, oval rings of strip or wire are more easily made by rolling up and soldering perfect circles and then bending the circles into proper oval shapes. They can be bent on an oval mandrel or in a jig. Specific sizes can be made by calculating the circumference of the oval (**A.4**). This length is then used to make the circle.

11.13

Bending a Rectangular Box from Sheet   The process of making a box requires precise layout. Saw out a sheet of metal in a rectangle equal to the width plus twice the height of the box and the length plus twice the height. Lay out the sides of the ends of the box, using a divider to scribe the lines along all four edges (Fig. 323). The squares at the four corners should be sawed out carefully, leaving the scribed lines on the end and side pieces. They should be sawed with a 45-degree bevel, so that, when the sides and ends are bent up, they will come together with mitered ends. Now take a V-scraper and cut a V-channel along each bend line around the box base. This channel must be cut just on the line and to half the thickness of the material.

Bend up the sides and ends squarely. If properly prepared, the sides and ends should fit evenly together at the corners. The seams are now soldered evenly, and a flat top is made to fit.

If the lid must be part of the box (Fig. 324), the box can be made either from one strip that is bent around for the sides or from two separate strips,

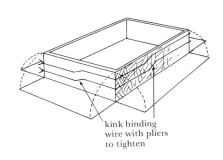

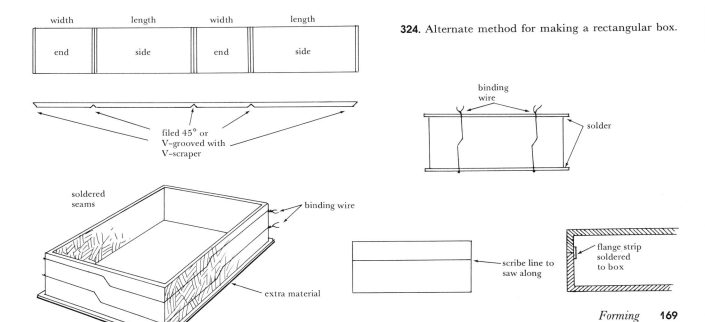

324. Alternate method for making a rectangular box.

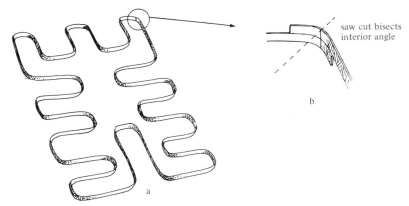

325. Strip ends are joined by overlapping, sawing through the double thickness, and soldering the cut ends together.

saw cut bisects
interior angle

b

a

each of which has one bend and beveled ends. These strips are soldered together squarely and finished. With dividers, scribe a lid line at the proper height around the side strip and then fasten on a top and bottom plate, each cut with just a slight amount of extra material all around. Binding wire of 20 gauge will hold them in position. Before soldering, make a small cut on one corner of the box at the lid line to allow gas to escape during the soldering process. The top and bottom plates are then soldered to the side strip. Afterward, the excess metal on the top and bottom plates is filed off, and the sides are finished. Then the box can be sawed apart at the lid line and the sawed edges filed and finished. A flange strip soldered to the box as shown serves to hold the lid in position.

11.14

Bending a Corner for a Solder Joint in a Strip Shape   Closed shapes made of strip should, whenever possible, be soldered together at a corner rather than on a flat side, but this corner seam should be made in such a way as to correspond to other bent corners of the shape. This means that each end of the strip should be bent completely around the corner. The excess material at each end, running past the mid-point of the corner, should be cut with the saw on a plane that bisects the interior angle of the corner (Fig. 325). When the ends are then brought together, a perfect corner, identical with the others, will be attained.

11.15

Bending Up Jump Rings   *Jump ring* is the trade name for a perfect circle of wire. It is used as a connector and in chains of various kinds.

For bending up jump rings, select a round mandrel of the proper diameter. The mandrel may be made of welding rod, carbon-steel drill rod, the back end of a drill bit, a metal knitting needle, or a nail with the head and point cut off. Place the end of the mandrel in a hand drill, and set the handle of the drill in a bench vise so that the mandrel points upward. Make a right-angle bend about $\frac{1}{4}$ inch from the end of the wire, and hook this down against the mandrel between the jaws of the drill chuck. Hold your left thumb against the wire at the drill chuck (Fig. 326). Place the end of your forefinger against the mandrel, and squeeze the wire between the finger and thumb. Now crank the hand drill to wind the wire around the mandrel. With a little practice you will learn how to control the wire so that each loop lies snugly against the loop below. There should be no space between loops. When you have enough loops, slide the spiral off the mandrel.

If you are using annealed wire, you may have difficulty in removing the coiled wire. Therefore, it is a good idea to wrap about two layers of tissue paper smoothly around the mandrel *in the direction you are going to wind the wire.* Wind the wire over this paper. After the spiral has been made, the mandrel is

326. Wire being wrapped around a mandrel, rotated in a hand drill.

removed from the drill, placed in the annealing pan, and heated with a torch. As the wire is annealed, the paper will burn away and the spiral can easily be removed. If you are winding wire around an oval or square mandrel, it is absolutely essential to wrap three or four layers of tissue paper around the mandrel.

To cut the rings apart, grasp the upper end of the spiral firmly between thumb and forefinger, resting your hand against the file block or edge of the bench (Fig. 327), and saw at a shallow angle straight down the center of the spiral. The angle of the saw should be flat enough to saw through three or four rings at the same time. Fine saw blades should be used on fine wire. You can also set the spiral horizontally in the bench vise and saw through the coils in the same manner. If you are using a wooden mandrel, it does not have to be removed before the rings are sawed. With oval rings, be sure to do the sawing on the narrow end so that the soldering will not show on the finished link, fastening, or length of chain.

In order to close each jump ring, seize each side with a pair of square-nose pliers and press the ends past each other; then pull them back into alignment so that they press against each other (Fig. 328). When this is done correctly, the wire ends will be in spring tension against each other, so that there will be no problem in getting the solder to flow into the seam and close it. If the ends are not together, the ring cannot be soldered. (For the procedure of soldering jump rings, see **10.26**).

Forming Metal

Forming is distinguished from bending by the fact that formed metal is warped out of a flat plane by being stretched. Metal hemispheres, spoon bowls, and hollowware are examples of formed metal.

11.16

Repoussé   For jewelers, the process of repoussé is probably the single most important means of forming metal. The term comes from the French verb meaning "to push," and the process consists of working a flat piece of metal on its reverse side with hammers and punches, pushing it into low relief so that it has three-dimensional design. The hammering is usually done with the metal supported on a bowl of pitch. For jewelry, the technique of repoussé is generally combined with chasing (**13.8**), which involves working directly on the front surface of the metal, rather than pushing it out from behind, as in the repoussé process. Chasing as a separate skill will be treated fully in Chapter 13, and it is suggested that you become familiar with the process before attempting repoussé.

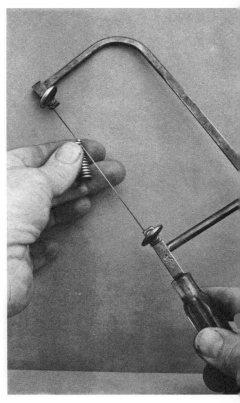

above: 327. Jump rings are cut from a coil of wire.

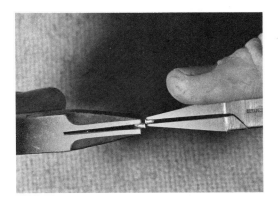

left: 328. Two pairs of pliers are used to bring the ends of a jump ring into alignment and give it spring tension.

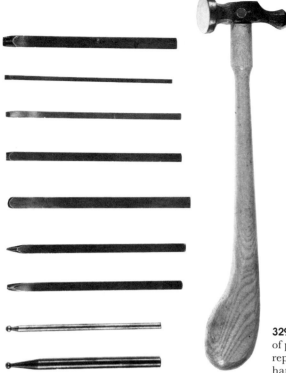

329. Repoussé equipment: bowl of pitch (with work in position), repoussé punches, and chasing hammer.

11.17

Materials and Process for Repoussé   The following materials are needed for the repoussé process:

- a pitch bowl, generally made of cast iron, hemispherical, and about 6 to 8 inches across. A lighter metal bowl tends to skid around as the work is being done unless the bottom is weighted. The bowl is set firmly in:
- a holding ring made of leather or hemp, or a hardwood holding block.
- pitch—a combination of burgundy pitch, plaster, and tallow; this can be purchased readymade.
- repoussé or chasing punches, and a chasing hammer (Fig. 329).
- a torch for warming the pitch and annealing the metal.
- pickling equipment for finishing the work.

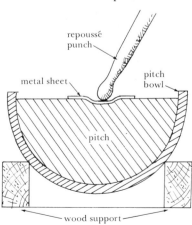

330. The repoussé punch pushes metal into a bowl of pitch.

First, fill the bowl with pitch, slightly mounding it at the center. Warm the pitch with a large soft flame, being careful not to burn it. Anneal the metal to be worked, and place the warm metal, outer side down, on the pitch. It will sink very slightly into the surface. When starting a new sheet of metal, it is sometimes useful to bend the corners down so they penetrate into, and are held by, the pitch. Do not begin hammering until the pitch has cooled, or the metal will soon sink beneath it. You can let cold water run over the pitch bowl and metal to cool them quickly. Now use the special repoussé punches with the chasing hammer to press the metal down into the pitch. The pitch gives the metal support, yet yields where the punch drives the metal down (Fig. 330). Hold the repoussé punch in the left hand (if you are right-handed), perpendicular to the surface of the metal. The first three fingers and thumb grasp the tool, while the little finger acts as a sort of spring to raise the tool off the metal between blows of the hammer (Fig. 331). The tool is not pushed along the surface of the metal; rather, the hammer blow carries it forward slightly.

In general, the full depth of a given form is hammered with large rounded punches in the first step. The metal is then heated, removed with tongs or soldering tweezers, and annealed to soften the work-hardened metal. In the annealing process the adhering pitch is also burned away. Do not pickle the work until all the pitch has been removed. Benzine or turpentine will remove any pitch still adhering after annealing.

After pickling, rinsing, and drying, the hollow that has been made in the first step is refilled with pitch, and the shape is set in the center of the pitch, with the pushed-out form upward. Punches (Fig. 329) and chasing tools (Fig. 382) are now used to work the metal back and to define the boundary of the shapes. By working in this manner, back and forth, any form can be developed. Details are finally added with chasing tools, and lines or edges defined as required.

The development of special forms, such as hollow rings, requires considerable practice and experience, but this is the basic approach that is required in repoussé. Remember that, as you stretch the metal down into the pitch, you are also thinning the metal. Therefore, you must learn to use the punches in such a way as to stretch and thin the metal evenly over a large surface. You cannot make a deep hollow by driving the punch directly down the full depth. The deeper the hollow is to be, the farther out from the center you must gather the metal. To create a deep hollow, first push down a broad area to perhaps half the depth. Then from the other side drive the pushed-up metal toward the center. After a second or third reworking, the final shape and depth can be achieved (Fig. 332).

331. Form for repoussé work. The punch is lifted after every blow.

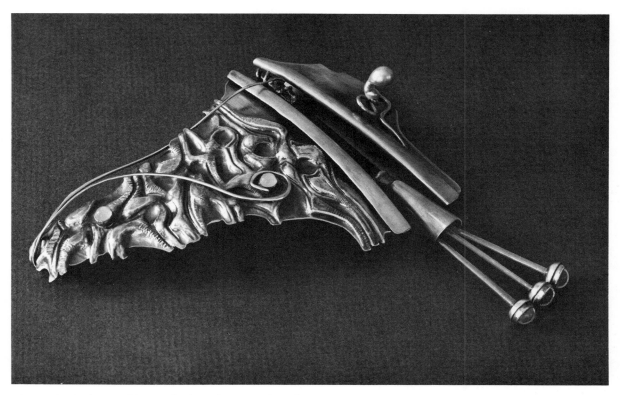

332. Nilda C. Getty. *Electra,* pin forged, repoussé, and constructed of sterling silver and 14k gold, with moonstone, baroque pearl, and tourmaline crystal, 1973.

Figures 333 through 338 illustrate the complete start-to-finish process of creating a hollow ring from copper tubing by means of repoussé. The copper tubing is set on a metal stake held in a vise, overlapping the stake to the point where the first depression will occur. With a forming hammer, the jeweler necks in the tube at the end of the stake (Fig. 333). This process is repeated at another point along the tube (Fig. 334). Next, the jeweler compresses the tube with its depressions by hammering it with a nylon mallet (Fig. 335). The tube is then filled with pitch; masking tape across the bottom prevents the pitch from running out (Fig. 336). With the copper tube supported on a wooden jig that has been hollowed out to size, the jeweler chases details into the surface with a dapping punch (Figs. 337, 338). Plate 10 (p. 152) illustrates the finished tube ring.

333–338. A hollow ring is made by repoussé from a length of copper tubing, as demonstrated by Elliot Pujol.

above: 333. The tube is placed on a stake, and a forming hammer is used to form a pinched neck in the tube.

left: 334. Detail showing a second necking being hammered at another point on the copper tube.

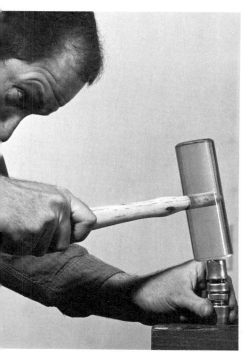

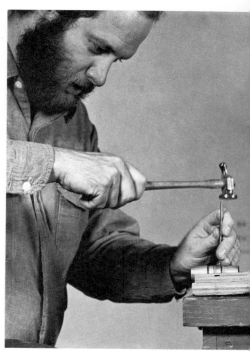

above left: 335. Hammering the tube with a nylon mallet compresses the neckings and shortens the tube.

above center: 336. The tube, stopped by masking tape, is filled with pitch to allow surface decoration by chasing.

above right: 337. The dapping punch is used to chase details onto the outer surface of the tube.

below: 338. Detail of the chasing operation, with pitch-filled tube supported on a specially cut wooden jig.

11.18

Sandbag and Block Forming   Metal can be shaped also by using a canvas or, better yet, leather bag filled with fine sand. The sandbag does not allow the delicate forming possible with the pitch bowl, but it can be used for larger, more generalized hollows and simple warped shapes.

Another means of forming is to carve depressions or hollows in wood or stone or in a tin or lead block. The metal is then shaped by driving it into the hollow with rounded punches. Thin sheets of metal can be pressed into such hollows.

11.19

Embossing and Dapping   Embossing is a shaping process in which small punches are used to drive simple forms into sheet metal from the back. Embossing can be done on a pitch bowl, a wood block, a tin block, or a lead block. Dapping, the traditional method of making hollow beads, involves punching hemispheres out of sheet metal and soldering two halves together. Special round-headed dapping punches are available, together with a dapping block (Fig. 339). With this outfit hemispheres of various sizes (Fig. 340) can be made by cutting disks of appropriate size, starting them in the larger depression in the dapping block, and then moving the curved disk on to successively smaller depressions. A dapping block is made of soft steel and must be treated carefully so that nicks are not put into the depressions.

When making beads or any hollow form by soldering two halves together, always drill an air hole in the center of one hemisphere to allow air to escape during the soldering operation; otherwise the work may explode as a result of air expansion.

After pickling such hollow beads, the pickle must be removed by boiling the beads in soapy water. The water can then be removed by warming the beads with the torch until the water evaporates. Also, when oxidizing hollow forms, be sure to remove the sulphur solution in the same manner.

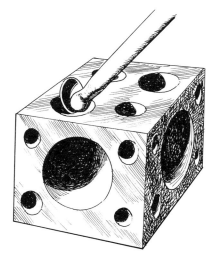

above: 339. Dapping block, with a disk of sheet metal posed in a depression of appropriate size.

right: 340. Philip Morton. *Saturnalia,* pendant of dapped copper and chased sterling, set with quartz, tourmaline, carnelian, crazy-lace agate, and black jade, 1975.

176

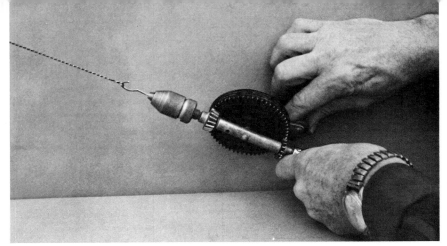

341. Wire being twisted in the hand drill.

11.20

Hardening Wire by Twisting   When you need wire to be rigid or springy, as, for example, in the case of a wire pin tong (Fig. 302), it can be hardened by twisting. Twisting is a special aspect of bending, in which a single wire is bent around its own axis. This is done by grasping each end of the wire with a pair of pliers and turning the pliers in opposite directions, meanwhile pulling on the wire to keep it in tension. For a long piece of wire, you can place one end in a vise and attach the other to a hook that is bent up and placed in the chuck of the drill. The wire is then twisted by cranking the hand drill while pulling on the wire to keep it tight (Fig. 341).

11.21

Twisted Wires   Elaborate twists of wire have been used in traditional jewelry. Contemporary jewelers have not utilized this technique to any great extent, but one sees twisted wire occasionally in rings, bangle bracelets, and as links in necklaces. Interesting experiments can be carried out with wires of various gauges or shapes—square, triangular, rectangular, oval—arranged in different combinations (Fig. 342). To form a length of twisted wire you need:

- annealed wire of medium weight—13 gauge is suitable
- a hand drill for working thinner wire
- a brace or hand vise for working thicker wire

342. Twisted wires.

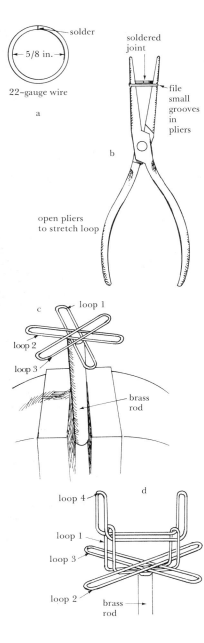

To make a simple twist, take two equal strands of wire or a single strand bent in two. Clamp one end of the wire in a bench vise, and fasten the other in a hand drill. Maintain tension on the wire while cranking the drill.

Variations can be achieved by twisting wire alternately to the left and to the right, by leaving some sections untwisted, by hammering the twisted wire flat, or by putting the twisted wire through the rolling mill. Square, triangular, and rectangular wires can be twisted individually before combining with other wires, to form complex patterns.

11.22

Making Chains Chain making is probably as old as the process of wire drawing, and a study of jewelry history will reveal many fascinating and elaborate chains. The contemporary jeweler has yet to explore the full range of possibilities residing in this process. Exploration of chain making may start with the assembly of simple, circular jump rings (**10.26, 11.15**). Since all rings in a chain must be soldered, chain making is a wonderful procedure for mastering delicate soldering operations.

To make oval rings or links for a chain, use an oval mandrel. Wrap the mandrel with three layers of tissue paper before rolling the wire around it in a spiral. After the mandrel has been wound with wire (Fig. 326), it is annealed with a soft flame. This annealing will burn off the tissue paper and allow the oval spiral to be drawn off the mandrel. The oval rings are then sawed apart.

A small number of contemporary jewelers have experimented with chain-making techniques that go back to ancient Roman times or earlier. One such technique, employed by Chuck Evans to create a classic "triple loop-in-loop" chain, proceeds as follows (Fig. 343):

1. Solder up about 300 loops of 22-gauge sterling wire (*a*), formed around a hardwood dowel of $\frac{1}{2}$- to 1-inch diameter. (Three hundred loops of $\frac{5}{8}$-inch diameter will yield about 9 inches of woven chain.)
2. Insert a pair of round long-nose pliers into each loop and pull open to stretch the loops into elongated shape (*b*). The soldered joints should be in the center, so that they will not be visible on the finished chain.
3. Take three elongated loops, and solder them together in a star pattern (*c*). Solder the group of three loops to the end of a brass rod, $\frac{1}{8}$ inch in diameter and about 3 inches long. The rod is secured in a vise to hold the chain during the weaving.
4. Beginning with the bottom loop, bend up each end, insert a new loop, and bend its ends up as well (*d*). Then repeat the process for the middle and upper loops (in that order), adding two more loops to make a total of six.
5. Push down the new loops to make room for the next three, each of which is threaded through the previous *two* loops in the corresponding position (*e*). Thus loop 7 passes through loops 1 and 4; 8 through 2 and 5; and 9 through 3 and 6. Continue the procedure in the direction established, taking each new loop in its proper sequence, and pull the chain tight after every three-loop pass.
6. After weaving, anneal, planish with a rawhide mallet, and draw the chain through a hardwood or steel drawplate just enough to ensure a uniform, round shape. Then anneal again and pickle. The brass rod can be sawed off, after which the ends of the chain are normally soldered inside a pair of tubular, thimblelike caps.

Once understood, this basic procedure affords almost endless variations. The experimental jeweler might try using thicker or thinner wire, a different size loop, or another material. A variety of nonferrous metals—silver, gold, brass, and copper—can be employed, singly or in virtually any combination: Every third or ninth loop might be of contrasting color, for example, or 1-inch

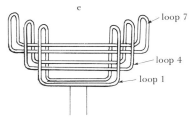

343. Steps illustrating an ancient Roman loop-in-loop chain technique, provided by Chuck Evans.

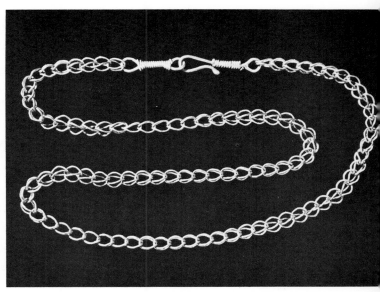

above left: 344. Kulicke-Stark Academy of Jewelry Art. Classic loop-in-loop chains of fine silver (*top to bottom*): single, double, sextuple, and quadruple loop-in-loop; single loop-in-loop with amethyst beads; single loop-in-loop with one end of each loop flattened. Links were prepared by granulation, according to a technique dating from as early as 3000 B.C.

above right: 345. Robert Kulicke and Jean Reist Stark. Single loop-in-loop chain of fine silver, c. 1971–75.

left: 346. Jean Reist Stark. Silver browband for a horse's bridle, made from single and multiple loop-in-loop chains, with cloisonné enamel, lapis lazuli cabachons and bead, and a granulated silver ball, 1974.

lengths of different materials could be interwoven one after another. The *double* loop-in-loop chain, based on a simpler sequence (four loops instead of nine), follows essentially the same procedure.

To make a chain from any kind of link, solder half the links closed, then attach pairs of closed links with an open link. This cuts in half the number of links that must be soldered in place in the chain.

Chains of round links can also be twisted in the same manner as wire is twisted. Completed chains can be hammered or put through the rolling mill. Other possibilities include combinations of different-shaped links or of links and twisted wire.

There is no limit to the variety of relationships that can be attained by varying size of link, size of wire, and shape of links, or by using multiple links, interlocking links, textured links, massive links (Figs. 344–346). The field is open to the curious and interested jeweler.

Filigree   There are two kinds of filigree—that in which the characteristically fine wires (either round or twisted) are soldered to each other to form a delicate open design, usually within a frame of heavier wire; and that in which fine wires are formed in an intricate pattern and soldered to a flat base. Naturally, great care must be taken during such fine soldering not to melt the wire. Easy solder is used, and the torch is equipped with a very small tip to make a tiny pointed flame. This is particularly important if the soldering is done in the normal way, that is, if the flame is applied at the point of the join.

There is an easier way to solder filigree, for which the necessary equipment is as follows:

- filigree wire
- easy-grade solder filings
- iron sheet
- gum tragacanth and a camel's-hair brush to apply it
- torch
- pickling equipment
- kiln or furnace

First, anneal the filigree wire. Bend it into shape with fingers or pliers, and cut the pieces apart with a sharp chisel, pressing the cutting edge against the wire supported by a copper plate. Now take the cut pieces of filigree wire and assemble them into the shape you want on top of a clean iron sheet. As you put the pieces together, apply a small drop of gum tragacanth at each join with a camel's-hair brush (Fig. 347). Before the tragacanth is dry, sprinkle a little easy-grade solder filings on each joint. When the assembly is complete, warm the iron plate gently to evaporate the tragacanth, and then place it in a furnace until the solder fuses. Then remove the work and pickle it.

Filigree is an impractical process for commercial work, at least in the United States, although craftsmen in other parts of the world have developed the technique to an art (Fig. 348). It is very painstaking and time-consuming, so that it must be sold at relatively high prices to compensate for the jeweler's time and effort. Unfortunately, filigree jewelry is also mass-produced by machine, and this type, which is hard to distinguish from the handmade variety, is fairly inexpensive.

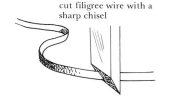

cut filigree wire with a sharp chisel

apply gum tragacanth to cement wires in place

above: 347. Filigree wire is cut with a sharp chisel, bent to the desired shape, and placed on a flat sheet of iron coated with gum tragacanth.

right: 348. Luis Guillermo Trespalacios Meza. Filigree earrings made from coin silver, with stones.

With all the effective and convenient means of cutting metal that we possess today, it is hard to imagine the primitive metalsmith cutting shapes and strips with a stone chisel. Nevertheless, surprisingly fine work was accomplished with this crude tool. Cutting metal is one of the most basic and important of the metalworking processes. It includes such simple skills as shearing sheet metal and clipping wire, as well as more complex tasks such as wielding the different kinds of drills. The most common method of cutting metal is sawing; often the saw will be used to create part of the design of a piece of jewelry. Also, there are the types of cutting that serve to embellish the surface of a piece of metal—carving in preparation for inlaying wire or stone, and scraping to enrich the texture. All of these techniques form the subject matter of this chapter.

12.1

Shearing, Clipping, and Chisel Cutting   *Shearing* is the simplest and most rapid means of cutting simple curved or rectangular shapes or strips of sheet metal. When using the hand shears, always cut *on* the line. Silver sheet of 16 gauge or smaller (**C.20**) can be cut quite easily with hand shears having a 4-inch blade (Fig. 349) or with the bench shears.

One disadvantage of cutting with any shears is that narrow strips of sheet metal are often twisted by the cutting action of the blades. This twist can usually be taken out with the fingers or pliers. A long strip should be seized at each end with a pair of square-nose pliers and pulled during the twisting. Another disadvantage of shearing is that one face of the cut is beveled by the

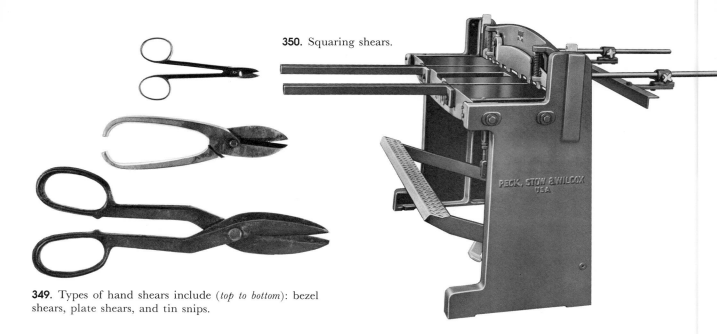

350. Squaring shears.

349. Types of hand shears include (*top to bottom*): bezel shears, plate shears, and tin snips.

action of the shears, and this face must be filed square. A large workshop will have squaring shears (Fig. 350) and a cutter, operated by a foot pedal, with a blade 30 inches long or more.

Clipping is simply the process of cutting strip or wire into lengths with cutting pliers.

Chisel cutting is a method rarely seen today, but at one time it was the sole cutting method available. Chisel cutting is still useful for many purposes; cloisonné and filigree wire are most often cut with a chisel. To use a chisel, you should first be sure that it is quite sharp and ground with a single bevel on one side. With a scribe, mark the cutting line on the metal sheet. Place the chisel exactly on the line, with the bevel side facing away from the piece to be saved. Strike the chisel with a blow that carries it about halfway through the metal. Shift the chisel along this slot half or three-quarters of the way, so that part of the chisel is held in line, and strike again. Continue this process along the line. To follow an outside curve, the chisel must be placed tangent to the curve at every point. Inside curves require a curved chisel. After the boundary has been traced, it is retraced by striking the chisel through the sheet. The work should be done on a soft iron anvil.

Sawing with the Jeweler's Saw

Sawing is by far the most accurate and the most generally used method of cutting metal. To handle the jeweler's saw accurately and easily, a very precise form must be developed. The following instructions should be studied thoroughly and applied with consistency if you wish to saw effectively.

12.2

Stringing the Saw Frame   The saw frame used by professional jewelers has an adjustable length, to a maximum of about 4 inches. Saw blades are quite inexpensive and are purchased by the dozen or the gross. Jeweler's saw blades are graded by number from fine to coarse as follows: fine, 8/0 to 0; coarse, 1 to 14.

With fine blades it is difficult to see the teeth, but you can determine the direction of the teeth by running your finger lightly over the blade. For most silverwork a No. 3 blade is good; No. 2 or finer should be used on goldwork. Place the upper end of the blade, teeth pointing to the handle, in the upper clamp of the frame. Make sure that the end is set in as far as it will go and that it is set in a straight line toward the handle; otherwise it will twist and break.

There are two ways of setting the blade in the handle clamp. One way is to adjust the handle piece of the saw along the front piece by loosening the slide clamp on the back and sliding the handle piece to such a position that the blade falls about $\frac{3}{8}$ inch short of reaching the back of the clamp. The slide clamp is then tightened. The front clamp of the saw is held against the edge of the bench, and by leaning against the handle with your chest, you will be able to bring the back clamp into position while the blade is set and tightened in the handle clamp (Fig. 351).

The other method is to loosen the back slide clamp and set the handle piece so that the blade can be fastened into the handle clamp. Then, by squeezing between the handle clamp and the end of the front piece, bring the blade under tension and tighten the back slide clamp.

The purpose of both methods is to place the blade under tension. When properly strung, the blade should give a high "ping" when plucked with the finger. *A slack blade will always break.* Never tighten the clamp screw with pliers, or you will strip the threads.

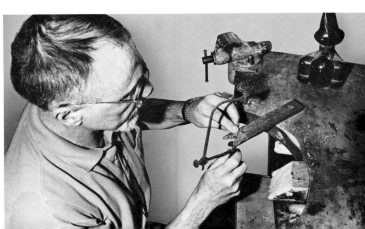

351. Saw frame and blade.

12.3

Position for Sawing For general sawing, it is necessary to arrange a V-block at the proper height in your jeweler's vise or at the edge of the workbench, so that it is not more than about 6 inches below eye level when you are in a normal sitting position (Fig. 352). This allows you to view your work closely without bending over or straining at the back and neck. It also places your arms in a natural and easy position for sawing. If the height of the bench is fixed, you can make the proper adjustment by sawing off the legs of the stool or chair. With the V-block set in position, you should sit so that your arm and right shoulder (left shoulder if you are left-handed) are lined up in a normal and relaxed position for working. Relaxation is important, because a strained position is difficult to hold for long periods of time and leads to muscular tension.

The saw handle is held firmly at its throat, between the inside joint of the thumb and the inside joint of the index finger. The remaining fingers should not grasp the handle but merely lie against it to keep the saw in a vertical position.

The saw blade must always be held in a vertical position, perpendicular to the plane of the work, unless you are purposely sawing a beveled or slanting edge. The metal you are sawing is held clamped to the V-block with the four fingers of the left hand on top and your left thumb beneath the block. A ring clamp, which is a wooden device that holds work steady without scratching it, is useful for small pieces. If you allow the metal to be pulled up or out of this position while sawing, you may break the blade.

352. Position for sawing. The V-block is about 6 inches below eye level and directly in front of the jeweler.

12.4

Form for Sawing   The reason for these detailed instructions, which will enable you to develop correct form in sawing, will become apparent after you have broken a number of saw blades. Do not let the breakage discourage you, however, because it seems to be a part of the learning process. Save broken blades; they can be used in short saw frames. The following suggestions will help you perfect your form:

- Using a scribe, mark the line you are going to saw. Always saw along the outside of the layout line, *leaving the line on the work.* This will allow you to file-finish right to the line.
- An alternate method of marking the metal for sawing is to paint the surface of the metal with a water-base white paint, draw or trace your design onto the painted surface using carbon paper, and spray with a plastic-base fixative. This can be filed and burnished off when the work is complete.
- Cut on the downstroke only.
- Always keep your saw blade under tension.
- Always keep your saw blade vertical.
- Always keep your arm, wrist, and hand relaxed.
- Avoid twisting the saw blade sideways in the metal.
- Take long, steady strokes, using the full length of the blade. When sawing a fine area of the design, however, short strokes are better.
- Always keep the saw in motion up and down, both when you are sawing and when you are backing the blade out of a cut. To preserve blades, unstring the blade and pull it through, instead of backing out.
- In order to saw a curved line, swing the back of the saw around in the correct direction *as you saw.*
- To change directions at a corner, hold the blade in the location of the corner and swing the back of the saw around in the correct direction as you saw *at that stationary point.* Twist the saw frame around slowly, since the saw teeth must cut their own space for turning. Otherwise, you will only twist the blade, and it will break. Or, you can drill holes at the corners before beginning to saw. This takes time but will make turning easy.
- Run the saw blade through a lump of beeswax now and then for lubrication.
- The saw blade is a delicate and subtle tool. Think of each saw tooth as chiseling out a small piece of metal.

Most broken saw blades result from undue haste or from the failure to hold the blade in a vertical position, which causes pinching or kinking. You will save yourself many additional broken blades if, when you remove broken ends from the frame clamps, you tap the frame against the bench. This shakes small broken ends out of the clamps. If they are allowed to remain, a new blade will immediately slip out of the clamp and break.

12.5

Using the Bench Tray During Sawing   Every jeweler's bench is equipped with at least one tray that has various uses depending upon the work being done. Sometimes it keeps tools being used close at hand. During sawing, however, it is pulled under the work so that it catches all the filings of precious metal. Better workbenches have a tray just for this purpose. Gold and silver sawdust (called *lemel*), in particular, should not be mixed with lesser metals. Save them carefully, and when you have a sufficient amount, cast them into ingots and reuse the metal. If you do not wish to cast your scrap, there are commercial dealers who will purchase it or cast it for you.

353. Sawing an inside cut in sheet metal.

354. Tapio Wirkkala. Pierced silver pendants, 1973.

12.6

Sawing an Inside Hole in Sheet Metal   Drill a small hole near the boundary line of the inside hole or shape. String the blade through the hole and fasten it to the saw frame. Set the work on the V-block and saw in the usual manner (Fig. 353). *Piercing* is elaborate cutout work done with the jeweler's saw. Such work involves careful layout of lines and accurate cutting (Fig. 354).

Drilling

Drilling is a process in which metal is cut away in a spiral. Drilling holes in metal is usually accomplished by a hand drill, an electric bench drill, or a flexible-shaft drill (Fig. 355). The hand drill will be satisfactory as long as you are not going to be drilling very much. It is neither versatile nor flexible. The high-speed electric bench drill is a better choice; it requires much less force to do the work, which lessens the chance of drill breakage resulting from putting too much pressure on a fine drill. The flexible-shaft drill is the best choice of all because it serves many purposes besides drilling (**19.5**). It is fast, highly accurate, and requires only that the jeweler give proper direction to the drill point. The chuck will accommodate a wide variety of different cutting and finishing attachments (Figs. 356, 521).

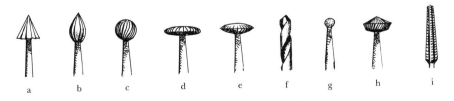

a   b   c   d   e   f   g   h   i

The drill itself is the threaded metal tool that fits into the chuck of the hand, bench, or flexible-shaft drill. The higher the number of the drill, the smaller it is in diameter.

Never begin drilling on the flat surface of the metal. First, rest the metal on a steel or lead block. Use a center punch to set the position of the hole you wish to drill. The small depression made by the punch will hold and position the point of the drill (Fig. 357).

355. Flexible-shaft drill, composed of motor, flexible shaft, and chuck for attaching different drills, burs, buffs, and grinding stones.

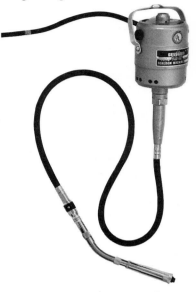

below left: 356. Cutting attachments for the flexible-shaft drill include the point bur (*a*), bud bur (*b*), ball bur (*c*), round-edge cutter (*d*), knife-edge cutter (*e*), twist drill (*f*), diamond-impregnated point (*g*), setting bur (*h*), and a reamer bur (*i*). For finishing attachments, see Fig. 521.

below: 357. A center punch is used to fix the position of the drill.

12.7

Form for Drilling The following suggestions will help you to develop a successful technique for drilling:

- Keep your drill lubricated with machine oil.
- Never place the metal to be drilled on a metal anvil. Use a wood support in order to protect the point of the drill.
- To drill a large hole through metal, drill a smaller guide hole first.
- To avoid raising a burr on the metal when using a large drill, first drill a smaller guide hole, and then drill the larger hole partly through from each side.
- Never apply too much pressure to the drill. Allow it to cut its own way. If it will not cut, the drill needs sharpening.
- Fine-number drills will break easily. Therefore, brace and support the hand drill carefully as you work, or snap the drill bit in half to reduce its length. The bit should protrude from the chuck as little as possible.
- Take particular care when the drill is emerging from the back side of the metal. This is the time when it tends to break easily.
- Holes can be drilled through wire by first flattening the wire slightly with a planishing hammer and center-punching exactly in the center.
- When drilling through thick metal, thrust the drill point into a lump of beeswax first for lubrication.

above: **358.** Scorpers are available with a variety of different points.

below: **359.** The pointed tip of the scorper, shown in end and side views (*a*), carves a groove in sheet metal (*b*), in which a wire can be inlaid.

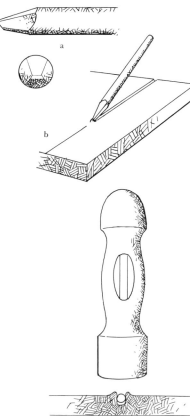

Carving and Scraping

12.8

Carving with Scorpers Carving can be done directly in the surface of the metal by means of scorpers (Fig. 358) or chisels, which are used with the chasing hammer. This is a delicate and refined process requiring considerable practice. Paved settings (**21.3**) often require carving with scorpers.

Wire can be inlaid in sheet metal by carving the patterns with a scorper, as shown in Figure 359, or with an engraving tool (**17.24**). Wire is then bent to fit into the cut and hammered in (Fig. 360). Niello, a black mixture of lead, silver, and sulphur (Figs. 49, 99; see also **C.6**), can also be fused into chiseled patterns.

12.9

Scraping Metalworkers use an assortment of very sharp scrapers for cutting away metal. The scraper (Fig. 361) serves to clean metal along seams to be soldered, to cut away excess solder, or to clean out pits or imperfections in the surface of metal being planished, forged, or rolled. Generally, after a surface has been scraped clean, it has to be polished further by filing and burnishing before the smoothness is restored. Before scraping a piece of metal, fix it in a horizontal position. Hold the blade of the scraper as flat as possible against the surface of the metal, controlling the pressure with your thumb. This will prevent the scraper from making nicks in the metal.

360. Section view of the inlaid wire setting. The wire is placed in the carved groove (*a*) and hammered in (*b*).

a   b

361. Scraper.

Hammering

Beating metal with a hammer is a subtle and exacting process, although it is often considered to be a gross muscular activity in which the arm is swung up and down with great force. This is perhaps true of blacksmithing. It is not true of nonferrous metalwork. In silversmithing and jewelry, hammers (Fig. 363) must be used as delicately as the jeweler's saw or the needle file.

There are four general types of hammering: striking, punching, forging, and planishing. The term *striking* (also known as *forming* or *bossing*) means any kind of hammer-shaping other than forging and planishing. *Punching* is the texturing of metal by hammering a tool called a punch into the surface. It is done primarily during chasing, in which a variety of punches are used to mark designs on metal. *Forging* is the process of forming, thickening, or thinning metal by the impact of the hammer head. *Planishing* means smoothing and evening a piece of metal by striking it with a highly polished tool called a planishing hammer.

13.1

Forging   In simple forging, a piece of metal is placed on an anvil or stake and then thinned and stretched with the hammer (Fig. 362). The necessary tools for forging are: a torch for annealing, forging hammers (available in many sizes and weights, a bench anvil, and one or two polished metal stakes to support your work (Fig. 379). Before forging, anneal and cool the metal to be worked. During the forging, further annealing will be necessary when the metal begins to resist the blows of the hammer. (If a hard or springy end-product is desired, omit the final annealing.) The primary forging ham-

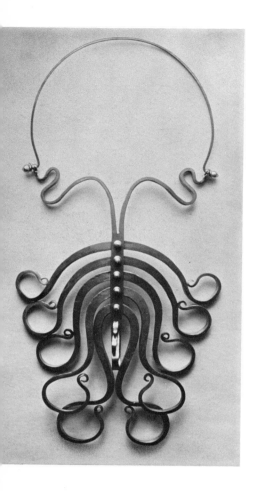

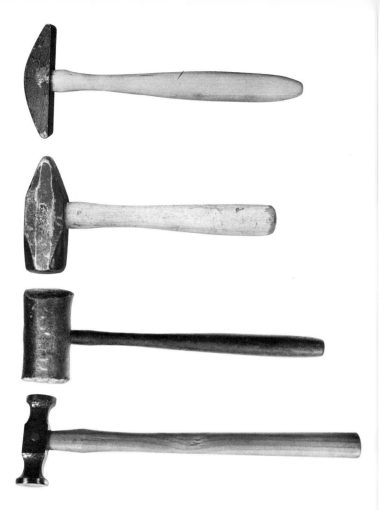

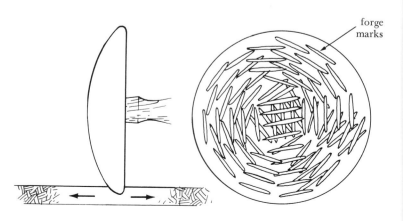

above: 362. Thomas R. Markusen. Pendant of forged copper and sterling, 1975.

above right: 363. Types of hammers (*top to bottom*): cross-peen forging hammer, short-handled sledge hammer, rawhide mallet, planishing hammer.

below right: 364. The cross-peen hammer spreading metal in two directions, and a metal disk spread out by forging in a radial pattern.

mer has a head with a cross-peen face (Fig. 363). When the face is driven down into the metal, it spreads the metal in both directions perpendicular to the cross peen (Fig. 364). Other commonly used hammers have a crown, or rounded, face that spreads the metal around the point of impact. In any case, forging moves the metal and thins it between the hammer head and the anvil. In forging heavy wire or rod such a hammer may accomplish a specific operation more effectively. A short-handled sledge hammer can be converted into an effective forging hammer with one crown face and one

forge marks

365. Richard Mafong and Jon Eric Riis. *Pin #4,* of forged, repoussé, and chased silver and gold, with carved ivory and wrapped metallic threads, 1975.

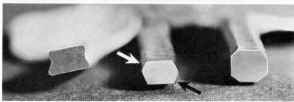

366. Three common errors in forging (*upper row*), and how to correct them (*lower row*), as demonstrated by Paul Mergen. *Left:* If the hammered side of a copper bar spreads more than the anvil side, turn the bar over and hammer to equalize the difference. *Center:* If the bar takes on a parallelogram cross-section, hammer the two most projecting edges. *Right:* If vigorous hammering of top and bottom produces grooves in the sides, avoid bothersome folds by hammering down all projecting edges.

cross-peen face. The cross-peen face offers maximum control. Forging hammers should be used only for forging.

Forging is a subtle operation in that sensitive variations in the weight of blows must be distinguished. To develop a smooth, tapered form (Fig. 365), the weight of the blows must be graduated to suit the form. The heavier blows should be directed to the part of the metal to be thinned the most.

In forging, the angle of the hammer-head axis must be controlled. If the forging hammer is tipped slightly to the right, the effect will be to spread the metal on the right side more than on the left. If a strip or wire is being forged, the result will be a curving of the metal to the left. Unless such curvature is desired, the axis of the hammer must not be allowed to depart from the vertical. Tipping the hammer is thus a means of controlling the curvature of a strip or wire. Three common forging problems, and ways to correct them, appear in Figure 366.

13.2

Forged Textures   In recent years, an interest in forging has led to the development of forged textures as a means of enriching a metal surface (Fig. 367). This sort of texture is made by laying down with a rather sharp cross-peen hammer very closely packed marks, often quite sharp and deep. Such marks show directional movement and give a natural warp to the metal. You may want to try texturing with a variety of forging hammers, including some with specially prepared faces.

367. Ed Lund. *Homage to Suzi/Kaneohe,* pendant of fused and forged copper, constructed with leather and pali tear, 1973.

368. The end of a copper wire forged by a cross-peen hammer into a thin, wide petal shape. Extra thickness at the edges provides strength and allows maximum control of spreading.

Forged Forms   The development of a forged form depends on experience with the forging process and on experiment, for shape cannot be arbitrarily imposed upon a material. The shape must be drawn out of the metal by the action of the forging hammer in displacing the metal, blow by blow. It is a good idea to begin forging experiments with a short length of 6-gauge or 8-gauge copper wire and see how much variation in width you can make in the center and at one end (Fig. 368). In forging a taper from thick to thin along a bar of metal, one soon learns to adjust the weight of the blows to the tapered thickness of the material.

The following sequence, illustrated in Figures 369–375, gives step-by-step procedures for forging a simple bracelet:

1. Cut a 7-inch length of $\frac{1}{4}$-inch-square sterling or copper rod.
2. Work on a clean, dent-free anvil with a cross-peen hammer of about 2 pounds. Both ends of the hammer should be reshaped, with the flat face slightly crowned, or rounded, the edges rounded, and the cross-peen end also slightly crowned and round-edged. Set the anvil in a stump at a comfortable height; if the stool is 30 inches high, for example, the anvil surface should be about 40 inches above the floor.
3. First forge the middle of the bar for the top of the bracelet. Figure 370 shows how the cross peen of the forging hammer is held parallel to the rod and worked from the center outward in both directions. Avoid striking the very edge of the rod. Taper the metal from thicker on the inside to thinner—but not too thin—on the outside. When the shape has been achieved, use the flat face of the hammer to planish out the forging marks and smooth the surface.
4. Bend the sides symmetrically over a small rawhide mallet, and forge the ends down to long, thin tapers (Figs. 371, 372). In this operation, the cross peen is worked across the width and on all sides of the rod, with blows becoming heavier toward the tips. Smooth out the tapers by planishing with the flat face of the hammer.
5. Now place the bracelet on the horn of the anvil, and forge out the flaring sides or "ears" in a plane perpendicular to the top (Fig. 373).
6. If irregularities remain, shape and true up the bracelet on the stump with a rawhide or wooden mallet (Fig. 374).
7. If forging has been done carefully and symmetrically, only a little filing should be required to smooth the edges. Use a No. 2-cut file first and finish with a No. 6-cut file.
8. Polish the work with tripoli on a 6-inch-diameter muslin buff. Begin by holding the piece at right angles to the plane of the wheel and move it

369–375. Sequence of steps in forging a bracelet, demonstrated by Chuck Evans.

369. Cross-peen forging hammer, and a rod of sterling silver 7 inches long and $\frac{1}{4}$-inch square in section.

370. Parallel strokes of the hammer spread the middle of the rod outward to shape the wide top of the bracelet.

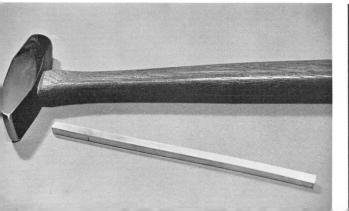

371. The sides of the bar are bent down symmetrically and drawn out to long tapers by forging all sides.

372. With one end forged and planished to a long taper, work proceeds on the other end.

373. The flaring sides of the bracelet are widened by forging over the gentle curve of the anvil's horn.

374. Forging completed. The work is then filed, emeried, and buffed before the tapered ends are bent into spirals.

from one end to the other, bearing down hard. Then rotate the piece 180 degrees to come at it from the opposite direction. Do the same for all surfaces, wipe off the excess tripoli, and, if desired, add surface texturing with the half-round bastard file.

9. Stamp your name or hallmark and the quality of the silver on the underside (**B.1**), and polish again on the loose muslin buff. Use clean, white cotton gloves to hold the piece for this final polish.

10. Finally, after all polishing, take a pair of round-nose pliers and carefully bend the tapered ends into spirals (Fig. 375).

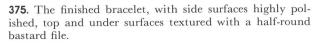

375. The finished bracelet, with side surfaces highly polished, top and under surfaces textured with a half-round bastard file.

376–378. Forging a tie clip.

right: 376. A 2½-inch length of 8-gauge sterling wire is hammered into shape on the T-stake.

below: 377. Forged, polished, and stamped, the piece is ready to be bent into final shape.

below right: 378. Completed tie clip.

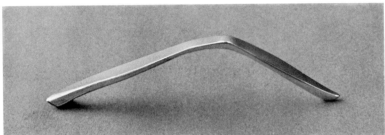

A tie clip can be made by forging a piece of 8-gauge sterling wire. A piece of wire about 2½ inches long is flattened down at one end (Fig. 376). The unhammered length is bent over the edge of the T-stake and flattened by planishing. The entire piece is then shaped and made symmetrical by filing, and then finished. A double bend is made with the round-nose pliers. The back is stamped with the sterling stamp and the jeweler's hallmark and then cut to length and polished (Fig. 377). The final shaping is made with the round-nose pliers, and the clip is given its final spring (Fig. 378). A large number of variations can be made with this shape of clip.

13.4

Hot Forging   Hot forging is the forging of heated metal. Usually a kiln is set at a temperature that will keep a metal blank at a very low, red heat. Sometimes a small metal canopy, open at the front end, is set over a gas burner. The forging blanks are set on an iron screen over the burner and heated to a very low red heat. The blank is seized by a pair of square-nose tongs (a variety of blacksmith tongs is best), and the forging is done on a suitable anvil. Hot forging is most often used for handcrafted flatware, because the pieces require a wide variation of thickness as well as width. Blanks heated to a low red heat are easily "upset." The term *upsetting* means increasing the thickness and reducing the width of the metal by hammering on its edges.

13.5

Planishing   Planishing is the process of smoothing the surface of metal by beating down its hills and bumps with a planishing hammer, which has a flat face on one end and a slightly crowned face on the other (Fig. 363). Planishing also thins the metal. The faces of the planishing hammer should be kept highly polished and protected from moisture, nicks, and scratches. Every nick or scratch in the face of this hammer will put a corresponding mark in the metal. Many jewelers make little copper caps to snap over the faces of their planishing hammers for protection. What is true of the planishing hammer is true for all hammers that are applied to metal. Never use the planishing hammer for anything but planishing. Keep a bit of crocus cloth handy to polish the hammer faces each time they are used. Polish the faces on the tripoli and rouge buffs occasionally.

A general rule for planishing is to keep the blows lighter than in forging and as even as possible. The blows should overlap slightly and go from the middle to the outer part of the work. Properly planished metal surfaces require no further polishing, but if there are any indentations left in the metal after you have finished, sanding on the wheel will remove them.

13.6

Stakes and Anvils   Almost all hammering is done on some sort of anvil or stake (Fig. 379). The jeweler usually has one or two small bench anvils on which to do general hammering work, as well as one or two stakes that are kept highly polished and free from nicks, on which it is possible to forge or planish work without marring the underside. The T-stake is generally one of the most useful stakes for both silversmiths and jewelers. It should be considered as basic equipment, and stakes of other sizes and shapes can be added to the collection as specific needs arise.

13.7

Form for Forging and Planishing   The main problem of hammering is that of control. Complete control can be achieved by the development of a proper form, and form can be learned by careful observation of the following general guidelines:

- Adjust the height of the stake or anvil so that, when the hammer face is resting in a plane normal to the surface of the stake, your forearm is in a natural and horizontal position. This allows you to take a relaxed posture that you could hold all day if necessary.
- Stand or sit so that your right shoulder, arm, and hammer are in line with the stake. (Left-handed craftsmen will adjust their positions appropriately.)
- Set your upper arm against your side, and do not move from that position except to alter the relationship of the hammer face to the anvil.
- Be sure that the metal is always parallel to the anvil before striking. If the metal is not resting firmly on the support, it will twist in your fingers or give a hollow sound when struck.
- Grasp the hammer firmly, but not tensely, at the end of the handle. Do not hold the hammer close to the head and push the hammer head up and down. *Swing* the hammer head up and down.
- Use your wrist, not your elbow, as the pivot of your hammer swing. Do not try to strike extremely heavy blows, but allow the weight of the hammer head to do the work, accelerating the downward fall of the head with a slight snap of the wrist.
- Pick up the hammer head on its bounce after striking the metal.
- The force of the blow will vary with the distance the hammer head travels. For a light blow, swing with a short arc. For heavy blows, use a longer arc. For a hammer head of a given weight, the rate of hammer blows will vary with the arc of travel. The force can therefore be controlled by controlling the length of the arc. You do not need great strength.
- Pay attention to the angle between the hammer face and the anvil. To change this angle, you either twist your forearm slightly or shift the position of your arm and shoulder to another set position.
- Do not thin out the edges of a piece too much. From both a structural and a design point of view, the edges are best left a little thick instead of being tapered to a fine edge.

With practice you will develop a feeling for position, and these rules will become incorporated by habit.

379. A variety of anvil heads, mushroom stakes, and T-stakes.

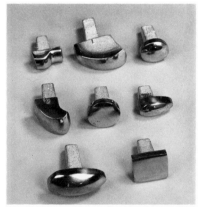

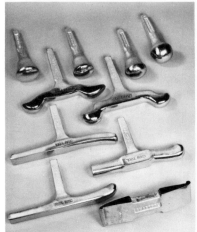

Chasing   Although it is treated here as one of the hammering processes, chasing can be considered in two other ways. It is very often used in conjunction with repoussé (**11.16–17**). The chasing hammer, together with chasing or repoussé tools, is then applied to the underside of metal to produce a low-relief design on the outer surface (Fig. 380). Chasing also serves as a direct method of surface texturing (Fig. 381), for which a great variety of chasing punches are available. However, since hammering skill is an essential prerequisite for successful chasing, the process will be discussed here. The skill involved is slightly different from forging and planishing, and a wider range of tools is needed to do the work (Fig. 382).

Chasing is usually done on sheet metal prior to any other construction or soldering operations. The sheet of metal is placed on a chasing plate—a soft iron plate of any reasonable dimensions and about 1 inch (25.4 mm) thick. The plate is provided with clamps that can be screwed down to hold the sheet metal in place during chasing or texturing operations. Note that in Figure 386 the clamp is bound with a copper strip to protect the surface of the sheet being chased.

Chasing tools are specifically designed for making marks in metal. The chasing hammer with its broad, flat face is standard equipment, and a wide variety of punches are necessary or useful. These punches are commonly available from suppliers (**B.8**), or they can be made by the jeweler (**22.13**). The large, rather heavy sizes serve for chasing bronze and sterling, the more delicate sizes for goldwork. However, because the working ends of these tools are often unsatisfactory, and because chasing demands such a large quantity of different punches, it is a good idea for the jeweler to learn to make them (see Chap. 22). Commercially made punches are spikelike tools, generally about 5 inches long, wider in the middle for easy gripping and tapered toward the ends, with a working point $\frac{1}{8}$ to $\frac{1}{4}$ inch wide and a broad head for

below: 380. Richard Mafong and Jon Eric Riis. *Sarcophagus,* of raised, repoussé, and chased sterling, with tapestry-woven metallic threads, c. 1973.

below right: 381. John Marshall. Chased and repoussé pendant, granulated with gold chips.

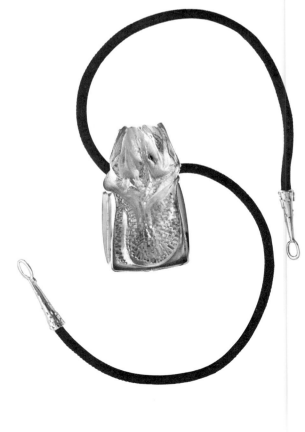

hammering. There are four standard kinds: tracers or liners for defining lines; rectangular or rounded planishers for smoothing the surface; background, or matting, punches for texturing background areas with fine designs; dapping and hollow, or ring, punches for making spherical marks. The dapping punch pushes the metal into a hemisphere from the back, and the hollow punch completes the shaping process from the front surface. Professional jewelers use dozens of these punches, purchasing or making them as each project requires.

13.9

Form for Chasing   Chasing requires the development of a certain form, which can be mastered by the observance of the following rules:

■ Hold the chasing tool firmly, but not tightly, in the left hand (Fig. 383), or the right hand if you are left-handed. Notice that the little finger rests on the surface of the sheet. The other three fingers are spread along the tool, one finger near the top, one in the middle, and one near the bottom. The tool is tilted back slightly, away from the direction you wish to move, but its sides are in a vertical plane.

■ Using a chasing hammer or a small ball-peen hammer, strike the upper end of the tool with steady, continuous light blows.

■ As each blow strikes the tool, it will be driven into the metal, and, if the angle is adjusted correctly, it will also move along the surface.

■ The impressions in the metal help to hold the point of the tool in line as it moves along.

■ Straight lines should be chased with a straight liner. All but very flat curves must be chased with a curved liner. Flat curves can be made by gradually rotating the straight liner as you move the tool along.

■ Do not expect too much from yourself at first. Chasing is a delicate technique and requires much practice. Skill will increase in relation to time spent.

■ When striking with the hammer, remember that the face of the hammer must always be held in normal relationship to the axis of the tool; otherwise, each blow will deflect the tool out of line and the force of the blow will be lost. When hammer and tool are held in proper alignment, the force of the blow goes directly into the metal.

The striking of all punches, as well as chasing and repoussé tools, should be done with a chasing hammer or a ball-peen hammer. Never use the planishing hammer for this purpose, because this will mar the polished face of the hammer. Punches with a large surface area may require a heavy ball-peen hammer.

As a variation, chased lines and textures can be inlaid by filling the depressions with solder and then filing off the surface.

13.10

Tool Texturing   A tooled texture results from massing tool marks closely enough together over an area to create a visual effect richer than that produced by single tool marks (Fig. 384). Every tool makes its own mark on metal. You can explore the possibilities of new textures when a new tool comes to hand. Experiment with the characteristic marks of each tool on scraps of copper. Try methods of handling the tool that go beyond the obvious and normal usages. For instance, the edge of the hammer makes a mark normally avoided in planishing. Perhaps it could be used in an unusual way for textural effects. The teeth of an old file might be hammered into the surface of metal. A rasp could give just the right quality of texture for some particular piece. These experiments, of course, should always be carried out with regard for

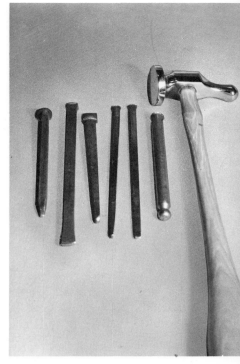

above: 382. Chasing hammer and punches.

below: 383. The chasing tool tipped slightly for hammering.

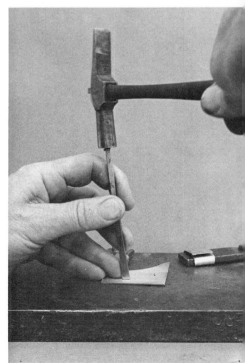

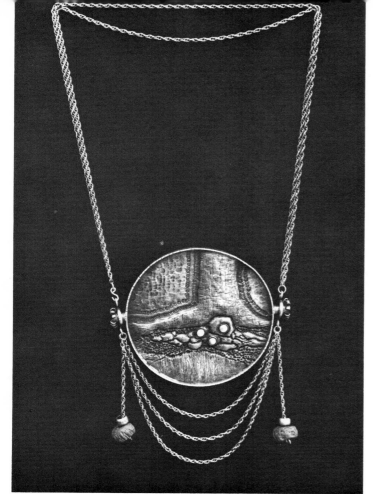

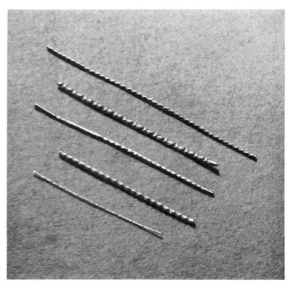

left: 384. Anne Echelman. Pendant of repoussé copper and silver, with chased textures, 1972.

above: 385. Examples of gallery wire, created by stamping stock wire with various punches.

below left: 386. Example of a border stamped on a sheet of sterling, clamped in the chasing plate.

below: 387. Egyptian gold collar, constructed from stamped units, with inlays of carnelian and feldspar; from Thebes, c. 1500–1450 B.C. (18th Dynasty). Metropolitan Museum of Art, New York (Purchase, 1926).

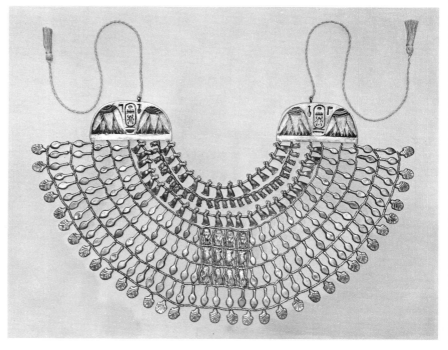

the safe use and proper care of the tools. For example, files are brittle and will break under the force of a sharp blow, so good files should not be used in such experiments.

13.11

Form for Chasing-Tool Texturing   When areas must be closely covered with chasing-tool marks, a method slightly different from standard chasing form yields the best results:

- Hold the tool with the same firm grasp, with the little finger on the metal sheet, but keep the tool slightly above the surface of the metal.
- Strike the tool with the hammer to drive the point into the surface of the metal, but lift it out each time the hammer rises.

This method increases the rapidity with which an area can be textured, since it eliminates two additional motions: that of placing the tool in each new position and that of removing the tool afterwards. The method also allows a flexible movement of the tool over the surface and permits it to be rotated between the fingers in order to create varying effects.

13.12

Stamping Sheet Metal and Gallery Wire   Areas of sheet metal or the surface of wire (Fig. 385) can be enriched by stamping with punches made especially for that purpose (**22.14**). The mark of a stamp or punch can serve as a border or create a textural area. Experiment with punch marks on a thick sheet of lead or aluminum. Try rotating the punch 90 or 180 degrees with every blow or every other blow. Try all the positional relationships to see whether more interesting patterns arise. When punch marks are grouped, you will discover that the area between the punch marks becomes a significant design pattern. Explore the possibilities of such reserved areas.

If a sheet of sterling is to be stamped, clamp it in the chasing plate so that one side or part of the area is accessible. When you want a border, scribe a light line along the edge with dividers, and carefully position the punch each time. It is important to keep the punch marks straight along the guideline and evenly spaced (Fig. 386).

Two observations will be of use to the beginner. First, punch marks will be sharp and deep if the gauge of the metal is fairly thick—16-gauge, at least, and preferably 14-gauge or thicker. Second, punch marks will be sharp and deep if the face of the punch is fairly small in area. Much early jewelry was made by stamping completely through the metal to create multiple units of the same form (Fig. 387). A punch face that is $\frac{1}{4}$-inch square will probably fail to make more than a small imprint on a piece of 18-gauge silver, even with a heavy hammer. A punch face $\frac{1}{8}$-inch square, more or less, should make a satisfactory mark in 16-gauge sheet. The weight of the hammer head is important in attaining good imprints. A little experience will provide a basis for judgment.

Gallery wire can be made by stamping nonferrous wire with any punch or chasing tool. Punches especially made for the purpose will give the most interesting effects. The punch face should be as wide as the wire, or wider. If a groove is filed across the punch face before the pattern is filed, the punch will stay on the wire in a constant position. It is useful to planish your length of wire so that it is slightly flat along the top edge; this will help prevent the wire from rolling as it is stamped. Stamping should begin at the end clamped in the chasing plate and proceed in a direction away from you, so that the preceding mark is visible for positioning the next punch mark.

Gallery wire can be used as a border around a high bezel, around a shape, or in combination with plain wire for a ring.

Casting

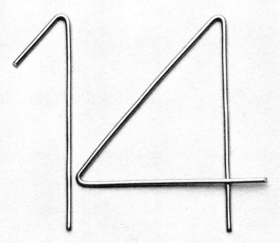

Casting is the process of pouring molten metal into a mold that has been fashioned to a predetermined form. It is one of the major techniques of working metal, as well as one of the oldest. No doubt it arose out of the earliest discovery of smelting metals, which seems to have occurred independently in various cultures of the Old and New Worlds.

Because metal melts at relatively high temperatures, special equipment is needed to hold it during melting—a container or crucible that can withstand the high heat without cracking or breaking apart. The fire must be concentrated around the crucible and raised to approximately 2000° F. Once both of these problems had been solved by ancient metalworkers, casting became possible. In primitive times crucibles were made of clay or loam mixed with roughly ground charcoal and organic matter such as straw. When baked, this material became *refractory*—that is, able to withstand high temperatures without cracking. Although much early casting was done in steatite molds, just as the Navajo still do today, many early cultures made lost-wax molds of clay and charcoal.

Today a graphite crucible is usually used in the melting furnace, while the hand crucible is made of a ceramic material. Modern technology has made possible a variety of methods of making molds for one-time use and for casting the same pattern many times over (Fig. 388). Some of the major improvements in casting methods arose from the need for better dentures; jewelry is cast in the same way that precious metals are formed into precisely fitting dentures.

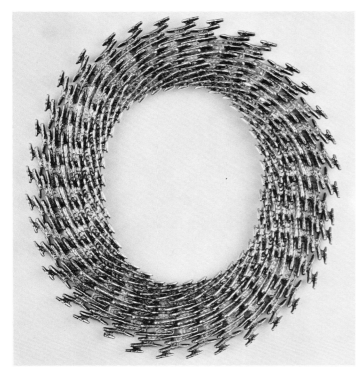

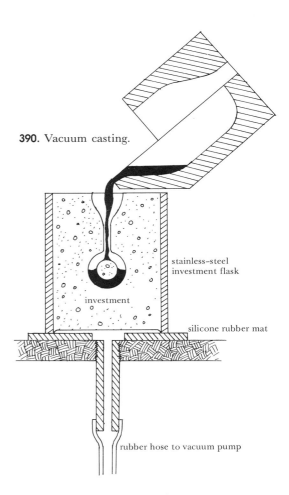

left: 388. Anthony Hawksley. Gold-plated silver collar, centrifugal-cast from a cuttlebone mold formed by 38 impressions of a single motif, 1973.

below left: 389. Centrifugal casting machine.

390. Vacuum casting.

stainless–steel
investment flask

investment

silicone rubber mat

rubber hose to vacuum pump

Casting Methods

In the jewelry shop of today a number of different ways of casting can be used. If classified according to the method of pouring the molten metal into the mold, there are four ways of casting:

■ *gravity casting,* in which the molten metal is drawn into the mold by gravity; that is, the metal is poured by hand into the mold.

■ *centrifugal casting,* which throws the molten metal into the mold by centrifugal force (Fig. 389).

■ *vacuum casting,* in which a vacuum at the base of the mold draws air and gas out of and molten metal into the mold (Fig. 390). This is usually combined with one of the other methods of pouring.

■ *pressure casting,* in which air or steam is applied at the sprue of the investment to force the molten metal into the investment cavity.

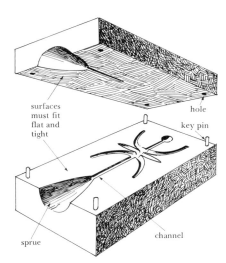

above: **391.** Open stone mold, showing pattern, channel, sprue, and key pins.

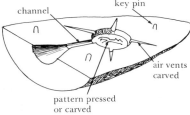

392. Cuttlebone mold, shown open (*above*) and wired to a charcoal-block crucible (*below*).

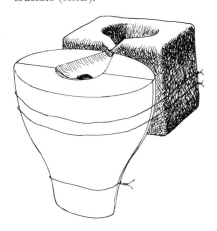

If the methods of casting are classified according to the type of mold, there are at least six ways of casting:

- *stone mold,* which uses gravity casting
- *cuttlebone mold,* also gravity casting
- *plaster mold,* gravity casting
- *charcoal mold,* gravity casting
- *sand mold,* gravity casting
- *investment mold,* which utilizes gravity or centrifugal casting, with or without vacuum casting

Sand casting using hand pouring, and investment-mold casting by means of gravity or centrifugal force, are the major methods of casting jewelry, and they will be described in detail in the sections to follow. This does not mean, however, that other methods might not offer interesting design possibilities for the contemporary jeweler—particularly if expensive casting equipment is lacking. For this reason all the methods will be discussed.

14.1

Steatite or Stone-Mold Casting   No method should be automatically excluded from consideration simply because it is traditional and relies on painstaking handwork. The Navajo have done some exquisite bracelets and buckles cast in stone molds, and there is nothing to prevent the contemporary jeweler from exploring the possibilities of chiseling and carving out designs in steatite. The mold is made of two halves (Fig. 391). The pattern, the pouring channel running to it, and the sprue are carved in the lower half. The other half of the sprue is carved in the upper half of the mold, which must be keyed to the lower half by drilling matching holes in each half for key pins.

14.2

Cuttlebone-Mold Casting   Cuttlebone is a traditional mold material made of the dried shell of a squidlike mollusk. It takes very fine impressions and is used for casting duplicates of small jewelry items, such as emblems, or even rings having no *undercuts* (projections outward from the parting line). The precise detail that can be reproduced is almost unbelievable. Cuttlebone can be purchased in jewelry supply houses in sizes from 4 to 9 inches long.

To make the mold, take the two halves of the cuttlebone, and file each half flat on one side with a coarse file or sandpaper until the filed sides fit together evenly and perfectly. Saw one end flat so the mold can be up-ended later when the molten metal is poured in (Fig. 392). Now trim the two sides so that they are identical, and make metal pins from heavy wire to hold the sides together during casting. To do this, cut three pieces of wire, about 8 gauge, to an appropriate length, and press them into one of the bones at the three corners. Then take whatever metal pattern you want to reproduce, and press it into the center of the same bone where the thickness is greatest. Place the upper bone over the lower one and squeeze the two together gently but firmly. The pattern presses into each half of the mold, and the key pins press into the upper mold. Carefully separate the bones and delicately remove the pattern. Cut a small channel from the pattern impression up to the flat end of the lower mold, and at this top end carve out half of the sprue. Knife cuts around the impression can serve as air vents, when necessary. Align the upper mold over the lower mold by the key pins, and mark the position of the half-sprue on the upper mold. Separate the parts again, and carve the other half of the sprue into the upper mold.

Check the pattern cavity and channels to be sure they are clean. Fit the two halves together and fasten with tape or wire. Now carve a piece of charcoal to fit snugly against the upended mold, and carve a cavity into the

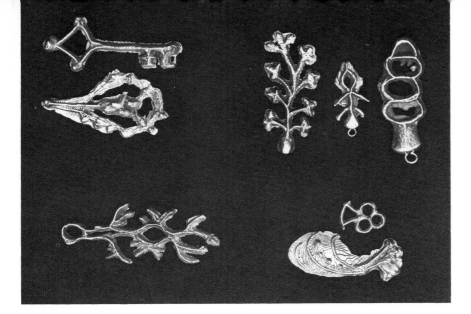

393. **Max Weaver.** Yellow-bronze pendants, cast from directly carved cuttlebone molds, 1975.

top with a small channel running over and into the sprue in the cuttlebone (Fig. 392). This piece of charcoal is wired to the mold in such a position that the metal, placed in the cavity and melted, will run into the sprue when the mold is tilted. This charcoal, then, becomes the crucible, and the process of melting the metal and pouring it into the mold is facilitated.

Cuttlebone can also be carved directly, and the rippled natural texture of the bone can be brought out by brushing the carved impression with a soft bristle brush (Fig. 393).

14.3

Plaster-Mold Casting   For the plaster mold two halves must be prepared, with the pattern centered at the parting line. To begin the mold, embed the pattern halfway into the center of a small, smooth pad of water clay or Plasticine. Build a wall of clay around the pad, perhaps an inch higher than the top of the pattern. Pour into this a smooth, creamy mixture of plaster, made by sifting powdered plaster into a small pan of water. If the mold within the clay wall is about 2 inches in diameter, about $\frac{1}{2}$ cup of water should be sufficient to mix enough plaster to a creamy mixture. The plaster must be thin enough to flow around the details of the pattern.

After the lower half of the mold has set—at least four hours later—the clay can be removed from the plaster. Trim the surface if necessary, and coat with a mixture of shellac and alcohol in equal proportions. After the shellac has dried, paint the surface with a mixture of equal parts of stearic acid and kerosene. (Melt the stearic acid in a small pan on a hot plate.) This coating will keep the plaster of the second half of the mold from sticking to the first. Prepare the second half in the same way as the first but with the other half of the pattern. Be sure that the two halves of the mold fit together evenly.

Place your mold on the table, with the pattern in it, and build a clay wall around it. Then pour plaster over the mold and flush with the top of the clay wall. If available, a vacuum pump (Fig. 394) can be used each time to remove air bubbles from the plaster in the mixing bowl just before it is poured. After the mold has set, separate the two parts gently, and remove the pattern. Shellac the mold on the joining surfaces but not in the pattern cavity. Now cut a channel in one half and a sprue in both halves, as for stone molds (**14.1**).

Plaster molds can be used only for casting metals with low melting points, such as pewter with its melting point at 400° F. Molten lead, with a melting

394. Vacuum pump.

point at about 620° F., will usually crack a plaster mold. One precaution must be observed if molten metal is to be poured into the plaster mold. *The mold must be completely dry.* A wet plaster mold will explode molten metal dangerously. Therefore, either bake the mold in an oven or allow it to dry for several days before casting with it.

14.4

Charcoal-Mold Casting   Charcoal-mold casting is similar in method to stone-mold casting, except that charcoal is much softer and therefore easier to carve. The only real technical difficulty is that it may chip out along the grain, but this often adds crisp textural patterns, which are all the more interesting for being accidental. The aesthetic virtue of working the mold itself rather than a wax model is that characteristic textures emerge that are unlikely to emerge from wax. Forms can also be carved in charcoal and then used as patterns for rubber-mold duplication (**14.8**).

A word or two should be said about the charcoal block. Since it will crack apart under heat, it is wise to take a length of 16-gauge iron binding wire, wrap it around the block, and twist the ends tightly together. Then take a pair of square-nose pliers and twist a kink on each side of the block to tighten the wire. This will extend the life of the block considerably and will even hold the block together should it crack apart.

It is important that the two blocks of a charcoal mold be flat and smooth, so that they fit together tightly when wired together for casting. The fastest way to ensure a tight join is to place a sheet of coarse sandpaper on a flat surface and carefully sand the surface of each block until perfectly flat. Check them for fit. If they are not absolutely flat, your molten metal will run out. As shown in Figures 395 and 397, the channel and the pattern are both carved

395–398. Casting a pendant in a charcoal mold.

above: 395. Charcoal mold, with pattern and channel carved in one block only.

above right: 396. Pouring molten silver into the charcoal mold.

right: 397. Open charcoal mold, with casting formed in the carved block.

into one block only. The pattern is carved into the lower part of this block so that the sprue can be as long as possible. This will give the greatest momentum to the flowing metal and force it fully into the pattern. The other block is left plain except for a matching sprue-half.

If a fully rounded form is desired, the carved block may be pressed onto a flat layer of talcum powder until the joining surface is smoothly covered, leaving the carved form cleanly black. This block must be keyed to the upper block and pressed against it to make a talc imprint, which will locate the pattern and channel on the uncarved block. This may then be carved to match the lower block. Keys made of round sterling beads about $\frac{1}{8}$ inch in diameter, or of 6-gauge silver posts, are set in holes drilled into the blocks.

After the pattern is completed, the blocks are wired together and the metal is poured from a hand crucible (Fig. 396). When the metal has cooled somewhat, the mold is opened (Fig. 397) and the casting extracted. After pickling and finishing, the piece is complete (Fig. 398).

14.5

Sand Casting   Sand casting is a simple method that uses a minimum of equipment to make small, uncomplicated pieces of jewelry (Figs. 399, 400). In this process, a pattern is set into a two-part mold, with half the pattern pressed into each side to form the impression. When the impression has been made, the mold is opened, the pattern is removed, the mold is clamped shut again, and the metal is poured in. The pattern should not have any undercuts; you should be able to lift the model out of the sand without disturbing the sand. The description below applies to casting a ring, which is about as complex as the sand-casting procedure becomes. If you know how to cast a ring, you can adapt the method to any simple piece.

The materials for sand-casting a ring are:
- *casting sand*—a fine sand with roughly the consistency of clay that is specially formulated and is sold in supply houses. It is generally mixed with glycerine. Test for moistness by squeezing a handful. The sand should retain the print of your fingers without oozing or cracking.
- *casting flask*—a rectangular metal frame, without top or bottom, that separates into two halves. The top part, the *cope,* has projections on the sides with holes, into which fit two metal pins. The bottom part, the *drag,* has pins that fit into the cope and hold the frame together.
- *parting powder*—a special powder that is dusted around the pattern to prevent it from sticking to the sand.
- a *sieve* for sifting the sand onto the pattern.
- *pattern*—a model of metal, hard wax (such as File-Wax), plastic, or almost any other material with smooth, polished surfaces, which is pressed into the sand to form the impression into which molten metal will be poured. The finished casting is always slightly smaller (about 10 percent) than the pattern.
- *crucible*—a ceramic flask for holding the molten metal.
- *jeweler's torch* for melting the metal in the crucible.
- *metal* for casting. This can be filings or small scrap.
- *flux* (borax) for mixing with the metal to be cast.
- two wooden *ring mandrels,* each the same length—about 2 inches—and the exact diameter of the model ring. Saw one mandrel in half to make a half-round mandrel. These support the *ring model* in the mold.
- a piece of *metal tubing* of the same length and *inside* diameter as the ring mandrels.
- two smooth rectangular *boards,* just a little larger all around than the casting flask.

398. Completed pendant.

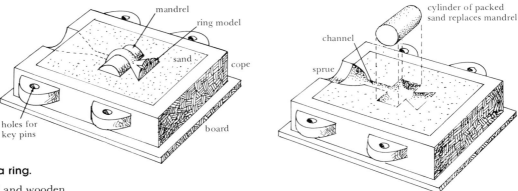

399–400. Sand-casting a ring.

left: 399. The ring model and wooden mandrel are sunk halfway into the sand, which has been leveled flush with the sides of the cope.

right: 400. After the ring model has been removed, channel and sprue are carved, and the mandrel is replaced by a cylinder of casting sand.

The procedure for sand-casting a ring is as follows:

1. Center the cope with hole projections downward on the board, and place the half-round mandrel, flat side down, horizontally in the center of the cope.
2. Sieve the sand onto the mandrel until it is covered. Then gently pack more sand around it and around the rest of the cope, using another mandrel or similar rod to tamp it down very firmly. Take the other board and run the edge over the surface of the sand to smooth off the excess from the flask.
3. Place this board on top of the flask, and invert the flask so that the bottom board is now on top. Remove it. You will see the half-round mandrel.
4. Carefully remove the mandrel without disturbing its impression.
5. Slide the ring model onto the round mandrel. Press mandrel and ring onto the spot where the half-round mandrel was (Fig. 399).
6. Sprinkle the parting powder thoroughly over the ring, mandrel, and surface of the sand.
7. Set the drag onto the cope, and fit the pins into place.
8. Sieve sand over the ring and mandrel until they are covered, and then overfill the drag, tamping down firmly as before. Using the edge of the board, smooth off the excess sand.
9. Place the board on top of the drag, invert the mold, and gently separate the two halves of the mold. The parting powder will make the two halves come apart easily.
10. Remove the mandrel and ring from the sand.
11. Using any pointed tool, carve a channel from the sprue at the upper end of the flask to the ring impression. Carve another passage from the ring impression to the surface of the sand at any point between the cavity and the sprue. This is called a riser and will allow gases to escape during the pouring. Blow excess sand away.
12. Pack the hollow metal tube full of sand. Ease the core of sand out, and fit it into the impression left by the ring mandrel (Fig. 400).
13. Fit the two halves of the flask back together. Replace the two boards, one above and one below. Using two C-clamps or binding wire, sandwich the boards and flask together firmly. Stand the apparatus with sprue-end up for casting.
14. Follow the general procedure for melting and pouring the metal into the sprue (**14.6**). Allow the mold to cool for about half an hour before separating the halves of the flask. The casting can then be lifted out to cool at room temperature.
15. Clean and pickle the casting, then cut and file away the projections formed by the sprue and riser, and finish those surfaces.
16. Store the sand in a tightly closed container for re-use.

Procedures for Casting Metal

14.6

Melting and Pouring Metal   All of the preceding methods of casting have one thing in common: the metal used in the casting is melted and poured by hand. The following discussion will help you to handle molten metal in a more efficient manner.

Smaller pieces of metal can be melted in a ceramic hand crucible supported on an annealing pan. The oxygen-gas torch best serves the purpose, because it gets hotter than the air-gas torch. Two rules should be observed when nonferrous metals are melted to a molten state:

1. *The metal should not be overheated.* Overheating bronze or brass will vaporize the zinc content, thus changing the characteristics of the metal. Overheating silver or gold will increase the absorption of oxygen, thus making the metal more porous than necessary.
2. The flame used to melt the metal should be a reducing (or nonoxidizing) flame if a hand crucible is used. An oxidizing flame is one with an excess of oxygen (**10.2**). Such a flame, if played over the surface of nonferrous metal, will greatly increase the absorption of oxygen, and the cast metal will be full of small pits and pinholes. A reducing flame is yellowish in color.

Melting can also be done in a graphite crucible in a small melting furnace. In Cellini's time (Fig. 56) it was the practice to cover the surface of the metal with a layer of charcoal to seal off the air's oxygen. In bronze casting today, the practice is to throw a handful of a chemical called *phos* into the crucible and stir it well just prior to pouring, as a means of eliminating absorbed oxygen.

401. Melting metal in the hand crucible.

When melting metal in the hand crucible, a large, feathery flame, in which the bright blue cone of gas has not been brought to sharp definition, will give a nonoxidizing melt. The flame should be pointed into the crucible at a low angle, so that the front pouring lip is heated at the same time as the metal (Fig. 401). As the metal scraps melt, the surfaces become oxidized, and this prevents the metal from flowing together. To counteract this, $\frac{1}{2}$ teaspoon of borax should be added to a new crucible as a fluxing agent. For later meltings, a pinch of borax should be added if necessary.

When the proper melting temperature approaches, nonferrous metals draw together into a liquid pool in the crucible, with a slightly convex surface that becomes brilliantly mirrorlike. As this condition is reached, the crucible

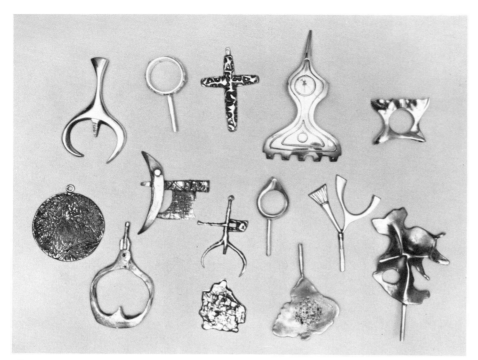

402. Metal patterns with sprues attached.

should be rocked gently in order to stir up the metal and ensure an even mixture of even temperature. When the metal is liquid and well mixed, the flame should be specially directed to the pouring lip, so that it will become glowing hot. The pour must be made with the flame playing on the pouring lip, as well as on the metal, until the last moment. Care must be taken to position the crucible properly, so that once it is tipped, the molten metal will flow continuously into the mold. Any excess of flux at the pouring lip should be scraped away with an iron rod just before pouring, so that the flux will not run into the mold. This is true also for the graphite crucible.

Once started, the pour must be uninterrupted, so that a continuous flow of metal runs into the mold. A large investment mold should be supported by a steel shell, embedded in a box of loam (not sand), or buried in the ground up to its neck, so that molten metal will not leak through cracks or break the mold apart by its pressure.

Safety precautions should be observed whenever molten metal is handled. Large pours should be made close to the ground; safety goggles, shoes, gloves, and aprons should be worn. Small pours can be made at table height but should be done over an annealing pan in case of spilling. If a centrifugal casting machine is used, it should be installed in a countersunk box below the surface of the counter, or a sheet-metal shield should be installed around it.

14.7

Making Patterns for Casting   Jewelry patterns for casting are usually made of metal, although many other materials can be used under special circumstances. Patterns for sand casting might be made of metal, plastic, wood, paper, or even wax. Wood patterns should be sanded, shellacked, and polished with steel wool to provide a sufficiently smooth surface.

Patterns for lost-wax casting (**14.14–20**) are made directly in wax by some jewelers (**14.13**). The wax pattern is invested and cast in metal, and the casting is then either finished as a final piece of jewelry or prepared as a metal pattern (Fig. 402) for making a rubber mold, as described below (**14.8**). Otherwise, patterns for lost-wax casting are generally made of metal. Silver is most often used for sterling or gold jewelry, but sometimes tin is used because it works more easily. A metal pattern should always be made about 10 percent (or more) larger than the desired final size to compensate for the shrinkage that takes place. Because of its softness, sterling jewelry should be made somewhat more massive than gold jewelry. Prongs, particularly, and ring shanks should always be made larger for both gold and silver in order to allow for filing and finishing. When the pattern is finished, a sprue channel of 8-gauge sterling wire should be soldered to the pattern at a point from which (1) it can most conveniently be removed from the cast piece, or (2) the molten metal will most logically flow into the entire pattern. Patterns should never be designed so that the metal must flow backward from the sprue channel in order to fill the mold (Fig. 403). If this situation cannot be avoided, a separate channel must be led directly to the inaccessible areas.

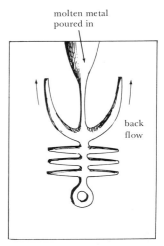

molten metal poured in

back flow

403. Example of a pattern to be avoided because of the backward flow of metal that it would require.

Wax Patterns

Since the casting technique most widely used today is the lost-wax method, in which a wax pattern of the object to be cast is melted away and replaced by molten metal, ways of making wax patterns will now be presented. If many pieces of the same design are needed, as for example in a commercial operation, the most efficient way of producing them is to make a rubber mold. With this mold any number of patterns can be produced. If only a single copy of the design is wanted, a piece of special hard wax (called File-Wax) can be carved to specifications, or a piece of softer wax can be modeled by hand or with the aid of a heated tool (**14.10**).

14.8

The Rubber Mold   A metal jewelry pattern can be used to make a rubber mold in which wax patterns can be formed. These wax patterns are then invested in a casting flask (**14.16**).

The rubber mold is made in an aluminum vulcanizing frame. The vulcanizing frame consists of two pieces, similar to the sand-casting flask but much smaller. At one end of the frame is a small hole into which the sprue is set in order to suspend the pattern at the center of the frame (Fig. 404). The length of the sprue channel may need to be adjusted in order to place the pattern at the center of the frame.

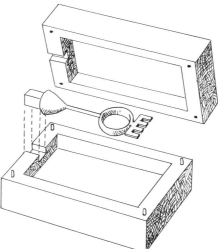

404. Pattern set into the vulcanizing frame for making a rubber mold.

There are two methods of making a rubber mold. To prepare the mold by the first method, fill the lower part of the frame with Plasticine so that the pattern is half embedded along a logical parting line. Then place the upper frame in position and pour in plaster to fill the upper frame. After the plaster has set, clean out the lower frame and the plaster around the pattern if necessary. Carve two or four small depressions into the plaster to serve as keys. Turn the mold over so that the plaster and the pattern are in the bottom frame. Then fill the upper frame with sheets of heavy mold rubber cut to fit snugly in the frame. Place the vulcanizing frame in the electric vulcanizing press (Fig. 405). Screw the upper press down tightly on the frame, and vulcanize the mold. The time of vulcanizing depends on the size of the mold; recommendations for times come with the vulcanizer.

After the rubber has been vulcanized, remove and open the frame, remove the plaster from the lower half of the frame, sprinkle the surface of the rubber with talc, and place sheets of rubber in the upper half. Again, place the frame in the vulcanizing press, and vulcanize the other half of the mold. After vulcanizing, the two halves of the rubber mold can be removed from the frame and opened, then the pattern extracted. When cool, the mold is ready to use for casting a wax pattern.

The other way to make a rubber mold is a bit simpler. Place the metal pattern in the vulcanizing frame and fill both sides with rubber sheets cut to size. Then place the frame in the vulcanizer in the usual manner. After vulcanizing, remove the rubber mold from the frame. It is in one piece, however, and the pattern is embedded within. Use a very sharp knife, such as the Exacto knife, to cut the mold in half. This is somewhat complicated, for keys must be cut at all four corners as the mold is bisected along the sides. Begin cutting at the sprue channel, come down along the channel on one side, exactly on the center, then along the high edge of the pattern, all around, and up the other side of the sprue channel. When the mold is finally cut in half, the pattern can easily be removed. Undercuts are no problem with the rubber mold, which can be pulled and stretched somewhat to release undercut parts of the pattern.

405. Vulcanizing press.

<h2 style="text-align:center">14.9</h2>

Casting Wax Patterns in a Rubber Mold   There are two ways to cast wax patterns. The old way is to place the mold in a small rubber-mold frame, which supports the mold and prevents distortion. The frame is then put into a special centrifugal casting machine with an aluminum crucible (Fig. 406), which is used only for casting wax patterns. The machine is wound up on its spring, liquid wax from a wax pot is put into the crucible, and the arm of the machine is spun to throw the wax into the rubber mold. The crucible of the machine has to be kept warm to prevent the wax from cooling. This is usually done with a torch, between castings. After each casting of the pattern, the mold is removed from the machine and from the rubber-mold frame, and the wax pattern is extracted.

A newer method of casting wax patterns uses a wax pressure injector (Fig. 407). A cast-aluminum pot is electrically heated and thermostatically controlled to hold the wax at a constant temperature. The rubber mold is placed in a rubber-mold frame and then pressed against a nozzle; air pressure forces the wax into the mold. It is important to hold the wax at the lowest temperature that will keep it molten. If the wax is too hot, the mold becomes heated, and it then becomes more difficult to extract the wax patterns, since they do not cool sufficiently to solidify.

There are several kinds of casting wax available, each with its special qualities. A hard, brittle wax is more desirable for use with simple patterns that are easily removed from the rubber mold. Dark-green casting wax is quite

406. An electrically heated centrifugal casting machine.

407. Wax pressure injector.

brittle and casts well, but it will break easily. The light-green wax is tougher and less brittle. Blue casting wax is tough and somewhat flexible. Red wax is also an ideal casting wax. Fragile and complex patterns require a tough, less brittle wax.

Temperature and pressure are both extremely important factors. These waxes melt at anywhere from 90° to 165° F. Each wax must be held at its lowest possible molten temperature in order to avoid excessive expansion of the molten wax, which will in turn lead to excessive shrinking of the cooled wax pattern. Injection pressure, if excessive, will tend to bulge the wax pattern in the rubber mold. Optimum temperatures and pressures are always specified by the manufacturer.

14.10

Modeling Wax Patterns with a Heated Tool   A wax pattern, whether cast, carved, pressed, or modeled, is often completed with a small spatula, knife, or carver to shape and form it. These tools can be heated in a Bunsen burner for carving, cutting, or texturing action. Also available now are wax welders, which are adaptations of the electric soldering iron, with a small, electrically heated tip at the end of a light handpiece. This handpiece is wired to a box having a temperature regulator, on-off switch, and pilot light. The wax welder is more convenient to use than the spatula that requires constant reheating.

A ring pattern is made by pouring a wax sheet to a thickness of about 12 gauge and then cutting a strip of the correct width and length for a ring band. This is rolled around a thin brass tube. The size of the tube should be about size 6 for a woman's ring or size 10 for a man's (**C.19**). The rest of the ring is then built up on this band. It is useful to have a little pot of melted wax on hand for modeling. A special Bunsen burner on the market has a small pot for wax built into it.

When the wax pattern is finished, a short channel about $\frac{1}{8}$ inch in diameter is joined to it for attaching to the "tree" (**14.15**).

14.11

Carving Patterns in File-Wax   File-Wax is a very hard, brittle wax that can be sawed, filed, or cut. It is not sticky and does not clog a file but comes away in clean filings. The wax-filing method of designing rings has become extremely popular in recent years. Such rings are made by cutting a short cylinder of the appropriate thickness, drilling out the ring center to the proper ring size, and then shaping the form with saws and files. Very accurate surfaces and edges can be attained, and for this reason most File-Wax rings tend toward geometric forms. The sequence in Figures 408–415 illustrates the steps of the process.

File-Wax comes preformed in many kinds of ring shapes, which can be cut off in small slabs. It can also be procured in rods and bulk slabs. File-Wax is difficult to model, but it can be formed with a wax welder or heated spatula.

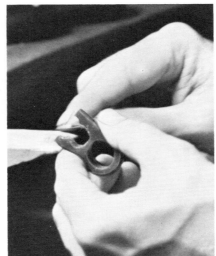

408–415. Procedure for casting a gold ring from File-Wax, as demonstrated by Olaf Skoogfors.

far left: 408. Filing out shape after sawing block and drilling finger hole.

left: 409. Cutting out the prongs, and further shaping.

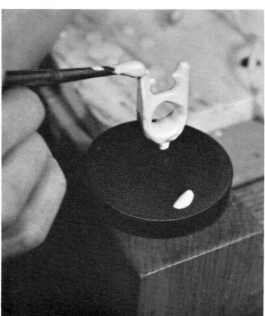

far left: 410. Painting on investment over a coating of debubblizer.

left: 411. Pouring investment into flask over ring model.

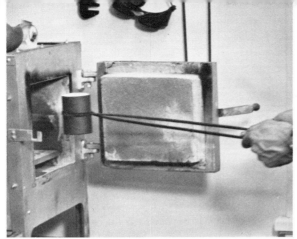

412. Inserting flask into kiln for burnout.

413. Melting 14k gold on centrifugal casting machine.

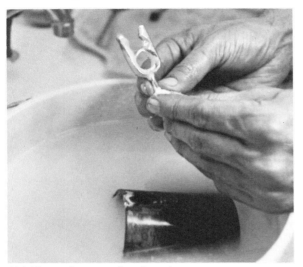

414. Removing cast ring from investment.

left: 415. Completed ring, with constructed gold "bearing" and a synthetic blue zircon.

below: 416. Alvin Pine. Pin of gold-plated sterling cast from a press mold.

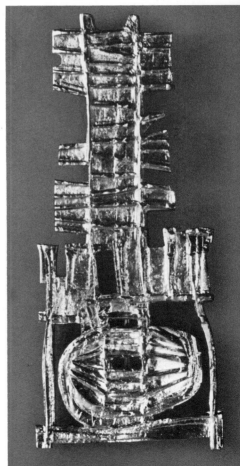

14.12

Press-Mold Wax Patterns   Taking a leaf from the potter's book of techniques, the metalworker can devise a *press mold* of lead, clay, or other impressionable material and squeeze or imprint its relief design on a sheet of soft wax (Fig. 416). The procedure, as perfected by Alvin Pine, is as follows:

1. Take a lead cake, perhaps $\frac{1}{2}$ by 3 by 5 inches. Using stamps, chisels, chasing tools, and any other tools that promise interesting effects, work out a negative relief design that will give sharp and crisp patterns. These should not be less than $\frac{1}{8}$ inch deep, but should vary in depth in different parts of the design.

2. Paint the surface of the lead mold with detergent, and cover it with a piece of plastic wrap. Paint the plastic wrap with more detergent. Then place a sheet of soft wax over the design. The thickness of the wax should be enough for the relief design to register without cutting through. Place another sheet of plastic wrap over the detergent-moistened wax, and lay a piece of thick (8 oz.) wet leather on top. Place this sandwich between two $\frac{1}{2}$-inch plates of aluminum. Clamp the entire package into a heavy vise, and tighten it until the wax is squeezed completely into the pattern.

3. Disassemble the press mold, peel the wax impression out, and rinse off. You can then trim and prepare it for lost-wax casting in the usual manner.

14.13

Direct Modeling of Wax Patterns   Although many casting patterns are made first in metal, it has increasingly become the practice to model patterns directly in wax. The wax used for direct modeling is fairly soft, but combinations of harder and softer waxes are likely to prove useful. One manufacturer supplies a "mold-and-carve" wax that becomes pliable with a light amount of heat. A mixture of beeswax and paraffin in equal proportions makes a good pattern wax. Adding powdered rosin and lampblack gives this wax a better working color. Another supplier offers a "utility wax" that is plastic at room temperatures. These waxes, and combinations of them, work well for direct modeling.

It does not take long to discover the peculiarities of wax. Bear in mind that wax has a crystalline structure. When it is melted, this structure disappears. The wax becomes rigid only when it has cooled to a point at which re-crystallization takes place. For this reason, when wax has been welded to another piece of wax, it must not be disturbed until the melted wax has cooled to the point of recrystallization. If disturbed, the joint will break apart. The term "welded" here refers to the process of fastening two pieces of wax together with melted wax. Liquid wax from a heated wax pot can be introduced between the two pieces, or a hot knife blade can be inserted briefly between the two pieces, causing them both to melt and fuse together.

One commercially available water-soluble wax, called Solu-Wax, can be used to build up hollow forms of modeling or casting wax. The Solu-Wax is built up into the desired matrix form; casting or modeling wax is then painted over it and built up as desired, or the Solu-Wax form can be dipped in wax. When the form has been completed, it is soaked in water to dissolve away the Solu-Wax. The hollow wax pattern can then be invested (**14.16**) and cast.

The above-mentioned waxes can be modeled with just the fingers, but it is more common to use a heated tool along with finger modeling.

Lost-Wax Casting

Lost-wax casting, one of the oldest and most sophisticated methods of casting metal, employs an investment mold together with gravity or centrifugal force. A brief summary of the lost-wax process will help you understand the rather complex procedure outlined below (**14.15–20**).

417. Philip Fike. *Fibula,* silver pin cast by lost wax, with separately forged pins, 1974.

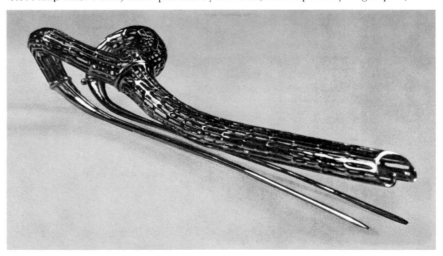

<h2 style="text-align:center">14.14</h2>

The Lost-Wax Process   In lost-wax casting, a wax model is melted away and replaced by molten metal, which hardens to become a permanent duplicate of the vanished wax pattern. Briefly, the process is as follows. A wax model is made of the object to be cast. A sprue with channel is attached to the model. The pattern is then placed in a cylinder called a *casting flask* lined with asbestos, and a plasterlike substance called *investment* is poured in to cover the wax model. After the investment hardens, the casting flask is turned upside-down and heated slowly in a kiln. Eventually, the wax melts and runs out through the sprue. The casting flask is removed from the kiln. When the investment is cool, molten metal is poured or forced into the investment to fill the cavity left by the melted wax. After cooling, the investment is broken up, leaving the cast metal object. Finally, the sprue is cut off and the metal finished (Fig. 417).

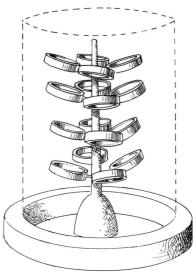

418. Multiple patterns set up on a tree, shown resting on the sprue base, with casting flask indicated by dotted lines.

<h2 style="text-align:center">14.15</h2>

Setting Up the Wax Pattern   Wax patterns are always set up on a *sprue base,* a heavy disk usually made of rubber that holds the stainless-steel flasks in which patterns are invested. Bases come in sizes to match the flasks, which range from $2\frac{1}{2}$ to 4 inches in diameter, and $2\frac{1}{2}$ to 7 inches in height. A small flask is used for single patterns. Larger flasks are used when patterns are set in a "tree" (Fig. 418): that is, when wax patterns are set circularly in two or more rows around a small, tapered wax "trunk" at an angle of about 45 degrees. Up to twelve pieces can be cast at once on such a tree.

The sprue base has a small, conical sprue form at the center, in which there is a small hole. This hole is filled with wax, to which the sprue channel (the tree trunk) is attached. Wax pieces are welded to each other by using a heated narrow blade to melt the surfaces to be joined. With practice, these welds can be made solidly, so that joints will not break apart when the investment is added. Wax patterns can be set up so that they come within $\frac{1}{4}$ inch of the sides of the casting flask. They should not come closer than $\frac{1}{4}$ inch to the top.

<h2 style="text-align:center">14.16</h2>

Investing the Wax Pattern   After the wax pattern or patterns are set up, the casting flask is placed on the sprue base. A 1-inch strip of asbestos sheet is placed half-way up around the inside of the flask. It will stay in place if it is moistened first. This strip allows for easier removal of the investment material.

Now mix the investment material in a rubber bowl. This material will consist of water mixed with one of the special powdered investments prepared by various manufacturers. All of them are developed to maintain a minimum expansion at burnout temperature, which is about 1000° F. Most manufacturers have made elaborate tests to determine exactly the correct proportion of water to investment powder that will yield maximum strength and lowest expansion. Most of these investments were developed for dental or commercial work, in which the finished size of the casting is critical. Hence the extreme concern for expansion. It is advisable for the jeweler to follow closely the recommended proportions of water to investment. Once measured out, the mixture is stirred until the investment is smooth and creamy.

The bowl of investment is then placed under the bell jar of the vacuum pump for "debubblizing." A properly equipped casting shop will have a machine that pumps air out from a bell jar. When the bowl of plaster is placed under the bell jar and a vacuum created therein, all the bubbles of air trapped in the investment plaster are drawn out. This prevents bubbles from forming on the wax patterns and thus appearing as part of the cast objects.

It is also standard practice to paint the wax patterns with a degreasing or "debubblizing" solution, so that the liquid investment will flow freely around

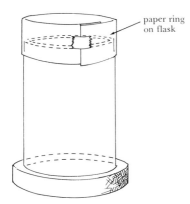

419. Casting flask with paper-strip extension.

the surfaces of the patterns. Sometimes, if there is a great amount of detail in the patterns, investment is painted over the surface of the patterns—or the patterns are dipped in the investment—before the casting flask is placed on the sprue base. Otherwise, pour the investment, after "debubblizing," into the flask, but to one side, so that it flows to the bottom and rises up and around the patterns. The flask must be filled to the top. This is best accomplished by taping a strip of paper around the top of the flask so that it projects about 2 inches above the top of the flask (Fig. 419). Investment must be poured to at least $\frac{1}{2}$ inch above the flask.

Then place the flask under the bell jar and turn on the vacuum pump again, in order to exhaust any air trapped in the investment around the patterns. The investment will froth up, but it will not run over and down onto the table of the bell jar, because the paper strip retains it.

When the investment plaster has set, the paper strip can be removed and the sprue base pulled off. Investment now extends past the top of the flask. This excess is necessary, because, when it is cut off with a hacksaw blade (Fig. 420), the top surface is flush with the edges of the flask. If any depression is allowed in this surface, the investment may cave in from the weight and pressure of the molten metal when it is cast in the centrifugal casting machine. Then the metal will leak out the back end of the investment, and the cast will be lost.

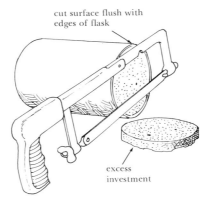

420. Casting flask with excess investment cut off with a hack saw.

14.17

Investment Burnout   A gas burnout furnace is superior to an electric furnace, because the vent of the gas furnace will carry off the wax fumes. The investment calcinates at about 800° F., but burnout temperatures should not exceed 1300° F. Overheating tends to expand the investment excessively, and this causes cracks during the cooling stage and produces flashings on the pattern. The length of burnout depends on the size of the furnace as well as the size and number of investments. Burnout should be continued until the sprue shows no trace of odor and the color is a pure rose red with no patches of black carbon. It is desirable to burn out at the lowest possible temperature in order to avoid unnecessary expansion cracks. You can start your experimentation with a temperature of about 1000° F. and a burnout time of one to four hours. The investment is placed in the furnace, sprue down. The bottom of the furnace is ridged, providing spaces under the investment where wax can drip out and fumes escape. In jewelry casting no attempt is made to save wax. The hot investment is removed from the furnace with special casting-flask tongs that fit around the flask.

Investments should be allowed to cool somewhat before casting. Cooling prevents the possibility of boiling the metal in the mold and yielding rough castings. For white gold, many jewelers cool the investment down to 1100° F.;

for yellow gold, down to about 850° F. For silver, the investment can be cooled to about 600° F. Some jewelers burn out for eight hours, cool down for casting, and then, after casting, leave the investment overnight before opening.

14.18

Centrifugal Casting   Centrifugal casting should be carried out quite systematically if consistent results are to be obtained.

1. First, the casting arm of the machine must be balanced (Fig. 389). One end of the arm carries a crucible. The other end carries an adjustable weight that can be moved forward or backward along the arm to balance the weight of the casting metal and the investment. Place the investment in its frame at the end of the casting arm. Move the crucible up against the investment.

    Place sufficient metal in the crucible to make the pour after melting. This quantity must be estimated in relation to the size and number of patterns to be cast and must include enough metal to fill the sprue. The estimate may be made by guessing, or by calculating first the weight of the wax in the pattern and the channel. Silver is about fourteen times heavier than wax. The specific gravity of silver is about 10.5, that of gold about 19.3. Gold is therefore about twenty-six times heavier than wax. The specific gravity of wax is about 0.75, which means that wax is lighter than water (whose specific gravity is 1.0). When the correct amount of metal is in the crucible, the weight at the opposite end of the casting arm must be turned toward or away from the crucible until the two ends balance.

    Balancing is easier to do on a machine that rotates vertically. It can be done just before each investment is cast. For systematic casting, number the investments and do the balancing of each in advance, so that the exact amount of metal can be recorded for each one. The machine is usually wound up on its spring after balancing but before the investment is placed in position for casting. Balancing is less critical for the horizontal casting machine than for the vertical casting machine.

2. Heat the metal in the crucible. If the amount of metal required is known in advance, the metal is usually heated with the torch to the melting point before the investment is removed from the furnace and placed in the machine. After the investment is in the machine, which has already been wound up on its spring, heat the metal until it reaches the proper melting temperature (**C.1**).

3. At the proper moment, remove the torch, and at the same time pull the rotating arm away from the catch and release it. This process is done in one sweeping movement. The rotating arm will now spin around, throwing the metal into the investment. It should be allowed to come to a stop, so that the metal will have some chance to solidify.

4. Remove the investment with the tongs and place it in a bucket of water. When casting silver or gold, this can be done as soon as the red glow of the sprue is no longer visible. When casting bronze, a little more time must elapse for the bronze to solidify. Bronze seems to cool more slowly than silver or gold. Plunging the investment into a bucket of water breaks out the investment quickly and frees the casting. The casting is then pickled and cleaned, and the channels are clipped away.

There are several variations in the process of centrifugal casting, depending upon the type of machine used. Some machines are spun by an electric motor; some have an electrically heated crucible in the casting arm (Fig. 406). Manufacturers provide detailed instructions for the operation of their own particular machines.

The great advantage of centrifugal casting is the delicacy and complexity that can be attained. Commercial precision casting is an extremely technical process, wherein variable factors must be controlled exactly.

The foregoing description of centrifugal casting is at best a brief summary of the process. Those who wish to pursue casting seriously should research the field thoroughly.

14.19

Vacuum Casting   Vacuum casting is not new, but it is becoming increasingly popular with contemporary jewelers for three reasons. First, there is a growing opinion that castings are more uniform with this process. Second, the cost of equipment is lower. And third, the casting operation is simpler and faster.

Vacuum casting requires a steel table with a central hole, over which the investment is placed. A pipe leads from the hole to a vacuum pump. A heavy silicone-rubber mat (with a similar hole) that can withstand temperatures to 1000° F. is placed under the investment, so that a tight air seal will be possible when the vacuum is applied to the flask. The procedure is as follows:

1. When the investment has been properly burned out and has cooled to the proper temperature, melt the metal in a hand crucible or bench furnace.
2. When the metal is molten, remove the investment from the furnace and place it on the casting table. Turn on the vacuum pump. Then, take up the crucible and pour the metal. The vacuum is already drawing air out of the investment flask, and as the metal enters the flask, vapors and gases are withdrawn, enabling the molten metal to flow in with decreased resistance. With a 4-inch flask, the rubber mat should have about a 1-inch hole under the flask for best results. To ensure a good seal between flask and silicone mat, about $\frac{1}{8}$ inch of the investment should be cut out before firing.

An excellent vacuum casting outfit, which also includes a vacuum bell-jar table, can be procured from Swest, Inc. (Fig. 421).

14.20

Pressure Casting   Pressure casting uses pressure to force molten metal into the investment mold. At a primitive level, pressure casting can be tried by placing the burnt-out investment right side up on an asbestos block and putting the unmelted metal into the sprue. The sprue channel should not be larger than about $\frac{1}{8}$ inch in diameter. A torch is then applied to the metal. When the metal is molten, a board covered with a thick layer of wet cloth is pressed firmly against the top. The steam generated by the heat of the metal exerts a pressure that forces the molten metal into the mold.

A more sophisticated device for pressure casting can be made from a small tin can a bit larger than the casting flask. Nail a wooden handle to the center of the back of the can. Fill the back end with about a $\frac{1}{2}$-inch layer of wet asbestos sheet cut to fit the diameter of the can snugly. When the metal in the sprue is molten, quickly press the can down upon the casting flask. The compressed steam forces the metal into the flask.

Small air-pressure casting outfits (Fig. 422) are available for very small castings. (The largest casting flask is only $1\frac{1}{2}$ inches in diameter and 3 inches high.) One reason for the diminutive size of such outfits may be that only a small channel is permissible from the sprue; otherwise the metal would run down the channel as soon as it became molten. This outfit includes a small cylindrical pump with which to build air pressure; it is placed over the investment when the metal is molten. When the machine is pressed down against the flask, compressed air is released, forcing the metal into the mold.

Casting with Plastics

Plastics provide a tremendous opportunity for experimentation in contemporary jewelry (Pl. 11, p. 153). Since the 1940s, industrial chemists have developed a wide variety of plastic resins, which together offer an almost limitless range of qualities and potential uses. The two major groups are *thermoplastics* such as acrylic, nylon, and polystyrene, which soften and become formable with the application of heat; and *thermosets* or *thermosetting plastics,* which, once set, can be heated with little distortion up to the burning point. The plastics best suited for casting jewelry are *epoxy resin* and *polyester resin,* both thermosets. Suppliers of plastics are listed in Appendix **B.7**.

14.21

Epoxy and Polyester Resins   *Epoxy* is the name chemists have given to a linkage between molecules of carbon and oxygen—an *epoxide linkage.* The resulting polymer can be converted into a thermosetting, nonmeltable material.

Epoxy resins possess strength, durability, transparency, and great adhesive properties. They can be modified to provide a wide range of physical qualities by the addition of colorants and flexibilizers (such as Benzoflex 9-88) as well as sand, sawdust, marble dust, metal powders, and almost any other inert filler. Epoxies are available in consistencies ranging from a thin liquid to an adhesive paste; the best type for casting comes as a viscous syrup. Uncured

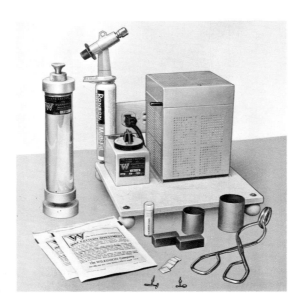

422. Pressure-casting outfit.

epoxy gives off toxic fumes and may irritate the skin, but after curing the material is chemically stable and safe for human contact. Epoxy resins are induced to set into solid form by the admixture of *curing agents* or *hardeners*.

Of the many epoxy resins available, one of the more popular types for crafts is CIBA Araldite No. 502. This is probably similar to the Epoxy E-1201 produced by The Plastics Factory. Curing Agent No. 956 should be used with the Araldite 502; for the E-1201, try Type-C hardener E-1209.

Polyester, the principal ingredient of fiberglass, is virtually interchangeable with epoxy for casting, laminating, and embedment. Both plastics use the same colorants and fillers, but polyester is less expensive and less toxic in its uncured, syrupy state. Unlike epoxy, however, polyesters will not adhere to metal or other polished or painted surfaces. Polyester resins are set by the addition of a *catalyst* (such as methyl ethyl ketone peroxide), whose solidifying action can be hastened by the admixture of an *accelerator*.

14.22

Molds for Resin Casting   In general, molds for resin casting can be made from plaster, Tamastone, Dura-Rock, Latex rubber, silicone RTV rubber, clay, or wax. An open-back mold is usually most convenient, but a piecemold or flexible mold must be used for patterns with undercuts.

A clay mold can be made quite easily by forming a slab of clay about 1 inch thick and then pressing and carving the negative form in it. By the same procedure, molds can be made from various waxes. Microcrystalline Wax 1290Y, produced by the Sun Chemical Company, is a yellow petroleum wax with a low melting point. A mold of Latex rubber usually requires a "mother mold" around it for support. If plaster is used, it must be thoroughly dried, and the mold surface must be sealed with a filler and then coated with a *release agent* (to prevent sticking) before the plastic is poured in. Good release agents include carnuba wax, Dupont Zelec UN Int-54 (for glass molds), and the aeresol 1711 Release Agent made by the Contour Chemical Company.

14.23

Preparing the Resin Mixture   Plastics with additives must be weighed out accurately, for which you will require a balance scale with gram weights. For jewelry, quantities will not be great, and you should be able to mix all ingredients in a single cup. The first step is to place a clean, empty cup on the scale, weigh it, and note the cup weight on a slip of paper. For example, assume that your cup weighs 80 grams. If your formula calls for 100 grams of polyester resin No. 32–032, add this figure to the cup weight to get 180 grams. Set the balance weight of the scale to this amount, and carefully pour your resin into the cup until the scale balances. Then, if the catalyst is to be 1.2 grams of MEK-Px, add this amount to the total, increase the balance weight to 181.2 grams, and pour in the correct amount of catalyst.

The materials will not react properly unless they are stirred carefully and thoroughly. The mold will have been prepared in advance, so you can pour the mixture immediately after stirring. One of the advantages of epoxy and polyester resins is that they can usually be poured at room temperature.

14.24

Curing and Finishing Resin Castings   Once poured, resin castings will cure at room temperature overnight. For unusually thick pieces, however, you should allow at least 24 hours for curing. A heat lamp set about 3 feet away will hasten solidification. After a resin casting has cured to a solid state, it can be carved and filed as well as sanded, emeried, and polished. For polishing, use a muslin buff with tripoli after fine emery. All cast resins can be finished to a high polish (Pl. 5, p. 150).

Fastenings

Historical practice has developed an infinitely broad range of fastening methods whose effectiveness usually cannot be surpassed. The necessity of finding new methods of fastening arises, for the most part, only when new materials or new techniques are developed. Nevertheless, experimentation may reveal unsuspected possibilities in the specific design relationships that the jeweler devises. Also, historical practice is often confined to conventional or well-established methods. New solutions therefore lie within a fresh or unconventional approach to old problems.

In jewelry, a fastening is not successful unless it is both durable and simple, as well as being visually suitable. Fastenings that can be incorporated as part of the design are superior to those that are simply "stuck" on. For example, devising the catch for a necklace is usually regarded simply as a functional problem, the featured part being the front. But why should the catch not be made the featured element of the necklace design, wherein the mode of fastening becomes the form of the design? The creative jeweler constantly reappraises ideas about what a piece of jewelry should be.

Direct Methods of Fastening

Methods of fastening in which metal is set against metal are the simplest and most effective. Examples of this type are flanges, clips, rivets, interlocking joints, catches, and hinges. The following solutions are presented as a basis for working out fastenings for your own particular needs.

219

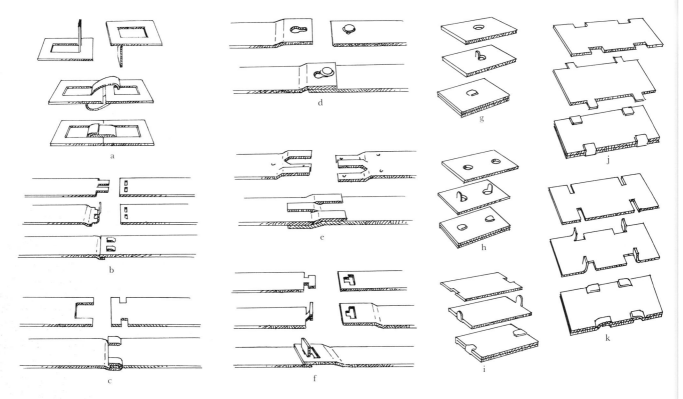

423. Various types of flanges for joining two sheets of metal.

15.1

Flanges Flanges are so simple in design and construction that they are used wherever possible in all types of metal construction. A flange is a rim of metal allowed to extend beyond the normal boundary line of a sheet-metal shape sufficiently to permit bending it up and around or over another piece of metal. This device allows great variation in size, shape, and location of the flange (Fig. 423). No additional, separate pieces are required, and the mechanical process is simple and suitable for either hand or machine fabrication. All the basic positional relationships can be accommodated: edge-to-edge, edge-to-surface, or surface-to-surface. In jewelry the flange method has many creative applications and could probably be used more than it is. The claw setting (**21.2**) is a special variation of the method.

15.2

Clips Clips are small pieces of metal that, when fastened to one piece of metal, hold another piece in position (Fig. 424). The spring clip is a special variation, in which the clip is a spring or is fastened to a spring that allows displacement of the clip for attaching or releasing one piece of metal to or from another piece. The spring clip is part of a catch. Spring clips always require a certain amount of tension in metal. Therefore, avoid annealing any jewelry that has been fitted with such a clip. To increase the tension in a piece of metal to be used for a clip, perform any of the processes that result in work-hardening—forging, striking, or twisting, for example. In almost all ancient cultures, brooches were used to hold garments closed. These had a wire spring clip. We retain the same idea in the safety pin.

15.3

Rivets A rivet is a small pin used to hold two sheets of metal together in a surface-to-surface relationship. The rivet pin runs through holes in the two plates, and the ends of the pin are flattened carefully to form heads, which prevent the two pieces from separating. In some pieces the rivet heads act as surface decoration (Fig. 425).

Select an appropriate size drill, and drill a hole through the pieces of metal to be fastened together. Choose a wire that is just slightly larger than the hole, and, using a pin vise, file a fairly long, flat taper, so that the tapered end will wedge snugly through the hole (Fig. 426). Clip the ends off on each side of the metal with the cutting pliers, leaving a length of wire projecting beyond the

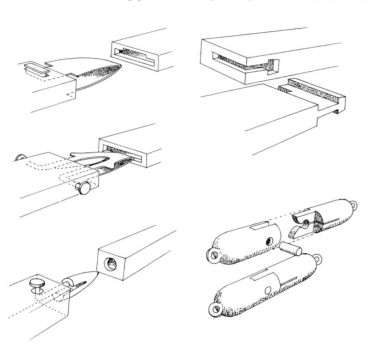

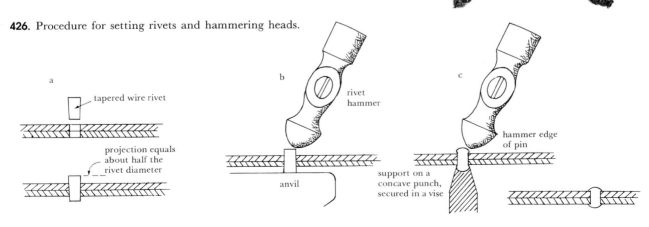

above: 424. Five examples of clips.

right: 425. Richard Mafong and Jon Eric Riis. *Baby Jane,* silver and bronze brooch, die-punched, pierced, and riveted, with woven metallic threads, 1974.

426. Procedure for setting rivets and hammering heads.

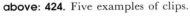

a
tapered wire rivet
projection equals about half the rivet diameter

b
rivet hammer
anvil

c
hammer edge of pin
support on a concave punch, secured in a vise

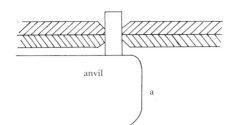

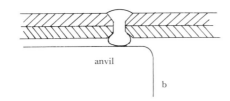

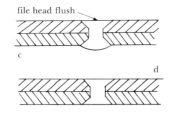

427. Procedure for setting and hammering a flush rivet.

surface of each side equal to about half the diameter of the wire. The pliers always pinch a crest in the wire ends, and these should be filed flat. Now set the rivet on an anvil and, with a small rivet hammer, strike very light blows around and around the edge of the rivet. As soon as the wire end has begun to spread over the edge of the hole, turn the work over and repeat the process on the other end of the rivet. Work back and forth until the rivet heads are driven down snugly and tightly against the surface of the metal.

If the rivet wire that you use is too long, if it does not fit the hole in the metal snugly, or if you strike too heavily with the hammer, the rivet is likely to bend over.

15.4

Flush Rivets   If an invisible rivet is desired, a countersunk hole should be drilled to an appropriate depth (Fig. 427). The rivet head, made by fusing the end of a wire into a bead (**10.5**), can be filed to a cone that fits the countersunk hole or can be placed directly in the rivet hole. In either case, the rivet is closed by hammering until the rivet metal fills the countersunk hole uniformly and completely. Excess material is then filed away, and the surface of the plate is finished. Such rivets, when properly made, are invisible.

428. Procedure for setting and hammering a tube rivet.

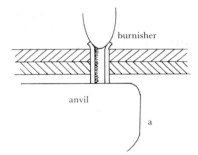

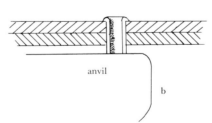

15.5

Tube Rivets   In certain situations a tube rivet may be a necessary fastening. A metal tube of the proper diameter is placed in the rivet hole. The ends of the tube should be cut to extend above the surface sufficiently so that, when the sides of the tube are bent over, they grasp the edges of the hole securely (Fig. 428). A bend in the edge of the tube can be started by twisting the point of the burnisher in the end of the tube, gradually pressing farther down as the sides are pressed out until they finally rest snugly against the surface of the metal. A few blows of the hammer will then secure the rivet.

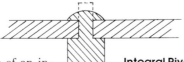

15.6

429. Section view of an integral rivet.

Integral Rivets   The integral rivet is made from a part of one piece of material that projects through another piece (Fig. 429). The projecting end is then closed in a typical rivet fashion, flush or domed.

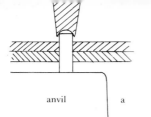

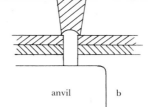

anvil   a   anvil   b

left: 430. A normal rivet head can be hammered round by means of the rivet set, struck with a ball-peen hammer.

below: 431. Two examples of interlocking joints.

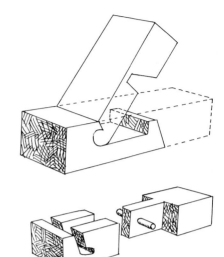

15.7

The Rivet Set   When a normal rivet has been set, cut, and filed to proper height, domed rivet heads can be made with a rivet set—a small punch with a tapered end in which a concave hemispherical hole has been made. Set the point over the rivet, and rotate the rivet set as it is struck lightly with a hammer (Fig. 430). The rivet head is thus rounded and polished.

15.8

Interlocking Joints   Interlocking joints are fasteners designed to block the separation of two pieces of metal in every direction except the one along which the pieces must move to be joined or parted (Fig. 431). Usually the direction of the joint opposes the normal pull or movement of the pieces away from each other. When a spring clip is added, this joint becomes a clip-catch. The Egyptians made beautiful interlocking joints for their bracelets and necklaces.

15.9

Catches   Catches are the means of fastening temporary closures (Fig. 432). The basis of the catch is the displacement of one piece of metal to allow two other pieces of metal to come together, after which the displaced piece moves back to its original position, in order to block the separation of the two pieces.

432. Catches of various types: (*a*) peg and fork with screw-on casing; (*b*) bayonet mount; (*c*) screw mount; (*d*) hinge with sliding bolt; (*e*) interlocking slide catch; (*f*) rotating cylinder for a pin tong; (*g*) pin cap mounted on a sliding tube; (*h*) hook and link; (*i*) toggle and ring.

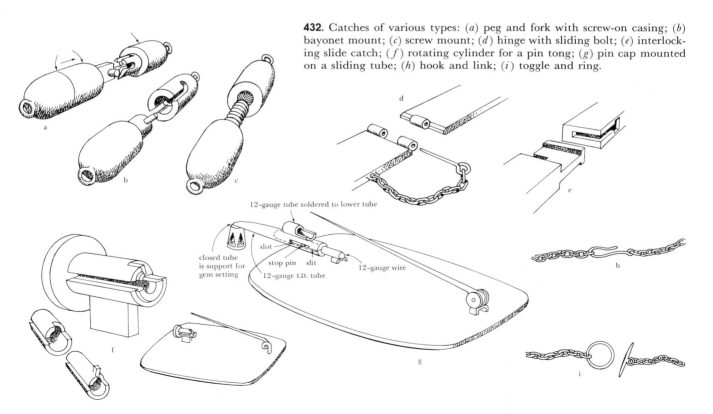

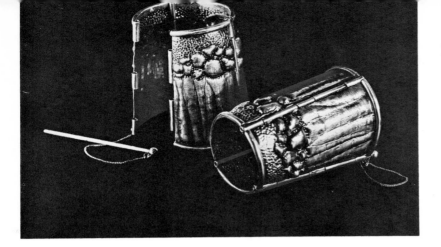

433. Anne Echelman. Pair of silver cuff bracelets, repoussé and chased, 1975.

Displacement can be made possible by a slide, hinge, twist, radial rotation, or a spring (Fig. 433).

15.10

Silversmith Pin Set   A pin set requires a pin tong, a hinge to fasten it to the back of a jewelry piece, and a clasp to hold it in place (Fig. 434). One method for quantity-producing pin sets rests soundly in silversmith tradition: Make a sterling-silver tube (**11.3**) about $3\frac{1}{4}$ inches long, and draw it down to a 1-millimeter inside diameter (I.D.). This should yield an outside diameter (O.D.) of about 2 millimeters (roughly $\frac{3}{32}$ inch) if you start with a strip of 20-gauge sterling. Remember that when you draw a tube down to a smaller size, the tube wall thickens.

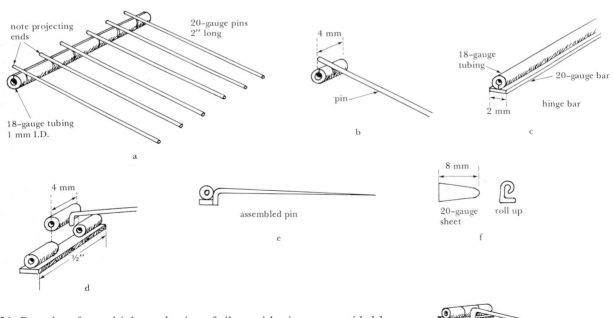

434. Procedure for multiple production of silversmith pin sets, provided by Heikki Seppa: Several pin tongs are soldered at regular intervals to a length of tubing (*a*), which is then cut apart (*b*). A length of identical tubing is soldered to a bar (*c*) and cut to form a three-section hinge with the pin (*d*), whose projecting end is bent down to provide spring tension against the bar (*e*). Finally, a simple clasp is rolled from sheet (*f*) and positioned on the work to receive the pin tong (*g*).

224   *Technique*

Now place your tube, seam up, on a soldering block, and lay on it at 4-millimeter intervals a number of wire pins of 18-gauge nickel-silver wire (Fig. 434*a*). The pins should be of uniform length—perhaps 2 inches. Be sure to let each pin project past the tube seam about 2 millimeters. This projecting end will be bent up to serve as a stop, so that the pin will have some spring in the clasp.

Solder the pins to the tube, then saw the tube apart in sections with a pin centered on each section (*b*). If soldering has annealed the pins, making them too soft, it will be necessary to work-harden them by taking each end in a pair of pliers and twisting the pin once or twice around its own axis. Pull on the pin from each end as you do the twisting to keep the pin straight. When needed, each pin will be cut to a suitable length and filed to a tapered point.

For the other half of the hinge, take another tube of the same size and solder it, seam down, on a small bar of 18-gauge sterling about 2 millimeters wide (*c*). Saw off a section of this tube-bar, perhaps $\frac{1}{2}$ inch long, for the hinge, and in the center cut out a section of tubing just the size of your pin hinge (*d*). Finish and polish both parts until they fit together comfortably. Finally, bend the short projecting end of the pin to form a spring stop (*e*).

The clasp is simply a triangular sheet of 20-gauge sterling, as shown in Figure 434*f*, with a flat bottom soldered to the jewelry and a curled top to hold the pin tong (*g*).

15.11

Fastening Wire   The end of a wire can be fastened to metal by running it through a hole and then fusing a bead on the end, hammering a rivet head to close the end, or merely bending and spreading the end of the wire that projects beyond the hole.

left: 435. Nilda C. Getty. *Nosy Priest,* hinged triple container in sterling silver, Plexiglas, and sodalite, 1973 (shown in closed position).

right: 436. Container of Figure 435 shown in open position.

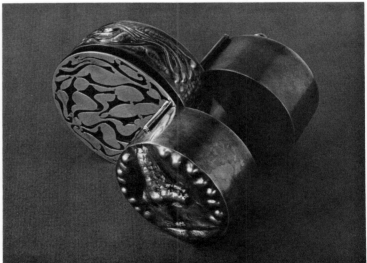

Hinges

The hinge is a device that allows one part of a piece of jewelry to swing on an axis fastened to another part (Figs. 435, 436). One might regard the jump ring between two links of a bracelet as a hinge. As a structure, however, the hinge is usually more complex than this. The construction of a hinge may be simple or complex. Both are presented here, though the complex type is seldom used.

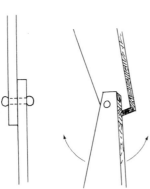

above: **437.** Rivet used as a simple hinge.

right: **438. Vada Beetler.** *Lichen Ring,* cast and constructed of sterling, bronze, and gold, 1974. Tube-rivet hinges permit the inner hemisphere to close over the bronze form cast from a lichen.

15.12

Simple Hinges The simplest type of hinge can be achieved by merely riveting one piece of metal to another (Figs. 437, 438). Another simple type of hinge consists of a supporting tube through which a rivet runs and fastens to another piece of metal.

A slightly more complex hinge can be made by soldering a small tube to each of two pieces of metal, drilling a hole through the metal to which the tube is soldered, and fastening the two tubes together with a rivet (Fig. 439).

A normal hinge has at least three sections of tubing in line around a rivet or hinge wire (Figs. 440, 441). The outside tubes are soldered to one piece of metal, the middle tube to the other piece of metal.

You will find it difficult to file the ends of a short piece of tubing exactly square, as they should be in order to fit well together. In practice, jewelers and silversmiths use a joint tool (Fig. 442), which clamps the tubing squarely while its end is being filed (Fig. 443).

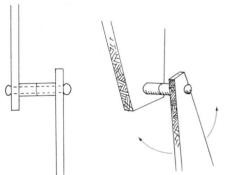

439. Double-tube hinge, with a rivet running through two short tubes, each soldered to a separate piece of metal.

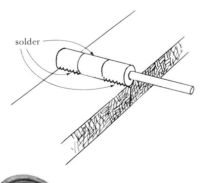

solder

left: **440.** Simple three-section hinge.

below: **441. Harlan W. Butt.** *Container Ring #2,* cast and constructed of sterling and gold-plated silver, 1973 (shown open).

right: 442. Joint tool.

below: 443. The joint tool holds tubing square for filing.

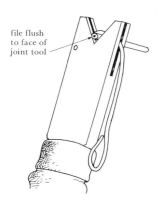

file flush to face of joint tool

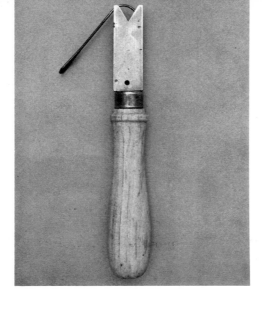

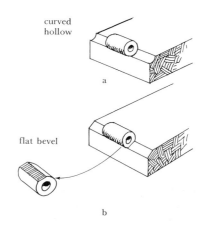

curved hollow

a

flat bevel

b

444. Beveled edges or a concave groove help secure a hinge tube to its base.

15.13

Procedure for Soldering Hinge Joints   Certain precautions must be taken to avoid soldering the sections of hinge tubing together:

1. When the sections have been cut to size and their ends filed square, string them together on a straight iron wire that fits the tube snugly.
2. Set the tube sections between the edges of the two pieces of metal that are to be hinged together. A more accurate and pleasing job can be done if the edges of the pieces to be hinged are either beveled or filed with a hollow to fit the curvature of the tubes (Fig. 444). The individual hinge knuckles should be beveled where they touch the metal pieces, so that solder will not flow between the knuckle joints.
3. When the work is in position, flux the seams and set a single piece of solder in the center of each hinge section at the seam. Now heat the work until the solder just begins to flow, tacking the hinge section to its proper piece of metal. This can be done by heating the large piece of metal to a temperature just below the melting point of the solder and then using a very small, hot flame at the particular hinge joint to melt the solder. Stop soldering as soon as the joint has been tacked and before the solder has a chance to spread along the entire seam. After all the sections have been tacked in place, withdraw the iron wire and take the hinge apart. The hinge joints are now correctly located, and the soldering can be completed (Fig. 445).
4. Take care that the relative position of the hinge joints is not disturbed or allowed to slip when the final soldering is done. A special setup is sometimes required on the soldering block to hold the hinge sections and the piece of metal in position.

15.14

The Full Hinge   The full hinge traditionally has five hinge sections (Fig. 446). The two outside sections and the center section are soldered to one side, the other two sections to the other side.

Any of the above hinges can also be made by using flanges on each piece of metal. These flanges are cut out to correspond to the joints of the tube hinge and are rolled around a rivet or hinge pin. Although characteristic of cheaper construction, such hinges may sometimes have a legitimate design use.

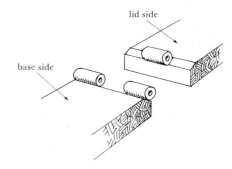

lid side

base side

above: 445. Sections of a three-section hinge tacked in position for final soldering.

below: 446. The full hinge, with five sections.

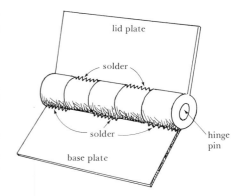

lid plate

solder

solder

hinge pin

base plate

15.15

The Silversmith Hinge   The silversmith hinge (Fig. 447), with stop plates, is the lord of all traditional hinges and requires considerable skill to construct. Prepare two tubes, one fitting snugly into the other. Split the outer tube lengthwise into three equal sectors, and finish two of them accurately and perfectly. Cut the inner tube into five, seven, or nine sections. Then fit these into the two sectors of the outer tube, and cut and finish these two pieces to the proper length.

Now cut the two pieces of metal to be hinged together to receive the lengths of outer tubing. The cuts must be made exactly in order to accommodate the desired relationship of the two pieces when assembled. Keeping these positions in mind, solder each sector of outer tubing to its respective piece.

Place the sections of inner tubing accurately in position in one of the outer sectors, and tack the appropriate number of alternate sections in place. Remove the sections belonging to the other piece, place them in their positions by matching against the first piece, and tack them in place.

Test the hinges by assembling. When the hinge assembles perfectly, complete the soldering separately on each piece. The purpose of the outer shell of tubing is not only to cradle the hinge sections but also to provide a stop as they come together when the hinge is opened. Check the position of the pieces when opened before the final soldering.

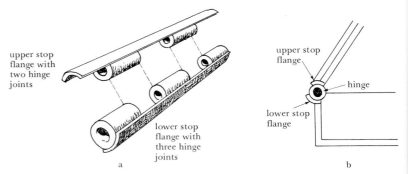

447. The silversmith hinge. After soldering alternate inner sections into the two outer sectors, paint the inside with yellow ochre, assemble the hinge with a steel pin, and fit it to the work. After positioning, solder each half of the hinge separately.

upper stop flange with two hinge joints

lower stop flange with three hinge joints

upper stop flange

hinge

lower stop flange

a

b

Other Fastenings

15.16

Cementing   Cementing is seldom used in jewelry except in "junk" jewelry. One exception is in the case of pearls, which are too soft to be set by means of claws or bezels. The pearl is usually drilled halfway through and cemented to a small metal post. For cementing pearls, a paste of litharge mixed with glycerine is a traditional and effective substance. This cement is impervious to water, once it has set. Epoxy cement, of course, is universally used these days for almost every kind of cementing job.

15.17

Riveting Metal to Soft Materials   Riveting can be used successfully for fastening almost any material to metal. In the case of soft materials, such as bone or wood, a small washer of metal (this can be part of a metal shape) comes between the material and the rivet head for protection. Also, a metal shape to be placed over a stone may have rivets soldered to it that will penetrate through holes drilled in the material and through another metal shape on which the rivet heads are formed.

Electroplating
and Electroforming

Electroplating and electroforming are two closely related processes that work by electrolytic action. In electroplating a very thin coating of metal is deposited onto a piece of jewelry to enhance, renew, or unify the surface or to make the piece more durable (Fig. 448); in electroforming a thick layer of metal is deposited onto a matrix of some material, such as wax or polystyrene, to actually form a piece of jewelry. Both processes require the same type of equipment. It will be useful for the jeweler to acquire a basic knowledge of the electrochemical activity that causes the metal transfer to take place.

Electroplating

Electroplating is done in a solution called an *electrolyte*. The piece of jewelry to be plated is suspended in this solution, which conducts low-voltage DC (direct current) electricity. The process is made possible because a salt dissolved in the solution separates into positive and negative electric particles called *ions*. The positive ions move from a positive terminal, the *anode,* to a negative terminal, the *cathode*. The negative ions move in the opposite direction. For electroplating purposes, the anode is a strip of the metal that is to form the plating, while the cathode is the object to be plated. During *electrolysis,* oxygen is discharged at the anode, and a coating of metal forms around the jewelry at the cathode. This coating is very thin, somewhere between one-millionth and two-thousandths of an inch, so the anode can be used many times.

If, for example, the jeweler wants to silver-plate a piece, the general procedure is as follows. The electrolyte is a water solution of sodium argento-

229

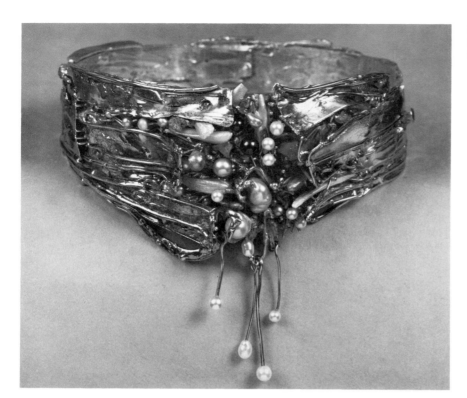

448. Glenda Arentzen. Choker of cast, constructed, and gold-plated silver, with pearls and natural minerals, 1971.

cyanide. The silver of the anode passes into the solution, and silver ions in the solution are deposited on the object to be plated, the cathode. This process is called *electrodeposition.* In this way a coating of metal can be built up as a thin, even layer. Theoretically, the thickness of a plated coating is determined by the time of plating and the *current density,* which can be expressed in amperes per square foot of cathode surface. Thus, if an electric source of 5 amperes is used to plate an object with a surface of 0.1 square foot, the current density is 50 ampere-feet.

The metals typically used for plating are gold, silver, copper, nickel, and rhodium. Gold is the most common plating, since it resists tarnish as well as contributing an attractive finish. Silver and copper also serve as decoration; nickel is often used as an underplating, to cover brass, silver, or other metals that corrode easily, before a rhodium plating is applied. Rhodium, a bright, tarnish- and corrosion-proof metal, resembles platinum in color and chemical composition.

16.1

Technical Analysis of Electrolysis   The process of electrolysis was discovered by Humphry Davy in 1807 when he isolated a series of elements—sodium (Na), potassium (K), calcium (Ca), and others—by passing an electric current through their molten compounds. For those who wish to understand what is happening at the molecular level during electrolysis, a brief analysis is presented here. It can be ignored by those who are interested primarily in the practical application of electroplating.

When certain salts are dissolved in water, the positive and negative molecules separate out in the solution as *ions.* Positive ions are called *anions;* negative ions, *cations.* The term ion means "wanderer," and the ions do wander throughout the solution on given paths.

For example, copper sulfate ($CuSO_4 \cdot 5H_2O$) separates into anions of $(Cu)^+$ and cations of $(SO_4)^-$. (The five molecules of water can be disregarded here.) Potassium cyanide (KCN) molecules separate out into $(K)^+$ anions and $(CN)^-$ cations. Sulfuric acid (H_2SO_4) molecules separate into $(H_2)^+$ anions and $(SO_4)^-$ cations.

The English physicist Michael Faraday, who conducted experiments with the process of electrolysis, formulated two laws that established the relationship between ions in a solution and the electrons flowing through the electrolyte. According to the first law,

> The mass of a given element formed by electrolysis is proportional to the quantity of electric current passing through an electrolyte.

In the cgs (centimeter-gram-second) system of units, the unit of quantity of electricity is known as the *coulomb*. Faraday found that 1 coulomb will deposit 0.001118 grams of metallic silver on a cathode when an electric current is passed through an aqueous solution of silver nitrate. As you can see, this is the fundamental basis for relating the flow of electricity to the quantity of metal deposited upon a cathode.

In order to discuss this question further, we must digress to explain the meaning of a *gram-atomic* weight of silver. The *atomic* weight of silver is 107.879. Chemists find it convenient in dealing with chemicals quantitatively to consider a quantity of a chemical in grams equivalent to its atomic weight. This is called its gram-atomic weight, and is also designated as 1 *mole*.

If we wish to know how much electricity is required to deposit 1 mole of silver on a cathode, we need only divide the figure 0.001118 (see above) into 107.879 grams, and we get 96,500 coulombs of electricity. This amount of electricity is designated as 1 *faraday*. And this leads us to Faraday's second law of electrolysis:

> For each 96,500 coulombs (1 faraday) passing through the electrolyte, one gram equivalent weight is chemically altered at each electrode.

But 1 faraday of electricity consists of 6.023×10^{23} electrons. (This quantity is known as *Avogadro's number*.) Obviously, when 1 faraday of electricity passes through a silver-salt electrolyte, 6.023×10^{23} silver anions $(Ag)^=$ must be deposited upon the cathode.

The terms *equivalent weight* and *Avogadro's number* require further explanation. The *equivalent weight* of an element is its atomic weight divided by its valence. For example, let us examine the amount of calcium in calcium chloride ($CaCl_2$) that is equivalent to a gram-atomic weight of chlorine. It must be noted that calcium $(Ca)^{++}$ takes up two chlorine (Cl) molecules. Thus, only 20 grams of calcium is *equivalent* to a gram-atomic weight of chlorine. (The atomic weight of calcium is 40.) You can see that in making calculations for electrolysis, account must be taken of the valence of the ions involved.

In making experiments with gases, Avogadro came to the conclusion that equal volumes of gases contained equal numbers of molecules under fixed conditions of temperature and pressure, regardless of the atomic weight of the molecules. A mole of gas was found to contain a fixed number of molecules, no matter what gas was considered. This number was determined finally to be 6.023×10^{23}. We see that this number also applies to ions in solution in the process of electrolysis.

One final relationship you must grasp is that 1 ampere is equal to 1 coulomb of electricity flowing past a fixed point per second. Thus, an ampere represents a unit of electric *current*.

16.2

Equipment for Electroplating   Quite a bit of material is needed for electroplating (Fig. 449). First, the object to be plated must be immaculately clean. Any remnants of previously plated metal must be removed. *Electrostripping* (the process that removes the old plating) and *electrocleaning* both use the same equipment as electroplating (see below) plus the following:

- brushes and detergent for preliminary cleaning
- pickling equipment to remove oxides
- an ultrasonic cleaning machine (Fig. 450), available at supply houses
- an electrostripping solution, if necessary, to remove old plating
- Pyrex beakers, of at least 1 quart capacity, for electrostripping
- a 1-quart stainless steel tank, for cleaning
- an instant-reading thermometer, available at photo equipment stores
- copper wire and self-locking tweezers, to handle the jewelry during cleaning
- household abrasive cleanser, for use during electrocleaning

For electroplating, the following equipment is needed:

- Pyrex beakers—a separate one for each solution
- electrolyte solutions—concentrated liquids that come with directions for mixing and recommended temperatures (Stopper tightly and store carefully when not in use.)
- an anode: high-karat gold, fine (not sterling) silver, pure copper, pure nickel, or platinum or titanium (for rhodium plating), and a wire of the same metal to be attached to the anode. (Both should be carefully rinsed, dried, wrapped in paper, and stored immediately after each use.)
- hot plate for heating most solutions and hastening the action
- a magnetic stirrer, used with the cold copper-plating solution to keep the solution moving
- an eyedropper, calibrated in milliliters
- plating machine (rectifier)

The plating bath always consists of a compound of the metal to be plated, mixed with a colloidal *addition agent*, which appears to act in a catalytic

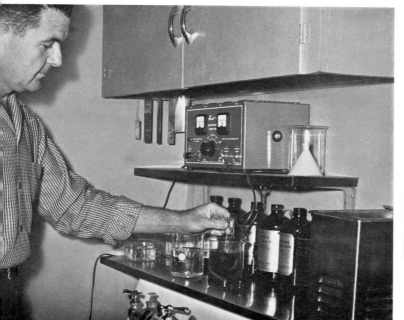

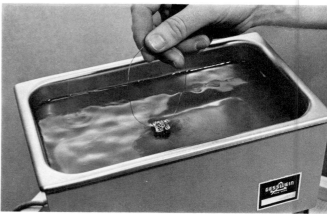

left: 449. Electroplating equipment.

below: 450. Ultrasonic cleaning machine.

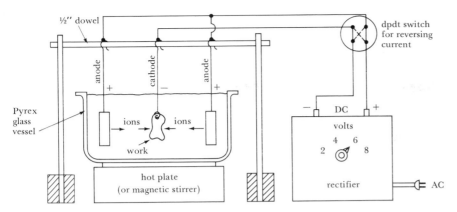

451. Schematic diagram of the electroplating process.

manner. The addition agent is usually glue, gelatin, albumin, or in some cases an aldehyde or ketone. The temperature of the plating bath is critical for commercial operations, although room temperature in a comfortable shop will probably be satisfactory for the individual craftsman.

Direct current must be used, for the simple reason that a continuous flow of positive ions must be maintained toward the cathode. Alternating current, which switches back and forth, would merely apply some ions and then on its reverse cycle take them off again. For a small shop operation, one or more storage batteries, yielding up to 5 amperes, might be quite satisfactory. For medium-size operations, a source yielding 5 to 1000 amperes would be adequate. The electroplating machine is nothing more than a rectifier, which changes alternating current (AC) to direct current (DC). The amateur electrician could well put a simple rectifier together from directions in a reference book. Copper-oxide, copper-sulfide, or selenium rectifiers can be used to convert AC to DC.

Electroplating machines for shop operation are available from many supply houses. They consist of the rectifier circuit, a fuse to protect against overloads, connections for anode and cathode, and a method of stepping up the voltage. The method may be merely a set of anode connections offering a choice of 2, 4, 6, 8, or 10 volts, or a more elaborate circuit with a switch and perhaps even an ammeter and voltmeter. The cost of these machines varies, usually according to the power available and the sophistication of the design. The expensive machines also include an automatic circuit-reversing system, which carries out the periodic reversal during the plating process. On simple machines this can be done manually, or a "dpdt" (double-pole double-throw) switch can be wired to reverse the current merely by flicking the switch.

16.3

The Electroplating Process   A typical setup for electroplating is shown schematically in Figure 451. First of all, before electroplating is started, the piece should be completely finished; that is, all soldering, polishing, and stone setting should have been done. Electroplating will not hide the tiniest scratch or imperfection; on the contrary, it will preserve even the finest gradations of texture (Fig. 452).

The procedure for plating begins with a thorough cleaning of the object to be plated. It must be free from grease, dirt, oxides, and all other foreign matter. Scrubbing the object with a brush and soapy water is followed by pickling to remove any oxide deposits. Then the piece should be immersed in an ultrasonic cleaning machine (Fig. 450), which uses a detergent solution.

452. David Laplantz. *Excelsior Pin*, of cast, constructed, and silver-plated brass and copper, 1975.

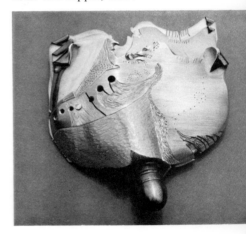

Finally, the piece can be electrocleaned in a cleaning bath. The piece of jewelry is suspended by copper wire in a stainless-steel tank in which 1 quart of water and 1 ounce of abrasive cleanser have been mixed. (You can also use a commercial cleaning solution.) The piece is wired to the negative (cathode) terminal, the steel tank to the positive (anode) terminal, and the machine is set for 6 volts. The solution is then heated over the hot plate to 82°C, or 180°F (check the temperature with a thermometer), and the machine is switched on. The piece is agitated until it is clean, which should take less than one minute. Then the jewelry is removed, rinsed, and left in cold water until the electroplating setup is ready.

The actual plating process is accomplished by suspending the object in the plating solution by the cathode wire (negative terminal) and the plating bar (anode) by the anode wire (positive terminal) and hooking these wires up to the correct terminals on the plating machine. At 2 volts a small piece of work will plate with reasonable speed. Higher voltage will be required for larger pieces, or for more than one piece. To hasten the plating of a small piece, the anode can be bent around it. If the piece is large or requires plating all around, it is best to hang at least two anodes at opposite sides of the piece being plated—perhaps even three or four.

During the plating the current should be periodically reversed for a short time in order to build up a uniform layer of metal over the entire surface.

After plating, rinse the work thoroughly in water. If cyanide solutions are being used, take care to avoid splashing the liquid. Then boil the work in soapy water and polish on a scratch brush, which burnishes the deposited metal. Afterward, a final polishing may be given, if desired.

Caution: The plating bath for gold and silver is a deadly poison, consisting of salts of cyanide. The process therefore must be handled carefully. Electroplating should never be done in the presence of children or unwary visitors. The equipment should be kept in a locked room or locked cabinet and must never be set up at higher than bench level. Extreme care must be used to avoid splashing the solution onto the bench or near the mouth, nose, or ears; also, solution should never be contacted directly with the hands. Always wear rubber gloves and a rubber apron, and wash the hands thoroughly after every operation. Only advanced students or mature and careful craftsmen should use these chemicals.

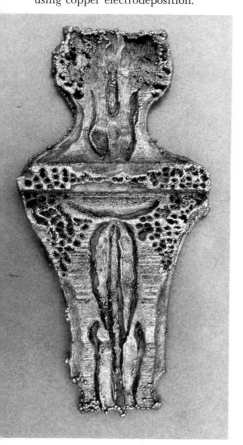

453. Chuck Evans. Experimental form using copper electrodeposition.

16.4

Electrostripping   The process of stripping old plate from the surface of a metal by electrolysis consists of placing the work on the cathode, as in regular electroplating, but reversing the current flow so that the work in effect becomes the anode. If your equipment lacks a reversing switch (Fig. 451), then you will have to put your work on the anode and hang a plate of the same metal on the cathode to receive the deposit of ions from the solution. In the stripping process a special solution is used. Stripping solutions are carried by most supply houses.

The most satisfactory method of removing fire scale (9.3) is also by means of electrostripping; for this purpose, too, a special solution is available from the supply houses. Both solutions must be kept in separate beakers or vessels to avoid contamination of the plating solutions. Keep in mind that these are dangerous cyanide solutions.

16.5

Copper Electroplating   Although plating with cyanide solutions is regarded as a process strictly for production workshops and professional educational programs, there is every reason for the typical school program to introduce electroplating with copper (Fig. 453). The formula given in Appendix C

(**C.17**) using copper sulfate and sulfuric acid is simple to mix and as safe as the pickle solution to use. This electrolyte does not need to be heated, but it should be kept moving by means of a magnetic stirrer. Otherwise, the procedure is exactly the same as that described for general plating.

16.6

Silver Electroplating in a Noncyanide Bath   The difficulties and dangers of plating with cyanide solution—particularly for schools and small work-shops—have led to a search for practical, noncyanide silver plating. The procedure outlined below, researched extensively by Charles W. Lewis, relies on the following formula:

silver sulfate (Ag_2SO_4)	30 g
potassium iodide (KI)	600 g
ammonium hydroxide, 25% (NH_4OH)	75 ml
distilled water (not tap water)	1 liter

This solution must be kept out of sunlight and should never be used with metal containers or stirrers. The solution is prepared as follows:

1. Weigh out 30 grams of the reagent silver sulfate in crystalized or powdered form, and place this material in a clean 1-liter Pyrex beaker. Install a clean glass stirring rod.
2. Pour in distilled water (pH 7) at room temperature to the 500 milliliter mark on the beaker, and stir for about three minutes. Only about 2 grams of the silver sulfate will have dissolved by this point.
3. Measure out 15 milliliters of ammonium hydroxide and pour it quickly into the beaker solution. Stir the solution rapidly during and after this addition for about ten minutes. Most of the silver sulfate should dissolve by this time. If not, add more ammonium hydroxide—a few drops at a time—until the silver sulfate dissolves.
4. While continuing to stir, add distilled water to make 700 milliliters of solution. Leave the glass stirring rod in the beaker at all times.
5. Weigh out 600 grams of potassium iodide, and, while stirring, gradually add it to the 700-milliliter solution.
6. A centigrade thermometer should be installed in the solution. Use a steam bath or a sand heater to heat the beaker solution gradually toward a temperature of 85°C. Stir at each 10°C temperature rise. All substances and surface foam will have dissolved. The solution may turn a pale lemon color. Leave the rod and thermometer in the solution.
7. Remove heat, and allow the temperature of the solution to fall normally to about 70°C.
8. Rinse the stirring rod and thermometer, and set them aside.
9. Let the beaker remain in the steam bath or heater. Cover the beaker with a clean plastic lid, such as a coffee-can lid, and allow the solution to settle overnight. About 100 milliliters of the solution will evaporate. Icelike crystals will grow out of the concentrate on the bottom of the beaker, and all traces of surface foam and crust will vanish. The total cool volume will be about 900 milliliters.
10. To rejuvenate, reinstall the centigrade thermometer and glass rod, stir in distilled water to make about 1050 milliliters, and reheat to 65°C, stirring at each 10°C temperature rise. All crystals should dissolve at about 60°C. Rinse the thermometer and rod as before.
11. Pour the entire concentrate directly into a clean 1-liter Pyrex Erlenmeyer flask at a temperature of about 50°C. Rinse the beaker with 10 milliliters of distilled water from an eyedropper to wash its walls, and pour the rinse into the storage flask.

The following steps apply to noncyanide silver electroplating with the solution prepared as above:

1. Use a *pure silver* anode ($+$) for the source of silver. This will prevent the introduction of any other metal into the concentrate. (Cleanliness is extremely important to avoid plating stains.)
2. When you are ready to plate, reheat the entire contents of the storage flask to a minimum of 65°C to redissolve all the crystals. You can utilize any portion of the solution as a plating bath.
3. The steam-bath technique is preferable for maintaining a plating-bath temperature above 35°C. The plating process works well at temperatures as low as 40°C.
4. Rejuvenate the total quantity of solution only when you are adding distilled water to compensate for evaporation loss.
5. In a separate flask prepare a *dip solution* with 2 tablespoons of household ammonia in 300 milliliters of distilled water. Immerse all objects that have had contact with the silverplating bath into the dip to recover chemical solutions. Also use the dip solution to clean the bath vessel, after rinsing it with 10 milliliters of distilled water. Store and save the dip. When it contains a considerable quantity of chemicals, use it to remanufacture the total concentrate: heat to above 90°C and hold above that temperature while restoring volume to about 1 liter. Cooling (steps 7–9), to allow for evolution of excess ammonia, and rejuvenating (step 10) will be necessary. In this way the expensive concentrate is preserved rather than wasted.
6. After the plated object has been dipped, soak it for a few minutes in tap water with a teaspoon of soap powder. Then scrub with a nylon brush.

In all other respects, follow the regular plating procedures as outlined.

Electroforming

The process of electroforming is a means of electrodeposition utilizing electroplating equipment and following the technical process of electroplating, except for the special plating baths that must be used. The steps of the process are shown in Figures 454 through 468.

Prepare a matrix from wax, expanded polystyrene, or some other suitable material. Then firmly embed a piece of fine copper, silver, or gold wire into the pattern. This piece of wire can be bent into a small ring at the end for fastening to the cathode connection, which should also be of fine metal wire, depending on the metal used for plating. Stanley Lechtzin often uses a frame around the outside of his matrix to increase conductance. Both cathode and anode wires should be annealed.

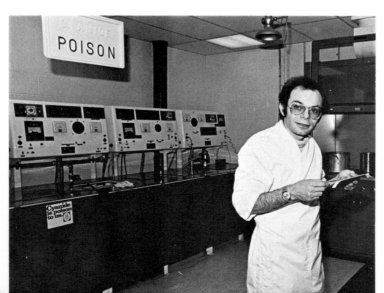

454–468. Stanley Lechtzin demonstrates electroforming procedure in making a gold-plated silver brooch with agate.

left: 454. Stanley Lechtzin in the electroforming lab at Tyler School of Art, Philadelphia.

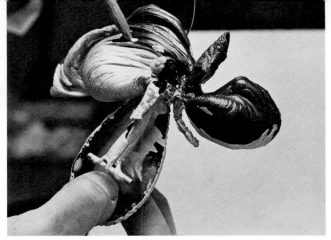

455. The wax matrix being attached to a copper wire.

456. Coating the matrix with conductive silver lacquer.

457. Placing the coated matrix into an acid-copper solution.

458. The matrix suspended in the silver-electroplating bath.

459. Removing the electroform from the silver bath.

left: 460. Dissolving the wax matrix in boiling water.

below: 461. Electrocleaning.

462. Water rinse.

463. Acid dip.

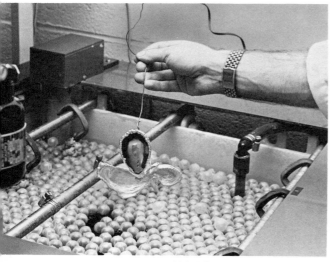

464. Nickel-electroplating dip.

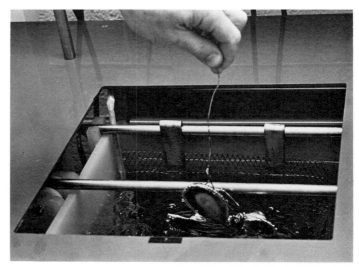

465. Gold electroplating.

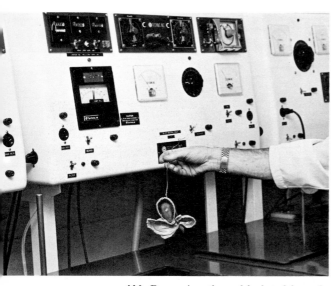

466. Removing the gold-plated brooch.

467. Scratch-brushing.

468. Completed brooch.

Spray the pattern or paint it carefully with a conductive silver coating. The silver lacquer used for printed circuits and sold in radio shops can be used. Dip the matrix in an acid-copper solution to deposit a thin coating of copper, which protects the silver coating from being dissolved by the silver-cyanide bath. Afterward rinse the matrix and place it in the silver electro-forming bath, where a silver coating is deposited.

If you want to electroform in gold, the silver-coated matrix can be transferred, after cleaning, to a gold-cyanide bath. When a sufficiently heavy coating of silver has accumulated the matrix can be boiled out before the gold plating takes place. The jeweler must distinguish, however, between solid gold electroforms and gold-veneered electroforms.

To prevent the deposition of metal at certain points on the pattern, paint on copal varnish with a small amount of chrome coloring. This can be used for cyanide solutions. The process is known as *stopping off*.

After the electroforming process, rinse the piece thoroughly and dissolve the matrix in boiling water if it has not been removed at an earlier stage. Gold and silver are usually finished by scratch-brushing with a brass or nickel-silver scratch brush, which has the effect of burnishing or smoothing the surface.

The electroform, once cleaned, can be treated like any other piece of metal—sawed, drilled, or soldered. Electroforming seems to result in an unusually dense metal. Annealing will soften it and release its compactness somewhat. One of the great advantages of the electroform is its unusual lightness (Pl. 12, p. 153; Fig. 469).

469. Lee Barnes Peck. Copper-electro-formed pendant, plated in 24k gold, with blown and fumed glass, 1971.

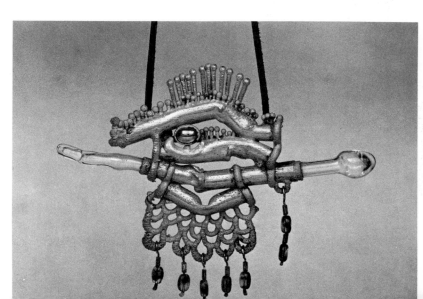

Surface
Treatment

Surface treatment applied to jewelry imparts texture—a visual or tactile element. Actually, texture can derive from two sources: it may be a natural feature of the material itself, or it may result from tool marks or any other treatment applied to the surface. Some textures, such as tool texturing (**13.10**), have been discussed in previous chapters. More advanced techniques—torch texturing and reticulation, granulation, engraving, etching, photoetching, roll printing, inlay work, and the ancient Japanese technique of mokume— will be explored in this chapter.

Torch Texturing and Reticulation

17.1

Torch Texturing   Some experimentation with the torch in fusing scraps of metal will lead directly to the discovery of torch textures. It is possible to bring the surface of a sheet of metal to a molten state while preserving the overall shape of the piece. The pin in Figure 470 was torch textured by the following method: a sterling silver disk was placed on a cold asbestos block, and the surface was hit with a very hot flame, removed quickly once the surface wrinkled. The natural oxidized color was left on the disk. (The fish design was chased on later.) An alternative way of torch texturing is to fuse filings, small chips, and beads to the surface of the metal. A torch-textured necklace by Harry Bertoia appears in Figure 226.

17.2

Reticulation   Reticulation is the term for a type of torch texturing that involves a more complex procedure. The process is based on the fact that a coating of oxides, free metal, or sometimes loam or yellow ochre will help to hold the surface in place when a sheet of silver or gold is heated to the molten state. Normally, when a piece of metal is heated to the melting point, molecular attraction pulls the metal into a globule or flat ball. If a reducing flame is used, if only a small part of the metal is melted at one time, and if the surface is well coated, the original form of the sheet metal will hold against the molecular pull. The surface of the sheet metal will tend to ripple into a texture that varies according to chance and the manner in which the surface has been coated (Fig. 471). Too thin a sheet cannot be used, because there is a tendency for holes to be melted into the metal. The usual procedure is to prepare a larger sheet of metal as stock from which shapes are cut out as needed.

To do reticulation you need a sheet of silver alloy; yellow ochre or loam; a sheet of asbestos; a torch; and a strong pickle solution. Sterling silver can be used, but a somewhat lower-grade alloy works better. One refinery will supply a silver alloy 820/1000, which is ideal for reticulation. It is available in a 3-inch width and any reasonable length (see Appendix **C.2**). Alternatively, you can prepare the alloy by heating in a graphite crucible from 800 to 925 parts of fine silver with enough pure copper to make 1000 parts by weight. This should be done in a furnace. Add the silver to the molten copper, and when the resulting metal has melted completely, stir thoroughly and pour it into an ingot mold. When the ingot is cool, roll it down to about 18-gauge thickness. Take this sheet through several stages of annealing and pickling in order to build up a good white coating of free silver oxide. It is best not to handle the silver with your fingers in order to avoid getting the surface greasy or marked. If you are planning to try a coating of loam or yellow ochre, now is the time to paint the sheet on both sides. Let the coating air dry; otherwise it will flake off when the torch is applied.

To reticulate the surface, adjust the torch to a small, medium-hot flame fed by equal amounts of air and gas. Set the metal on a clean, flat, and thoroughly dry asbestos or bismuth block. Play the flame on one small area at a time until the metal is molten. When the surface of the metal begins to wrinkle, add more air to the flame and begin playing the torch back and forth over the entire surface until the metal is completely textured. Even with utmost care,

left: 470. Philip Morton. Pin of torch-textured and chased sterling, 1945.

right: 471. Olaf Skoogfors. Pin of fused, reticulated, and gold-plated sterling, 1972.

small holes may appear, but these can sometimes be made a part of the design. After the surface has been reticulated, do the final pickling in a weak solution. The reticulated piece will be fairly brittle, and it will not be easy to forge, twist, or otherwise change in shape. Also, the metal will have a fairly low melting point, which you should keep in mind if any soldering is necessary.

Reticulation works well on gold (Pl. 13, p. 154; Fig. 259). Since it is already an alloy, 14-karat gold can be textured readily.

Granulation

Granulation is a process of surface enrichment whereby very small beads or chips are fused onto the surface of a metal to form designs or a very rich texture (Fig. 472). It is accomplished without the use of solder. The art of granulation is a very ancient one (Fig. 29), and the history of how the process was reinvented in modern times is interesting.

17.3

The Development of Granulation Techniques   The ancient practice of granulation by which the Etruscans were able to organize extremely fine beads (as small as 1/200 inch) into patterns and then fasten them so neatly and cleanly to a background metal surface remained a mystery for a very long time. Until recent times it was believed that these granules were soldered, each on its own pedestal, to the background metal. Yet no one was able to reproduce this feat.

In modern times the first successful granulations were accomplished by an Englishman named H. A. P. Littledale, who used metallic salts of the metals rather than solder alloys of those metals. For gold granulation Littledale proposed using 1 part gold oxide, 1 part copper hydrate, and 2 parts dried glue. These materials were mixed with water and applied to the work. The glue furnished excess carbon to the process and served to hold the granules in place. The work was then heated in a reducing atmosphere. By this process, Littledale reproduced some of the finest granulation of antiquity and also did original work in fine gold.

In recent times, John Paul Miller, one of the outstanding contemporary jewelers, has achieved marvelous success with granulation—even granulating with 14-karat gold (Fig. 473). Miller makes granules of gold alloyed with copper and, by his own secret process, uses the copper within the granule to form the fused attachment. He does not follow the Littledale process of applying metal salts. The essence of Miller's principle is that using gold in conjunction with copper has the effect of lowering the melting point of both.

In 1950 Patrick F. Mahler and Donald Tompkins, two students of Ronald Pearson, set to work on the problem of granulation. After reading the available literature, they finally arrived at the following procedure:

1. Use two grades of metal—for example, fine silver for the parent metal and sterling (925 parts silver, 75 copper) for the granules.
2. Prepare the parent metal for shape and finish.
3. Prepare the granules in an iron box layered with charcoal (**10.6**).
4. Heat the box in the kiln to above 1640° F.
5. Remove and wash the granules.
6. Affix the granules to the parent metal with Elmer's glue or gum tragacanth.
7. After the glue has dried thoroughly, fire the work with a carefully controlled reducing flame. This is the critical point in the process: only a few degrees separate the fusing of the granules from the melting of the piece.
8. Finish the work by pickling and then pumicing, buffing, or scratch-brushing. Finish the work gently so that the granules are not scraped off.

472. John Marshall. Diamond ring of gold and silver, with granulated gold chips, 1969.

A reducing atmosphere is created in a gas furnace by providing slight excess of gas over oxygen. In an electric kiln, the addition of small blocks of wood or the introduction of nitrogen gas into the furnace will have the same effect.

17.4

The Principle of Eutectics   In 1961 William Haendel wrote a beautifully clear and accurate technical paper on the process of attaching granules to jewelry forms. He called this process "eutectic soldering." The term *eutectic* refers to an alloy that has a melting point lower than any of its constituent metals. In the process he describes, granules are coated with copper by immersing them in an iron pan containing a sulphuric-acid pickle solution (about 1 part acid to 10 parts water) to which copper carbonate has been added.

As an example of the eutectic characteristic of metals, Haendel points out that if fine gold is alloyed with fine silver to 14 karats, the melting point of the alloy drops from 1945° to 1869.8° F. If the gold is alloyed to 14 karats with copper only, the melting point drops to 1691.6° F. When alloyed to 14 karats with equal parts of silver and copper, its melting point drops to 1540.4° F. If the admixture is composed of about 18 percent copper and 82 percent silver, the melting point of the 14-karat alloy drops to about 1342.4° F.—the lowest possible melting point of a gold alloy.

Thus, the principle of granulation by means of fusing small granules to a mother metal depends on the principle of eutectics. And the problem of granulation depends on successfully depositing on the granules a coating of copper sufficient to lower the melting point of the alloy of gold and copper, or of silver and copper, to a point below the temperature at which the mother metal begins to melt.

17.5

Granulating in the Workshop   The process of granulation is divided into four major stages:
1. Prepare the piece to be granulated. If it is to be of fine silver (Fig. 474), only a high-melting-point solder should be used—for example, I.T. grade, which is also used for enameling. The work should be finished to its final polish, since after granulation finishing will be limited to burnishing or light polishing of the granules.

left: 473. John Paul Miller. Pendant/brooch of fine gold, granulated in 18k gold, c. 1969.

right: 474. Jean Reist Stark. Granulated ball of fine silver on a double loop-in-loop chain, 1975.

2. Prepare the beads to be adhered to the work. Whether there are several or many, the manufacture is the same (**10.5**).
3. Make the solution in which to soak the granules and the gum tragacanth solution that will adhere them to the work. Two different methods of copper-coating granules are explained below: the iron-pan method and the copper-ammonia method. These are two of several different methods for coating the granules that have been used successfully. The recipe for gum tragacanth is also given below.
4. Glue the coated granules to the work, and heat it in the kiln until the granules adhere.

17.6

Iron-Pan Method
1. Mix a solution of sulphuric acid with water in a ratio of 1 to 10. Stir the mixture well, and add to a pint of pickle 1 tablespoon of copper carbonate. The solution will bubble and turn blue, emitting a gas, so wait until the action stops before stoppering the bottle.
2. Pour $\frac{1}{2}$ cup of this solution into an iron pan, and stir in the granules. The solution should be used cool, not heated, since the granules will become coated almost immediately. When they all reach a strong red-orange color, transfer the granules to a glass container, and rinse them to wash away the solution. Place them on a paper towel and dry them.
3. Granules can now be applied to the metal surface with a small sable brush and a solution of gum tragacanth.

17.7

Copper-Ammonia Method
1. File a small pile of copper filings equal to about $\frac{1}{4}$ of a penny. Put these filings into a jar with a tight screw lid, and add 1 cup of household ammonia. Allow this preparation to rest for about five days, stirring occasionally. Then pour the blue liquid into another container and discard the filings. Keep the solution tightly corked. This will be a stock solution.
2. Make a gum tragacanth solution by adding one heaping tablespoon of powdered gum tragacanth to a quart of distilled water. To do this, sieve the powder through a kitchen sieve to break up the lumps, then make a paste with a small amount of water before adding the rest of the water. Stir well to break up lumps. Now bring the solution slowly to a boil, while stirring and working out all lumps. Strain the solution through a double thickness of old nylon stockings placed in the sieve, and store it in a quart bottle with a tight lid. This is a concentrated solution.

   To mix a 1-to-20 ratio solution, measure out 1 teaspoon of concentrate to 20 teaspoons of distilled water, and mix well.
3. You must prepare a fresh granulation solution for each project. Mix $\frac{1}{2}$ teaspoon of stock solution with 5 teaspoons of gum tragacanth solution (mixed 1 to 20 ratio) if you are granulating fine silver. Mix 1 teaspoon of stock solution with 5 teaspoons of gum tragacanth solution (mixed 1 to 20 ratio) if you are granulating with gold.
4. Dip each granule into the granulation solution with tweezers, and fix it in position on the work. After all granules are in place, the work must be allowed to dry.

17.8

475. Granules in position on the mother metal, placed on a sheet of steel for handling.

Fusing Granules to the Mother Metal   Work should be placed on a sheet of steel. Bend up a corner of the sheet (Fig. 475), so it can be seized with a pair of tongs. Small work can be done in an enameling kiln, but more ambitious pieces will require a larger kiln. Place the work in a hot spot of the kiln, and

leave it until a soft pink glow spreads over the work. Then remove the lid and apply a medium-size, slightly reducing flame to the work with an air-gas or oxygen-gas torch. When the surface suddenly becomes shiny and molten, remove the torch immediately and blow on the piece. Timing is crucial, for the work can be overheated easily.

Engraving

Engraving is one of the oldest artistic techniques known. Not only engraving on bone or ivory, but the petroglyphs found on rock cliffs throughout North America reveal efforts by primitive peoples to scrape line images on durable materials. Although ancient jewelers used gravers of bronze or flint, the thin gold sheets they fashioned for their decorative jewelry were really suitable only for chasing, stamping, or repoussé.

Both as a method of illustration and as a technique for creating rich surface decoration, engraving achieved a remarkable level of development that was maintained until the mid-19th century. Thereafter, with the advent of photographic processes for illustration and of machine manufacture, the demand for engraving died away. In the 1940s Stanley Hayter revived gravure as a contemporary means of graphic expression, but engraving has elicited only limited interest among jewelers (Fig. 476). This is partly because engraving usually requires years of artistic training before any sort of elaborate surface decoration can be attempted. However, it would be possible to master the craft sufficiently to add accents or minor embellishment to a piece of jewelry (Fig. 477). The following treatment of engraving is necessarily brief, just touching on the use of the tools and techniques.

17.9

Gravers Gravers are made in a wide range of shapes, each with a distinctive name and purpose. Pointed gravers are used for gouging away small sections of metal; square- or diamond-headed gravers make fine lines. Some lining tools have as many as twenty lines set in the cutting surface. The graver used for monogramming wide block or English letters is flat. A graver's cutting surface extends its whole length in the same way that a saw blade is sharp for the length of the saw. After the blade is fitted into a handle, the length can be adjusted to the comfort of the jeweler. The major problem with gravers is one

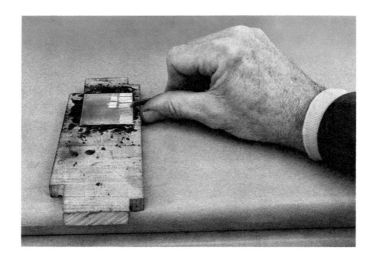

478. Form for engraving, with thumb against the block to guide the movement of the graver.

of control: the tool is extremely sharp, and pressure in the wrong direction will cause it to dig an unwanted trough in the metal or skid away from the direction you want your line to take.

17.10

Form for Engraving   For elaborate and skilled engraving a jeweler's engraving block is required, but most work can be accomplished with the sheet metal cemented to a shellac stick or a shellac block, or placed in a diemaker's ball.

To cement the metal to a shellac stick or block, place a small handful of shellac chips on the block or stick, melting them down with the torch. Place the metal on the shellac, and heat it with the torch until it sinks into the shellac. Allow it to cool, and, if you are using a block, place the block in a vise or diemaker's ball. The metal can be removed from the shellac block by striking the block sharply with a mallet. Shellac is scraped or burned off the metal or, if other methods would be damaging, dissolved away in alcohol. Before engraving, buff the metal to remove unwanted dents or scratches.

The procedure for engraving is as follows:
- Hold the graver in the hand as illustrated (Fig. 478), with the handle well back against the heel of the palm. Place the end of the thumb against the block and apply pressure. Release pressure from the thumb, and apply it to the graver by using hand muscles to push the graver forward.
- The angle of the graver must be adjusted in relation to the plate so that with a given pressure the point will be driven into the metal at a constant depth, neither going deeper nor slipping up.
- The advantage of using the hand muscles to adjust the pressure is that you have complete control of the graver. At any point cutting can be halted merely by shifting the pressure from the graver to the thumb.
- To assist you at the beginning in preventing the point from slipping out and across the metal, place the index finger of your left hand on the end of the graver. A slight pressure will hold the point down.
- When you engrave, always keep fingers and hands all on the handle side of the point.

17.11

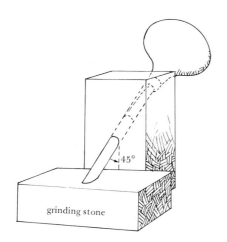

479. Graver sharpener. A hole drilled through a block of wood holds the graver in position as it is scraped against the stone.

Adjusting and Sharpening Gravers   New gravers, when fitted into the graver handle, may be too long for some hands. When the graver is held as described above, the point should not extend much beyond the end of the thumb. If it does, the excess should be taken off. This is done by setting the graver point in a vise, so that the excess length is above the vise jaws, draping an old piece of heavy cloth over the graver end, and striking the graver end sharply with a ball-peen hammer. It should snap off readily. A bevel is then ground on the end of the graver at the angle of the original tip. This should be done on a coarse grindstone. *Be careful not to burn the steel* by grinding too fast. When the correct bevel has been attained, shift to the fine grindstone for a careful smoothing. Be sure to keep the bevel in a single, true plane. Then transfer to the hand stone for sharpening and finally to the Arkansas stone for polishing.

The graver is normally sharpened *only on the beveled face.* If gravers are kept oiled and dry, there should be no rusting and consequently no need to smooth and grind the sides. Sharpening a graver consists of grinding a perfectly smooth *flat* surface on the end bevel. This can best be done with a special tool called a bevel sharpener. Otherwise you can do it by hand in the following manner: Hold the graver in your right hand so that the heel of the hand rests on the table and the end bevel is pressed against the face of the sharpening stone. A drop of oil should be used on the stone. Now carefully slide the graver point sideways along the stone, keeping the end bevel surface flat. Grind the bevel until a clean, uniform plane has been attained.

A simple graver sharpener (Fig. 479) can be made from a block of wood by drilling a hole through it at the proper angle. This angle should be identical with the angle of the face of the graver point. The graver is inserted through the hole and thus held in fixed position for grinding.

When a new graver is to be fastened into a handle, a hole must be drilled into the handle. This hole should be of a diameter about equal to the width of the tapered end about halfway up the taper. The point is then set against a hardwood block and the handle driven with light blows of a mallet.

Etching

The popularity of etching on metal dates back to Renaissance Europe, where it was a prime technique for decorating armor and weaponry. Today, most art students are familiar with the basic process, but until recently few contemporary jewelers have exploited it, possibly because of limited interest in graphic surface effects.

In the last decade or so, jewelers in Europe, particularly Ohl Ohlsson of Denmark, have shown an increasing interest in etching (Figs. 480, 481).

left: **480. Ohl Ohlsson.** Hinged bracelet of silver and gold, with etched decoration, jasper settings, 1973.

above: **481. Katie Cleaver.** Pendant of etched sterling, 1974.

Surface Treatment **247**

482. **Arline M. Fisch.** *Torso II,* pendant/brooch of chased, etched, and gold-plated silver, with ivory inlay, 1974.

Also, the extreme popularity of fantasy designs has encouraged jewelers in Europe and the United States to reexamine the potential for surface effects (Fig. 482). Besides its decorative capacity, etching prepares depressions in metal for champlevé enameling.

The jeweler can do simple etching on metal with a minimum of equipment; more sophisticated effects, such as soft-ground textures, require more elaborate tools. The brief discussion that follows will serve to introduce the general nature of the etching process. References listed in the Bibliography will provide more detail.

17.12

Materials for Etching   All of the following supplies are available at most art supply stores:

- *Asphalt ground* covers the surface of the metal to be etched and stops out the acid. Store the brush used for asphalt ground in turpentine.
- *Turpentine* thins or dissolves the asphalt ground.
- *Resin,* in lump or powdered form, is used for making the *varnish* that covers the back and edges of the work, as well as for dissolving in the aquatint process. Make the varnish by putting $\frac{1}{2}$ pound of resin in a quart jar and filling it with wood (methyl) alcohol. (Denatured alcohol will not dissolve the resin.) Keep the varnish tightly stoppered, or the alcohol will evaporate.
- *Methyl alcohol* serves for making stopping-out varnish (above) and for dissolving the varnish from the back of the plate.
- *Gasoline* dissolves asphalt ground and cleans the plate after etching.
- *Nitric acid* is the basis of the etching bath. Mix one part acid with two parts water; for better biting, put a small scrap of copper in the bath until the bath turns pale green.
- A *feather* or *sable brush* clears away bubbles that form on the surface of the copper while it is in the bath.
- A *Pyrex plate* holds the nitric-acid bath.
- *Coarse sawdust* is required for scrubbing varnish or asphalt ground off the plate.
- *Tallow* or *grease* makes soft ground.

17.13

Etching Procedure

1. Clean a small sheet of copper with gasoline to remove grease, wash in soap or detergent, and rinse thoroughly. Avoid fingerprinting the surface to be etched.
2. When the plate is perfectly dry, paint the surface evenly and smoothly with asphalt ground. Dry the ground by placing the copper on an electric hot plate, but keep switching off the current so the plate doesn't overheat. (It is hot enough when just past comfort to the touch.) This will dry and harden the asphalt ground. If you have the time, the ground can air dry.
3. Take any kind of point—needle, knife-blade, scraper—and scratch the design or texture through the ground to expose the bare copper.
4. Where errors occur, repaint with asphalt ground.
5. Paint the back and edges of the plate with varnish, and allow it to dry completely.
6. Place the plate gently into the etching bath, design-face up so that you can observe the process of the "bite."
7. Brush away any bubbles that form on the surface of the copper as it rests in the bath. These will cause the etching to be uneven if they are allowed to remain.
8. If you notice that portions of the ground are breaking away, it means that the acid bath is too strong. Remove the copper, let it dry, and repaint as necessary. Weaken the solution slightly and try again.
9. The length of time the plate is left in the acid bath will determine the depth of the bite. You can gauge this by removing the copper from the acid and testing the depth with your fingernail. When the depth is satisfactory, remove the plate and rinse under water. The biting process will take at least an hour and probably more.
10. To clean the varnish off the back of the plate, sprinkle on a little alcohol and scrub with sawdust.
11. To remove the ground from the plate, pour a little turpentine or gasoline on the plate and scrub with sawdust. Finally, wash the plate with soap.
12. To get the full impact of the etching, color the plate with liver of sulphur and polish with powdered pumice, the scratch brush, or tripoli.

17.14

Safety Notes for Etching

- When mixing the etching bath, always pour the acid carefully into the water.
- Nitric acid is corrosive to skin and clothing, and to the nose, throat, and lungs. Therefore, rinse your hands well immediately after you have handled the plate in the bath. Avoid dripping the solution onto the counter, the floor, or your clothing.
- If you splash the solution into your eyes, rinse them out immediately with a solution of bicarbonate of soda.
- Do not carry out the etching process in a closed, small, or poorly ventilated room. Put the etching bath outside, if necessary.
- Keep fire away from the solvents used for cleaning the plates. Do not smoke anywhere near the solvents.

17.15

Aquatint   Aquatint offers the possibility of an interesting variation on the etching process. After the copper plate has been cleaned, sprinkle a resin powder over the surface. To do this, crush some lumps of resin and tie the powder in a double layer of discarded nylon hose. Shake the bag of resin over the plate to sift a fine layer of resin particles onto the surface. Then set the copper on an electric hot plate to melt the small grains in place. If the copper is overheated, the grains may run together, so heat it just to the point where each separate grain fuses to the surface. Then paint the edges and back of the plate with varnish. After the varnish has dried, the copper is ready for biting.

Aquatint produces a finely stippled texture. Obviously, if one were to sprinkle particles of assorted sizes, the texture could be varied accordingly. Areas that are to remain clear of texture should be stopped out with asphalt ground.

17.16

Soft-Ground Etching   Soft ground is made by melting together asphalt (hard) ground with tallow or grease in equal proportions. Apply the soft ground to the copper in a small dab, and spread it around while the copper is heated. Then remove the copper from the hot plate, and roll the soft ground evenly over the surface with a hard rubber or leather roller. The plate must be quite cool before rolling.

Texture is achieved by laying various types of material—lace, screen, burlap, string—on top of the soft ground. A piece of felt about $\frac{1}{4}$-inch thick should be placed on top of the textured material. Sandwich the plate between two $\frac{1}{4}$-inch plywood boards, and then roll it through the rolling mill or press (Fig. 309). Adjust the rolls so that a moderate pressure is exerted on the felt. This pressure will force the textured materials into the soft ground. When the imprint materials are pulled carefully away from the copper, they will leave a clear impression. After the copper has been varnished on the back, it is ready for etching. The soft ground must be handled carefully to avoid disturbing the textured surface. The range and variety of potential materials is almost unlimited.

17.17

Hard-Ground Rollprints   Using a hard ground (asphalt) rather than a soft ground allows imprinting with hard materials, such as wire screen, sandpaper, or clusters of fine wire. As with the soft ground, a felt pad must be placed on top of these materials. If sandpaper is used for texturing, it may need to be rolled through several times. The two plywood boards will protect the rolls of the rolling mill.

17.18

Etching by Reverse Electrodeposition   If you have access to electroplating equipment (Fig. 449), etching by reverse electrodeposition may prove far more convenient and rapid than the conventional process. William Haendel has pointed out that this method eliminates the problem of corrosive fumes in the small workshop and attains direct, deep bites without the usual undercutting of acid etching. The procedure is essentially that of electroplating (**16.3**) for copper, except that the poles are reversed, as outlined below:

1. Prepare your work just as you would for acid etching, except that you must soft-solder (**10.8**) the end of a copper wire to an exposed place on the back of the work. The wire is attached to the cathode terminal of the DC source. It would be well to make this attachment before applying any ground to the surface of the plate.
2. After the ground has been air dried or baked on the plate and the design scratched through, varnish the back and edges of the plate, including the length of the copper wire, with stopping-out varnish, and allow it to dry.
3. Suspend the plate in the solution as a cathode. Copper plates are also suspended in the solution in front of the etching surface as anodes. *But the current is reversed* (note switch in Fig. 451).

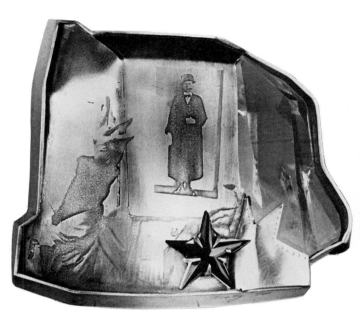

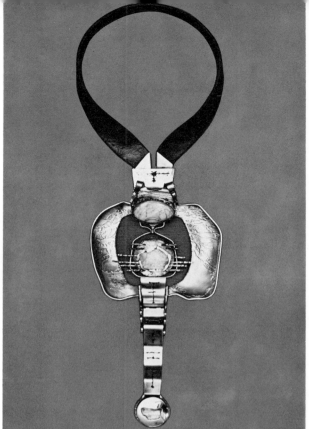

above: 483. Eleanor Moty. *Dual Image Pin,* of photoetched sterling, with quartz crystal and obsidian star, 1974.

right: 484. Thomas Berglund. Pendant of forged and photoetched copper and silver, with leather neckpiece, set with Oregon jasper and raw turquoise, 1975.

4. The solution is the regular solution for copper plating (**C.17**).
5. The depth of the bite will depend on the voltage used and the duration of the charge.
6. Clean the plate as for any regular etching process.

Photoetching

The wide-ranging exploration of technological processes has led some contemporary jewelers to experiment with registering on metal textures and images derived from photographs. Photoetching (or photofabrication) has been researched by the Eastman Kodak Company for industrial applications, and the process is now available to the experimental jeweler as well (Figs. 483, 484).*

17.19

The Photoetching Process   In the photoetching process a piece of metal (copper or silver) is coated with a special ultraviolet-light-sensitive resist, which is then baked or air dried on. Since the resist is light-sensitive, all work must be done in a darkroom with a safelight. After the metal has dried, a contact print is made on it with a black-and-white negative. Negatives from high-contrast film (such as Kodak High-Contrast Copy or Kodak Ortho) will

*Eastman Kodak Company pamphlet P246, *Photofabrication Methods,* provides introductory technical information, and individual specification sheets describe the various metal-etch resists available. Requests should be sent to Department 454, Eastman Kodak Company, Rochester, New York 14650.

give stronger images than those from conventional films in which grays predominate. The contact print is made by exposing the resist-coated plate and the negative to ultraviolet light.

After exposure, the plate is developed in a special developer solution in the darkroom. This bath removes the resist, thus exposing the metal for the etching process. Etching proceeds in the normal manner (**17.13**) with a solution of nitric acid or by the process of reverse electrodeposition (**17.18**).

Just as a photographer who is printing a negative makes test strips of the print using different developing and exposure times, so the jeweler should try at least one experimental run before attempting a final piece. For the experimental run you might use several pieces of copper plate with different exposure and developing times, recording the procedure for each. Practice will help you to estimate what kind of treatment different types of negatives require.

17.20

Photoetching on Copper   The following materials and equipment are required for photoetching on copper:

- KRP-3 Kodak Photo Resist, Type 3 (for copper)
- Kodak Ortho Resist Developer
- Kodak Ortho Resist Thinner
- varnish and alcohol
- stainless-steel or glass tray
- darkroom safelight
- sheet of ultraviolet-light-transmitting glass
- 2 black-light fluorescent tubes fitted to an exposure box

Note that there are two kinds of resist: negative-working and positive-working. With the *negative-working* resist, the *exposed* areas of the resist remain on the surface after development; with the *positive-working* resist, the *unexposed* areas remain on the surface after development. When ordering resist, you must specify the type.

All the solutions used in the photoetching process are corrosive to skin, lungs, and eyes. You should wear rubber gloves whenever handling the solutions, and if any solution should come into contact with the skin, wash the affected areas immediately. Avoid working in an unventilated room for prolonged periods.

Steps in the photoetching process for copper are as follows:
1. If possible, drill a small hole in a corner of the copper plate so that a wire can be inserted for dipping and hanging to dry. You can also use a metal clip if you have one strong enough. Another method is to construct a cradle of wire or masking tape to support the work during dipping and drying.
2. Prepare the copper by cleaning with detergent to remove grease or oil. After it has been cleaned, do not handle the surface. Dip the plate in nitric acid solution to put a tooth on the surface for the resist. Then, air dry the plate completely, so that the resist will hold.
3. Transfer the work to a darkroom, and turn on the safelight. Using rubber gloves, pour about 1 inch of KRP-3 resist into the tray. Dip the copper plate into the resist, taking care that a smooth film, with no bubbles, covers the surface. Should bubbles appear, you can brush them away with a sable brush or the tip of a feather. Let the excess resist drip into the tray, then hang the plate to dry for at least 24 hours. Since the plate is now light-sensitive, it must remain in the darkroom (or in a light-tight box) until ready for exposure.

4. Prepare the work for light exposure by laying the negative directly on the coated copper plate. Place a sheet of clean, ultraviolet-transmitting glass over the negative in order to hold it flat and maintain contact with the plate. If the copper plate is smaller than the negative and/or the glass plate, you can add a piece of cardboard under the copper to make a compact "sandwich" arrangement. Elastic bands at the edges will hold the pieces together.

5. Expose the plate to a source of ultraviolet light. On very bright days, you can expose the plate by setting it on a support in a safe place in direct sunlight. The sun's rays, of course, will be strongest at midday and in the summer. Give the plate an exposure of fifteen minutes or more to the direct sunlight. Experiment will determine the correct exposure.

   If you are using black-light fluorescent tubes, exposure should be 30 to 40 minutes. Generally speaking, overexposure is preferable to under-exposure. Exposure should take place in the darkroom. Black-light fluorescents must be used with extreme caution, because the ultraviolet radiation they emit is *damaging to the eyes.* Therefore you should construct some sort of light-tight box to contain both the tubes and the plate for exposure. A cardboard box will do if it is long enough to hold the tube housing (Fig. 485). Set the two tubes in the bottom of the box at the center, about 1 inch apart. Devise a sling of cords to cradle the plate-negative-glass assembly at a level about 7 inches above the tubes. Wire the fluorescent tubes together in parallel, and run the cord through a tight hole in the box end. When the carton is closed, it may be necessary to place a cover of heavy paper or cardboard on the top to seal the seam. A weight will hold the lid in position. *Close the box tightly* before turning on the switch for exposure, and do not open the box until you have turned off the switch.

6. At completion of the exposure period, remove the source of ultraviolet light. For black-light tubes, turn off the switch; when sunlight has been used, transfer the plate immediately to the darkroom.

7. To develop the plate, pour about 2 inches of Ortho Resist Developer into the tray, using rubber gloves. Run a clean wire through the corner hole in the plate or set the plate in its wire cradle, and immerse it. Agitate the plate gently by moving it up and down through the tray as you would in developing a print. Developing time should be no more than three minutes for KRP-3 resist. Kodak specifications will give the time for other resists. Still wearing rubber gloves, rinse the plate with water, then hang it to dry for at least 24 hours. Eastman Kodak recommends baking the plate, but this involves certain difficulties and should not be necessary at an experimental stage.

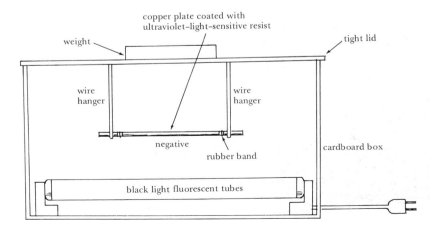

485. Diagram showing the arrangement of copper plate and black-light tubes for copper photoetching.

left: **486.** Rollprints made from a work-hardened penny in soft sheets of annealed copper, as demonstrated by Heikki Seppa.

right: **487.** Rollprint in soft copper (*above*) made from a pattern of heavy iron wire wound over an iron strip (*below*), as demonstrated by Heikki Seppa.

8. Prepare the plate for etching by painting the back and edges with stopping-out varnish wherever the resist may have dissolved or peeled off. Then proceed with the usual method of etching (17.13) in the nitric-acid bath. Take care with the length of the bite, for overbiting will tend to undercut the resist. However, this overbiting can create very interesting textural effects.
9. When the etching is complete, remove the resist with kerosene, turpentine, or thinner. Alcohol will dissolve the varnish on the back of the plate.

17.21

Photoetching on Sterling Silver   The procedure described above for copper can be followed for sterling silver, *except* that you must use KMER Metal-Etch Resist and Metal-Etch Resist Developer. The solutions used for copper cannot be applied to silver.

Rollprints

The rolling mill has long been used to roll out gallery wire with many kinds of designs engraved into the rolls themselves. By extension, one can use the rolling mill to impress a textured material into a soft metal plate. This idea leads to what Heikki Seppa calls "rollprints" (Figs. 486, 487). The textural possibilities are limited only by the size of the rolls and the necessary concern for protecting the rolls themselves.

17.22

Texturing with the Rolling Mill   Almost any hard material can be rolled between two sheets of annealed nonferrous metal, as long as it promises an interesting textural result: wire screens, arrangements of wire, string, thread, woven materials, even organic forms such as leaves, seed pods, grasses, and bark.

To make double rollprints, first select, size, and anneal two sheets of nonferrous metal. Place your textural material between the sheets. For even rolling, adjust the rolls to accommodate the double thickness of the sheets, and run them through the mill (Fig. 488). Only one pass can be made, because the sheets will become elongated as they are rolled. If you want only a single print, use a sheet of half-hard or hard-rolled brass, of perhaps 16-gauge thickness, for a back plate.

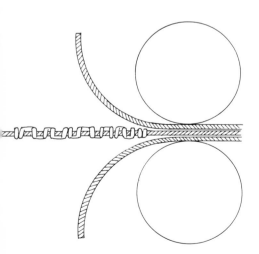

488. Diagram showing a pattern like that of Figure 487 being rolled in the rolling mill between two sheets of annealed metal.

Inlay

Inlay, sometimes called the "marriage of metals," is a traditional jewelry form in which one metal is set into another, usually by a painstaking file-and-fit process. Its chief decorative property is the contrast in color between two or more materials (Figs. 489, 490). No matter what is being inlaid—sheet metal, metal strips, wire, or solder—the basic principle is the same. Of course, other materials besides metal can be inlaid, including plastics, stone, and wood. Enameling, another form of inlay—indeed, one of the most important—is treated in Chapter 18. This discussion will be limited to the use of metals. Three processes will be described: *sheet metal inlay, wire inlay,* and *solder inlay.*

above: **489. Barbara Becker.** *How ya gonna keep 'em down on the farm after they've seen Paree?,* pendant of cast and constructed bronze, with sterling-silver sheet inlay, tintype (c. 1860), and glass, 1975. Animals were cast from plastic by lost wax.

right: **490. Katie Cleaver.** Necklace of copper and brass, with sterling inlay, 1973.

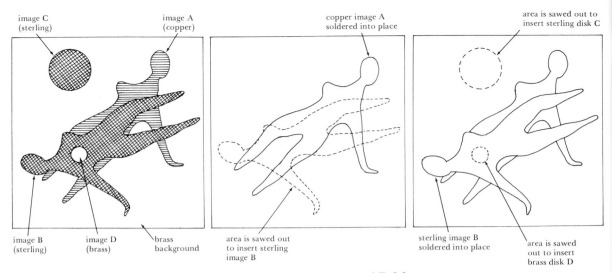

image C
(sterling)

image A
(copper)

copper image A
soldered into place

area is sawed out to
insert sterling disk C

image B
(sterling)

image D
(brass)

brass
background

area is sawed out
to insert sterling
image B

sterling image B
soldered into place

area is sawed
out to insert
brass disk D

17.23

491–494. Procedure for sheet metal inlay.

left: 491. Layout for a brass pendant inlaid with sterling, copper, and brass.

center: 492. The area for image B is sawed out through the brass plate and through image A, already soldered in place.

right: 493. After image B has been soldered in place, the circular holes for images C and D are cut and filed to shape.

Sheet Metal Inlay   One way of learning a method of sheet metal inlay is to observe, step-by-step, the actual inlaying of a fairly complex design. The technique used here can be adapted to any similar type of inlay. Three metals of contrasting colors—copper, silver, and brass—were used to make this experimental pendant (Figs. 491–494).

The procedure was as follows:
1. The design was worked out and the sequence of inlay planned (Fig. 491).
2. The background plate of brass was prepared.
3. Image *A* was transferred to a piece of 18-gauge sheet copper. The image was sawed out, making certain that the traced outline was left on the piece. Then the edges were filed down just *to* the traced line. A very sharp pointed scribe was used for all tracing. Then, with this image serving as a template, another image was traced, which we will call image *B*. The edges were file finished.
4. Image *A* was placed on the background plate in the correct design position. The image was traced with a sharp scribe, in such a way that the line followed the contours at all points. A small hole was drilled on the inside of the image near the traced outline. The image was pierced out, leaving the traced line *on* the background plate.
5. Next, the image was filed down carefully to the traced line. Then began a process of "try-and-fit-and-file," until all the high points on the background plate had been filed away. (The image *A* plate was not filed.)
6. When the image fit the background plate perfectly, the two were placed together upside down on a flat charcoal block and soldered, using the strip method of applying solder (**10.18**). Care was taken not to spread solder all over the back seam. After soldering, the metal was pickled clean and dried.
7. On the front side of the background, image *B* was placed in its proper position and carefully traced. This image was pierced through the plate and the soldered image *A* (Fig. 492), leaving the scribed line on the plate. Then the edges were filed down to the scribed line.
8. Now followed the process of filing and fitting until image *B* fit into the background plate.
9. Image *B* was soldered in place in the background plate.
10. Image *C*, a sterling disk about $\frac{3}{4}$ inch in diameter, was prepared. This was set on the background in the correct design position and traced accurately.
11. A small hole was drilled inside the circle, and the shape was pierced, leaving the traced line on.

12. The pierced hole was filed to the traced line. Then followed the process of filing and fitting until the disk fit snugly (Fig. 493).
13. Image D was cut—a brass disk about $\frac{1}{4}$ inch in diameter. The edges were filed and placed in position on the image for tracing. This circle was pierced and filed until it fit into the figure.
14. The piece was placed upside down on a charcoal block, and both disks were soldered into place.
15. After all soldering, the seams on the front side were inspected for gaps. A corrective procedure for gaps is to flux the entire piece on both sides, then place it upside down, and flow additional solder at the points of the gaps. If this fails, it may be necessary to take a small ball-peen or chasing hammer and a small ball-point punch and work along each side of the seam to force down the metal from the back side in order to close the seam on the front side. After this has been done, it will be necessary to flux each side and again reheat the piece, so that solder flows into the seams that have been planished together. The front side is always placed down on a flat charcoal block to prevent the separate pieces from shifting out of position when the solder melts.
16. Finally, the entire plate was planished in order to create a slightly arched surface in both directions. Then the surface was filed smooth and emeried to remove the file marks and prepare for a tripoli finish (Fig. 494).

The finish of an inlaid piece is important. Since highly polished metal surfaces tend to lose color contrast, some kind of coloring is generally called for in finishing. When you are experimenting with finishes, try liver of sulphur mixed with detergent and applied with a scratch brush of brass. Dip your piece alternately in pickle solution and in liver of sulphur solution. Be sure to rinse off each solution before immersing the piece in the other solution. The final finish will depend on whatever effect pleases you. The solution of liver of sulphur should be relatively weak, or you will get a flaky coat on the copper.

17.24

Wire Inlay   In wire inlay, the problem is to keep the wire from falling out of the groove into which it has been hammered. This is accomplished by making the groove narrow at the surface and wide underneath, and forcing into the groove wire that is slightly bigger than the surface of the cut. In effect, the wire is held in place by two ledges of metal. The procedure is as follows:

1. Prepare the base metal by scribing the design you wish to inlay.
2. Using a hammer and the engraving tool called a *liner,* make an even groove, hammering at an angle all along the scribed line. (Remember that only a curved liner can cut curves effectively.)
3. Hammer the liner along the groove again, this time aiming the point in the opposite direction. You are cutting a wide-bottomed, narrow-mouthed trough in the metal (Fig. 495).
4. Hammer the wire into the trough, and planish it smooth.

Similar results can be obtained by carving the channel with a scorper (Figs. 359–360).

17.25

Solder Inlay   Solder can also be used in small, shallow, inlaid areas such as are made with chasing tools. After the areas have been prepared (**13.8**), paint them with liquid flux, and set the paillons of solder in place. The solder must have a melting temperature considerably lower than that of the base metal, so that the base will not melt before the solder. Allow enough solder to compensate for the slight shrinkage that will occur when it cools. After the piece has been pickled, file off any solder that may have escaped the line.

494. The finished pendant, with surface planished to a slightly convex shape.

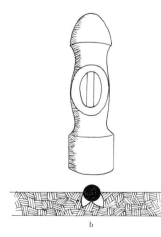

495. Section view of wire inlay procedure: A double-grooved trough is cut into the metal with a liner (*a*), and the wire is hammered in (*b*). See also Figs. 359–360.

Mokume

Mokume is an ancient Japanese technique of creating a moiré or "wood grain" pattern on the surface of metal (Pl. 14, p. 156; Fig. 496). Thin layers of several different metals are combined into a sheet and then pushed out shallowly from the back in various patterns by means of repoussé. When the small projections are filed off on the front side of the sheet, a moiré effect appears, consisting of wavelike contour patterns created by the exposed layers of metal.

Mokume has become popular in recent years because of the increasing interest in organic textures. The process is not difficult if carried out correctly. What is essential is absolute cleanliness, flatness of sheets, and a uniform and thorough soldering between each pair of sheets.

17.26

Preparation of Metal for Mokume   The procedure described below is planned so that the gold sheet will remain on top in the final mokume surface. If you wish one of the other metals to be on top, adjust the directions accordingly.

1. Prepare a small sheet of 18-gauge metal, perhaps $1\frac{1}{4}$ inches square, from each of the following materials: sterling silver, bronze, copper, brass, and gold. A small size is preferable, because it simplifies the problems of cleaning, soldering, and rolling.
2. Anneal and pickle these pieces.
3. Hammer each piece with a rawhide mallet on a flat anvil to make sure there is no curving or warping.
4. Lay each piece on a paper towel, and scrape the surfaces uniformly with a scraper to remove oxides and fire scale. To avoid getting oil or dirt on the metal, do not handle the sheets with your fingers, but use tweezers or a paper towel.
5. The object of the first stage of mokume is to solder the sheets together, gold uppermost, with thin, even layers of solder. To ensure that each sheet is completely covered and that there are no gaps in the solder, solder each sheet separately before sandwiching it with the others. Place sheets of silver, bronze, copper, and brass side by side on a flat charcoal block, and apply borax flux. Make certain each surface is completely and evenly covered with a light coating of flux. (The gold sheet is reserved for use as the top sheet of the sandwich.)
6. Flow medium-grade silver solder onto each of the plates. If you are using sheet solder, cut $\frac{1}{4}$-inch square pieces and space them all over the surface. For strip solder, apply it with tweezers to the heated plate until every part is covered. If there are gaps in the solder, take a soldering pick and spread the solder to close them. *Do not overheat the metal.*
7. Soak the four soldered plates in *hot water, not pickle solution,* until the flux is removed.
8. Check to make sure that the surfaces are uniformly covered with solder. If they are not, go back to the charcoal block and resolder.
9. Scrub both sides of each sheet with pumice powder and an old toothbrush. Rinse and dry.
10. Place the silver sheet on the charcoal block, solder side up, and cover with a *light* coat of flux. Place the bronze sheet exactly on the silver, also solder side up, and cover it with a light coat of flux. Repeat this for the copper and the brass sheets. Finally, position the gold sheet on top.
11. Paint all the *edges* with a light coat of borax flux.
12. Stack the sheets, with the gold on top, on a very flat, heavy, iron-wire soldering screen on top of a tripod (Fig. 497a).

496. Chuck Evans. Pendant of forged and turned brass and copper, with laminated sections hammered and filed in mokume technique, 1974.

13. For soldering the plates together, use a large, bushy annealing flame, and play the flame alternately underneath and on top of the sheets, all around. This will heat them uniformly.

14. When the solder begins to flow, take a long iron-wire soldering pick and press gently on the top plate. Wiggle the top plate slightly and very carefully. This action will squeeze out excess solder and ensure that no air will be trapped underneath. Do not apply excessive pressure on the top sheet until solder appears at all the seams; then maintain the pressure after the flame is removed until the solder has solidified.

15. Soak the solder plates again in *hot water, not pickle solution,* until the flux has dissolved. Then inspect to make certain that all seams are full of solder.

16. If any gaps are found in the seams, these must be painted with flux, reheated, and soldered.

17. This sandwich of sheets is now run through the rolling mill (Fig. 497*b*). Put the same end through the mill each time, and keep the same side up each time. Roll this laminated sheet out until it is twice its original length. Anneal the sheet often to avoid brittleness and cracking.

18. Saw the rolled sheet into two equal shapes. Flatten each piece with a mallet on a flat anvil, as you did before.

19. Scrape the two surfaces that are to be soldered together—the top of one half and the bottom of the other (Fig. 497*c*).

20. Repeat all the necessary steps to solder the two sheets together (step 5 through step 19). If you carry out the rolling operation three times, you will have forty layers. A greater number than this will probably create unnecessarily complex results.

21. On the final rolling, roll your plate out in two directions until you have a sheet of 18-gauge thickness. Anneal often during this final rolling out.

17.27

Creating Mokume Patterns

1. Mokume patterns are achieved by repoussé—hammering out a pattern of indentations (Fig. 498). This can be done on a lead cake. The punch marks can follow any arrangement—random or ordered. They must not be too deep, that is, not past the middle of the sheet. As the diagrams in Figure 499 show, all that is necessary is that several layers are pushed up so that they can be cut across. Indentations that are too deep will result in holes through the plate.

2. After the repoussé process is complete, take a No. 2 hand file to cut away the bumps and level the entire surface. This is more easily done if, at the final rolling, the piece is left in a slightly curved shape rather than perfectly flat.

3. If desired, the plate can then be rolled to smooth out the indentations underneath.

4. If any additional soldering needs to be done to complete the piece, be sure to use easy solder so as to avoid melting the solder that joins the mokume layers together. Finish the surface with a fine file, emery, and tripoli.

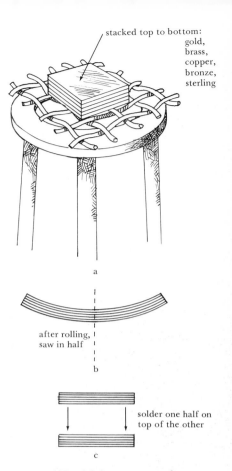

stacked top to bottom: gold, brass, copper, bronze, sterling

a

after rolling, saw in half

b

solder one half on top of the other

c

above: 497. Mokume procedure: Sheets of five metals are laminated and soldered (*a*), rolled and sawed in half (*b*), and joined to make a ten-layer sandwich (*c*).

below: 498. Sample mokume plaque, after repoussé hammering but before filing and finishing.

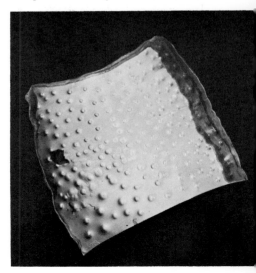

499. Indentations for mokume should be hammered deep enough to displace a few layers of metal (*left*), not so deep that holes will be cut in the surface (*right*).

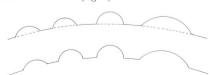
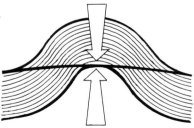

Enameling

The art of enameling has been practiced in almost every developed culture. Its origins are obscure, but enamels dating from the 13th century B.C. have been found in Cyprus, and from the 9th century B.C. in Asia Minor. Both Chinese and Japanese artists practiced enameling at an early time, and the art was known throughout Europe during the Middle Ages. Particularly fine are Celtic enamels, such as the famous 9th-century "Alfred Brooch" (Fig. 500).

The different enameling techniques emerged separately in various places. Byzantium became an important center for cloisonné during the 10th century (Fig. 45); enamels from Limoges and from the valleys of the Rhine and the Meuse began to appear in the 12th century; we find the basse-taille technique in the 13th century and plique-à-jour in the 15th. Throughout the Middle Ages and into the Renaissance, enamels flourished in Europe. Nearer to our own time, enameling enjoyed great popularity in the 19th century (Fig. 65), and the art is currently undergoing a healthy revival (Fig. 501).

In essence, enameling is a means of adding color to jewelry or other objects by fusing a glassy substance to metal. The actual enamel is a combination of several chemicals—soda or potash, flint, lead, and potassium hydroxide. To this colorless mixture, called *frit,* are added the metallic oxides that form the enamel colors. These may be transparent, translucent, opalescent, or opaque.

18.1

Materials and Equipment   Not much equipment is needed to make a modest beginning in enameling. The following items, some of them pictured in Figure 502, will serve the needs of most jewelers involved in enamel work:

- a kiln for firing, probably the small table model used by hobbyists. If you need a larger kiln, you should obtain one with a door that opens forward on a horizontal hinge, for this controls escaping heat better than a door that opens laterally on a vertical hinge.
- sable brush, No. 1 or No. 3 size, for applying enamels
- small metal tools—enameling spatula, pointer, and spreader—for applying enamels.
- firing fork, tongs, or household spatula for placing enamels in the kiln and retrieving them
- trivets and wire mesh racks to support the work in the kiln. These should be of nichrome or a similar material that will not form fire scale (**9.3**) to flake off on the enamel. The edges of the wire racks should be turned under on two sides so that the firing fork can be inserted underneath.
- asbestos board at least 1 foot square on which to lay fired work
- asbestos glove to protect the hand when loading or unloading the kiln
- glass or ceramic jars or containers to hold the enamels while work is in progress
- ground enamels, 80 mesh, in opaque and transparent varieties in a range of colors, plus transparent flux and opaque white
- gum tragacanth in solution (**17.7**) or Klyrfire for adhering the enamels to the metal
- pickling equipment for cleaning the base metal (**9.2**). The pickle should be one part nitric acid to five parts water, mixed in a glass bowl.
- Scalex to prevent fire scale (**9.3**) from forming on copper
- Carborundum stones in medium and fine grades for grinding and polishing fused enamels
- sheet of base metal (**18.2**)

Beyond this basic list, jewelers who are interested in specialized methods of enameling or particular effects may want to consider the following additional equipment:

right: 501. Garry L. Sherman. *FBI Belt Buckle (Standard Director's Issue),* of cast bronze with prong-set cloisonné enamel, 1972.

below: 502. Enameling equipment (*from upper left*): Klyrfire and Scalex (in larger jars), ground enamels, glass containers, copper sheet, brush, spreader, pointer, enameling spatula, household spatula, medium and fine Carborundum stones, wire racks, trivets, asbestos board, and kiln.

above: 500. *Alfred Brooch,* of gold filigree with cloisonné enamel. English, found 1693 at Athelney, Somerset; 9th century. Ashmolean Museum, Oxford.

- mortar and pestle for grinding one's own enamels
- sieves and sifters, in 80- and 200-mesh sizes, for sifting dry enamels onto large pieces
- stiff bristle brush for cleaning sieves
- glass fiber brush for finishing, polishing foil, or thoroughly cleaning a stoned surface
- emery paper in four or five fine grades for special finishing
- pyrometer, which measures the temperature in the kiln and aids in determining when the correct temperature has been reached

18.2

Metals for Enameling   The metals used for enameling are gold, fine silver, and copper; each has its particular advantages. Being the most precious metal, gold may be especially desirable for fine jewelry. A special gold alloy that bonds well with enamels can be purchased in sheet form wherever precious metals are sold (**B.4**).

The silver used for enameling is fine (pure) silver, which does not become discolored by oxides during heating, as sterling silver does. Also, fine silver has a higher melting point than sterling (1762°F as compared to 1640°F), which acts as an advantage, since the metal is subjected to frequent reheating during the enameling process. Because fine silver does not wear very well, the finished enamel piece can be set into a base of sterling with some device that does not require soldering—a bezel or claw setting, for example (**21.1, 21.2**). With such a setting the enameled piece becomes the focal point. However, many contemporary jewelers have ingeniously used enamels for secondary decoration. Plate 15 (p. 154) shows a complicated gold form by John Paul Miller in which both enamel and granulation serve as integrated decorative effects.

The third possibility, copper, has as its chief virtue a relatively low cost, so it might be a good choice for the beginner who wishes to experiment.

18.3

Types of Enamels   The art of enameling depends to a great extent on the different effects that can be achieved by mixing or overlaying materials. To get an idea of the infinite combinations that are possible, one need only consider the variables: base metal; transparent flux or opaque white ground; transparent, opaque, translucent, or opalescent enamels; a complete range of colors; the use or absence of foils; and different types of finish. For example, transparent enamels applied over a transparent flux will allow the base metal to show through, thus creating a gemlike sense of depth with subtle colors. This combination makes it difficult to obtain intense colors. However, when the same transparent enamels are used over an opaque white ground, the colors will be more intense and slightly flatter but still jewellike. Opaque enamels always result in a flatter effect, with the colors seeming to be right at the surface; there is no sense of depth, but the colors can be quite vivid. Opalescent colors are neither opaque nor transparent but in between; a mat finish will produce interesting stonelike qualities on these enamels. At the other extreme, an unusual brilliance can be achieved by applying transparent or translucent enamels over foils. The color of the metal, too, can contribute to the overall result. Transparent or translucent colors placed over silver may seem sharply brilliant, whereas copper or gold will impart a warm tone, bringing different hues closer together and muting them. The various types of enamel work (**18.6**) also yield strikingly different effects.

Enamels differ in the temperatures at which they will fuse, so problems sometimes arise when the enamelist has not become familiar—by means of exploratory tests—with the various hard and soft properties of the enamels. Very hard enamels layered over very soft ones (and the reverse) often cause flaws. Soft-fusing enamels melt at 1450°F., medium enamels at 1500°F., and hard at 1550°F. Experience will show which layering combinations to avoid.

18.4

Handling and Storage of Enamels   Absolute cleanliness is vital to enameling, for the slightest contamination with dirt, ashes, or another color can ruin your materials. Ground enamels cannot be used just as they are purchased but must be washed thoroughly in order to yield clear, strong colors.

Place the colors in shallow glass or ceramic containers, cover with water and stir the mixture; then pour off the milky water. Repeat this process several times until the water is absolutely clear.

Some enamelists who are particularly concerned with pure, strong colors prefer to grind their own enamels. The materials are purchased in cake-lump form and ground with water in a mortar and pestle. In this process the washing and grinding take place simultaneously, since the water is poured off and replaced each time it becomes milky. After the enamels have been ground and dried, they must be graded by passing through an 80-mesh sieve. Grinding is a very tedious process, and most jewelers find purchased ground enamels, after careful washing, to be entirely satisfactory.

Ground enamels should be stored in glass bottles with airtight screw lids, for moisture in the air will cause them to deteriorate. Each bottle should be labeled with the manufacturer's name, the number of the enamel, the color, and the type (soft, medium, hard) if it is known. Leftover waste enamels can be mixed together in a jar; with an equal volume of hard flux added, this becomes a *counterenamel* (**18.8**) suitable for inconspicuous backs of pieces.

18.5

Color Test for Enamels   Until you know by experience exactly what color will result from firing a given enamel onto a particular metal, you should undertake the test described below. Ideally, you should make a test for each color you possess—especially the transparent colors, which will show varying aspects over metal, over a white base, over gold or silver foils, and over opaque colors or other transparents. Make the test piece as follows (Fig. 503):

1. Prepare a sheet of copper, approximately 4 by 4 inches, as shown in Figure 503, and on it lay four different grounds in horizontal bands.

enamel colors

	1	2	3	4	5	6	7	8	9	10
transparent flux										
opaque white over flux										
silver foil over flux										
gold foil over flux										

503. Plan for a test piece for transparent enamels. Ten different colors are laid over four different grounds; the results are preserved permanently in the fired piece.

2. Apply the different-colored enamels in vertical strips, using the procedures described below (**18.7**, **18.8**).
3. As you apply the colors, label a coded chart in your notebook that duplicates the checkerboard of the test piece.
4. Fire the test piece (**18.9**).

18.6

Classic Forms of Enameling   Enameling has many traditional forms as well as some modern ones. This chapter will outline basic techniques; jewelers who require more sophisticated knowledge of the processes should consult books devoted specifically to enameling (see Bibliography).

Although the different forms of enameling offer varied decorative effects, they share a similar general procedure.

Cloisonné is a French word meaning "partitioned," and this describes the divided effect of cloisonné enamels. A framework of flat metal wires is shaped into a design, with the wires adhering to a metal base. The spaces in the framework are filled with enamel, so that each color is bordered by a thin strip of metal.

Plique-à-jour resembles cloisonné, except that there is no base metal. The enamel portions are translucent, giving the effect of a stained-glass window.

The technique of *champlevé* combines inlay and enameling. Indentations are engraved, punched, or etched into the surface of metal and then filled with enamels.

Limoges enameling, named for the French city that once specialized in this very basic technique, is like cloisonné enameling without the wires. It is often called "painting with enamel," since the results look like tiny paintings.

Basse-taille, a French term for low relief work, designates a kind of enameling in which the metal is textured by gravers or punches and transparent enamels allow the texture to show through.

Grisaille, the French for painting with only black, white, and shades of gray, is the application of light-and-dark effects to enamels. Successive coatings of white enamel are applied to a dark background to create a rich spectrum of values.

18.7

Preparation for Enameling   Some basic steps should be taken before you begin any actual enameling work.

- Complete all soldering, except of findings. You must use hard solder, since anything else will be melted in the intense heat of the kiln.
- Roughen the surface of the metal with medium emery paper or fine (00) steel wool. This helps the enamels to adhere.
- The metal you are enameling should be thoroughly clean, free of oxides, oils, and dust. Copper and gold can be pickled in a solution of 1 part nitric acid to 5 parts water; silver in one of 1 part sulphuric acid to 10 parts water. The piece should then be rinsed in water and scrubbed with a household cleansing powder.
- Enamels should not be fired onto perfectly flat metal, which tends to crack the enamel since it has no resistance to warping. If a small plaque is being formed for later setting in a bezel, it should be domed slightly with a round-end mallet on a round anvil or repoussé bowl.

18.8

Applying Enamels   There are two basic methods of applying enamels to a base metal: *wet application* with a brush or spatula, and *dry application* by sifting. The latter helps to achieve a large, even surface in one color and is practical mainly for such pieces as trays or plates.

The process of applying enamels consists of a series of steps—interspersed with firings—that are repeated until the desired effect has been attained. Usually, the jeweler begins with a layer of *counterenamel* on the reverse of the piece. This is necessary because the expansion rates of metal and enamel differ. If enamel were applied only to the face, the stresses of firing could produce cracks. The waste enamels already referred to (**18.4**) can serve as counterenamel when the back side of the piece will be concealed by a bezel or similar setting. Otherwise, the jeweler can treat the reverse as a design area and use whatever colors are desired.

The next step in the wet-inlay method takes place on the face of the work. A thin coat of transparent flux is applied to the piece, after which it is fired. Any exposed areas of metal should be protected with a coating of Scalex before firing. Next the jeweler lays on a coat of opaque white enamel, if desired, and again the work is fired. At this point begins the process of applying the colored enamels. The enamels are placed in shallow porcelain or glass dishes, and water is added to create a pastelike consistency. Either a brush or a spatula can be used to spread the colors onto the piece uniformly. After each layer has been applied, the piece is dried and fired. As layers build up on the face, they should be balanced with additional layers of counterenamel on the reverse.

For some types of work the enameler may wish to place foils under the layers of transparent enamel. Foils are extremely thin metal sheets, available in several colors, which come packed in "books." The procedure for working with them is as follows:

1. Prepare the work with a ground coating of enamel, and fire it.
2. From your book of foils remove the desired sheet with its two protecting layers of paper. Place this "sandwich" of sheets on a cardboard mat, and with a sharp needle punch an allover pattern of tiny holes into the foil, about fifty holes per square inch. This will allow gases to escape during the firing and prevent the foil from buckling.
3. Trace the desired pattern on the paper and cut it out, being careful to touch only the protective paper. If your fingers touch the foil itself, they will leave traces of oil that will prevent the foils from adhering properly to the enamel.
4. With a brush, paint a coating of gum tragacanth on the work, and, while the tragacanth is still wet, lift the foil with the same brush and set it in position. You can use tweezers to adjust the position as you set the foil down.
5. Brush out any air pockets that may have formed under the foil, and allow the piece to dry.
6. Fire the work quickly to the point that the foil sinks into the enamel. If ripples form in the foil, you can press them down with a spatula as soon as the work is removed from the kiln. Then polish the foil with a glass fiber brush.
7. Apply a layer of transparent enamel, then fire as usual. Several more layers of enamel can be added if you wish.

The sifting method of application begins with the spraying of a fine layer of gum tragacanth on the surface of the work. Next, the enameler holds the work over a sheet of paper and, with the sifter, sifts a light coating of ground enamel onto the piece. If the tragacanth solution was sprayed uniformly, the enamel should adhere evenly all over the surface and along the edges. After drying, the work is fired and cleaned in the usual manner. Several layers can be sifted onto a piece, but each must be preceded by a spraying with gum tragacanth and followed by a firing.

The sifting method lends itself to a number of variations, including stencil enamels and sgraffito. In the first of these, a layer of base enamel is fired onto the metal, then a stencil made from paper toweling or other absorbent paper is placed over the work before the next layer is sifted on. Sgraffito is a technique borrowed from ceramics. After the first coating of enamel has been fired onto the piece, a second and contrasting coat is sifted on. A design is scratched through the second layer with any kind of pointed scribe to reveal the contrasting enamel underneath.

18.9

Firing and Cleaning Enamel firing can be tricky at first, but with experience the various steps will become almost automatic. The three most important considerations are: supporting the work in such a way that no enamel surface comes into contact with the kiln or the trivet; moving the pieces in and out of the kiln quickly to minimize heat loss; and removing the enamel just when it has fused properly.

The kiln should be preheated to about 1500°F. (or about 1400° if you are working on gold or silver). Then the enamel is set on a trivet and the trivet lifted by the firing fork into the kiln. The necessary firing time can be approximated only; medium-size objects fuse in about two to seven minutes. You must watch the piece through the peephole in the kiln. When it takes on a cherry red glow and looks smooth and slick, the fusing should be complete. The trivet must be removed immediately and placed on the asbestos board.

Whenever pieces are to be fired more than once—which is nearly always the case—any exposed metal that is not protected by Scalex will have to be cleaned after each firing. Place the cooled work in the pickle solution. The acid will attack some enamel colors, but further firing will restore the surface. After pickling, rinse and dry the work. You can also clean exposed metal with an abrasive, either steel wool or cleanser.

It is possible to fire enamel work with a jeweler's torch, having the piece set on a wire mesh supported by a tripod. A clean oxidizing flame is applied directly underneath to fuse the enamel, taking care to keep the flame off the enamel itself. Jewelers who want to add a touch of color to their work without getting involved in the entire process of enameling may wish to investigate this method of firing.

18.10

Finishing After the final layer of color has been fired and the work has cooled, you can begin whatever finishing you desire. A common process, known as *stoning*, consists of grinding with a flat emery stone under running water (Fig. 511). Fill in the depressions revealed by the stoning, fire, and repeat this sequence as many times as necessary. When the piece is level and smooth, begin the final stoning and finishing. If you want a glossy finish, stone with coarse, then medium and fine emery stones; then rub with wet sandpaper in different grades from medium to very fine. Rinse thoroughly, using a glass brush to remove any particles of emery that might adhere. Do a final high firing, and let the piece cool very slowly. The finished enamel will gleam like a highly polished gem (Fig. 504). If you prefer a mat finish, you can continue the wet sandpaper treatment and omit the last flash firing. A soft surface results from hand-buffing with moist cerium oxide.

18.11

Cloisonné This description of the process of cloisonné on a copper plaque base can be adapted to all the other types of enameling, since the preparation of the metal, the application of enamels (by the wet inlay technique), and firing in the kiln are carried out in practically the same manner.

504. Hiroko Swornik. *Corsica,* pin of sterling and fine silver, with cloisonné enamel, 1975.

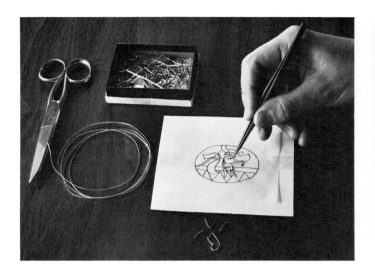

1. Draw the design.
2. Cut and form cloisonné wires of fine silver, arranging them directly on the design (Fig. 505). Cloisonné wires are rectangular in section, usually 18 by 30 gauge. They can also be purchased in 1-foot lengths.
3. Cut the desired base form from copper, and anneal it to make the shaping easier and eliminate impurities. This can be done either with a soft flame of the jeweler's torch or by covering the piece entirely with Scalex and, after drying, putting it in the kiln.
4. Shape the metal as described above (**18.7**). The domed shape will enhance the appearance of the enamel, rendering it more gemlike.
5. If the edges are rough, file them a little. Roughen the surface of the metal, then pickle and clean it as described above. After this, handle the metal only by the edges.
6. The top will be enameled first, so protect the underside with a coating of Scalex, for otherwise fire scale will form on the copper.
7. Arrange the wires on top of the metal, adhering them with gum tragacanth or with Klyrfire applied with a brush.
8. When the Klyrfire has dried, the first coat, the special flux, can be applied. Like all the enamels, it must first be washed.
9. Apply the resulting pastelike substance very carefully between the wires and all over the piece, using a brush or a tiny metal spatula. Take care to break any bubbles that may form in the corners near the wires.
10. Dry the piece. You can facilitate drying by applying a blotter or strips of paper toweling at the edges of the panels and then setting the piece over the pilot light of a gas stove. Or you can set it at the open kiln door for a few seconds.
11. Place the work in the kiln. Upon removal, the wires will be fused to the base (Fig. 506).
12. Cool the piece slowly, preferably in a warm place.
13. Clean the underside of the piece, using pickle, cleanser, and water. Apply flux to the underside as a *counterenamel*, and fire.
14. Since the object is now coated on both sides, the only place where fire scale can form is at the edges. Before applying the enamel for each subsequent firing, clean the edges with medium emery paper and wash with household cleanser.
15. If you do not want the base metal to show through the enamels, put a layer of washed opaque white enamel on the top side, and fire (Figs. 507, 508).

505-511. Procedure for cloisonné enameling.

above left: 505. Forming and positioning cloisonné wires with tweezers.

above: 506. Wire fused in place, after being coated with flux and fired.

below: 507. White enamel undercoat applied with a brush.

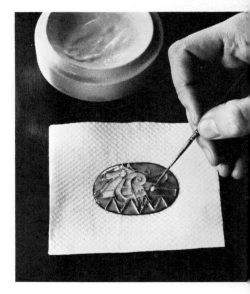

16. Apply a second layer of counterenamel to the underside, and fire.
17. Begin building up layers of color on the face of the piece (Fig. 509). It is possible to use all the various kinds of enamel on a base of flux and opaque white. The more transparent the enamel, the greater care should be taken with the washings, so that the transparency does not become flawed.
18. Put a third and final layer on the underside of the piece.
19. When using 18-by-30 cloisonné wire, you will need to apply at least three full layers of colored enamel to reach the tops of the wires.
20. With each application of enamel, you must pack the wet enamel slightly higher than the cloisonné wires; when the piece is fired, the resulting convex surface sinks (Fig. 510). Actually, the surface can be utilized to great effect, as Mary Kretsinger did for the piece shown in Plate 16 (p. 155), where metal ridges rather than wires separate the areas. However, the traditional result is a surface built up flush with the wires. After each layer has been fired, examine the colors to see whether changes are necessary. Corrections are easy. Naturally, an opaque color will hide the color beneath, while a transparent one will modify the undercolor.
21. Finish the piece as desired (Fig. 511).

below: 508. Firing the white under-coat after it has thoroughly dried.

below right: 509. Beginning to apply colored enamels over the white ground.

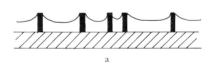

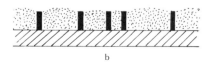

above: 510. Because firing causes them to sink and cling to the sides of the wires (a), enamels are always applied mounded in the center (b).

right: 511. Stoning with medium, then fine, Carborundum stone—performed under running water, so that waste is washed away and not ground in.

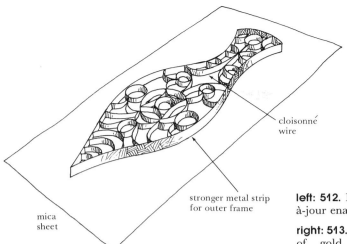

left: **512.** Preparing for plique-à-jour enamel on a mica sheet.

right: **513. Dvora Horvitz.** Links of gold and plique-à-jour enamel on a gold chain, 1976.

18.12

Plique-à-jour The design of plique-à-jour enamels utilizes cloisonné-type wires in much the same way as just described, except that there is no base metal (Fig. 512). This technique requires a heavier outer frame to hold the delicate inner wires in place. Spot soldering or gum tragacanth aids in the adhesion.

If you wish a more massive look, you can pierce or saw and file a piece of base metal to create openings for the enamel (Fig. 513). Do not make the individual partitions too large. To ensure that the enamel will stay in place, undercut each of the partitions with a pointed tool.

If the piece is flat, place the framework on a piece of mica, then clamp it to a thin piece of steel to prevent warping. Enamels will not adhere to mica. Build up layers of transparent enamels, taking care that they are very clean. After the final finishing and hydrofluoric dip, set the piece on edge and arrange some kind of support for the final firing. This must be done with extreme care so that the piece does not overheat. As soon as it becomes glassy, remove it from the kiln and cool slowly.

To make a curved plique-à-jour surface, begin with the cloisonné method on a metal base. The metal will later be eaten away by acid, leaving only the wires, glass, and a frame structure. In all plique-à-jour work, the wires must be arranged so that they are touching one another and the frame, or else the structure will collapse.

18.13

Champlevé To do champlevé, follow the technique for etching as described in Chapter 17 (**17.12–14**). The metal will be designed for separated colors much as it is in the cloisonné process, but here the partitions are to be cut out by the etching acid (Fig. 514). Acid cuts for enameling should be deeper than for normal surface decoration—about $\frac{1}{16}$ inch. Be careful to remove all traces of acid—and of the turpentine and alcohol used to dissolve the ground and varnish (**17.12**)—before beginning the enameling.

When the design has been filled in with enamel, the effect is that of inlay (Fig. 515). The cavities must be filled and fired several times, and then stoned down to the surface of the metal. Finally, the work is given a flash firing to smooth the enamel surface. If the base metal is copper, the portions of bare metal around the enamel must be protected by Scalex during firing to prevent formation of fire scale.

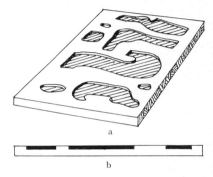

a

b

above: **514.** Champlevé enameling: sunken areas are etched out of the metal plaque (*a*), then filled and fired until enamel becomes flush with the surface (*b*).

below: **515.** Champlevé medallion, of enameled and gold-plated copper; French, from Limoges, 12th century. Louvre, Paris.

18.14

Limoges   Since limoges is the most basic enamel technique, it can also be the most flexible, offering endless opportunity for experimentation by the contemporary jeweler. The process is the same as for cloisonné enameling, but there are no separating wires. Layers of color are built up one on another until the desired effect has been attained. If the enamels have been ground very thin and the proper tool is used, the colors can actually be painted onto the base metal, thus justifying the term "painting with enamel." The base metal can be covered with a coat of flux enamel, so that the transparent colors reveal the metal, or with an opaque white base. A combination of the two can result in interesting effects. Often, a final layer of flux is fired on the surface to give a smooth, lustrous, and protective finish.

18.15

Basse-Taille   Basse-taille could almost be considered a secondary decorative technique, since its purpose is to enhance and reveal a relief carving under the transparent enamel. The first step is to do the relief work in the base metal, by means of chasing and repoussé techniques. Then transparent enamels are applied and fused on in the usual manner. Even if only one transparent color is used over the piece, the effect may be one of several subtle colors, because of the shadows and highlights glinting through the enamel (Fig. 516). If the base metal is gold or fine silver, the overall effect may be one of preciousness.

A similar appearance can be obtained by using tool-worked gold or silver foil under the transparent enamel.

18.16

Grisaille   Grisaille is a form of "painting" in neutrals—black, white, and grays. Work begins on a dark background, and the jeweler builds up light values by repeated coatings of white enamel until a rich chiaroscuro effect develops (Fig. 517). The ground is generally sifted onto the work to provide an absolutely smooth surface. Then opaque white enamel (about 200 mesh) is mixed with lavender oil and painted on the ground in the manner of china painting. Repeated applications and firings build up a range of values from black through all the grays to white. Touches of pastel color are occasionally added. Since this technique is really one of surface painting, the grisaille enamel is fragile and easily scraped off. A final coat of flux enamel will help protect it.

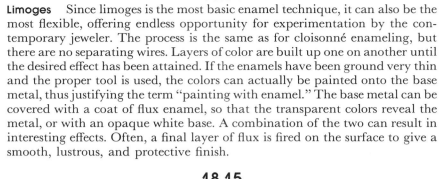

left: 516. Mary A. Kretsinger. *Sun, Moon, and Venus,* pendant of sterling silver, with brass mountings, basse-taille enamel, Petoski stone, and Cave Creek jasper, 1975. Transparent enamel reveals the chased texture of the base metal, parts of which project through the enamel layer. Collection Dr. and Mrs. John Visser, Emporia, Kan.

right: 517. Jacques Huon. Watch decorated in grisaille enamel; Paris, c. 1660. Victoria & Albert Museum, London.

Finishing

Filing and Polishing

Finishing should always be a systematic process wherein, by stages, successively finer tools are applied to the surface of the metal until it has acquired the desired degree of polish. Filing is the most common means of shaping and finishing a sawed edge. In general, coarse cutting tools should be used first. A coarse file smooths the surface but leaves coarse file marks. These should be removed by a finer file and the finer file marks by a still finer file or a coarse emery stick. Coarse emery scratches should be removed by a medium emery stick and medium scratches by a fine emery stick. In carrying out this entire process, it is advisable to work crosswise over the preceding file or scratch marks, rather than parallel with them. After the fine emery process, the piece is ready for the buffing or polishing lathe.

19.1

Files   The file is often considered to be the single most important tool for the jeweler. Without it, little metal forming or finishing could be done. A great many different types of files are available in many sizes and cuts. The beginner should consult a supplier's catalogue in order to become familiar with the full range of files. The general types are as follows (Fig. 518):

■ A *hand file* is a flat file with parallel edges. One edge is cut, while the other is smooth and therefore called "safe." In much filing the thumb serves as a guide to control the position of the file on the work. The "safe"

518. The types of files used in jewelry (*left to right*): flat hand file, half-round file, half-round ring file, round or rat-tail file, barette file, and three needle files.

side of the file is always put against the thumb. The hand file is used on convex and flat surfaces.

- A *half-round file* has one flat surface and one round face. The side edges are sharp intersections of the two sides and run to a tapered point. This tool is used chiefly for working on concave surfaces.
- A *half-round ring file* has a proportion better suited than the regular half-round file to fit inside ring bands for filing and finishing.
- A *round file,* as the name indicates, is a round, tapered file, also called a *rat-tail file.* It is used primarily to smooth, enlarge, or alter the shapes of the holes in openwork.
- A *barrette file* has one flat face and very narrow, thin edges, making it possible to file closely against a corner. The back is smooth.
- *Needle files* are very small, slender, tapered files used for small or intricate shapes. They are available in many styles, such as barrette, crossing, equaling, half-round, knife, round, square, triangular (or "three-square"), marking, and slitting. The handle of the needle file also can be used as a round file.

File cuts (Fig. 519) are numbered from 00, the coarsest, to No. 6, the finest. The jeweler eventually selects according to individual preference, but the beginner might well begin with two cuts—a No. 1 for rough shaping and finishing, and a No. 3 or 4 for final smoothing and finishing. Needle files, too, should be selected on this basis—a No. 1 for rough filing and a No. 4 or 6 for final smoothing. The file faces illustrated in Fig. 519 are all double cut; that is, they are formed of lines that intersect to make little diamond shapes. This is the type most commonly used on hard or precious metals. Other types of files used on wood and plastic and such soft metals as pewter and aluminum have single rows of curved teeth (the *vixen cut* file) or short, raised teeth (the *rasp*).

19.2

Position for Filing   Your workbench should be provided with a file block or bench pin, set about 6 inches below the level of the eyes when you are in a normal sitting position (Fig. 520). This places your work at a comfortable distance from your eyes. In most cases filing should be done by holding the

	teeth per inch (up cut)	30	38	51	64	79
length of files 10″ and over	00		0	1	2	3
length of files 4″ to 8″		00	0	1	2	
escapement files				0		
needle files 4″ to 7¾″				0		
regular rifflers				0		

teeth per inch (up cut)	97	117	142	173	213
length of files 10″ and over	4		6		
length of files 4″ to 8″	3	4		6	
escapement files	2	3	4		6
needle files 4″ to 7¾″	2	3	4		6
regular rifflers	2	3	4		6

work in your left hand, which is supported on the bench pin. The edge of the file rests against the bench pin (which eventually becomes worn and has to be replaced). Small work, as well as rings, can be held in either end of the ring vise or in the hand vise. One way of handling very small cast objects during finishing is to hold them by the sprue. After all other filing and polishing has been completed, remove the sprue and finish the area where it was attached.

19.3

Form for Filing Files are made with teeth that cut only on the forward stroke; therefore, if you must draw the file across the work on the backstroke, do so very lightly. Apply pressure on the forward stroke only. To accomplish the greatest amount of work in the least amount of time, use the whole tool when you file, pushing it down from the tip to the handle. Make efficient use of the surface of the file. If you are smoothing a long surface, move the file sideways as well as forward. When evening a broad surface that has high spots, use the same slanting motion to hit as many of the spots as possible with one stroke. When the surface begins to show grooves on the angle at which you are filing, reverse the angle and file in the opposite direction. Remember to round the edges of the underside of your work to give it a quality finish. The following advice will help you make good use of the file for different types of work:

■ Hold the arm and wrist relaxed, and let the file follow the work if the shape is curved.

■ When filing the edges of a sheet or strip, slap the file gently against the edge so that it will find the flat surface. You will thus avoid filing new planes across the edge.

■ The coarsest appropriate file should always be used to begin a cutting or smoothing operation. When filing across the edge of a sheet, however, select a file with teeth somewhat smaller than the thickness of the sheet.

■ Flat files should be used for straight edges and outside curves. Half-round files are necessary for inside curves. When filing an inside curve, slide the file along the length of the curve as you make the forward stroke. This will help to avoid filing irregular grooves in an edge, particularly when needle files are being used.

above: 519. File cuts (actual size) and the file lengths in which they are available.

below: 520. Position for filing.

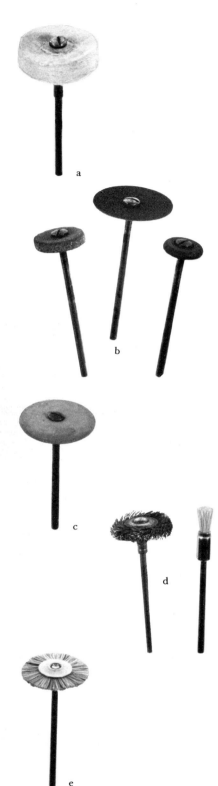

19.4

Care of the File   All files have handles and should be held by the handles. If you put your fingers on a fine file, the oil from your hands will make the file slide across the metal. From time to time when you are filing, hit the file against the bench to knock out any metal dust that may be lodged between the teeth, or clean it with a wire brush. Never use your regular files on lead or solder, for this will clog the teeth. Keep old files for this purpose. Remember that a particle of lead solder, should it adhere to a piece of silver, will soak into the silver if it is heated to the annealing point—another reason for keeping your solder files separate from those you use on other metal. Files on the shelf should not be allowed to rub against each other, since this will eventually dull them. They should be kept clean and dry to avoid rust.

19.5

Flexible Shaft for Grinding, Emerying, and Polishing   One of the most useful tools for cutting away metal, smoothing with emery, and polishing is the flexible-shaft drill (Fig. 355). This tool consists of a flexible shaft that is attached to a small motor capable of speeds up to 14,000 r.p.m. Several designs of chucks are available for the flexible shaft, in which drills, burs, grinding stones, and polishing buffs can be fastened. Some of these are especially good for reaching areas that cannot conveniently be finished with larger hand tools. In some models one end of the motor is geared down so that the flexible shaft can be operated with more power at lower speed. The motor is controlled by a foot rheostat to provide variation of speed.

Most suppliers (**B.8**) carry a wide selection of small attachments that can be used with the flexible shaft (Fig. 521). Burs are made in many shapes: round, cone, bud, wheel, reamer, (Fig. 356). The setting bur (Fig. 568) will cut a shoulder in the metal, into which a stone can be set. Small grinding wheels, brushes, and crystal and pumice wheels, as well as small muslin buffs, can be attached to mandrels for use with the flexible shaft.

Some experiment is necessary to learn control of the cutting burs. Cutting is done on a forward stroke, and it is advisable to hold the thumb in a solid position to anchor the handpiece to the work. The speed of the shaft must be adjusted so that the momentum of the cutting balances the pressure exerted on the metal. If too slow a speed is used, or if a backward stroke is taken, the bur is likely to run over the work. The flexible shaft is intended for use by experienced craftsmen and can easily ruin a piece of work if it is not properly controlled. Practice first before using it on a good piece of jewelry.

19.6

Special Tools for Cutting, Grinding, and Emerying   A number of special tools or attachments can be used with the flexible shaft for cutting, grinding, or emerying. There are, of course, many shapes of carbide burs, abrasive wheels, and polishing points—for example, a very serviceable carbide ring bur in three grades, which speeds up the inside finishing of a ring casting and can also be used for surface grinding. Rubber pumice wheels and mounted carborundum stones in several shapes also facilitate grinding operations. These have a long life span, for when they are worn down, they can be saved for use in small or recessed areas. Small steel mandrels are available, and to these various types of felt, leather, muslin, or emery disks can be attached as needed.

left: 521. Flexible-shaft attachments for finishing: muslin buff (*a*), three emery wheels (*b*), pumice wheel (*c*), a pair of steel brushes (*d*), and a bristle brush (*e*).

522–523. **Construction of an emery dowel.**

far left: 522. A birch dowel of $\frac{1}{2}$-inch diameter is screw-mounted on a steel mandrel for attachment to the chuck of a flexible-shaft drill.

left: 523. A slot in the dowel receives a strip of emery paper, which is wound around the dowel in several layers. When one layer wears thin, it can be torn off to expose a fresh section of emery.

One of the most useful little emery mandrels that a jeweler can make consists of a short length of $\frac{1}{2}$-inch-diameter birch dowel fastened solidly to a steel mandrel so that it can be attached to the flexible-shaft handpiece (Fig. 522). A narrow slot is sawed into the side of the dowel to allow the attachment of a small strip of emery paper (Fig. 523). This little mandrel is used to finish the inside of a ring and works better than an emery shell.

19.7

Emery Paper   Emery paper is a refined type of abrasive sheet coated with powdered emery, carborundum, or garnet. It comes in grades from No. 3, the coarsest, through Nos. 2, 1, 0, 2/0, 3/0 to No. 4/0, the finest. Most jewelers manage with three grades: No. 3 or 2 for initial smoothing of filed surfaces; No. 1 for medium finishing; and No. 3/0 or 4/0 for fine finishing. Crocus cloth, an emery cloth coated with iron oxide, is also used for fine finishing.

19.8

Emery Sticks   The jeweler uses emery paper fastened to a flat stick, called an emery stick or emery buff. The emery stick can be purchased in all grades or can be made with strips and dowels of various sizes. A good size for an emery stick is about 1 inch wide, $\frac{1}{4}$ inch thick, and 12 inches long. Smaller and thinner flat sticks may also be useful, as well as dowels of from 1 inch to $\frac{1}{4}$ inch diameter.

To make an emery stick, use a flat piece of wood with smooth surfaces and sharp edges. Lay the stick on the paper, and line up the outside edge of the stick exactly on the narrow edge of the paper (Fig. 524). With a scribe, score a line along the inside edge of the stick. Fold the paper up along this scored line. The emery paper will crease easily and sharply. Place the stick snugly against this fold, and scribe a line along the other edge of the stick. Fold the paper along this line also. Place the stick snugly in these folds, and continue the process until you have wrapped three or four layers around the stick. The paper should be cut off so that the last layer ends on one edge of the stick. Three small round-headed nails or three staples will hold this edge against the edge of the stick without interfering when you emery on the flat sides or the opposite edge (Fig. 525). The emery paper can be cut by drawing the scribe several times along the same line. As each layer wears out, trim it off, always along the nailed or stapled edge. Round and oval emery sticks of various diameters can have two or three layers of emery paper rolled up and stapled along the edge.

When using the emery stick (or files, for that matter), always work across the scratches made by the preceding tool and go from coarser to finer grades of paper. Emery finishing is never completed properly until all file marks have been removed. A file mark left in the work will show up immediately after

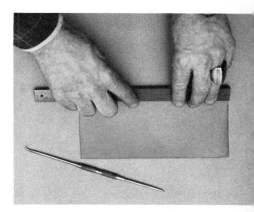

524–525. **Construction of an emery stick.**

above: 524. Emery paper, creased by a scribe, is folded several times around a wooden stick and stapled down on one edge.

below: 525. Completed emery stick. Worn-out layers can be torn off to expose a fresh surface.

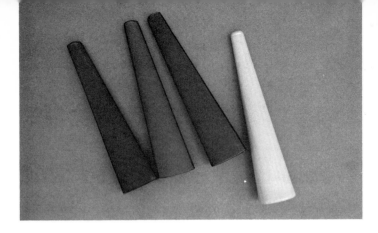

above: 526. Conical emery shells and a wooden ring stick.

right: 527. Buffing lathe, with a dust collector.

below: 528. Buffs and other lathe attachments: muslin cutting buff (*a*), flannel polishing buff (*b*), brush buff (*c*), laps (*d*), scratch brushes (*e*), and a pair of felt-covered ring buffs (*f*).

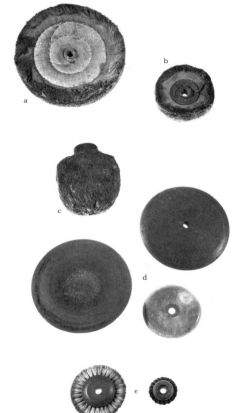

polishing on the buffing lathe. Do not attempt to polish out a deep file mark. Always go back to working with an emery stick until the file mark is removed. This way you will achieve perfectly finished work.

19.9

Emery Shells for Ring Sticks   Emery shells that fit on conical ring sticks (Fig. 526) are also commercially available. The stick is placed on the buffing mandrel, a tapered spindle, and the shell slipped on the tapered stick. These shells can be made easily by cutting the emery paper in the proper arc and gluing together. (For the layout of a cone, see **A.9**.)

When using the ring stick on the flexible shaft, never bring the ring up on the cone to where the diameter of the stick is equal to the ring size. The ring will be likely to catch and tear out of your hands. Always work just below that point. This will require that you rotate the ring continually as you press it against the stick, in order to avoid cutting a groove in the ring. Finishing the inside of a ring should also follow a sequence from coarse to fine emery and finally to a ring buff.

19.10

Cutting and Polishing on the Buffing Lathe   The process of polishing with the buffing lathe (Fig. 527) is a modern improvement that replaces the slow traditional method of working the metal smooth with scotch stone and polishing with burnishers. If you consult a jewelers' supply catalogue (**B.8**), you will find a wide range of specialized buffs (Fig. 528). These can be classified as *cutting buffs, polishing buffs, brush buffs, laps, scratch brushes,* and *ring buffs.* (There are many others, but they are not important to the jeweler).

Buffing is the process by which the surface of the metal is smoothed even further than it was during sanding. A tiny portion of the metal surface is cut away during buffing, so it should be done only as much as necessary. Polishing, on the other hand, will not remove any marks from the metal (rather it will serve to highlight them). Polishing simply makes the metal shiny. Both of these processes can be done on the same wheel, but wheel covers (called buffs) make the difference in what happens to the metal. Tripoli, an abrasive compound, is generally used with cutting buffs to remove scratches. It consists of fine, sharp particles that cut very fine scratches into the metal, thereby taking out the coarser emery-paper scratches. For polishing, the wheel is coated with one of the various types of rouge.

Cutting buffs are generally made of layers of coarse, hard materials such as wool, muslin, or leather, which are sewn together. Leather buffs made of walrus hide are commonly used with pumice and are called *sandbobs*. These are used by silversmiths mainly for fast cutting. Wool buffs are combined with coarse cutting compounds such as Hard White or Lea compound, muslin buffs with tripoli or White Diamond jewelry compound. The muslin buff will give a "butler finish" rather than a high polish to the silver. The butler finish is often preferred to a high polish, because silver scratches readily.

Polishing buffs are made of flannel and are used with white or red rouge for imparting a high polish to silver or gold. Rouge is made of flat particles that have a burnishing or smoothing effect on metal.

Brush buffs are appropriate wherever the work is irregular or has deep corners or crevices that cannot be reached by cloth buffs. Brush buffs are small wooden disks with one or more rows of bristles around the circumference. Both tripoli and rouge are used with them.

The scratch brush, made of fine brass or nickel-silver wire, gives a burnished, mat finish. The work is usually pickled several times before scratch brushing. By tradition, Scandinavian silversmiths dip their work in stale beer before scratch brushing and believe that this gives a superior finish. The scratch brush should be run at a speed of not more than 600 r.p.m.

The ring buff is a tapered cone of wood covered with a layer of felt. Tripoli or rouge is applied for finishing the inside surface of a ring band (Fig. 529).

19.11

Buffing   While most of the compounds used in buffing have been named, some further description may be useful. Compounds consist of a cutting or polishing material mixed with a thick grease or wax to hold them together (Fig. 530). When leather buffs (sandbobs) are used, however, loose pumice sand is fed into the buff as it is held against the work. To help keep the pumice sand from dusting into the air, mix a small amount of oil with the sand.

For most jewelry work you should have three types of compound on hand: a coarse compound such as Hard White, a finer compound like tripoli, and a stick of red rouge for high polishing. Applying compound to the buff is called *charging*.

For ideal buffing practice, your buffing lathe should have three speeds—slow for scratch brushing, medium for tripoli or other cutting compounds, and high for rouge polishing. In a permanent workshop, a dust collector should be hooked up to the buffing lathe, so that dust and lint are carried off instead of being thrown onto the face of the craftsman.

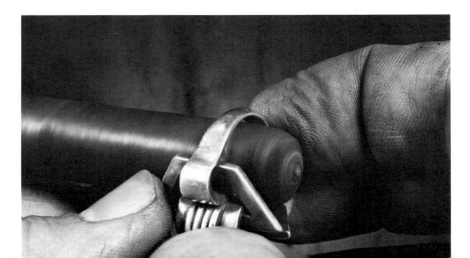

left: 529. Polishing the inside of a ring on the ring buff.

above: 530. Polishing compounds (*top to bottom*): tripoli, Lea compound, and sticks of red and white rouge.

The following general buffing rules will help the beginner to polish correctly:

- Use separate buffs for each compound. Do not mix them.
- A 4-inch or 5-inch buff is large enough for ordinary polishing. As buffs wear down, a row of stitching can be cut out.
- Apply compounds frequently, as you polish, by lightly touching the spinning buff with the compound (Fig. 531). Do not apply too much at one time; the excess will merely fly off the wheel and into the working area. Excess compound also causes the metal to become blackened.
- Wear goggles to protect the eyes from flying dust and as a precaution in case the work is accidentally pulled from your hands by the spinning wheel.
- Apply compound to the whole edge of the wheel, including the corners. This helps polish or buff recesses in the work.
- Pickle the work thoroughly before buffing to remove any other oxides or flux.
- Hold your work with the edge toward you and covered over by your thumbs (Fig. 532). This will prevent the buff from catching this edge and tearing the work out of your hands. The position of the work should be just below the center of the wheel. If the work is held too low or too high, the wheel will more easily tear it from you.
- If the work becomes too hot to hold, you may wish to wear leather finger guards or tight-fitting gloves.
- When cutting with tripoli, keep shifting your work around so that the buff works across the metal in many directions. If you continue holding the work in one position, the buff will cut wavy marks into the surfaces of the metal.
- As you hold the work up against the buff, keep sliding it back and forth.
- Chains, lengths of wire, and long jewelry pieces such as necklaces and bracelets may catch on the buff and break unless certain precautions are taken during polishing. The safest method for polishing chain is to wrap it around a mandrel, holding the ends tightly with the thumbs (Fig. 533).

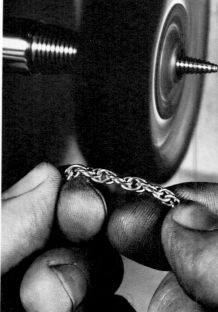

top: 531. Charging (applying compound to) the buff.

above: 532. Holding work against the buff.

right: 533. A length of chain is wrapped around a mandrel for polishing on the lathe.

far right: 534. Alternative method for polishing chain.

The mandrel is moved back and forth at the wheel and rotated slowly to cover all of the chain.

■ Another method of polishing chain is by the following practice (Fig. 534): The ends of the chain should be cradled tightly, one in the palm of each hand, with only a very short length—no more than 1 inch—suspended between the two thumbs and across the two forefingers. The fists are held together with the thumbs up and pointing toward the buff. The chain is exposed to the buff and supported by the forefingers, which curl back under the thumbs, pointing away from the buff. A small length of chain is thus polished, and since it is held tightly in the fingers, it cannot be caught and twisted around the buff. If this practice is not followed, there is danger that the chain will catch on the fingers and cut or break.

■ Small pieces of metal sheet or wire can be supported on a strap of leather, cardboard, or wood and thus be brought up against the buff. The upper end of the piece is pinched into the leather by the thumb and forefinger.

19.12

Burnishing   A traditional manner of smoothing and polishing the surface of a metal is to use a burnisher. The burnisher is a tool with a smooth and highly polished end, which is pressed against the surface of the metal and rubbed smoothly back and forth (Fig. 553). The effect is to smooth and compress the metal. Today the burnisher is used almost exclusively to press the surface of a closed setting snugly and smoothly around the cabochon (**21.1**), but there is nothing to prevent the jeweler from experimenting with the special surface that the burnisher produces on metal.

19.13

Finishing with Powdered Pumice   Whereas much traditional jewelry and most trade jewelry is finished to a high polish, the contemporary jeweler often finds a more refined richness in other types of finishes for certain designs. "Flash," or shine, is but one characteristic appearance of metal. When metal is rubbed with fine pumice, a more subtle quality can be produced. This is done after the final pickling of the piece, or after oxidation if the piece is colored. Powdered pumice comes in coarse and fine grades. One way of using it is to dip the thumb in water and then in pumice powder and rub the surface of the piece. This operation is repeated until the desired finish is attained.

Coloring Metal

While there are many methods of coloring metal to different tones, the most successful go only skin deep; that is, they are surface treatments and can be rubbed off easily. For this reason coloring often acts as a contrast in recessed parts of a piece of jewelry, while the surface parts are usually polished or given some other type of finish. Oxidized steel is used for humorous contrast in a brooch by Gilles Jonemann (Fig. 535).

19.14

Coloring Gold   Gold is difficult to color for the simple reason that, as an inert metal, it does not readily react to most elements. Gold can be colored black, insofar as it *can* be colored, by heating and then dipping it in liver of sulphur or a solution of ammonium sulfide. Commercial solutions for coloring gold are available from supply houses. These solutions, which should be applied with a steel rod or point, normally result in a deposit of iron salt that darkens the affected parts of the gold. An ancient formula for turning gold to a raw yellow color consisted of boiling the gold in a salt solution with ammonia.

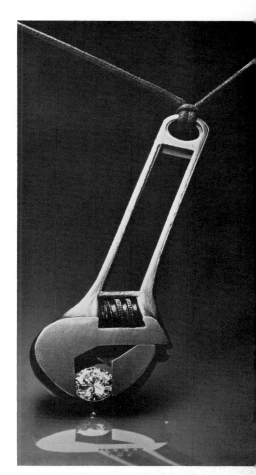

535. Gilles Jonemann. *La clef anglaise vue par un français,* pendant of oxidized steel, with 5-carat diamond, 1975. The miniature "clef anglaise" (the French term for monkey wrench) can be adjusted to grip stones of different dimensions.

19.15

Coloring Silver or Sterling Silver   The most commonly used agent for coloring silver or sterling is liver of sulphur. This solution is made by dropping one or two lumps of potassium sulphate into a pint of hot water. The solution should be kept in a tightly stoppered jar or bottle, since oxygen will cause it to deteriorate. The most common procedure is to place the article into the jar for a period of time, from five minutes to half an hour, depending on the darkness of color desired. The longer the metal is left in the solution, the thicker the coating of oxide; therefore the process should be controlled. Another method, which gives a uniform black or gray, is to bring the solution to a boil in a small pan, quickly dip the piece, and immediately rinse it under the tap. After oxidation, the color tone may be left as is or shaded by rubbing with fine pumice powder and water. Of course, the piece can be given a tripoli finish to contrast the dark recessed areas with polished surfaces.

Silver can also be oxidized by painting the surface with a solution of chloride of platinum, in proportions of 1 ounce chloride of platinum to 1 gallon of water. Only a small quantity is required. It should be kept in a stoppered bottle and applied with a brush.

Silver can be colored green by applying, or soaking the piece in, a solution containing 3 parts hydrochloric acid, 1 part iodine, and 1 part water, until the desired color is reached.

19.16

Coloring Brass and Copper   Liver of sulphur will color brass and copper as well as gold. Brass is more difficult to color uniformly because of the tin in the alloy. Often it just will not take color. When you are trying to color either brass or copper, however, use only a weak solution of liver of sulphur. Otherwise, you may get a heavy coating that tends to flake off. When coloring brass, dip the metal in a pickle solution reserved for brass (never use the silver or gold pickle) and rinse well. Then dip in a dilute solution of liver of sulphur. You will note an immediate response. If you want a deeper color, rinse off the liver of sulphur *thoroughly* and repeat the pickle treatment. Be sure to rinse carefully, since each solution will spoil the next if the two are mixed.

Copper colors readily with liver of sulphur, and the only problem is to avoid too heavy and flaky a coating. Hence, you must use a very dilute solution and repeat the dippings until the correct color is reached.

Both copper and brass can be colored by mixing dilute liver of sulphur with some detergent and applying the mixture with a brass scratch brush to get the desired finish. Such finishes have more subtlety than dipped finishes.

19.17

Coloring Bronze   Color treatment for bronze does not often occur in jewelry. However, it is possible to create an artificial patina on bronze by means of the following formula:

> 5 oz. copper sulphate
> 5 oz. cupric acetate-basic [Cu (CH$_3$CO$_2$)$_2$CuO$_6$H$_2$O]*
> 1 gal. water

When mixed properly, this solution attacks the surface of bronze, brass, copper, or silver directly to build up a warm brown color. The addition of copper carbonate gives the famous "antique" green.

---

*This specific formula for cupric acetate-basic must be given to a chemist, because there are two similar chemicals. The recipe is adapted from one given in Henry Wilson, *Silverwork and Jewellery* (London: Pitman, 1902).

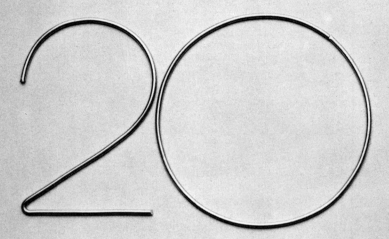

Gems and Semiprecious Stones

Gems and semiprecious stones have been an inseparable part of jewelry throughout history. From the very beginning they have been valued for color, pattern, texture, and transparency, as well as for the magical and protective qualities attributed to them in the past.

The oldest form of cut gemstone was the cabochon—a round or oval shape, generally with a dome face. Until the Renaissance, European jewelers used stones in one of three ways: *en cabochon,* like the star sapphire; carved, like the cameo with a design in relief; or intaglio, with an engraved design. The faceting of gems began when the technology for cutting them into symmetrical surfaces was developed. In 1476, Louis van Berquem of Antwerp first cut diamonds into facets, so that the light entering the stone from above reflected back through the top, giving it its characteristic fire. Other faceted stones had been brought into Europe much earlier. From the Renaissance onward, the qualities of transparent gems, enhanced by the technique of faceting, lifted them to the highest value in jewelry.

Beauty, durability, rarity, and size are the criteria for determining the value of gems and semiprecious stones. While there are a great many semiprecious stones, only the most brilliant and colorful gems—the diamond, ruby, sapphire, and emerald—are considered to be precious. Throughout history, individual gemstones have risen and declined in fashion.

The modern view of gems and semiprecious stones is somewhat different from that of previous generations of jewelers. The contemporary jeweler places as high a value on color, pattern, and texture as on brilliance alone, for the integration of the stone with the overall form of the jewelry has become an

above: **536. John Marshall.** Ring of cast green gold, with smoky topaz, 1972.

below: **537. Margaret De Patta.** White-gold dinner ring, with rutiliated quartz, 1954.

right: **538.** Profiles of low (*a*), normal (*b*), and high (*c*) cabachons, double cabachon (*d*), and special flat-top cabachon (*e*).

right: **539.** Top views of some normal and special cabachons: rectangular (*a*), oval (*b*), round (*c*), octagonal (*d*), and "antique" (*e*).

important design consideration (Fig. 536). Many jewelers today have expressed renewed interest in faceted stones, but the tendency is toward aspects of faceting other than the traditional one of pure brilliance. Margaret De Patta, for example, made a special study of such qualities as transparency, refraction, displacement, and distortion. She also experimented with freer transparent volumes and other facet relationships (Fig. 537). Asymmetrical volumes, structural settings, and natural crystals have become popular in the last two or three decades.

Plate 17 (p. 155) illustrates a broad range of stones and slabs of interest to the contemporary jeweler, while Plate 18 (p. 156) shows a selection of more conventional, commonly available gemstones. Appendix D lists the names of the most useful gemstones and other substances suitable for jewelry settings.

20.1

Gemstone Forms   The natural forms of gemstones have always aroused the interest of the jeweler. In contemporary times the appreciation of the "found" object has enhanced the aesthetic value of such things as coral, petrified wood, and bone, as well as gemstones. The baroque pearl, so popular in an earlier period, is again being used.

Tumbled stones have become popular since the development of the tumbling machine, which, by rolling the stones together with an abrasive powder and water, effects a mutual abrasion and gives a high polish at extremely low cost. Technology and tourism in America have greatly increased the popularity of "rocks." Although tumbled forms are frequently used in tourist jewelry of little value beyond the stone itself, this does not prevent the sensitive contemporary jeweler from adapting the unique tumbled gemstone in an original and expressive way.

Some stones, like the varieties of quartz, occur naturally as crystals, and as such can be cleaned and set without any polishing. The setting of such minerals is generally designed to reflect and enhance their forms.

Cabochon forms (Fig. 538) are the oldest to be fabricated from rough natural stones. They are especially suited for minerals such as turquoise, tigereye, moonstone, malachite, agate, and other opaque or translucent stones. There are four styles of cabochon: low, normal, high, and doublet. The double cabochon, or doublet, consists of two stones glued together with invisible cement just below the midpoint (*girdle*) to give the appearance of a larger stone. The higher-quality gem is set at the top (*crown*), while the lower-quality gem, or even a synthetic or imitation stone, serves as the base (*pavilion*). The

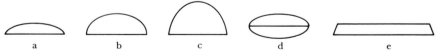

cabochon may be round, oval, rectangular, or square, but almost any special shape can be cut and polished into a cabochon style (Fig. 539). Figures 540 to 542 show standard sizes for various-shaped stones. The jeweler is likely to use small gemstones as accents where only color or contrast is required, and larger forms when the stone possesses an exciting pattern as well as color. The

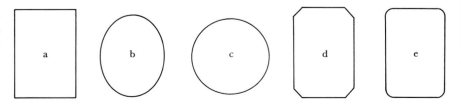

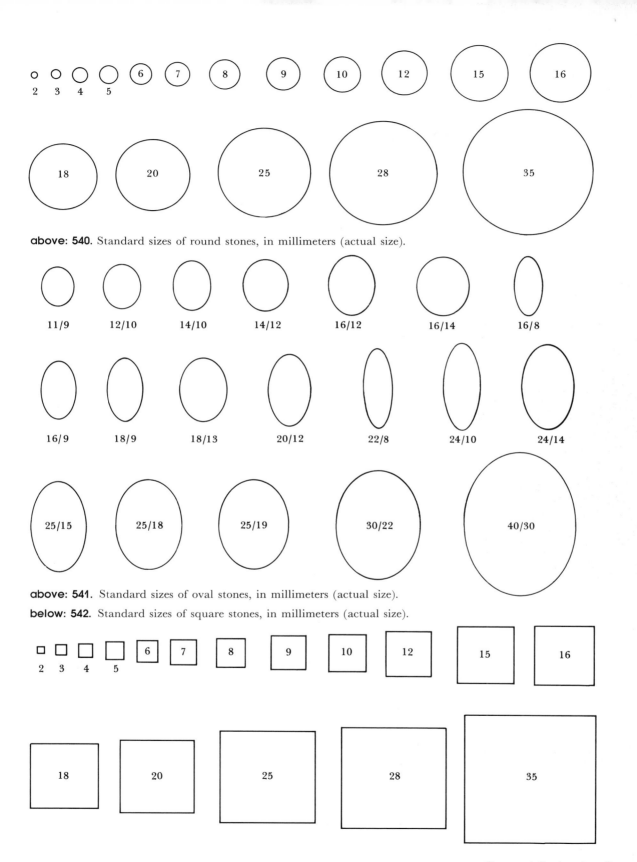

above: 540. Standard sizes of round stones, in millimeters (actual size).

above: 541. Standard sizes of oval stones, in millimeters (actual size).

below: 542. Standard sizes of square stones, in millimeters (actual size).

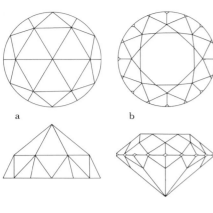

Faceted gemstones in traditional styles bring design restrictions that many jewelers are unwilling to accept, preferring to design their own shapes and forms. Those interested in faceting stones will sooner or later explore the problem independently of tradition. Some of the common and popular forms of faceted stones are illustrated in Figure 543.

20.2

Selecting Gemstones for Contemporary Jewelry   Pictures of gemstones are interesting to look at and will be of help to the beginning jeweler. Catalogues published by suppliers (**B.5**) sometimes provide a great deal of useful information, as well as illustrations showing a selection of types, shapes, and sizes. But a trip to a good lapidary is essential. At the lapidary workshop the jeweler

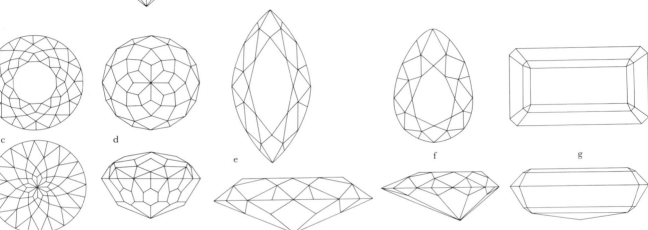

above: 543. Typical cuts of faceted gems: rose (*a*), brilliant (*b*), star (*c*), jubilee (*d*), marquise (*e*), pendeloque (*f*), and step (*g*).

below: 544. Arlette Baron. Hammered silver necklace, with smoky quartz, 1975.

right: 545. Arline M. Fisch. *Green Eyes,* necklace of 18k gold and reticulated silver, with green malachite, 1973.

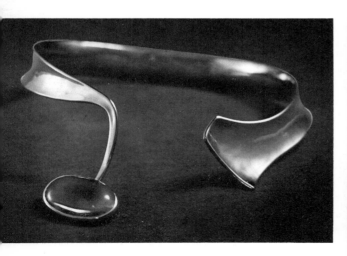

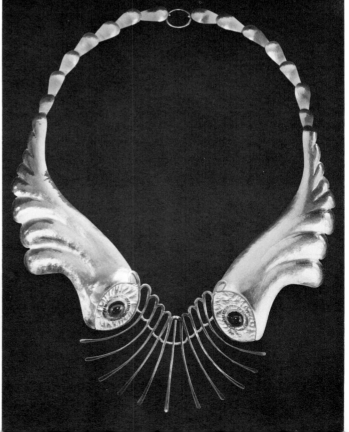

can see and handle all kinds of gemstones, in polished and rough form, and can begin to get an idea of the individual quality of each stone.

20.3

Designing Gemstone Forms   Creative jewelers are seldom willing to be limited by convention. They will eventually wish to determine gemstone shapes for their own jewelry (Figs. 544, 545). For cabochons, a sketched plan and side view, with dimensions indicated in millimeters, will usually give the lapidary sufficient information to go to work. The exploration of faceting for transparent gemstones can be done with Plexiglas. While careful drawings can be made, the advantage of Plexiglas is that it affords direct experience of the transparency and the facets. This material, while soft, can be filed and polished to approximate the faceted gemstone. The lapidary will be able to duplicate Plexiglas patterns in any gem—usually after a trial cut in quartz.

20.4

Designing Jewelry for Stones   Two qualities that the jeweler should consider when selecting a stone for a particular setting are hardness and toughness —terms that are not synonymous. *Hardness* means imperviousness to abrasion or scratching. On the Mohs' scale, named after its inventor, there are ten degrees of hardness, each defined by a characteristic mineral:

1. talc		6. orthoclase
2. gypsum		7. quartz
3. calcite		8. topaz
4. fluorite		9. corundum
5. apatite		10. diamond

In the Mohs' scale, talc is the softest stone and diamond the hardest. That is, a diamond will scratch another diamond or any other stone on the scale, while quartz, No. 7, will scratch only another No. 7 or softer minerals. It is unwise to design a ring set with any stone softer than No. 5 on the scale. Appendix D lists the hardness number of many common stones.

However hard it is, the diamond is not a particularly *tough* stone. It can be broken easily by the diamond cutter's cleaver or by a careless hammer blow when a jeweler is prong-setting it. The softer mineral jade is more easily scratched, but it is extremely tough and does not break easily.

When soft and/or fragile gemstones are used in rings, protective strips or other design features are required to guard them from bumps and abrasions. Most brooches and earrings are relatively safe from scratching and wear, and for these, softer gemstones can be used. The type of setting (see Chap. 21) should also be chosen in relation to the qualities of hardness and toughness. Whereas the closed or bevel setting (**21.1**) is appropriate for almost any stone cut as a cabochon, the paved (**21.3**) or any other setting that requires chasing metal against the stone may not be appropriate for stones that are soft or brittle, since a slight blow may crack or shatter them.

From the design standpoint, a gemstone is a specially differentiated shape that must be integrated into the composition of a piece of jewelry. It is distinguished from the other shapes by its color, texture, pattern, and unique characteristics as gem material. But it is as a *shape* that it must be integrated into the form of the jewelry (Fig. 546). Although gems of standard shape and size can be fitted into many designs, the jeweler may be interested in selecting unusual stones as they come to light at the lapidary or at a rock shop. These stones may be of unusual shape, and they call for a different approach. The jewelry piece must actually be designed around the stone, providing the form that will best complement its characteristics. The stone can be traced on paper and sketch designs made around the tracing; or, if casting is contemplated, a wax pattern can be modeled directly around the stone (Fig. 547).

above: **546. Marjorie Schick.** Two-finger ring in sterling silver, with smoky topaz, 1974.

below: **547. Hazel Olsen Brown.** Pin of cast gold, with black baroque pearl and blue-white freshwater pearls, 1967. The wax pattern was modeled around the pearls.

Gems and Semiprecious Stones   **285**

Settings

Gemstones and other nonmetallic materials have been an important part of jewelry from earliest times. This chapter presents the technical problems of setting gems, as well as a description of some traditional types of settings. The two requirements for a gem setting are that:

- The setting hold the stone securely and permanently
- The setting display the gem to the greatest extent possible, rather than conceal it

21.1

Closed Setting (Bezel Setting)   The closed setting (Fig. 548) is among the most commonly used for cabochons and irregularly shaped stones. A bezel is simply a band of metal that fits around the gemstone and is soldered to the base jewelry. It is generally curved but can be squared. Bezels can be made with or without a *seat* or *bearing* that fits inside to support the stone. Seats are used: when there is no metal backing to which the bezel is attached, as for instance in the case of a pendant; to raise a shallow stone; or to lift the bottom of a convex stone away from the base metal so that it sets firmly. Commercial bezel wire is available, with or without seats, in a variety of styles—plain, twisted, beaded, or otherwise decorated. You can also make your own bezel from sterling or, preferably, from fine gold or silver wire (about 20- to 26-gauge), which has a high melting point and therefore can be burnished easily against the stone.

The materials and tools necessary for making a bezel are:

- flat wire or commercial bezel wire
- jeweler's saw
- bench vise
- fine file (about No. 4) or emery paper
- round-nose pliers
- beeswax and a dowel for setting small stones
- bezel mandrel and rawhide mallet
- burnisher or chasing punch with a polished end
- pusher
- soldering, pickling, and annealing equipment

The procedure for making a bezel is as follows:

1. Determine the length of the bezel strip. If the stone to be set is circular, simply measure its diameter with your dividers, and, on the strip you are planning to use, mark off a little more than 3 diameters along the length. (Circumference equals about 3.14 diameters.) It is best to allow a slight amount of extra material, then roll the strip around the stone, locate the overlap precisely, and mark it with your scribe. Saw off the excess material exactly on the *outside* of the mark.

2. The height of the bezel, and thus the width of the strip, will depend upon how high you want to set the stone above the base on which you plan to mount it. You may wish to set a stone high above the base, close to it, or directly upon the base plate. In the latter case you may not need a seat, although this is not regarded as the best craftsmanship. Navajo jewelry is often set in this way. Turquoise, because it so soft, is usually set upon a layer of sawdust or disks of cardboard in order to provide a cushion during the burnishing.

3. The amount of bezel strip left above the seat as a burnishing flange will depend on the shape of the stone. A relatively flat or low-cut cabochon will have an edge that the flange can hold firmly when it is burnished over. In this case a fairly small flange is sufficient. Do not cover any more of your stone than necessary. A high-cut cabochon (Fig. 549), however, will have relatively vertical sides, so that the flange must be higher in order to lock it firmly around the stone by burnishing. Evaluating this problem calls for a little experience. The best way is simply to hold your stone against the bezel strip and estimate by eye the amount of flange required. On the inner side of the strip, mark the height to which the seat must reach from the bottom of the bezel. It pays to leave a little extra material on the flange so that you avoid losing essential flange height in the final filing.

4. When cutting the bezel strip, it is preferable to cut it slightly smaller than the exact size needed. After soldering, the bezel can be planished on a mandrel to the *exact* size of the stone, which should fit snugly but *not* tightly. If it becomes too large, you will save time by resawing and resoldering. Also, keep in mind that in the planishing stage, the final fit can be made by uniform filing inside with a fine, half-round needle file.

5. If you have planished the bezel ring to size, it will automatically have become perfectly round. In the case of an oval or irregular stone, the bezel ring can be fitted by bending it with the fingers or half-round pliers, or simply by holding the stone in the strip and rolling them together on a flat surface. When the stone fits properly, take a fine hand file and file the top and bottom edges to make them smooth and parallel. A No. 1 emery stick will take out file marks.

6. If you are setting a rectangular or square stone, it will be easiest to lay the stone out on the strip and, side by side, mark the corners on the inner

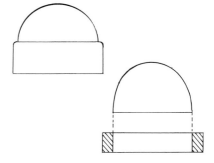

left: **548.** Bezel or closed setting around a cabochon.

right: **549.** Section of bezel with stone above.

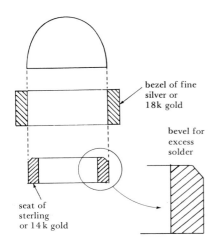

above: 550. Bezel, cabochon, and seat, with a bevel filed on the upper outside edge of the seat.

below: 551. Bezel, seat, and cabochon, with a bevel filed around the outside of the bezel.

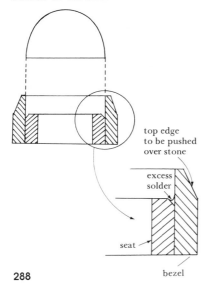

surface. At these corner marks, file notches no deeper than three-quarters of the thickness. The two ends should be beveled so that they come together and make the same kind of sharp, flush corner. Use binding wire to hold the ends together when soldering. Flux the notched corners and apply a small amount of solder (by the strip method) in order to give them strength.

7. When the bezel strip is prepared you can make the seat (Fig. 550). Usually a somewhat heavier metal is used for the seat. For stones up to $\frac{3}{8}$ inch in diameter, 18 gauge is usually sufficient. But you should increase the thickness of the seat as the size and weight of the stone increase. For example, if you are setting a stone $1\frac{1}{2}$ inches in diameter, it is wise to use 20-gauge strip for the outside bezel strip and 16-gauge for the seat. This is particularly essential if the bezel must be self supporting—if it is to be soldered against a supporting post, for example, and must float free in the air on this support. For 14-karat gold, all gauges can be made lighter because of the material's greater hardness. But 18-karat gold will be softer and more like sterling.

8. The height of the seat is determined, as described above, from the amount of flange required for a particular stone. Determining the length of the seat strip cannot really be done by measurement. A more direct method is to roll up the seat strip with round-nose pliers and by trial and error bring the ring to a size that fits inside the outer strip. Here, too, it is simpler to make the seat ring slightly smaller than necessary, since the relatively thicker gauge allows considerable planishing. After estimating the correct circumference, make a mark with the scribe and saw off the excess material. Bend the strip into a true circular shape, with edges matching neatly. If it slips into the outer ring with only a small gap, then solder it up. After soldering, pickling, and rinsing, you can planish the seat ring up to size. To get the best fit, planish the seat to slightly over size and then file the outside down to eliminate gaps between outer ring and seat. (Such gaps cannot be filled with solder, for this will leave a thick fillet of solder on top of the seat and thus prevent the stone from sitting properly.)

9. After the seat ring has been planished and filed to fit, file the top and bottom smooth. Be sure that top and bottom surfaces are parallel, so that the stone will sit squarely and evenly, without rocking. Many a stone set on an uneven seat has been cracked in the burnishing. Finally, file a bevel around the outside upper edge of the seat (Fig. 550) to allow for excess solder between the two rings.

10. After the seat has been soldered into the bezel shell, test the stone for fit and for the amount of flange available for burnishing. If you have allowed a bit of extra material, the excess can now be filed down. Use a fine hand file to finish, but be sure to keep the flange edge in a flat plane parallel to the seat. Next file the bottom of the completed bezel in order to even up the inner and outer rings. This is the operation that will reveal solder gaps if there are any. Then, with a fine hand file, file the outside surface of the bezel with even, flat strokes.

11. Now file a flat bevel around the outside of the bezel, extending from the top down to the height on the inside seat (Fig. 551). Do not file the top of the bezel down to a hairline. The purpose of the bevel is to remove excess metal in order to facilitate burnishing the flange over the stone.

12. Finish the bezel by emerying and polishing. Success in setting a stone always depends on the accuracy of the fit of the setting. If the bezel is too large, it cannot be burnished to fit smoothly around the stone but instead will become lumpy when you try to burnish it down. Resize the bezel if it does not fit snugly.

The stone is not set until the bezel has been soldered to its base, and all other soldering, coloring, and finishing have been done. Then the stone is placed in the bezel, squarely upon the seat. If the stone is small and you have difficulty maneuvering it into place, put some beeswax at the end of a dowel and pick up the stone with the dowel. Any wax that sticks to the stone can be melted off later.

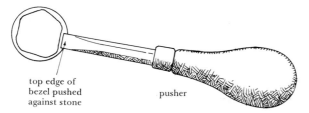

top edge of
bezel pushed
against stone

pusher

552. Plan view of a bezel being pressed against the stone with a pusher.

A pusher, which has a polished, flat face, is used to press the bezel firmly and evenly against the stone (Fig. 552). All the small corners that are formed must also be pressed against the stone. Then the burnisher is used to rub the bezel smooth and tight against the stone (Figs. 553, 554).

Many bezels may require something more than burnishing to bring the metal down around the stone. This occurs if the bezel is too heavy, or if a heavy bezel has been designed. The claws of a claw setting sometimes cannot be pressed down against the stone. In such cases the piece of jewelry is grasped in a ring vise and placed in the bench vise, or it is placed on the ring mandrel and supported. Then the bezel is brought against the stone with careful taps of a chasing tool with an appropriately shaped, flat end. The secret of setting the stone by this method is to use a small-ended chasing tool and very light taps of the hammer, so that a small amount of the metal is moved at a time. To keep the stone centered, the tapping must be done at regular intervals, first at four equidistant points, then between these points.

below: **553.** The edge of a bezel being burnished smooth and tight against the stone.

right: **554. Vada Beetler.** Sterling ring constructed with fold-over shank, with bezel-mounted green moonstone, 1975.

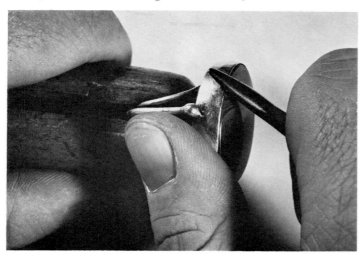

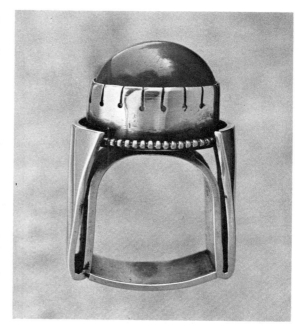

Claw Setting   The claw or prong setting was much used in earlier times and is still popular in trade jewelry. This method shows faceted stones to their best advantage, since maximum light can enter the stones from all sides and be refracted through the top. The contemporary jeweler seldom uses claw settings in their traditional forms, preferring to devise alternate arrangements that harmonize with the total design of the piece. Both conventional forms and some contemporary solutions will be discussed here.

One conventional claw setting is made from a bezel, as follows:

1. Prepare a bezel setting high enough to provide material to reach up and over the edge of the stone. The bezel ring should be made of heavier metal than would be used for a normal closed setting—18- or 16-gauge metal, depending upon the size of the stone.
2. When the bezel is complete and emeried, mark out around the top edge the center points of the claws, then their widths. (This can be done on a circle template, **A.5**.) With dividers, scribe a circle around the outer face of the bezel to locate the depth of the claws (Fig. 555). If the seat material is thick enough, the slots between the claws may extend below the top of it.
3. Outline the edges of the claws, and file away the metal between them with a needle file, or saw out the slots with the jeweler's saw. Take care to shape each claw exactly and to bevel the top and edges of each claw. With irregularly shaped stones the claw size and spacing may vary.
4. Emery and finish the edges with emery paper wrapped around a small mandrel or needle file.
5. After the bezel has been soldered in position, place the stone in the setting, remove excess metal on the ends of the claws, and finish the ends.
6. The stone is set in either of two ways. One is to make the claws in such a way as to bend them over or against the stone (Fig. 556). In this case the claws should not be too thick, but they must be wide enough to grasp the stone securely. The other way is to make the claws somewhat heavier and to file slots inside each claw to receive the stone (Fig. 557).

seat

scribed line

left: 555. Claw setting made from a bezel.

center: 556. Claw setting with claws pushed tightly around the stone.

right: 557. Heavy claw setting with stone held in slots filed into the claws.

Another simple claw setting for a cabochon can be made without first constructing a full bezel. To begin, scribe a tracing of the stone on sheet metal. Then, if the stone is round, lay out axis lines for the claws radiating from the center (Fig. 558). (For an elliptical stone, the axis lines must be spaced around the circumference.) Outlines for the claws are centered on the axis lines and sized to fit the stone. The outline for the seat, however, is usually cut back somewhat from the edge of the stone, so that the seat will not be visible, and the claw outlines are thus extended beyond the perimeter of the stone to this inner line. The claws are then sawed out to this inner line.

Next, an engraved line is made just outside each section of the line indicating the stone's perimeter, which will still appear running across each claw. The new line must be graved to about two-thirds the thickness of the

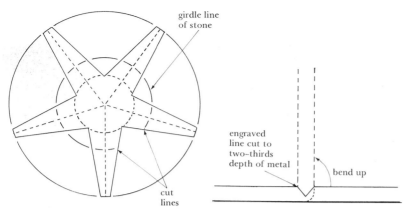

558–560. **Method for making a claw setting from sheet metal.**

girdle line of stone

cut lines

engraved line cut to two-thirds depth of metal

bend up

left: 558. Layout around a circular stone. Claws are laid out from axis lines radiating from the center.

center: 559. Bend lines are engraved to two-thirds the depth of the metal before the claws are bent up.

right: 560. Finished setting with claws bent up into position.

sheet metal (Fig. 559) and placed in such a position that when the claw is bent up into a vertical plane, the inner face of the claw is on the scribed circumference line of the stone (Fig. 560). If the face of the claw is outside this line, the stone will fit too loosely in the setting. Conversely, if the face of the claw comes within the circumference line, the setting will be too small for the stone.

Using the strip-solder method (**10.18**), heat the setting and touch the solder to the seam at the root of each claw. The setting can now be file-finished, emeried, polished, and placed in position on the piece. When all other work has been completed, the length of the claws is adjusted, the ends are finished, and the stone is then set.

Many imaginative variations of the claw setting have been devised by contemporary jewelers (Figs. 561, 562).

21.3

Paved Setting and Gypsy Setting   The paved setting is one in which the stone is set directly into the surface of the metal, which is chased up over the edge to hold it in place. Many stones can be set close together in this fashion, which is how the setting got its name. Since the paved setting necessitates hammering metal against stone, the gem should be able to withstand stress; this requires a hardness of at least 6 on Mohs' scale. Anything softer may be scratched or shattered while it is being worked.

To begin the paving, drill a small hole exactly in the center of the spot where the stone is to be set. This hole will steady the point of the larger drill that follows. Next, with a flat drill, enlarge the hole to the size of the base of the stone and to a depth of about $\frac{1}{32}$ inch. If the stone has a convex bottom, a

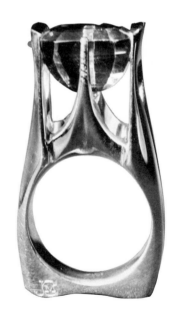

right: 561. John Marshall. Ring of cast green gold, with an amethyst in a claw setting, 1972.

left: 562. Margaret De Patta. Ring with flange setting, c. 1948.

round or tapered bur must be used next to make a depression for it. Set the stone in the hole. To facilitate chasing, carve or chase a groove around the edge of the hole, leaving a small flange for chasing up against the stone (Fig. 563).

An alternate method is to drill or saw a hole through the metal, to the exact size of the stone, and then solder a larger disk under the hole as a landing for the stone (Fig. 564). Or a small seat can be soldered within the hole, if the metal sheet is thick enough (Fig. 565).

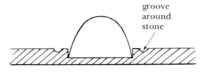

groove
around
stone

above left: 563. Section view of a paved setting, with groove cut around the stone for chasing the metal against it.

left: 564. Paved setting made with hole cut through the metal and a solid metal disk soldered under the stone.

disk

above left: 565. Paved setting with ring disk soldered into the hole as a seat for the stone.

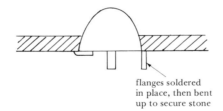

left: 566. Paved setting with cabochon held by flanges in a tapered hole.

flanges soldered
in place, then bent
up to secure stone

below: 567. Gypsy setting, with faceted stone held in beveled seat.

right: 568. The setting bur is used to cut the seat for a gypsy setting.

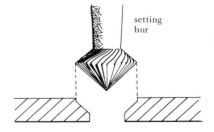

setting
bur

If the stone has tapered sides, as on a cabochon or high cabochon, a tapered hole can be drilled or sawed from the back and small flanges soldered in place, to be bent over against the bottom of the stone for setting (Fig. 566).

For the gypsy setting, which is used to set a faceted stone flush with the surface, a beveled seat is carved or soldered into a hole cut to fit the stone (Fig. 567). A cabochon can be set in the same way, by drilling a hole with a cone bur and then drilling a seat in the metal with a setting bur (Fig. 568).

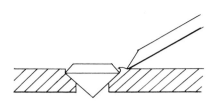

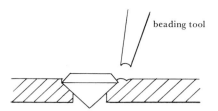

beading tool

569–570. Making a bead setting.

far left: 569. A curl of metal is rolled up with a graver against the faceted stone.

left: 570. The beading tool, a type of concave punch, forms beads around the stone.

21.4

Bead Setting   The bead setting is used to set transparent gems at the surface of the metal. To make this setting, drill a tapered hole with a cone bur, then put in a seat with a setting bur, so that the gridle of the stone is just below the surface. Mark the location of the beads to be burnished around the stone, and, with a graver, carry a small curl of metal up to the edge of the stone (Fig. 569). With a beading tool, burnish the curl into beads that rest against the edge of the girdle, thus holding the stone in place (Fig. 570).

The bead setting is normally used with platinum, palladium, and white or yellow gold. (Silver is usually too soft, unless the beads are relatively large.) Manufactured crowns (**21.6**) and standardized patterns have been developed for bead settings in the jewelry trade. However, there is room for much experimentation by the contemporary jeweler.

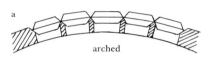

a

arched

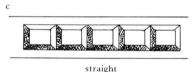

c

straight

right: 571. Channel settings can be arched or level in section, straight, curved, or tapered in plan.

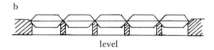

b

level

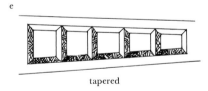

d

curved

21.5

Channel Setting   The channel setting is appropriate when rectangular or round-faceted gems are to be set in a solid line. The channel can be made along the surface of a metal sheet or raised above the surface in various ways: arched or level in section, straight, curved, or tapered in plan (Fig. 571).

The procedure is as follows: Saw out the shape of the stone with a bevel that matches the angle of the stone below the girdle, so that the girdle line is slightly below the surface (Fig. 572). Saw the next adjacent hole in such a way that the metal between the two holes supports the stones but will not be visible between them (Fig. 573). Continue the row in this manner to the desired length.

The stones are set along the row by chasing the edge over, as in the paved setting, or by bead setting.

e

tapered

572. Section view of a channel setting, with metal beveled to match the stone.

573. Channel setting for contiguous stones, with concealed support.

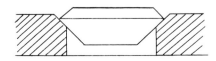

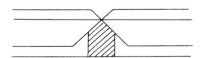

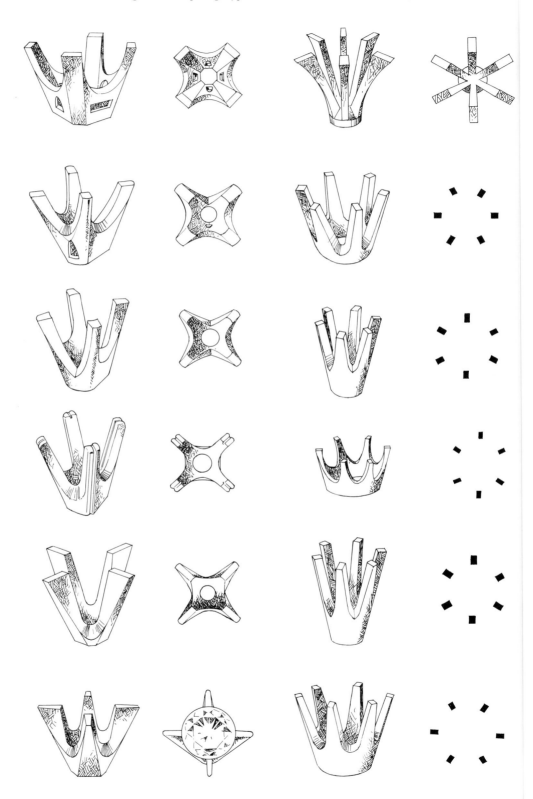

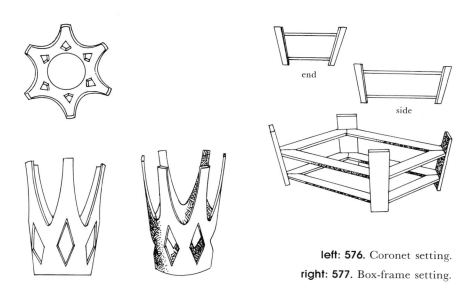

end

side

left: 576. Coronet setting.

right: 577. Box-frame setting.

21.6

Crown Setting   A wide range of forms and styles of crown settings are manufactured and available from the supply houses. As you will see from Figures 574 and 575, the crown is made with claws in which slots are filed to receive the stone, or it is designed for a bead setting.

In general, the crown setting is usually a variation either of the coronet setting (Fig. 576), which may also be developed from a truncated cone layout (**A.9**), or of the box-frame setting (Fig. 577).

Toolmaking

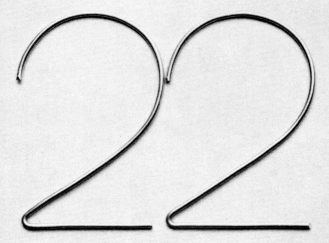

Blacksmithing is a complex art that requires not only specialized equipment but considerable study and practice. For those who have a small forge or are planning to install one, this chapter presents an introduction to simple blacksmithing techniques. The student who wishes to pursue the art beyond an elementary level should consult a specialized text (see Bibliography). However, the studio jeweler can learn to make punches and other small tools.

22.1

Heating Without a Forge   Even without a forge the jeweler can heat small carbon-steel drill-rod lengths sufficiently to form chasing tools. The oxygen torch is adequate for this purpose. Place a firebrick in the annealing pan as a back reflecting surface, and lay a length of tool steel beside it (Fig. 578). Heat the end of the tool steel to a bright red color, and work it immediately on the blacksmith's anvil. Strike several blows at once before the steel cools, and then replace in the annealing pan for reheating. In hammering the taper, work from one side to the other, holding to the same planes, and gradually develop an even taper. Make certain that each tool is straight and true before you complete your forging operation. If there is a bow in the tool, it will spring when struck—or at the very least you will have to do a lot of grinding to true it up. The fabrication of specific punches is described in greater detail later in this chapter (**22.14**).

22.2

Blacksmithing Equipment   A small portable forge, which is relatively inexpensive, will probably suffice for light work (Fig. 579). But the individual

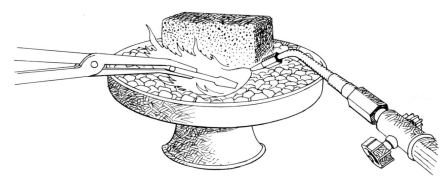

above: **578.** Tool steel being heated against a firebrick in annealing pan.

right: **579.** Buffalo portable forge.

who plans to do considerable forging or requires a permanent installation may find it more efficient to build up a forge from brick. Figure 580 shows how to build such a forge, with a layer of clay or mud between the double brick walls. A 3-inch cast-iron tue pipe, or *tuyere,* with holes drilled in it for a grate at the center point, will suffice to deliver the air blast. A vent hood must be hung over such a forge if it is to be used indoors, with a blower system for taking off the smoke and fumes.

The *anvil* is a magnificently designed tool and a great example of the functional intuition of folk design (Fig. 581). A solid base must be provided for the anvil. In the country workshop it can be set on a big log sunk 2 or 3 feet into the ground, but in the city or school workshop it will have to be mounted

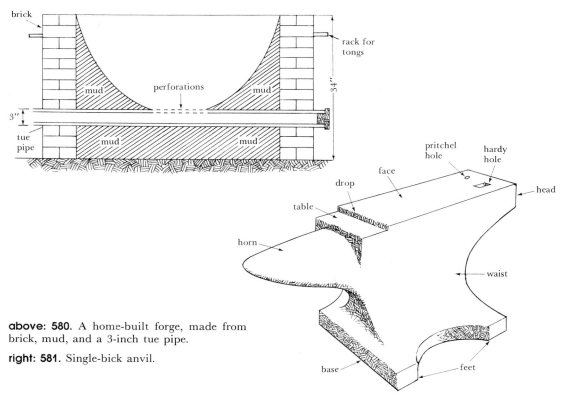

above: **580.** A home-built forge, made from brick, mud, and a 3-inch tue pipe.

right: **581.** Single-bick anvil.

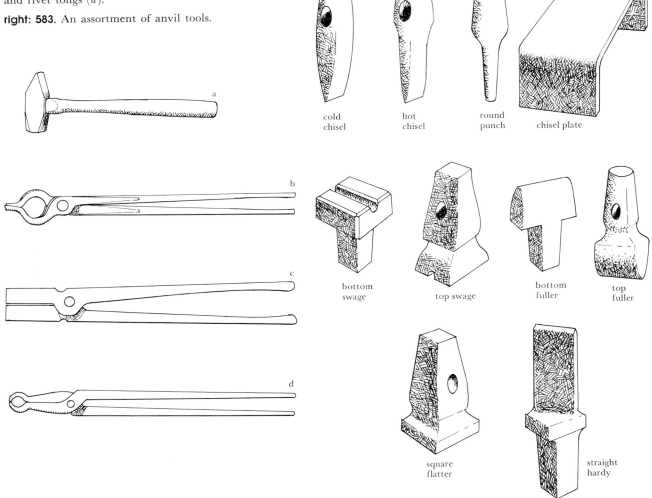

below: **582.** Blacksmith's hand hammer (*a*), curved-lip tongs (*b*), brazing tongs (*c*), and rivet tongs (*d*).

right: **583.** An assortment of anvil tools.

cold chisel

hot chisel

round punch

chisel plate

bottom swage

top swage

bottom fuller

top fuller

square flatter

straight hardy

on a rectangular post or box frame resting on a concrete floor. No anvil should be set on a wood floor unless there is a supporting column under the floor joists.

A *slake tub*—any tub that holds 5 to 10 gallons of water—should be set somewhere to one side but between the forge and the anvil. For extensive forging you will want a *brine bucket,* which in olden days was hung on two poles laid across the slake tub. The brine serves for tempering—a process that will be described later (**22.10, 22.17**). A *water can,* with holes punched in the bottom, will hang somewhere near the slake tub. This is used to pack down the coal or cool the fire.

Blacksmith's hand hammers are available in various weights from $2\frac{1}{2}$ to 12 pounds (Fig. 582). *Tongs* for handling hot iron come in assorted shapes according to function. The anvil tools are as follows (Fig. 583):

The *cold chisel* is used to cut cold iron; the *hot chisel,* with a somewhat sharper blade, cuts hot metal. The *chisel plate* is placed over the anvil to protect its surface during chisel cutting. The blacksmith uses chisels not only to cut metal apart, but also to split iron along its axis. A hole is often punched at the point or line where a split must be terminated. This prevents the iron from splitting along the grain beyond the terminal point.

Punches come in many different sizes and shapes. To punch, you should set the work over the pritchel hole and line up the punch over the hole before striking.

The *swage* provides one or more slots of various sizes and shapes in which iron can be formed. It is set on a shank that rests in a hole in the anvil. In a half-round bottom swage, for example, a square iron rod can be shaped into a round rod.

The *fuller* serves many forming purposes, but mainly it thins or draws out iron. The fuller has the same function as the silversmith's cross-peen forging hammer, namely: to thin and stretch the metal. After fullering, the surface of the iron is smoothed on the anvil with the *flatter*.

The *hardy* is a chisel with a square shank for insertion into the *hardy hole* of the anvil. The metal is placed over the hardy, and cuts are made from the underside by hammer strokes on top of the metal.

Many of the anvil tools will have holes through them and can be fitted with a handle, so that they can more conveniently be held in position and struck with a hammer.

Forge Operations

Forge operations can be broken down into four processes: 1) fire-making and setting; 2) heating; 3) forging; 4) heat treating and annealing. The best fuel for a forge is coke, which gives more heat with less smoke than coal. Coke can be purchased in 100-pound bags from a coal dealer. If you are using anthracite, pea coal or nut coal is handiest; lump coal will have to be broken up.

22.3

Building the Fire   Two tools will be necessary for fire building—a poker and a small hand shovel. If your fuel is coal or coke, begin the fire by setting a 6-inch post or log on top of the *duck's nest* or grate (Fig. 580). Then immediately pack wet coal against the post, followed by coke or more coal to a depth of about 5 to 8 inches. Withdraw the post, and build your fire in the hole, using shavings, paper, and small pieces of wood. As the fire catches, pack coke around and over the hole to create a hot cavity. Operate your blower during this period. When the fire is going well and has settled down to a hot, fiery glow, place your iron in the upper part of the cavity.

22.4

Heating the Metal   In heating a piece of iron, large or small, do not crank up a heavy draft through the forge. Heat the fire, set it right, and place your iron in the proper position. Then fan the fire sensitively and gently according to the size of the iron. If you are heating chasing tools or small tools of any kind, tuck them into the shallow fire in a circle and heat them all together. Avoid overheating and burning. You will be able to work from one to another, since they cool down rapidly. Remember that a large piece of iron takes longer to heat. Do not try to hurry.

When iron or steel is heated, changes in the temperature of the metal correlate with changes in its color. The sequence of colors during heating runs from light yellow through straw yellow to purple, then to blue and dull red. As the heat increases, the metal changes from red to glowing red and finally to white. Beyond white heat, steel turns a glowing yellow and approaches a molten state.

The heat range for forging iron and steel extends from glowing red to white heat. Further heating beyond white heat will force the metal to give off sparks, which indicate that the metal is burning. This is too hot for steel, although pure iron could be forged at this temperature.

The heat range for tempering (22.10) is lower in the sequence than that for forging, so the two scales should not be confused. As the silversmith knows, the colors can be seen better in a darkened or semidark room. Sometimes a small box into which the metal can be thrust for a color check will be set up near the forge.

Steel should be heated as few times as possible, since the structure of the steel will eventually be affected, and an oxidation scale will build up. The hotter iron is, the more malleable it becomes. Iron should not be hammered when it has cooled to below the glowing red stage, for below this temperature it will tend to crack along the grain.

22.5

Forging Forging demands a real understanding of the use of the hammer (Fig. 584). The anvil should be set at a height that allows you to set your hammer face "normal" to the anvil surface without undue bending. When you begin to hammer a piece of hot iron, you should automatically bring your hammer into a normal plane with respect to the anvil surface, so that the blows will fall squarely on the metal. For variations of hammering, the hammer is tilted right or left and the hammer handle is raised or lowered according to the form desired.

The various forging operations are as follows:
- *Cutting* is the process of cutting a bar or rod on the hardy or with a chisel on the chisel plate.
- *Dressing* is the heating and re-forming of a tool that has been beaten out of shape through use or misuse.
- *Drifting* is enlarging or shaping a hole with a tapered or shaped punch.
- *Flattening* is smoothing the surface of a forged piece by means of the flatter. The silversmith would call it *planishing*.

584. Forging tool steel on the anvil, as demonstrated by Eric Moebius. Portable forge and ventilating hood appear in the background.

- *Fullering* is the process of "drawing out" or thinning iron with the bottom or top fuller.
- *Packing* is the method of making the fingerlike grains of iron pack together more densely by hammering iron heated to the glowing red stage.
- *Punching* is driving a punch through hot iron.
- *Scarfing* or *beveling* is a hammering action along an end or an edge of a bar to create a tapered or diagonal plane.
- *Shrinking* is the fastening of one piece of metal to another. This is done by cutting or punching a hole in one piece of metal slightly too small for a bar or rod, which is inserted in the hole after the metal has been heated and expanded. As the metal cools, it shrinks firmly around the bar or rod.
- *Upsetting* is the process of thickening a piece of metal by hammering on the end or along the sides of the bar or rod.

22.6

Heat Treating (Annealing)   The process of heat treating immediately raises the question of what kind of iron is being worked. The possibilities include:

cast iron	2.2 percent carbon or more
steel	0.3 to 2.2 percent carbon
wrought iron	0.3 percent carbon or less

Wrought iron, or *black iron* as it was called in Colonial times, was in great demand for most agrarian tools, nails, and horseshoes. It also served, of course, for hinges, locks, ornamental grilles and frames, and other such products. Wrought iron could be work-hardened by hammering and annealed by heating to a low red color.

Steel is preferred for cutting tools and weapons, because it can be hardened or tempered to a great range of hardnesses. The process for hardening and tempering steel will be discussed in subsequent sections (**22.9, 22.10**). One thing to keep in mind about maintaining iron or steel in a state of softness is that it will cool more slowly in a box of dry earth than in the open air.

Metals for Toolmaking

22.7

Tool Steels   There are two general types of tool steels—*carbon steel* and special *alloy steel*. Of the alloy steels, Ryerson V.D. tool steel is excellent for making small punches and chasing tools, but it must be quenched in oil. Keep a gallon can of crank-case oil in the shop if you plan to use this alloy steel.

A good all-around tool steel for jewelry tools, hammers, punches, and chasing tools is a basic open-hearth, sulfurized carbon steel, such as 1942 SAE No. 1115. Its identification color is black. This steel hardens at about 1425° to 1450° F. and should be water-quenched. It can be purchased in squares and rounds from $\frac{1}{4}$ to 6 inches in diameter, or in hexagons from $\frac{1}{4}$ to 2 inches in diameter. Carbon-steel drill rod, either square or round, can be procured in 3-foot lengths in any diameter up to 2 inches. These rods are fine for making punches and chasing tools. A $\frac{3}{16}$-inch-diameter round or square steel drill rod is a good size for a chasing tool; it should be cut into $4\frac{1}{2}$-inch lengths.

22.8

Characteristics of Steel   It is characteristic of carbon tool steel that at a certain "critical point" in its temperature, the composition of the steel undergoes changes, both as the temperature increases and as it decreases. At normal temperatures, steel holds its carbon in a form called *pearlite* carbon. As the steel is heated to the critical point, called the *decalescence point,* its pearlite carbon becomes *martensite,* or hardening, carbon. If the steel is allowed to cool quite slowly, the martensite changes back into pearlite carbon. The critical point at which it changes back—the *recalescence point*—is somewhat lower in temperature than the decalescence point. These critical points have a direct bearing on the hardening and drawing of steel.

22.9

Hardening Steel   To harden steel, it is necessary to heat it to a temperature above the decalescence point and then quench it in a bath of water. When steel is heated above this point, it becomes nonmagnetic, and this is a simple test of whether your steel is heated sufficiently before quenching. Visually, the steel should be heated to a bright, whitish red; at cherry red it will still be magnetic.

After the steel has been hardened, it is very brittle and, therefore, not suitable for working, since a sharp blow will crack it apart. It must therefore be *drawn,* or tempered, to a suitable hardness.

22.10

Tempering Carbon Steel by the Color Method   Small tools can be tempered by holding them in annealing tongs and applying a small flame to the center of the tool until the desired color is reached, whereupon the tool is thrust into a bucket of water and agitated until it is completely cool. This is a subtle process, and the heat should be applied quite slowly. The hardened steel will be coated with oxides, which must be emeried off until the clean, bare metal is visible. As the steel is heated, a succession of colors will appear and move one after the other away from the center where the heat is applied. These colors are listed in the order of their appearance:

very pale yellow	Until it turns this color, steel is completely hard and brittle.
light yellow	
pale straw yellow	Draw twist drills and center punches to this color.
straw yellow	Draw chasing tools and repoussé punches to this color.
deep straw yellow	Draw chisels and scorpers to this color.
dark yellow	
brown yellow	
spotted red-brown	
brown-purple	
light purple	
dark purple	
full blue	
dark blue	At this color the steel begins to soften.

22.11

Grinding Tool Steel   Grinding wheels are available in a wide range of grades and sizes. If you consult supply catalogues, you will see that there are small, lead-centered grinding wheels for use on the tapered mandrel of the buffing lathe. When considerable toolmaking is done, a regular grinder, with standard-size grinding wheels, should be used. Safety goggles or a face mask should always be worn when grinding. For the buffing lathe, a 3-inch-diameter wheel is a good size. Both a fine and a coarse carborundum wheel are needed. Grinding tools are *never* used for grinding nonferrous metals, because such metals tend to clog the surfaces of the tools.

When grinding tool steel, certain precautions should be taken:

- Do all preliminary shaping on the coarse wheel.
- Avoid heating the metal on the grinder, for this will destroy the temper. Have a small can of water beside the grinder. Apply the tool to the wheel for an instant; then dip it into the water to cool it. Continue grinding in this way until the shape has been achieved.
- Use the fine wheel to finish surfaces and to sharpen edges. Even more care is required to avoid burning the steel with the fine wheel. Cutting edges and thin sections can become overheated very rapidly, and the tool must not be pressed too heavily against the fine wheel. It should be held very lightly in the fingers, so that, as a given plane is pressed against the wheel, it will not be cut into a new plane.
- Always move the tool across the face of the wheel. If you hold it in one place, you will wear a groove in the wheel.
- The coarse grinding wheel can be used to determine the quality of a given steel. The sparks from carbon steel fly off and burn in little sizzling stars, very brightly. The sparks from wrought iron or mild steel, which cannot be hardened, fly off as little round, dull red dots. Always make this test if you are not sure of the quality of the steel, since your tools should all be tempered and hardened.

Procedure for Making Specific Tools

22.12

Repoussé Tools   Repoussé work requires tools in a variety of shapes and sizes. Initial work should always be done with large, blunt, rounded tool ends. In general, the size of the tool is determined by the size of the work.

For jewelry work, one of the most useful tools is a punch made from $\frac{1}{2}$-inch round drill rod, which is ground to the general shape of the thumb and polished smooth. This shape can be achieved more quickly by forging first and then grinding the final form. The tool is used to do the main work of pushing out metal from the back.

Another basic repoussé tool is made from $\frac{3}{8}$-inch square drill rod, with the working end beveled to about $\frac{1}{4}$ inch square (Figs. 585, 586). The end is just barely domed, and the corners and edges are rounded. This tool is used to

585–586. Forging a repoussé tool.

right: 585. Drill rod forged with a flat taper.

below right: 586. Repoussé tool after forging is completed.

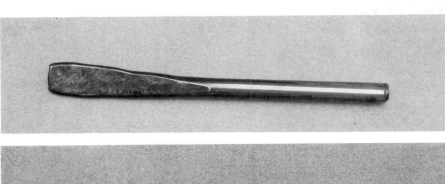

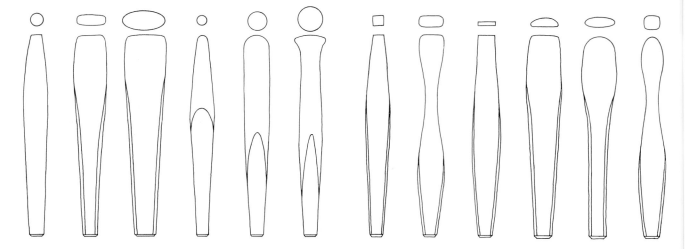

587. Repoussé tools of various kinds and sizes, with section views of their working ends.

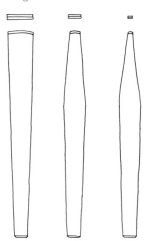

left: **588.** Flat repoussé tool, with rounded edges and corners.

below: **589.** Chasing tools: straight and curved liners.

flatten and smooth work. Other tools can be made in sizes and shapes according to need (Fig. 587).

Remember that the problem of repoussé is always to push the metal down without cutting into it; therefore, most tools should have rounded corners and edges (Fig. 588). Better-balanced tools and punches can be made if a taper is forged from the back end down about two-thirds of the length, and another taper forged from this point down to the working end. Such tapers should be made carefully and symmetrically around the axis of the tool. If they are forged and ground out of line, they will have a tendency to spring or bend when struck. After being forged, the tapered faces should be ground and finished perfectly and the working end shaped and file-finished.

22.13

Chasing Tools   Chasing tools should always be tapered as described above for repoussé tools. The two basic chasing tools are the *straight liner* and the *curved liner* (Fig. 589). Study the illustrations carefully, and note that the straight liner is ground perfectly symmetrical at the point of the two intersecting bevels, which are ground about 40 degrees off the axis of the tool (Fig. 590). The sharp edge is taken off the intersection of the two bevels so that it is not a sharp chisel, but this edge should not be rounded too much. The curved liner is made by first grinding one flat 60-degree bevel on one side. The other side is then ground to a curve by holding the tool at an angle of about 60 degrees

590. Faces on the point of a straight liner.

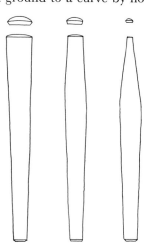

straight liners   curved liners   side   front

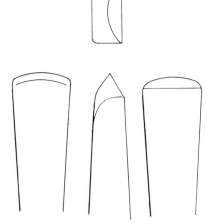

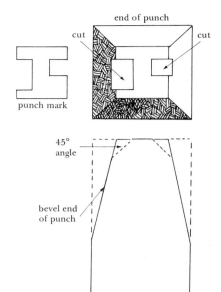

left: 591. Faces on the point of a curved liner.

right: 592. Pattern punch, with 45° cuts filed in the working end.

and rotating it on its axis against the wheel to grind a symmetrical curve across the tip (Fig. 591). Both of these tools must be made in an assortment of widths; other tools can be made according to special needs: square-ended, ball-point, flat-rounded, and so on.

22.14

Punches The size and proportion of punches vary with their purpose. Your own experience will help you determine the size and kind of drill rod to be used. For ordinary small punches, $4\frac{1}{2}$ inches is a good length, and $\frac{3}{16}$ inch is a good diameter. The square stock will give you a larger tip for special designs.

The first step in making a punch is to grind the ends flat and square. Then file the working end smooth with a fairly fine file. Never use your silver files for work on steel; use separate files reserved especially for this purpose.

Cutting designs and shapes in the end of a punch involves certain limitations. Cuts with files and the jeweler's saw, unless they run completely across the end, must be made into the punch from the sides, at an angle of about 45 degrees to the axis of the punch (Fig. 592). The purpose of this angle is to carry the cut back from the end so that, when the punch is driven into the metal to any given depth, the cut will register throughout the depth. Cuts made with saw or file, as well as holes drilled into the end, must be made a little deeper than the impression depth you wish to achieve. In the development of more elaborate designs, special punches must be made, hardened, and tempered to impress special shapes into the end of the main punch.

Punches for more permanent use should be made of slightly heavier stock, and a taper running back about 1 inch should be ground evenly around the working end. The back end of all punches should be ground to a small bevel, perhaps $\frac{1}{8}$ inch wide (Fig. 593). The purpose of this bevel is to eliminate the corners, which, under continual striking, tend to mushroom over. This can be dangerous to the eyes, because the edge may flake off as it spreads over the sides. Therefore, as the mushroom develops, take time to grind the flange away, so that the back end of the punch is always clean and safe.

22.15

Rivet Hammer A simple rivet hammer (Fig. 594) can be forged by the following procedure:
1. Select a piece of alloy steel, about $\frac{3}{8}$-inch square stock, perhaps $2\frac{1}{2}$ inches long, to serve as the hammer head.
2. Find the exact center along the length, and center-punch for drilling.
3. Drill a $\frac{1}{4}$-inch-diameter hole in the exact center. This hole must be true through the thickness.

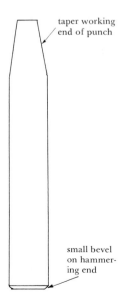

593. The working end of a punch receives a long taper, the hammering end a small bevel.

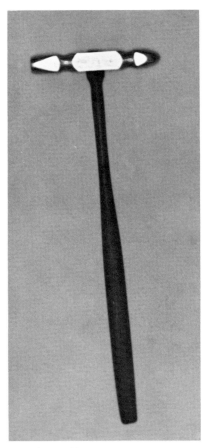

594. A small rivet hammer, forged from a length of alloy steel $\frac{3}{8}$ inch square.

4. About $\frac{5}{8}$ inch back from each end, cut a wide, shallow groove all around the stock. This can be done by rotating the head at a constant angle against the edge of the grinding wheel.
5. Now grind the tapered ball-peen end by rotating the end against the face of the grinding wheel.
6. If you want the flat face of the hammer to be round in section, rotate the head against the wheel until you have smoothed the corners of the flat face.
7. After the grinding process—which should be done with perfect symmetry—file down to remove grinding marks. The surface can then be finished with 80-J Metallite Cloth and further emeried to a fine finish with tripoli.
8. A round hole is not satisfactory for a hammer handle, so take a small rat-tail file, and file an oval shape in the $\frac{1}{4}$-inch-diameter hole that you have drilled in the head. At the same time, taper this hole from the bottom toward the top surface of the hammer head, so that when a handle is put in the top, a wedge can be driven into it, spreading it to fill out the taper and thus locking the handle in the head. The oval hole will prevent the head from slipping around the hammer handle.
9. There is no need to harden or temper this rivet hammer, since it is intended for use only on nonferrous metals. But if hardening and tempering are desired, follow the instructions for punches and chasing tools.

Final Finishing of Tools

22.16

Hardening   After the fine grinding of the tools, the sides and ends are always trued up and finished by filing. Strive to achieve perfect, true, and symmetrical finishing. To harden tools, a bucket of cold water and annealing tongs are needed. Place the tool in the annealing pan, and heat its full length cherry red. Now bring the working end up to a bright red or even white heat. At this temperature bright white specks will appear on the metal. When this point is reached, have the tongs ready to grasp the back end of the tool and plunge it into the water, agitating it slowly until all hissing and bubbling have stopped. It can then be taken out and dried.

22.17

Tempering   For tempering, polish the end of the tool at least halfway up from the working end, so that the bright, clean metal is visible. Now seize the back end of the tool with the annealing tongs. Hold a soft, small flame at the center of the tool, and from time to time run the flame up to the working end and back. If you heat the tool slowly, you will be able to get a very uniform straw color over the entire lower half. You must be careful not to apply too much heat to the working end, however. When the proper straw color has covered the working end, plunge the tool into the bucket of water. When the hissing stops, the tool can be withdrawn. If you apply too much heat, the color changes will appear and move down the tool too rapidly. As a result, you will get a very narrow band of straw yellow. Experience will enable you to control the heating properly.

22.18

Polishing   After tempering, the final surface is given to the working end of the tool. You can do this by emerying the faces of the tool with coarse and then fine paper. Then finish the tool on the tripoli wheel. Do not grind away the clean plane intersections of the chasing tools. Their marks should be crisp and clean, not blurred or rounded.

Appendices

appendix A
Elementary Layout for Jewelry

Layout is the graphic construction and division of circles, ellipses, squares, rectangles, lines, and other geometric figures into finished shapes of various sizes and proportions. It also includes the planning of flat shapes that can be rolled up to form volumes such as cylinders and cones. The jeweler often has occasion to divide a circle into equal sections or lay out an ellipse of a certain size. Geometry is a complex subject that cannot be extensively covered here, but certain basic geometric constructions should be mastered because of their practical value.

A.1 General Layout Guidelines   To duplicate one or more shapes, cut and file-finish one shape perfectly; then use it as a pattern to trace the other shapes with a sharp scribe. The resulting outline will be slightly larger than the original. Therefore, saw on the line, rather than outside the line as in normal practice.

Always center-punch the location of holes to be drilled. The center-punch hole will hold the drill exactly in place.

When laying out shapes on a piece of sheet metal, always locate the shape on or near the edges of the sheet, in order to reduce waste.

Lines on metal sheet are often difficult to see, whether scratched with a scribe or dividers, drawn with a pencil, or traced with carbon paper. To make scribed lines more visible, prepare a solution of whiting mixed with alcohol. This quick-drying solution can be painted over the surface. Lines scratched in the metal will then show clearly.

Lines and shapes can be transferred from a design drawn on paper by any of the following methods:

1. Trace the design, using carbon paper and a sharp pencil or stylus.
2. Lay the design in position on the sheet metal and make pin pricks along the lines with a sharp scribe.
3. Fix the design in place on the metal with rubber cement; then simply saw through both paper and metal. In this way scratch lines on the metal surface are avoided.

If a single pattern is to serve for more than one piece, use any of the preceding methods to make a template of 24-gauge brass (Fig. 623). Then, for each piece, trace the template with a sharp scribe and saw out on the scribed line.

A.2 Use of the Dividers   Dividers are very useful to the jeweler for laying out dimensions, as well as for drawing circles.

Lay out measurements on metal by setting the dividers to the exact dimension on the scale or steel rule, and then placing one point of the dividers on the edge of the metal and scratching a short mark with the other point.

To lay out a straight strip of given width along a straight side of sheet metal, mark the correct width from the edge of the sheet. Then, with the sheet laid flat on the workbench, place one point of the dividers against the edge of the sheet, and draw the dividers down along the edge, thereby scratching a line parallel to the straight edge of the sheet (Fig. 595).

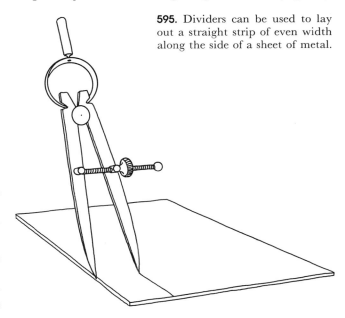

595. Dividers can be used to lay out a straight strip of even width along the side of a sheet of metal.

A.3 Basic Geometric Constructions

To divide a Line into Two Equal Parts (Fig. 596): Using the end points of line *AB* as centers and a radius greater than half the length of the line, draw circular arcs that intersect above and below the line at points *C* and *D*. *CD* divides *AB* into two equal parts and is also perpendicular to *AB*.

To Draw a Perpendicular to Line at a Given Point on That Line (Fig. 597): Using *A* as the center, draw a circular arc on each side across the line, locating *B* and *C*. Then, from points *B* and *C*, draw equal arcs that intersect the line at point *D*. Radii *BD* and *CD* must be greater than *AB* and *AC*. Line *AD* will be perpendicular to *BC*.

To Draw a Perpendicular to a Line from a Point above the Line (Fig. 598): Given the line *AB* and point *C* above it, draw an arc from *C* that intersects line *AB* at points *D* and *E*. Using *D* and *E* as centers, draw arcs of equal radius that intersect below the line at point *F*. Line *CF* will be perpendicular to *AB*.

To Divide a Line into Any Number of Equal Parts (Fig. 599): If, for example, it is desired to divide line *AB* into 5 equal parts, draw a line at an angle from *A* to some point *C* above the line. With the dividers, set off five equal parts of a convenient size from *A* along the line *AC* (*AD, DE, DF,* etc.). Draw line *BH* first, then draw lines parallel to *BH* that run through points *G, F, E,* and *D*. (Angles *d* through *h* must be equal.) These parallel lines intersect line *AB* to divide it into 5 equal parts.

A.4 Geometric Equations

$$\text{Area of a rectangle} = \text{length} \times \text{width}$$
$$\text{Area of a triangle} = \tfrac{1}{2} \times \text{base} \times \text{height}$$

$$\text{Diameter of a circle} = 2 \times \text{radius}$$
$$\text{Circumference of a circle} = 3.1416 \times \text{diameter}$$
$$\text{Area of a circle} = 3.1416 \times \text{radius} \times \text{radius}$$

$$\text{Circumference of an oval} = 3.1 \times (a + b)$$
$$\text{Area of an oval} = 0.7854 \times a \times b$$
$$\text{where } a = \tfrac{1}{2} \text{ major axis}$$
$$b = \tfrac{1}{2} \text{ minor axis}$$

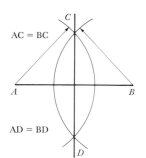

AC = BC

AD = BD

left: 596. Dividing a given line into two equal parts.

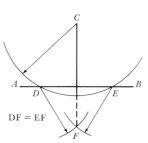

BD = CD

BA = AC

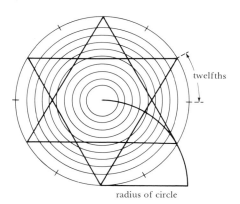

above: 597. Constructing a perpendicular through a point on a given line.

left: 598. Constructing a perpendicular to a given line from a point above it.

below: 599. Dividing a given line into any number of equal parts.

$\angle d = \angle e = \angle g = \angle h$

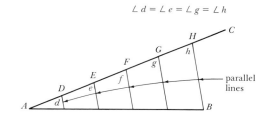

parallel lines

DF = EF

600. Constructing a circle template divided into equal thirds, sixths, and twelfths.

twelfths

radius of circle

A.5 Circle Division: The Circle Template

To Divide a Circle into Equal Thirds, Sixths, and Twelfths: Prepare a circle template as follows (Fig. 600). Take a small disk of brass about 4 inches in diameter and of 18 to 20 gauge. Punch a center point and inscribe concentric circles about $\frac{1}{8}$ inch apart all the way to the outside edge. Pick up the radius with the dividers, and step this distance around the circumference carefully. Bisect the one-sixth arcs to get twelfths.

To Divide a Circle into Eighths: Prepare a circle template as above. Construct a diameter through the center, carefully, with a scribe. Erect a perpendicular to this line through the center. Bisect the resulting quadrants with lines running accurately through the center of the circle (Fig. 601). You now have a template divided into eighths and quarters.

   If you wish to divide any small piece into halves, thirds, fourths, sixths, or twelfths, you merely set the piece in the center of the nearest scribed circle of the appropriate template and mark off the proper dividing lines.

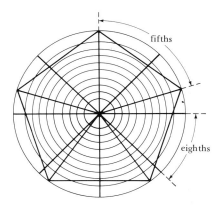

fifths

eighths

above: 601. Constructing a circle template divided into equal fifths and eighths.

below: 602. Circle template divided into thirds, sixths, twelfths, fourths, and eighths.

bottom: 603. Circle template divided into fifths and tenths.

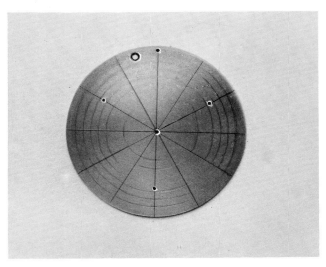

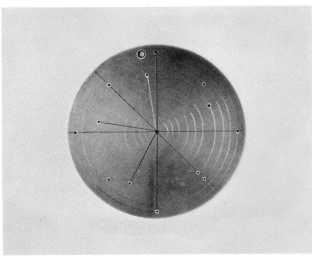

To Divide a Circle into Fifths: It is usually better to keep separate templates for eighths and fifths (Figs. 602, 603). For dividing the circle into fifths, it is most convenient to use a protractor and mark out the circle into units of 72°.

A.6 Ellipse Construction and Division The templates described above may also be used for dividing ellipses into symmetrical parts. In addition, there are templates now commonly available with an assortment of ellipses that can be traced. You may, however, wish to construct an ellipse with a specific major and minor axis. If so, proceed as follows (Fig. 604):

604. Construction of an ellipse using two pins and a loop of string.

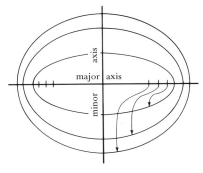

major axis

minor axis

1. Draw a straight line on paper and call it the major axis. Erect a perpendicular line across the major axis and call it the minor axis.
2. Set two pins on the major axis at an equal distance from the intersection with the minor axis, say 12 mm apart. Take a length of string about $2\frac{1}{2}$ times as long as the distance between the pins—30 mm, for example, if the pins are 12 mm apart. Tie the string into a loop, and place the loop over both pins.
3. Take a sharp pencil and push the point against one part of the loop, pushing it taut along the minor axis as far as the pencil will go.
4. Now draw a line by moving the pencil against the string, allowing the string to guide the pencil. An elliptical path will be produced.
5. To make a narrower ellipse, the pins must be set farther apart on the major axis. To make a wider ellipse, move the pins nearer to the center of the ellipse.

A.7 Calculating Ring-Band Lengths A simple and direct method of measuring the circumference of a ring band is to wrap a stick of paper around the ring mandrel at the desired size, mark the circumference, and measure with a ruler. Or you can multiply the diameter of the ring size by *pi* (3.1416). Either method, however, will yield only the circumference of the inner surface. A more practical circumference, giving the actual length of metal required, must take into account the thickness of the metal to be rolled up. This requires a diameter measured from center to center of the material, or the inner diameter plus one thickness of the metal. For example, 12-gauge silver is 2.05 mm thick (**C.20**). Calculation of the lengths required for a selection of ring sizes in this material proceeds as follows:

Size	I.D. (mm)		12 gauge (mm)		(mm)	_pi_		Length of band
4	14.88	+	2.05	=	16.93	× 3.1416	=	53.2 mm
6	16.51	+	2.05	=	18.56	× 3.1416	=	58.3 mm
8	18.14	+	2.05	=	20.19	× 3.1416	=	63.4 mm
10	19.76	+	2.05	=	21.81	× 3.1416	=	68.5 mm
12	21.39	+	2.05	=	23.44	× 3.1416	=	73.6 mm

Similar calculations for 18 gauge (1.02 mm thick) yield the following practical circumferences:

Size	_Length of band_
4	50.0 mm
6	55.1 mm
8	60.2 mm
10	65.3 mm
12	70.4 mm

It is usually a good idea to add another millimeter or so to all of the above dimensions, in order to have a little extra material to work with. After comparing such paper calculations with practical experiments in the studio, the jeweler may wish to make a composite table according to the ring sizes and gauges most commonly used. Standard ring and gauge sizes are listed in Appendix C, sections **C.19** and **C.20**.

A.8 Layout for Necklace Arrays Draw a circle of 6-inch diameter and draw a line straight down from the center. Construct two 60° angles on either side of this line to mark the practical limits of an array to be suspended around a chain (Fig. 605).

A woman's neck will range from about 12 to 15 inches in circumference. Only with a snug-fitting choker can an array be carried around the neck. Such a choker will fit higher on the neck and pass above the shoulders, whereas a chain type of necklace will rest upon the shoulders.

A necklace array that is flexible and consists of a lattice of spacing elements will drape well across the shoulders. But a necklace consisting of pendant elements hung from a single chain will not hold an array pattern. The pendants will simply hang straight toward the ground in an ungainly parallel formation.

A.9 Layout of a Cone The development of a simple cone is often necessary in jewelry making, as in the preparation of chain ends and special crowns. A simple but effective crown, for example, can be made from a truncated cone rolled from sheet (Fig. 606). First, draw a profile elevation of the truncated cone desired, and extend the sides of the trapezoid until they intersect at the apex of a triangle. In the example

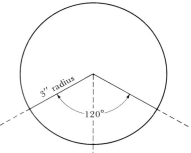

above: **605.** Practical limits of a necklace array.

below: **606.** Constructing a cone from sheet metal.

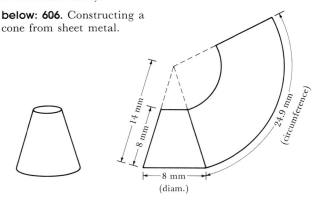

illustrated, the triangle has sides 14 mm long and a base (the bottom diameter of the cone) 8 mm wide. The line of truncation is 8 mm from the base, resulting in an upper diameter of approximately 5 mm. Given a constant base diameter, the upper diameter and height of a truncated cone can be varied according to a constant inverse relationship; one or both of these dimensions can also be changed by altering the angle or slope of the sides.

Once the profile of the cone has been established, place the point of a pencil compass at the apex of the extended triangle, set the pencil point at one of the corners, and draw an arc about four times as long as the base of the triangle. Then draw a similar arc from the upper corner of the trapezoid. Since the base diameter of the cone is 8 mm, the circumference of the base will be:

$$8 \text{ mm} \times 3.1416 = 25.13 \text{ mm}$$

This circumference must be stepped out in small intervals (say, 2 mm) along the outer arc. Then draw a line between the apex of the triangle and the point reached on the arc. The line will intersect the inner arc as well, and the resulting shape can be cut out of metal, rolled up, and soldered to form a truncated cone of the desired shape and dimensions. A relatively thin sheet of metal will yield the best results.

appendix B
Sources of Findings, Materials, Tools, and Supplies

B.1 Hallmarks In the United States the sterling stamp is required by law to be affixed to any piece of work that is sold as sterling. Likewise, gold work must be stampled according to its karat grade. These stamps can be secured from supply houses (**B.9**). In addition, most jewelers and silversmiths buy or make a hallmark—a stamp of identification for their own work. This mark is stamped near the karat or sterling stamp on the back of the work.

B.2 Jewelry Findings There is such a wide variety of jewelry findings supplied by so many different manufacturers that every jeweler should secure a set of catalogues in order to become acquainted with the types, kinds, and prices. Basic types of findings are described and illustrated here.

Ear Backs A large variety of ear backs are commercially available from supply houses. These designs vary in size, quality, metal, and type of fastening device. They are available in sterling, 14-karat gold, and cheaper alloy metals.

The screw back (Fig. 607) is perhaps the most common design but the clip (Fig. 608) is becoming more popular, because its greater surface area holds more firmly but with less pinching pressure on the ear lobe. Both these types are made with or without a small open ring to which a dangle can be attached. Those with such a ring usually have a small sphere or hemisphere covering the outer end of the clip. The type without an open ring usually has a small disk or cup with a small threaded post in its center, to which a bead or pearl can be cemented. The post is clipped off when the ear back is to be attached to a button type of earring. It is sometimes best to buy an ear back that has both the open ring and the cup and post, because the ring can be sawed off if it is not required.

Ear backs for pierced ears are made in two styles. One style, attached to the ear by threaded post and nut, has a small disk on which a button can be mounted (Fig. 609). The other common style features a continuous wire for use with dangle earrings (Fig. 610). There is also a pin-and-clip design for pierced ears, but this is seldom preferred over the type with post and nut.

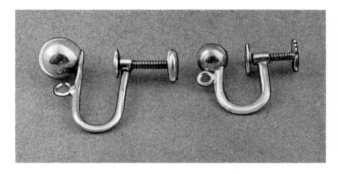

above: 607. Screw-on ear backs.

left: 608. Clip-on ear back.

below left: 609. Ear back with post and nut, for pierced ears.

below: 610. Ear wire for pierced ears.

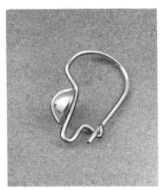

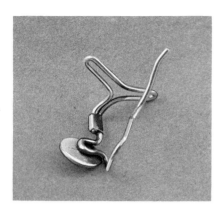

The wing back is an interesting type that fits into and around the ear, with no clip to pinch the lobe (Fig. 611). Although unusual in appearance, the wing back is functional and extremely comfortable.

Cuff-Link Backs The contemporary jeweler often tries to make the cuff-link back an integral part of the overall design. For many button-type designs, however, a simple readymade back will be satisfactory (Fig. 612). Such backs often have a small cup or depression at the base for soldering. One of the harder soft solders (**C.9**) should be used, and care should be taken not to overheat the spring in the swivel part. The best way to solder this back is to clip it to the button with self-locking soldering tweezers, position it with the swivel part up and the button part down, and then apply a small flame upward on the underside of the button. As soon as the solder flows, the cuff link should be quenched in water.

Pin Sets A variety of pin tongs, joints, and safety catches are available from suppliers (Fig. 613). The pin tong comes in a number of lengths ranging from 1 to $3\frac{1}{2}$ inches. The short lengths are of smaller-gauge wire, desirable for small pieces of jewelry. The 3-inch pin, however, can be cut down to any shorter length desired, and it is therefore the single most useful size to have on hand.

The type of joint illustrated always comes spread apart. The sides should be squeezed parallel, and the resulting rounded bottom should be filed flat before soldering. The most useful style of safety catch has its slot opening on the top. The catch can be used with pin tongs of any length. For directions on making a pin set, see **15.10.**

Sister Hooks The sister hook, composed of two hooks hinged together by a tube rivet, is a practical fastener for link bracelets (Fig. 614). Once closed, it will fall open only if the tube

613. Safety catch, pin tong, and joint.

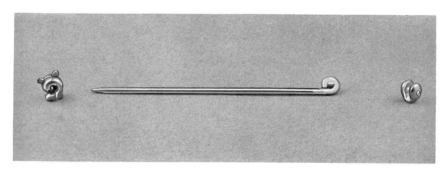

614. Sister hook.   **615.** Spring ring.   **616.** Tie tack.

rivet becomes too loose. If this happens, the hinge can be tightened simply by burnishing the tube.

Spring Ring   The spring ring (Fig. 615), a standard fastener for necklaces, comes in a range of sizes from $\frac{1}{8}$ to $\frac{3}{8}$ inch in diameter.

Tie Tack   The tie tack (Fig. 616) is popular for button-type tie clips. The flat disk on the pin is soft-soldered to the button.

Tie-Clip Back   The sterling tie-clip back illustrated (Fig. 617) is one of the best on the market. It should be soft-soldered to the tie clip.

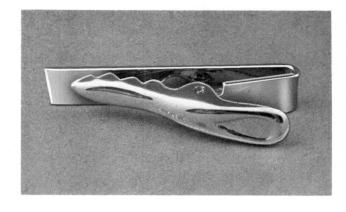

617. Tie-clip back.

B.3 Sources of Jewelry Findings

Allcraft Tool & Supply Co., Inc.
100 Frank Road
Hicksville, N.Y. 11801

American Handicrafts Co., Inc.
1011 Foch Street
Forth Worth, Tex. 76107

B. A. Ballou & Co., Inc.
800 Waterman Avenue
East Providence, R.I. 02914
(*wholesale only*)

Craft Service
337 University Avenue
Rochester, N.Y. 14607

Paul H. Gesswein & Co., Inc.
235 Park Avenue South
New York, N.Y. 10003

Grieger's Inc.
900 S. Arroyo Parkway
Pasadena, Calif. 91109

J. J. Jewelcraft
4959 York Boulevard
Los Angeles, Calif. 90042

Karlan & Bleicher, Inc.
195 Danbury Road
Wilton, Conn. 06897
(*wholesale only; ring findings*)

Kramer Studio
20 Bethune Street
New York, N.Y. 10014

Marshall-Swartchild Co.
2040 N. Milwaukee Avenue
Chicago, Ill. 60647

Metal Crafts and Supply Co.
10 Thomas Street
Providence, R.I. 02903

Montana Assay
610 S.W. 2nd Avenue
Portland, Ore. 97204

Swest, Inc.
10803 Composite Drive
(or P.O. Box 2010)
Dallas, Tex. 75220

B.4 Sources of Sheet and Wire Stock

American Handicrafts Co., Inc.
1011 Foch Street
Fort Worth, Tex. 76107
(*silver*)

T. E. Conklin Brass and Copper Co.
322–324 West 23 Street
New York, N.Y. 10011
(*brass, copper, alloys*)

General Refineries
292 Walnut Street
St. Paul, Minn. 55102
(*silver, gold*)

Paul H. Gesswein & Co., Inc.
235 Park Avenue South
New York, N.Y. 10003
(*silver, gold*)

Grieger's Inc.
900 S. Arroyo Parkway
Pasadena, Calif. 91109
(*silver*)

T. B. Hagstoz & Son
709 Sansom Street
Philadelphia, Pa. 19106
(*copper, brass, alloys*)

Hauser & Miller Co.
4011 Forest Park Boulevard
St. Louis, Mo. 63108
(*special 820/1000 silver alloy for reticulation*)

Hoover & Strong
119 W. Tupper Street
Buffalo, N.Y. 14201
(*silver, gold, platinum*)

J. J. Jewelcraft
4959 York Boulevard
Los Angeles, Calif. 90042
(*silver*)

Swest, Inc.
10803 Composite Drive
(or P.O. Box 2010)
Dallas, Tex. 75220
(*silver, gold, platinum, palladium*)

B.5 Sources of Gems and Semiprecious Stones

A-Plus Craft Supply Co.
93 Davies Avenue
Dumont, N.J. 07628

Ernest W. Beissinger
P.O. Box 454
Carnegie, Pa. 15106

Eugene Chaput
210 Post Street
San Francisco, Calif. 94108

Grieger's Inc.
900 S. Arroyo Parkway
Pasadena, Calif. 91109

T. B. Hagstoz & Son
709 Sansom Street
Philadelphia, Pa. 19106

International Gem Corporation
15 Maiden Lane
New York, N.Y. 10038

Kramer Studio
20 Bethune Street
New York, N.Y. 10014

The Lapidary Journal
Box 80937
San Diego, Calif. 92138

William V. Schmidt Co., Inc.
30 Rockefeller Plaza
New York, N.Y. 10020

B.6 Sources of Enameling Supplies

Allcraft Tool & Supply Co., Inc.
100 Frank Road
Hicksville, N.Y. 11801
(*enamels, cloisonné wire, kilns, equipment*)

Carpenter & Wood Co., Inc.
15 Cedar Street
Providence, R.I. 02903
(*enamels*)

William Dixon Co.
750 Washington Avenue
Carlstadt, N.J. 07072
(*enamels, kilns*)

T. B. Hagstoz & Son
709 Sansom Street
Philadelphia, Pa. 19106
(*cloisonné wire, foil*)

Metal Crafts and Supply Co.
10 Thomas Street
Providence, R.I. 02903
(*enamels*)

Stewart Clay Co.
133 Mulberry Street
New York, N.Y. 10013
(*kilns*)

Thomas C. Thompson Co.
1539 Deerfield Road
(or P.O. Box 127)
Highland Park, Ill. 60035
(*enamels, foil, cloisonné wire, kilns, equipment*)

B.7 Sources of Plastic Resins and Supplies

Resin Coatings Corporation
14940 N.W. 25 Court
Opa Locka, Fla. 33054

The Plastics Factory
119 Avenue D
New York, N.Y. 10009

Polyproducts Corporation
13810 Nelson Avenue
Detroit, Mich. 48227

B.8 Sources of Tools and Equipment

Allcraft Tool & Supply Co., Inc.
100 Frank Road
Hicksville, N.Y. 11801
(*jewelry tools*)

American Handicrafts Co., Inc.
1011 Foch Street
Fort Worth, Tex. 76107
(*craft tools*)

Anchor Tool & Supply Co., Inc.
231 Main Street (or P.O. Box 265)
Chatham, N.J. 07928
(*general tools*)

Craft Service
337 University Avenue
Rochester, N.Y. 14607
(*general tools*)

William Dixon Co.
750 Washington Avenue
Carlstadt, N.J. 07072
(*silversmith and jewelry tools*)

General Refineries, Inc.
292 Walnut Street
St. Paul, Minn. 55102
(*casting equipment and supplies*)

Paul H. Gesswein & Co., Inc.
235 Park Avenue South
New York, N.Y. 10003
(*jewelry tools*)

Grieger's Inc.
900 South Arroyo Parkway
Pasadena, Calif. 91109
(*jewelry and lapidary supplies*)

Kerr Manufacturing Co.
28200 Wick Road (or P.O. Box 455)
Romulus, Mich. 48174
(*casting equipment and supplies*)

Marshall-Swartchild Co.
2040 N. Milwaukee Avenue
Chicago, Ill. 60647
(*jewelry tools*)

M. McNamara Stamp & Stencil Works, Inc.
40 East 20 Street
New York, N.Y. 10003
(*sterling and special stamps*)

Metal Crafts and Supply Co.
10 Thomas Street
Providence, R.I. 02903
(*lapidary equipment and jewelry tools*)

Alexander Saunders & Co., Inc.
28 Chestnut Street (Route 9D)
Cold Spring, N.Y. 10516
(*casting equipment and supplies*)

Swest, Inc.
10803 Composite Drive
(or P.O. Box 2010)
Dallas, Tex. 75220
(*jewelry and lapidary supplies*)

Torit Division,
Donaldson Company, Inc.
1133 Rankin Street
St. Paul, Minn. 55116
(*casting equipment*)

Waldree Lapidary Shop
2267 N. Dearborn Street
Indianapolis, Ind. 46218
(*lapidary equipment*)

B.9 Other Common Supplies

Material	Supplier (See key)
barium chloride	L
Battern's Flux	J
beeswax	L
borax	L
boric-acid crystals	L
chloride of platinum	L
cuprous cyanide	L
emery paper	L
green copperas	L
gum tragacanth	L
Handy Flux	J
hydrochloric acid	L
iodine	L
Lea Compound	J
liver of sulphur	L
mold rubber	J
nitric acid	L
pitch	J
potassium cyanide	L
potassium iodide	L
powdered pumice	L
rouge	J
saltpeter	L
shellac chips	J
sodium carbonate	L
sodium cyanide	L
sodium phosphate	L
sodium pyrophosphate	L
sodium thiosulphate	L
soldering salts	L
sulphuric acid	L
tripoli	J
wax, blue	K
File-Wax	S
green	K
red	J
Solu-Wax	S
yellow ochre	L
zinc chloride (soldering salts)	L

Key		
	L	local dealer (drugstore, hardware, or craft shop)
	J	jewelry supply house (**B.3, B.8**)
	K	Kerr Manufacturing Co. P.O. Box 455 Romulus, Mich. 48174
	S	Swest, Inc. P.O. Box 2010 Dallas, Tex. 75220

Metals

C.1 Melting Points of Metals

aluminum	1218° F	lead	621° F
brass	1700–1850° F	platinum	3191° F
bronze	1675° F	silver, fine	1761° F
cast iron	2300° F	sterling	1641° F
copper	1981° F	tin	449° F
gold, fine	1945° F	zinc	787° F

C.2 Silver and Silver Alloys   Fine silver is used for such special purposes as enameling, because its reflective power under transparent enamels is greater, and because its melting point is higher that that of sterling. Fine silver is also preferred over sterling for bezel making, because it is softer and can be burnished over a gemstone more readily. For most purposes, however, fine silver is too soft, and it is therefore alloyed with copper.

In continental Europe the standard alloy is 900 parts fine silver to 100 parts copper. American jewelers and silversmiths use the British sterling standard, which is 925 parts fine silver to 75 parts copper. A somewhat lower grade alloy, such as that composed of 820 parts silver to 180 parts copper, works best for reticulation (see Hauser & Miller, **B.4**).

Silver can be alloyed with gold to produce some very interesting color qualities. Electrum, you will remember, was a natural alloy of gold and silver. Gold and silver in equal proportions, which would be 12-karat gold, has a beautiful, soft color that is quite rich for jewelry.

Silver solders are usually made from alloys of silver and brass. Formulas for silver solder are given below (**C.7**).

C.3 Gold and Gold Alloys   Gold is traditionally produced in a variety of alloy proportions reckoned in karats or twenty-fourth parts. Fine gold is equivalent to 24 karats.

18k gold	18 parts gold, 6 parts alloy metal
14k gold	14 parts gold, 10 parts alloy metal
10k gold	10 parts gold, 14 parts alloy metal

These are the standard gold alloys commonly used in the jewelry trade. The three grades exist for good reasons: Fine gold is so soft that it has poor wearing qualities; 18-karat gold is used in the most expensive jewelry, but it wears rather easily; 14-karat gold is the most commonly used grade for good jewelry, because it has better wearing qualities while still retaining most of the rich color and quality of pure gold; 10-karat gold appears in less expensive jewelry and in exposed parts of other jewelry where harder wearing qualities are needed. An alloy containing less than 10 parts gold cannot legally be stamped with the karat stamp (**B.1**).

Gold can be alloyed in various grades with several different metals; these combinations produce the different colors of the gold alloys:

Grade	Color	% Gold	% Alloy		Melting point (approx.)
24k	yellow	100			1945° F
22k	yellow	91.6	4.20 silver	4.20 copper	1860° F
20k	yellow	83.3	8.35 silver	8.35 copper	1820° F
18k	yellow	75.0	12.5 silver	12.5 copper	1660° F
14k	yellow	58.3	20.8 silver	20.8 copper	1565° F
10k	yellow	41.6	29.2 silver	29.2 copper	1515° F
18k	white	75.0		25.0 palladium	1660° F
14k	white	58.3		41.7 palladium	1700° F
10k	white	41.6		58.4 palladium	1760° F
18k	green	75.0		25.0 silver	1770° F
14k	green	58.3		41.7 silver	1600° F
10k	green	41.6		58.4 silver	1480° F
14k	red	58.3		41.7 copper	1670° F

C.4 Testing Gold   The touchstone method of testing gold requires the following equipment:

stone of slate or basalt, polished smooth
set of standard gold needles from 4k to 22k
nitric acid
aqua regia
(Gold-testing sets can be purchased.)

Procedure: Make a streak across the stone with the gold to be tested. Make streaks on each side of the first streak with standard gold needles. Choose two needles at random, estimating the possible karat of your gold.

Across the gold streaks make a streak of nitric acid and observe the reaction of each streak. Watch carefully the color changes and the speed of the reactions. A green color comes from the copper in the alloy. Fine gold gives a yellow color, masked by green. High-karat streaks are not affected by nitric acid, and therefore a special acid known as "aqua regia" (**C.14**) must be tried.

The testing is done by making a comparison of the acid reactions. Identical color reactions on the test gold and on one of the gold needle streaks will establish the quality of the gold being tested.

C.5 Alloys An alloy consists of a homogeneous mixture of metals. The composition of some of the nonferrous alloys is given below:

brass: 60% copper, 40% zinc (proportions variable)
bronze: 90% copper, 0.2% zinc, 9.7% tin, 0.1% lead
ormolu (mosaic gold): equal parts of copper and zinc
  (Melt the copper at the lowest temperature that will fuse it. Stir well and add the zinc little by little. This alloy first assumes the yellow color of brass, turns purple, and finally becomes white.)
pewter: 100 parts tin, 17 parts regulus of antimony
queen's metal: 9 parts tin, 1 part bismuth, 1 part antimony, 1 part lead
talmi gold: 86.4% copper, 12.2% zinc, 1.1% tin, 0.3% iron (may be eliminated)
tombac: 16 parts copper, 1 part tin, 1 part zinc
tombac (red): 11 parts copper, 1 part zinc
  (Melt the copper, then add the zinc.)
German silver: 41.2% copper, 32.6% nickel, 26.2% zinc

C.6 Niello Niello, a black metallic compound of silver, copper, lead, and sulphur, can be set in three-dimensional forms or used to fill engraved lines and walled areas. One formula employs:

  1 oz. fine silver
  2 oz. copper
  3 oz. lead

Melt the silver and copper in a crucible; then add the lead, and stir with a piece of charcoal held in the tongs. Clean off the scum caused by the lead. When the mixture is blended, pour it into a pottery jar that has been half filled with powdered sulphur. Ideally, you might commission a potter to make a pint bottle with a small neck that is not much larger than 1 inch in diameter. The purpose of the jar is to confine the sulphur fumes. Stopper the opening with a lump of clay, wrap the pottery bottle in burlap, and shake it vigorously as it cools.

Another formula for niello is:

  3 parts fine silver
  7 parts copper
  5 parts lead

Melt the silver and the copper in a crucible in a bench melting furnace; than add the lead. When the melt is thoroughly blended, pour it into a second crucible of the same size, which has been half-filled with sulphur. Stir the mixture with an iron rod as it cools. When stirring is no longer possible, remelt the mixture in the furnace and restir in order to mix the components completely and drive off excess sulphur.

This entire process of stirring the molten metal into the crucible of sulphur must be done under an efficient ventilating hood, because a good amount of sulphur smoke will be generated.

When the mixture is cool, the niello will be in small lumps. Break these up in a mortar and remelt them in a crucible, repeating the process several times.

Crush the niello into grains, rather than to a powder. Place the niello in a glass bottle and wash several times to remove dirt.

You can apply niello to three-dimensional work with a torch, provided the flame is not allowed to touch the niello directly.

To apply niello to engraved work, spread the niello evenly in lines about $\frac{1}{16}$ inch deep. Place the work on an iron plate and into the kiln. When the niello begins to melt, take an iron rod with a flattened end and spread the niello into all the grooves. Then remove the work and allow it to cool. The excess niello must then be filed away with a file or a stone.

As a final step, warm the work in the kiln until it is slightly hotter than the hand can bear. Remove it and go over the niello lines with a burnisher dipped in oil. The work can then be polished lightly with tripoli.

Solder and Flux

C.7 Silver Solders The five standard grades of silver solder are composed as follows:

I.T.	7 parts fine silver, 1 part brass
hard grade	5 parts fine silver, 1 part brass
medium grade	3 parts fine silver, 1 part brass
easy grade	2 parts fine silver, 1 part brass
Easy Flow	2 parts fine silver, $\frac{1}{2}$ part brass

C.8 Gold Solders Gold solders for the various gold alloys are made by increasing the alloy metal enough to lower the melting point sufficiently for soldering. Examine the table of alloys in **C.3** and note the differences in melting points of the various gold alloys. In yellow gold, for example, there is a difference of 50° between 10-karat and 14-karat alloy.

To make gold solder for any given gold alloy, take four parts of that alloy and add one part of fine silver. To make a gold solder for 18-karat gold, for example, take 4 pennyweights of 18-karat gold and 1 pennyweight of fine silver; put them together in a small hole in a charcoal block, add a bit of borax for flux, and melt them together. When the mixture is molten, stir slightly with a heated iron rod. Take the button, when cool, and forge or roll it into a thin sheet, and cut into paillons or strip.

This procedure can also be used to make gold alloys for special purposes; a 10-to-12-karat alloy is excellent for repoussé work in gold.

C.9 Soft Solders

common lead solder: 2 parts lead, 1 part tin
   (Add tin to melted lead.)
soft lead solder: 2 parts tin, 1 part lead
hard lead solder: 63% tin, 37% lead
   (This solder, hardest of all, melts at 175°C.)
Allstate No. 430 Soft Silver Solder (remains silver-bright)

C.10 Fluxes

Soft-solder fluxes:

for lead: 1 oz. zinc chloride in 1 cup water
for pewter: 1 part hydrochloric acid to 18 parts glycerin

Hard-solder fluxes:

Borax is prepared in sticks for use with a borax slate. A small amount of water is placed in the hollow of the slate, and the borax stick is rubbed in the hollow until a solution of flux is made. This is applied with the flux brush.

Borax powder is available in cartons in the grocery store. This is a convenient form of flux to use in the crucible or in solder powder.

Battern's Self-Pickling Flux is a fluoride flux much used by professional jewelers. It comes in small bottles or pint cans. Since it evaporates, it is best kept in a very small bottle on the workbench. An India-ink bottle, well cleaned, makes a good flux bottle, and the flux brush can be put into the rubber stopper.

Prip's Flux is an excellent flux that also prevents fire scale buildup (**C.12**).

Handy Flux, a special preparation, melts at 1100° F, which is just below the melting point of silver solders. It is especially good for soldering copper because copper oxidizes so readily. It is also a good flux for silver-soldering steel.

Sal ammoniac is used for lead-soldering iron and steel.

Cleaning and Protecting Metals

C.11 Pickle Solutions   The most common pickle solution for silver work consists of one part sulphuric acid and from six to twelve (usually ten) parts water. This solution can also be used for gold, copper, and brass, but pickles reserved for each metal should be kept separate. For special purposes, it is often best to use a solution of one part nitric acid and five or ten parts water. Another substitute for the sulphuric-acid pickle is a propriety product called Sparex.

A pickle solution is usually kept in a half-gallon crock or Pyrex jar with a lid. For jewelry, it is most convenient to keep a crock or container filled with no more than an inch or two of solution, so that only the fingers need be dipped in to retrieve the work. Many jewelers prefer to use copper or stainless-steel tongs (but never iron) for removing work from the pickle solution.

Always add the acid to the water! When acid and water are mixed, considerable heat is generated. Should water be poured into the acid, an explosion will take place. Therefore, pour the acid into the water very slowly and carefully, pouring close to the near edge of the crock in a small trickle. For a pint of water, you can estimate about 2 tablespoons of acid.

Silversmiths, who usually do large work, often have a special tank made of lead ⅛ inch thick, measuring 30 inches square and 12 inches deep. A gas burner is placed under the tank so that the pickle can be brought to a moderate heat for more rapid pickling action.

The jeweler who wishes to pickle something quickly can place the work in a special copper pickle pan with enough pickle to cover the work and then bring the solution to a boil over the hot plate. The solution is afterward carefully poured back into the crock, and the pickle pan and the work are rinsed under the water tap.

C.12 Fire Scale Protection   The buildup of fire scale or firecoat can be retarded by any of the following procedures:

1. Mix yellow ochre with a solution of boric-acid crystals dissolved in water to a light, fluffy paste. Paint this over the areas to be protected. When solder seams must be fluxed, do this first and dry the flux by warming the piece. Then the yellow ochre can be painted over the appropriate areas and up very close to the seams. If the yellow ochre is painted on first, the flux will tend to draw it into the seam, thereby obstructing the flow of the solder.
2. Boric-acid solution is mixed with alcohol to aid rapid drying.
3. Prip's Flux
       64 g borax
       64 g sodium phosphate
       96 g boric-acid crystals
   Make a paste with a little water and then gradually add 1 quart water. Bring the mixture to a boil. This will give a clear coating that protects against fire scale remarkably well and also serves as an excellent flux for gold and silver.

C.13 Stripping   Stripping refers to the process of boiling silver work in a stripping solution of nitric acid to remove fire scale. Stripping always takes place in the final finishing of work, after all soldering and annealing have been done. The stripping solution is made of one part nitric acid, poured slowly into one part water. *Always add the acid to the water.*

The solution is placed in a copper pickle pan and brought to a boil. This must be done either outdoors or in a ventilated booth that will exhaust the corrosive fumes.

The work is boiled for 1 to 3 minutes and inspected. Acidic action removes the surface layer of the metal. The longer the work is left in the pickle, the more metal is removed. This process should be timed carefully so that the least necessary amount of metal is removed.

Electrostripping is a far more effective method of removing fire scale, because it leaves a bright, polished surface (**16.4**). It is the standard method in the industry for cleaning gold castings before polishing, since it leaves inaccessible and recessed areas bright.

C.14 Aqua Regia   Aqua regia, or "royal water," is the most powerful of all acids and will dissolve or etch gold as well as silver. It can also be used to test high-karat gold (**C.4**).

Add one part nitric acid very slowly to three parts hydrochloric acid. Never keep the bottle tightly stoppered. The fumes are highly corrosive. *Use with care!* Aqua regia should be used outdoors or in a ventilated booth with a blower.

C.15 Removing Lead from Gold or Silver Lead or lead solder will soak into gold or silver if the latter metals are heated to annealing or soldering temperature. The lead that has thus soaked into gold or silver will cause pits and ruin the surface. If the lead cannot be scraped off, the following solution will dissolve the lead:

2 oz. green copperas
1 oz. saltpeter
10 oz. water

Procedure: Dissolve the chemicals in the water and boil. When cool, the solution will crystallize. Then dissolve the crystals in the hydrochloric acid in the proportion of 8 ounces acid to 1 ounce of the crystals. Finally, dilute this solution in four times its weight of boiling water. Articles to be cleaned should be boiled in this solution.

Other Metal Treatments

C.16 Buffs and Buffing Compounds Buffs, brushes, and laps are attached to the wheel of the lathe and used with compounds or by themselves for a variety of purposes:

cutting buffs: made from layers of coarse material sewn together; used with cutting compounds. *Leather* buffs or *sandbobs,* made from walrus hide, are used with powdered pumice. The *wool* buff is used with Hard White or Lea compound, the *muslin* with tripoli or White Diamond compound.
polishing buff: made of flannel and used with rouge.
brush buff: one or more rows of bristles mounted on a small wooden disk; used with tripoli for working in inaccessible areas that cannot be reached with cloth buffs.
scratch brush: wheel-mounted bristles of brass or nickel-silver wire; produces a mat, satin finish.
ring buff: tapered wooden cone covered in felt; used with tripoli or rouge to finish the inner surface of a ring band.
lap: wooden wheel for burnishing and polishing, used especially in lapidary work.

Compounds are mixtures of mineral particles held together by grease or wax (Fig. 530). They are applied to the buff, or "charged," as a means of cutting, burnishing, and polishing metal. There are three major types:

Lea compound: a coarse abrasive for cutting out deep pits and scratches from silver (grade A), brass, or copper (grade C). Similar types include Hard White and White Diamond. The jeweler should wear a respirator when using any of these compounds.
tripoli: a medium abrasive of fine, sharp particles that cut tiny scratches into metal; used to give silver a "butler" finish.
rouge: a compound of flat particles that burnish, rather than cut, metal; used to give gold and silver a high polish; available in several colors—white and green, as well as red—with slightly different characteristics.

C.17 Electrolyte Solutions The following formulas are mixed with distilled water to make baths for electroplating in copper, silver, and gold:

for copper (cyanide solution):

cuprous cyanide (CuCN)	22 g per liter
sodium cyanide (NaCN)	34 g per liter
sodium carbonate (Na_2CO_3)	15 g per liter
sodium thiosulphate ($Na_2S_2O_3 \cdot 5\,H_2O$)	2 g per liter

operating temperature: about 40°C
current density: 15 amperes per square foot

for copper (noncyanide):

copper sulphate ($CuSO_4 \cdot 5\,H_2O$)	$1\frac{2}{3}$ lbs. per gal.
sulphuric acid (H_2SO_4)	4 oz. per gal.

for silver (cyanide solution):

fine grain silver	2 oz. troy per gal.
sodium cyanide (NaCN)	3 oz. Av. per gal.

for silver (noncyanide):

silver sulphate (Ag_2SO_4)	30 g per liter
ammonia (NH_4OH)	75 cc per liter
potassium iodide	600 g per liter
sodium pyrophosphate	60 g per liter

for gold (cyanide solution):

metallic gold	1 g per liter
cyanide (KCN) (free)	0.1 to 15 g per liter
phosphate (K_2HOP_4)	15 g per liter
ferrocyanide (K_4FeCN_6)	10 to 11.5 g per liter

C.18 Pitch for Repoussé and Chasing

1 lb. green pitch
2 lb. plaster of Paris
1 oz. tallow

Melt the pitch in an old pan over a gas plate. Heat slowly until it is liquid. Gradually stir in the tallow, then the plaster; pour the mixture into the pitch bowl. Leave a little extra in the pan so that, if you need a small amount to fill up the back of a repoussé piece, you will not have to dig it out of the pitch bowl. In cold weather the pitch may harden, and additional tallow will be needed.

Sizes, Weights, and Measures

C.19 Ring Sizes Standard ring sizes progress at intervals of 0.032 inch or 0.8 mm between whole sizes.

Size		Inner Diameter (in.)	(mm)	Size		Inner Diameter (in.)	(mm)
0	=	.458	11.6	$6\frac{1}{2}$	=	.666	16.9
$\frac{1}{4}$	=	.466	11.8	7	=	.682	17.3
$\frac{1}{2}$	=	.474	12.0	$7\frac{1}{2}$	=	.698	17.7
$\frac{3}{4}$	=	.482	12.2	8	=	.714	18.1
1	=	.490	12.4	$8\frac{1}{2}$	=	.730	18.5
$1\frac{1}{2}$	=	.506	12.9	9	=	.746	18.9
2	=	.522	13.3	$9\frac{1}{2}$	=	.762	19.4
$2\frac{1}{2}$	=	.538	13.7	10	=	.778	19.8
3	=	.554	14.0	$10\frac{1}{2}$	=	.794	20.2
$3\frac{1}{2}$	=	.570	14.5	11	=	.810	20.6
4	=	.586	14.9	$11\frac{1}{2}$	=	.826	21.0
$4\frac{1}{2}$	=	.602	15.3	12	=	.842	21.4
5	=	.618	15.7	$12\frac{1}{2}$	=	.858	21.8
$5\frac{1}{2}$	=	.634	16.1	13	=	.874	22.2
6	=	.650	16.5	$13\frac{1}{2}$	=	.890	22.6

C.20 Gauge Sizes The B&S (Brown and Sharpe) gauge plate is a disk with slots of various sizes cut into the edge (Fig. 303). These slots are of standard sizes calibrated from 0 to 36. To find the size of a sheet or wire, merely find the slot into which the metal fits most neatly, and read off the number. A table of gauge sizes, with dimensions in both inches and millimeters, is given below:

Gauge	in.	mm	Gauge	in.	mm
0	.325	8.25	16	.051	1.29
1	.289	7.35	17	.045	1.15
2	.258	6.54	18	.040	1.02
3	.229	5.83	19	.036	0.91
4	.204	5.19	20	.032	0.81
5	.182	4.62	21	.029	0.72
6	.162	4.11	22	.025	0.64
7	.144	3.67	23	.023	0.57
8	.129	3.26	24	.020	0.51
9	.114	2.91	25	.018	0.45
10	.102	2.59	26	.016	0.40
11	.091	2.30	27	.014	0.36
12	.081	2.05	28	.013	0.32
13	.072	1.83	29	.011	0.29
14	.064	1.63	30	.010	0.25
15	.057	1.45			

C.21 Weights of Sheet and Wire Stock

Gauge	Sterling		14k Gold	
	Wire oz./ft.	Sheet oz./sq. in.	Wire dwt./ft.	Sheet dwt./sq. in.
4	2.15	1.12	54.2	28.1
6	1.36	.887	34.1	22.3
8	.852	.704	21.4	17.7
10	.536	.558	13.5	14.0
12	.337	.443	8.47	11.1
14	.212	.351	5.33	8.82
16	.133	.278	3.35	7.00
18	.0838	.221	2.11	5.55
20	.0527	.175	1.33	4.40
22	.0331	.139	.833	3.49
24	.0309	.110	.524	2.77
26	.0131	.0873	.330	2.19

C.22 Fahrenheit and Celsius Units of Temperature

$$T_C = \frac{5}{9}(T_F - 32) \qquad T_F = \frac{9}{5}T_C + 32$$

where:
T_C = temperature in degrees Celsius
T_F = temperature in degrees Fahrenheit

C.23 Comparative Weights in the Troy, Avoirdupois, and Metric Systems

	Troy	Avoirdupois	Metric
1 pound troy =	12 oz. troy	= 13.166 oz. Avoir. =	373.2 grams
	240 dwt.	.823 lb. Avoir.	
	5760 grains	5760 grains	
1 ounce troy =	20 dwt.	= 1.097 oz. Avoir. =	31.104 grams
	480 grains	480 grains	155.5 carats
1 pennyweight =	24 grains	= 24 grains	= 1.555 grams
(dwt.)	.05 oz. troy	.055 oz. Avoir.	7.775 carats
1 grain		= 1 grain	= .065 grams
			.325 carats

	Avoirdupois	Troy	Metric
1 pound		= 1.215 lbs. troy	= .454 kilograms
	= 16 oz. Avoir.	14.6 oz. troy	453.6 grams
	7000 grains	7000 grains	
1 ounce Avoir.		= .9115 oz. troy	= 28.35 grams
	= 437.5 grains	437.5 grains	141.75 carats
1 grain		= 1 grain	= .065 grams
			.325 carats

	Metric	Avoirdupois	Troy
1 kilogram	= 1000 grams	= 2.205 lbs. Avoir. =	2.666 lbs. troy
		35.26 oz. Avoir.	32 oz. troy
1 gram	= 5 carats	= .035 oz. Avoir. =	.032 oz. troy
		15.43 grains	15.43 grains
1 carat*	= 200 milligrams =	.007 oz. Avoir. =	.0064 oz. troy
		3.086 grains	3.086 grains

*Not to be confused with the *karat,* a twenty-fourth part, used to express the purity or fineness of gold (**C.3**).

C.24 Metric and U.S. Units of Length, Area, and Volume

Length

1 meter	=	100 cm	=	1.093 yds.	1 yard =	3 ft. = .914 m
		1000 mm		3.28 ft.		36 in. 91.4 cm
				39.37 in.		914 mm
1 centimeter =		10 mm	=	.394 in.	1 foot = 12 in. =	30.5 cm
1 millimeter			=	.039 in.	1 inch =	2.54 cm

Area

1 square meter	=	10.764 sq. ft.	1 square foot	=	.093 m^2
1 square cm	=	.155 sq. in.	1 square inch	=	6.451 cm^2

Volume

1 cubic centimeter =		.061 cu. in.	1 cubic inch	=	16.387 cc
		.010 liter			.016 liter
1 liter = 100 cc	=	1.057 U.S. qts.	1 U.S. quart*	=	.946 liter
		.254 U.S. gals.	1 U.S. gallon*	=	3.785 liters
		61.02 cu. in.			

*The British imperial quart equals approximately 1.2 U.S. quarts or 1.135 liters. Similarly, the British gallon equals 1.2 U.S. gallons or 4.54 liters.

abalone Mollusk shell of the genus *Haliotis,* greenish or bluish in color, used in small shapes or as pearls; usually small in size and of "baroque," or irregularly round, shape.

achrolite Colorless variety of tourmaline that is rare and expensive if over 5 carats and perfect.

agate Variegated form of compact silica, with stripes, bands, or cloudy patterns of various colors; in pure form called chalcedony. Sometimes found with moss or leaf patterns (see *moss agate*). Widely distributed throughout the world. Hardness 7.

alexandrite Green variety of chrysoberyl from the Ural Mountains, named after Czar Alexander II; under artificial or reflected light, the color appears red. Hardness $8\frac{1}{2}$.

almandine Hard variety of garnet, rich red, violet, or purple in color, the finest coming from Ceylon and India. Hardness $7\frac{1}{2}$.

amazonite Pale green variety of feldspar resembling jade, named after the Amazon River but found widely. Hardness 6.

amber Translucent fossil resin of yellowish to dark brown color, sometimes having insects or plant elements embedded; capable of being polished. Hardness $2-2\frac{1}{2}$.

amethyst Variety of crystallized quartz ranging from pale violet to dark red-violet in color; named from a Greek work for a remedy for drunkenness and in ancient times so used. Clear stones may be faceted. Hardness 7.

anatase Metallic or brown stone, also called octahedrite. Hardness 6.

andalusite Vitreous olive-green to brown stone, sometimes mistaken for tourmaline; named for Andalusia, where it was first found. Hardness $7\frac{1}{2}$.

Apache tears Popular name for obsidian pebbles.

aquamarine Transparent member of the beryl family, of cool bluish or sea-green color. Hardness 8.

aventurine Translucent variety of quartz, pale to dark green in color and spangled with mica and other substances; found in Brazil and India. Hardness 7.

azurite Compact copper mineral, opaque blue in color and often associated with green malachite. Hardness 4–5.

benitoite Crystallized sapphire-blue mineral, found only in San Benito County, Calif.; rare over 2 carats. Hardness $6\frac{1}{4}$.

beryl Transparent silicate of beryllium and aluminum, a mineral family name including aquamarine, emerald, goshenite, heliodor, morganite, as well as cat's-eye varieties in many colors. The term "beryl" is sometimes applied to various beryllium stones outside those in the above categories. Hardness 8.

beryllonite Rare beryllium mineral, transparent and pale. Hardness $5-5\frac{1}{2}$.

bloodstone Variety of chalcedony, of a dark, opaque green with red oxidized spots like drops of blood, which made it an important talisman in ancient days. Hardness 7.

bonamite Strong blue-green variety of *smithsonite,* of limited usefulness in rings, but good for other jewelry. Hardness 5.

brazilianite Brilliant stone, yellow to yellow-green, and transparent to translucent, recently discovered in Brazil. Hardness $5\frac{1}{2}$.

cairngorm Yellow or smoky gold member of the quartz family, available in large sizes. Hardness 7.

cameo Relief-carved gem of a stone such as agate or onyx, or shell, coral, etc., cut through contrasting layers of color.

carnelian Variety of chalcedony, reddish to orange-red in color, much used in ancient times. Color can be produced in gray agates by heating. Hardness 7.

cat's-eye Stone having an "eye," an internal reflection resembling a cat's eye, or chatoyancy. Term used in the gem trade to refer to chrysoberyl and as a prefix to names of other gems having an eye-like reflection.

chalcedony Translucent variety of quartz. Term refers to blue and gray shades, the red being called carnelian, the green chrysoprase, etc.

Chatham created emerald Synthetic emerald grown from a natural emerald by a proprietary process. Hardness 8.

chrysoberyl Brilliant, transparent stone, bright yellow to golden in color; alexandrite and cat's-eye are examples. Hardness $8\frac{1}{2}$.

chrysocolla Deep blue to bluish-green copper mineral; when translucent and clear, stones are of gem quality. Hardness up to 7.

chrysoprase Apple-green variety of chalcedony, of gem quality when translucent and pure. Dyed variety called "green onyx."

citrine Variety of quartz, pale yellow to golden in color, sometimes mistakenly identified as topaz. Hardness 7.

coral Hard skeletal material secreted by colonies of sea organisms; color ranges from white or pale red to deep red (oxblood) and, rarely, to black or blue shades.

cordierite Two-colored blue stone named for a French geologist; capable, when correctly oriented, of being faceted to produce a gem similar in color to the Ceylon sapphire. Also called iolite. Hardness 7 plus.

corundum Natural aluminum mineral occurring in various colors. When red, called ruby; when blue, called sapphire. Synthetic corundum can be produced in almost all colors. Hardness 9.

crocidolite Quartziferous mineral with fibers, often bluish or greenish, producing a chatoyant effect in cabochon cuts. When golden in color, called tigereye. Hardness 7.

crystal Colorless quartz, faceted for beads, pendants, and other uses; also called rock crystal. Colored varieties called amethyst for lavender, citrine for yellow, etc. Hardness 7.

danburite Transparent to translucent stone similar to topaz, but more yellow than golden; first found in Danbury, Conn., whence the name. Hardness 7.

demantoid Garnet varying in color from yellow to deep green, and very brilliant; the most expensive of garnets. Hardness $6\frac{1}{2}$–$7\frac{1}{2}$.

diamond Crystallized carbon of high brilliance, in colors from pink, violet, green, and yellow to golden; produces tremendous "fire" when cut correctly. Hardness 10.

dinosaur bone Textured fossil stone resulting from replacement of bone structure by silica; occurs in a mixture of reds, browns, and tans.

diopside Transparent pyroxene stone of bright green color, often faceted. Burmese variety is a cat's-eye. Hardness 5–6.

dioptase Copper silicate of bright green color, resembling emerald; must be used with caution in jewelry because of its softness. Hardness 5.

dumortierite Opaque, blue-violet aluminum silicate, named for a French paleontologist. Hardness 7.

emerald Rare and expensive variety of beryl, green in color. Hardness 8.

epidote Yellow-green to dark green stone, usually opaque, but sometimes found clear and sometimes mixed with pinkish feldspar. Hardness 6–7.

fibrolite Aluminum silicate of brown, gray, or greenish color, sometimes mistaken for jade. Hardness $7\frac{1}{2}$.

garnet Family name for silicates ranging from orange and red to purple and pink, as well as green (see *demantoid*). Deep red to black garnet is called pyrope. Hardness 6–$7\frac{1}{2}$.

goshenite Colorless beryl, named after Goshen, Mass. See *beryl*.

hematite Heavy, black crystalline iron mineral with considerable reflective quality; also called "black diamond." Hardness $5\frac{1}{2}$–$6\frac{1}{2}$.

hiddenite Yellow to yellow-green stone of the spodumene family, named for its discoverer in North Carolina; now also available from Brazil.

ivory Dense dentine substance from tusks and teeth of elephants, whales, and other large mammals; white, creamy, or brownish in color; readily carved and incised as beads and other jewelry elements but too soft for some purposes. Hardness $2\frac{1}{2}$–3.

jade Term used for two different minerals: (1) **jadite,** a pyroxene, also called "true jade" or "Chinese jade"; found mainly in Burma, in a wide range of colors, including white, green, violet, orange, red, and black; hardness 7; (2) **nephrite,** a variety of tremolite or actinolite, ranging from apple-green to green-black and black, found in many parts of the world. The name comes from the Greek word for kidney, and the stone was used as an amulet or remedy in ancient times. Hardness $6\frac{1}{2}$.

jasper Opaque varieties of quartz, usually found in strong colors of red, yellow, and brown; also, in antiquity, green chalcedony. See bloodstone.

jet Black fossil wood derived from decomposed and compressed driftwood; can be easily carved and highly polished; found mainly in England.

kunzite Brilliant but rather brittle type of spodumene, lilac or blue-violet in color. Hardness 6 plus.

labradorite Chatoyant variety of feldspar, first known from Labrador, generally gray with flashes of blue or, occasionally, yellow or orange.

lapis lazuli Dark blue stone, often spangled with iron pyrites; best varieties come from Russia and Chile. Hardness 6.

malachite Opaque, lustrous, green copper mineral, capable of a high polish but requiring protection if used in jewelry. Hardness 4.

moonstone Translucent variety of feldspar with pearly or waxy luster and sometimes with blue chatoyancy. Hardness 6.

morganite Member of the beryl family, named for J. P. Morgan, obtainable in delicate pink or subtle orange shades, the latter called peach morganite. Hardness 8.

morion Quartz of smoky black color.

moss agate Variety of quartz containing fibrous formations of manganese oxide resembling trees or moss. See *agate*.

nephrite One of the minerals often called jade. See *jade*.

obsidian Volcanic glass in varieties of color and pattern: jet black, snowflake, mahogany, rainbow. Hardness 5.

olivine Mineral group including peridot. Hardness 6–7.

onyx Banded agate; also dyed chalcedony known as "black onyx," "green onyx," or "blue onyx." "Mexican onyx" is a variety of alabaster.

opal Form of silica with fiery play of colors, found in many parts of the world, varying from almost black to pale bluish or greenish with flame-colored flashes.

peridot Member of the olivine family, of clear yellow-green color and high brilliance; expensive when over 10 carats.

pyrope Deep red, ruby-colored garnet. See *garnet, star garnet*.

quartz Crystalline silica occurring in a variety of colors and including many gemstones. See *amethyst, citrine, rock crystal, rose quartz, smoky quartz*, etc.

rhodolite Garnet of pale pink or lavender color, transparent and delicate.

rock crystal Clear, colorless quartz. See *crystal*.

rose quartz Delicate pink quartz, occasionally found clear enough to facet, but usually cut *en cabochon*. Hardness 7.

rubellite Tourmaline of rose-red or pink color, generally more expensive than green tourmaline.

ruby Red corundum that runs from pink shades to the rich, deep red of "pigeon-blood" gems; one of the most valuable of gemstones. Hardness 9.

rutilated quartz Clear quartz with slim crystals of rutile embedded in the stone. Hardness 7.

sapphire Blue corundum ranking next in value to the ruby; also found in colors of white, yellow, green, and pink. Clear varieties are usually faceted.

sard Carnelian of uniform brown-red color.

sardonyx Carnelian of dark red-brown color, banded with white or other colors.

siberite Tourmaline of deep red-violet color.

smithsonite Translucent stone of apple-green to blue color, named for the donor of the Smithsonian Institution; too soft for rings but fine for a protected setting. Hardness 5.

smoky quartz Brilliant but inexpensive stone, also known as *cairngorm*.

sodalite Stone somewhat like lapis lazuli, but less expensive. Hardness about 6.

spessarite Rare stone of brown-red to yellow or orange-brown color, similar to garnet.

sphene Light-colored titanite with varied color effects, showing green-yellow or red-yellow, depending on the axis on which it is cut.

spinel Transparent stone of dark color, ranging from orange to red, purple, and blue. Hardness 8.

spodumene Mineral family of good brilliancy, including *kunzite* and *hiddenite*. Hardness 6–7.

star garnet Garnet with star-shaped crystal reflection in four rays (or multiples of four); usually only in the red *pyrope*. Hardness $6-7\frac{1}{2}$.

star ruby Red corundum with six-ray star reflection. See *ruby*.

star sapphire Blue corundum with star reflection; other colors of star sapphire less valued. See *sapphire*.

Swiss lapis Dyed agate or jasper, somewhat lighter blue in color than genuine lapis lazuli. Hardness 7.

thomsonite Decorative stone of pink or red patterns, often in eye shapes; found near Lake Superior. Hardness $5-5\frac{1}{2}$.

tigereye Chatoyant silicified crocidolite with fibers turned to oxide of iron; generally golden yellow or brown in color but may be turned red by heating the yellow variety. Hardness 7.

titania Synthetic stone with fiery play of many colors. Hardness 6 plus.

topaz Clear, brilliant stone of fine golden yellow color, also occurring in less valued shades of pale to medium blue, pink, and colorless varieties; frequently imitated. Hardness 8.

tourmaline Group of gemstones occurring in almost every color; dichromatic. Hardness $7-7\frac{1}{4}$.

tugtupite Cyclamen-red ornamental stone discovered in southern Greenland in 1960.

turquoise Opaque, somewhat porous stone of sky-blue to greenish color, originally known from Turkey. Hardness 6.

zircon Transparent, lustrous stone occurring in brownish, golden yellow, green, red, and green-blue colors. White stones (resembling diamonds in brilliancy) and blue stones are made artificially by heating the naturally brownish-colored stones. Hardness $6\frac{1}{2}-7\frac{1}{2}$.

appendix E
Marketing and Production

This book is directed primarily to the studio craftsman involved with problems of design and technique and with developing a personal mode of expression. The issues of marketing and quantity production, however, bring the beginning jeweler out of the studio and face to face with economic realities.

The economic status of the artist-craftsman today remains marginal, although it has improved considerably over the past twenty or thirty years. Aesthetic standards, quality of materials and workmanship, originality of conception, and expressive power—all these tend to be undervalued by the masses of consumers. Only a relatively small percentage of the population will pay for them. Nevertheless, the handcrafts are surviving by reason of the peculiar relationship in which the craftsman stands to his or her work. The craftsman is a person who finds it essential to affirm the human values involved in working directly with the hands. In addition, the craftsman is one who strives to achieve the integrative benefits that result from carrying out a complete process of production from the initial stages of planning and design, through the various technical procedures, to the final product and its marketing. Few occupations in modern industrial society offer this kind of independent, comprehensive, and satisfying activity.

It is the demand for wholeness, then, that places the craftsman in a marginal economic position in today's society. The studio artist who becomes involved in quantity production for the public at large must learn to walk the delicate line between successful commercial operation and the integrity of the creative process.

On the whole, the current market position of the craftsman is rather favorable. There seems to be an unusually large demand for craft products of all kinds, due in part to the increased interest in the arts and the crafts that has developed since World War II and in part to the prosperity of the postwar period. On the other hand, the craftsman must be prepared to survive through unfavorable economic periods and must therefore cultivate the most advantageous methods of marketing and production.

Marketing

E.1 Finding a Market   The craftsman who survives must realistically meet the market in terms of price and performance without sacrificing artistic and personal values. This will require both efficiency and industry.

The student jeweler will eventually begin to sell early jewelry pieces to friends and acquaintances, usually at modest prices. This situation is very exciting, of course, because a new source of income suddenly appears. The problem of marketing seems fairly simple, and it may continue to be simple in certain favorable environments. The college community living on campus or in a college town offers a fairly good local market for the beginner. After graduation the student might well set up a small workshop near the campus and develop a good livelihood. This would be a most natural and satisfactory market solution. Even there, however, competition is likely to offer a challenge to the beginner.

It is extremely important to find a location where the market demand is potentially large. This point is dramatized by the example of one retail merchant, who doubled his sales volume by moving his shop one half-block nearer to the center of town! Traffic is vital in retail sales. The craftsman about to set up shop should really make a traffic study of the number of pedestrians passing a given location and compare it with the most populous section of the business district. Sometimes it is best to go straight for a proven area, such as a campus shopping center, where there is a captive market for jewelry.

In large population centers the contemporary jeweler may follow one of two marketing routes. The first is the gradual development of a personal following in a community large enough to support full-time activity. As the jeweler's reputation spreads from customer to customer, private commissions come in. The marketing program can be improved mailing flyers to previous and prospective customers, and perhaps by holding periodic clearance sales. The beginning jeweler can broaden his or her clientele by giving talks to local groups, by exhibiting in local shows, and by teaching courses in one of the community's education programs. This kind of marketing program can be carried out in the home studio on a personal basis, or it can be expanded to include a shop in the suburbs, a summer tourist location, or a downtown commercial location, depending on local conditions and the jeweler's personal preferences.

The second marketing route leads to a retail shop operated by someone else. Such a shop may be in a museum, gallery, department store, or gift shop. From the craftsman's point of view, this outlet is less desirable than the other, because work must be produced and sold at a wholesale price that will allow the retailer to cover overhead and make a reasonable profit. Theoretically, the craftsman makes half the amount of money on each piece that would be earned by selling the piece in his or her own shop. However, the established jeweler finds that it costs as much or more to sell out of a private shop as it does to sell through a retail outlet. Interrupting production sequences to wait on customers consumes time and seriously interferes with efficient production. The jeweler can, of course, set up a full-scale retail outlet, but this means hiring a staff to operate the shop and still spending some time—preferably not more than one afternoon a week—in supervision of employees and in appointments for custom work at the shop.

At the retail store the craftsman must relate output to the prevailing market for the product, which is now competing on the display shelf with other jewelry. A jeweler with a truly personal style never competes with other jewelers, for the work is unique. A craftsman who has nothing in particular to offer as personal expression might better become a bench-worker for a designing jeweler.

The work must also compete in price with other jewelry on the market, as well as in quality of design and execution. Those who work in sterling will automatically reach a broader but lower-priced market than those who work with gold and the more precious gemstones, for the latter will automatically restrict their clientele to buyers in higher income brackets. Aside from this distinction of competitive price, the other dominant factor that will determine sales to a retail shop is reliability. No retail shop will long endure a craftsman who cannot be depended on to produce consistently for the market that the shop has created and must continue to satisfy.

E.2 Pricing   Pricing a product requires familiarity with the market. First, the jeweler must have an accurate idea of how much the work costs to produce and must also be aware of the price that comparable merchandise commands. Whenever possible, the jeweler should set the retail price, but if it is set too high, the work may not move off the display shelf.

The retail price is arrived at by doubling the total "wholesale" price of an item, as derived from the average unit cost, calculated from the "production record" (Fig. 618). There will probably be some variations in labor cost from time to time or from worker to worker, as well as variations in cost of materials. The retail price should be held constant unless the unit cost begins to get too far out of line with the current retail price. When a price increase is contemplated, the retailer should be given the courtesy of advance notice with an explanation. An increase in materials or labor cost is perfectly understandable to a businessman.

Some retailers like to buy at wholesale prices and set their own retail prices. Many such retailers take more than a 100-percent markup on an item that will sell at a high price. It is to everyone's advantage to have the jeweler set the retail price in the invoice and then deduct 50 percent from the total amount to arrive at the wholesale price. By setting the retail price, the craftsman ensures that all outlets are on an equal footing. The jeweler must have a clear and frank understanding with each retail outlet on this question to avoid future misunderstandings. Once a price has been set, it must be held consistently for all purchasers. The jeweler cannot ethically sell the same piece at one price to one shop and at another price to another shop. Nor would it be fair to sell a production piece from the studio at a lower price than is set for the retail outlets.

Above all, the jeweler must establish a reputation for reliability and fairness. It is good policy to stand behind every piece that is produced. If any piece is found to be defective or to have come apart, for any reason, it is best in the long run to replace or repair the piece without question. Such problems will seldom occur with good work, but when they do, this sales policy generates goodwill and helps immeasurably in retaining customers.

There can be no production without sales. Therefore, the craftsman must appreciate and understand the role of the retailer as the other side of his or her economic existence. A retail outlet will work hard for a cooperative and appreciative craftsman.

E.3 Repairs   Occasionally the producing or designing jeweler may be asked by a customer or a retail outlet to do a repair job. Accommodating the request will help to create goodwill. As a guide for the beginning jeweler, typical prices for repair work are given in the table below. These prices are, of course, subject to change.

Repairs	
hard-solder (silver or gold)	$ 2.50 up
soft-solder	2.00 up
platinum	4.50 up
solder two rings together	3.00 up
solder in a new crown	7.00 up
change crown	11.50 up
Prong and Bezel Work	
repair less than four prongs	$ 4.00 up (each)
repair four or more prongs	3.00 up (each)
prongs on man's birthstone ring	12.00 up
repair bezel and set stone	16.00 up
Brooches	
replace pin tong (sterling)	$ 3.00
replace pin tong (10k gold)	4.00
replace joint or catch (sterling) plus soldering	2.00
replace joint or catch (10k gold) plus soldering	4.00
Ring Sizing	
woman's (sterling or gold)	$ 3.50 up
woman's (platinum)	5.00 up
man's (sterling or gold)	3.00 up
man's (platinum)	7.00 up

E.4 The Exhibition as a Marketing Aid The importance of exhibitions as historical records of the artistic status of contemporary jewelry and as a measure of individual craftsmanship is fairly well understood. Up to a certain point the exhibitions and the awards for craftsmanship establish a prestige that is useful for publicity and for a marketing program. Between two craftsmen of equal merit, the one represented in exhibitions and honored by awards may often have the marketing advantage. However, in submitting jewelry to exhibitions, the craftsman should beware of becoming preoccupied with producing "exhibition pieces" as something totally separate from the design of "bread-and-butter" items. An overemphasis on the prestige of exhibitions may lead to a deprecating attitude toward the work produced for sale, and thus the sustaining values of craftsmanship can be subtly undermined.

When approached with a certain caution, and regarded essentially as a record of individual artistic and technical progress in the field, the exhibition offers craftsmen another method of establishing or expanding the market for their jewelry among potential customers.

Production

Almost every jeweler enjoys making special one-of-a-kind designs, whether by commission or simply for the personal satisfaction involved. There is certainly a market for custom jewelry, particularly in the more expensive categories. Most jewelers, however, usually find themselves reproducing designs that for one reason or another have become popular, and selling them in a price range that commands a larger market. The production of such "bread and butter" designs requires accurate record-keeping, sensible planning, and efficient working methods.

E.5 Production, Job, and Inventory Records Three devices that help the jeweler organize and control production operations are the production record, the job card, and the inventory record.

The *production record* (Fig. 618) is a master ledger in which the design, materials, and actual production of each jewelry item are recorded. A separate page is allowed for each design, which is identified by a code number. This may be merely a

PHILIP MORTON, Goldsmith	PRODUCTION RECORD			Code Number 812 G

DESIGNED BY: P.M.	DATE: 4/15/76	PRICE: 75.00	ITEM Hand-Forged Necklace

Materials Required:
12" 14k Yellow Gold wire, 14 ga

See Photograph # 884

Pattern or Sketch

Date 1976	Job No.	Quantity	Customer	DIRECT COST Labor	Matls.	INDIRECT COST O. H.	Markup	TOTAL COST		UNIT COST	
4/15	291	6	Inventory	85.00	57.80	14.28	57.12	214	20	35	70
4/25	327	6	Marshall, Inc.	87.00	57.80	14.48	57.92	217	20	36	20
5/2	402	6	S. S. Roach	82.50	57.80	14.03	56.12	210	45	35	07
7/15	556	6	Contemporary Gifts	74.00	59.90	13.39	53.56	200	85	33	47
10/10	675	6	Marshall, Inc.	70.05	63.96	13.40	53.60	201	01	33	50
11/15	841	6	Inventory	72.00	63.96	13.60	54.38	203	94	33	99
11/18	860	6	Racing Gifts	73.25	63.96	13.72	54.88	205	81	34	30
12/1	880	6	Inventory	72.00	63.96	13.60	54.38	203	94	33	99

389 Number	Philip Morton			Goldsmith Jeweler	

Item:	Hand-Forged Necklace, 14k Y. Gold			Code:	812 G
Date:	12/1/76	Worker:	Staff	Price:	75.00

	Materials	Quantity	Unit Cost	Cost	
1	14k Y. Gold Wire, 14 ga	72" 1 oz 12 dwt	2.00 dwt	63.96	
2					
3					
4					
5					
6				63.96	
	Labor	Hours	Rate	Cost	
7	(P.M.) Forging & Planishing	9½	5.00	47.50	
8	(R.S) Forming & Stamping	3½	4.00	14.00	
9	(J.T.) Finishing, Polishing				
10	& Cleaning	3	3.00	9.00	
11	Packaging & Pricing	½	3.00	1.50	
12				72.00	
13			Total Direct	135.96	
14	Overhead		10%	13.60	
15	Factory Markup		40%	54.38	
16	Number Made: 6	Unit Cost: 33.99	Total Cost	203.94	

opposite: **618.** Sample page from a production record.

right: **619.** Sample job card.

consecutive number, but a more useful method is one that allows ready identification of the type of object, as in the following system:

100	wedding band
200	engagement or dinner ring
300	man's ring
400	earring, dangle type
500	earring, button type
600	earring, pierced-ear type
700	bracelet
800	necklace
900	pendant
1000	brooch
1100	cuff link
1200	tie clip
1300	tie tack
1400	barrette
1500	comb
1600	watch band
1700	buckle

If a particular design is to be produced in both sterling silver and 14k gold, the jeweler can let the plain number designate the silver version, adding "G" to indicate the gold. Also, matching sets can be given matching numbers, so that a gold set comprising earrings, a bracelet, and a necklace might be indicated by the code numbers 507G, 707G, and 807G.

In addition to the code number of each design, the production record includes a description and a sketch, tracing, or photograph of the item, as well as its current price. The production record also lists the kinds and amounts of materials needed, along with the sequence of operations to be performed and the approximate time they require. Except in the case of very simple designs, it is a good idea to add layout sketches with dimensions for all the separate parts that must be formed or bent. Finally, the production record serves as a ledger for production and cost data entered from successive job cards whenever new stock of an item is produced.

The *job card* (Fig. 619) is a simple device for keeping track of materials and labor cost with a minimum of bookkeeping. For every production order, the craftsman takes a job card to the bench. Each card is numbered and dated. The item of jewelry is listed with its code number and retail price. Its various materials, taken from the production record, are listed with sizes or weights at their unit costs. The hours of labor, labor rates, and total labor costs are recorded. In this manner the direct costs are kept on the production of the jewelry item. To this can be added an overhead percentage to cover such costs as rent, light, and heat, which will usually amount to 10 or 15 percent of direct costs (**E.9**). A profit margin must also be added to the direct costs and overhead to arrive at the established retail price for the piece. This markup can be as much as 100 percent of direct and overhead costs. If a dozen units are produced on the particular job card, then a unit cost can easily be derived and recorded. The name of the craftsman is recorded, so that production time comparisons can be made from job to job or from worker to worker. On the back of the card may be made a sketch of the jewelry item, with any detailed notes concerning methods or procedures that are time-saving or particularly useful.

The job card is filed numerically after the cost and labor information is transcribed in the production record. When another job order comes in for a particular jewelry item, earlier job cards for that item can be found from the production record, so that evaluations and comparisons of current costs can be made. As labor and materials go up, the jeweler is alerted to the necessity for increasing retail prices.

The craftsman will need to identify individual designs on invoices and purchase orders from retail outlets, and on the pieces themselves. Ideally in control of the retail prices, the jeweler should attach a price tag on each item as it is finished and then package it in a small plastic envelope. On one side of the tag the retail price appears. On the other side the code number is written in ink. The retailer can use the price tag for reordering by saving it as each item is sold and then writing out new purchase orders from the tags, periodically, as they

620. Sample inventory record.

INVENTORY OF MATERIALS

DATE 76		gold	silver	gems	castings	findings	copper	brass	total materials
Jan. 1	INVENTORY	2791.46	3088.64	801.84	567.66	122.59	128.00	100.49	7600.68
	PURCHASES	588.22	640.37	84.80	37.66	27.50			1378.55
	USED IN PRODUCTION	188.12	359.69	99.70	97.81	88.22	27.50	18.35	879.39
Feb. 1	INVENTORY	3191.56	3369.32	786.94	507.51	61.87	100.50	82.14	8099.84
	PURCHASES								
	USED IN PRODUCTION								
Mar. 1	INVENTORY								
	PURCHASES								
	USED IN PRODUCTION								
Apr. 1	INVENTORY								
	PURCHASES								
	USED IN PRODUCTION								
	INVENTORY								

621. Flow diagram for a jewelry workshop.

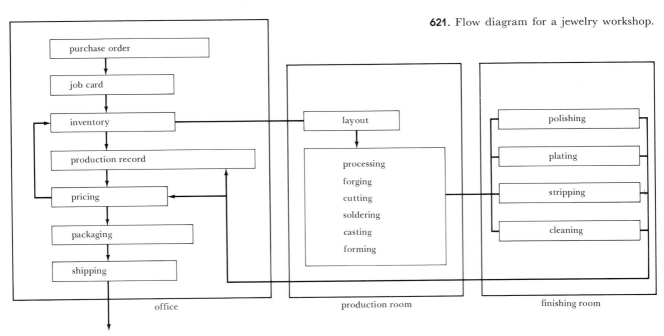

office   production room   finishing room

330

accumulate. Thus the craftsman should be sure that both the code number and the price are accurately recorded.

Another important record that the producing craftsman should keep is an *inventory record* for materials and supplies that have been purchased, used, or sold. Inventory totals should be brought up to date at the end of each month. Figure 620 illustrates a typical inventory record for a fairly well stocked jewelry shop.

To open such a record, the jeweler takes inventory of actual monetary values for each category of materials and posts these on the opening line of the record. At the end of the month the total purchases in each category of materials are recorded from the check register. The totals of the beginning inventory and the purchases for the month represent the total amount of available materials during the month. From this total must be deducted the amounts of each material used in production during the month. The difference in each category represents the inventory value for the beginning of the next month.

E.6 Workshop Layout   One of the first and most obvious methods of improving production is to organize the workshop in a convenient physical space pattern, so that a logical production flow is possible. The question of physical arrangement of equipment is important even in the small, one-person shop (Fig. 271). The single craftsman carries out all of the operations, and special separate space centers should be available for each. Regardless of the size of the shop, there will be a flow of production more or less similar to that shown in Figure 621.

When a workshop grows beyond the one-room size, finishing operations are usually the first to be segregated (Fig. 622), because of the fumes and dust arising from polishing, stripping, plating, and cleaning. The casting and forging operations would be the next to be segregated, because of the noise, heat, and fumes.

E.7 Production Design   All beginning jewelers have encountered the design that looks really good but takes 42 hours to make. Even at $1.00 per hour it is priced out of the market. It could be sold for $11.50, but the designer would be lucky to get back the cost of materials. Today a craftsman can hardly afford to work for less than $5.00 per hour. Therefore, as a first step in increasing production efficiency, designs must be evaluated in terms of marketability. Designs that cannot be produced efficiently must be discarded as production pieces. The jeweler's resources as a designer will be sharpened by experimentation. A search must be made for designs directly compatible with production means. Only those items that lend themselves to efficient multiple production, as well as to favorable market acceptance, should be selected.

Once a design has been projected for possible production, it must be analyzed carefully in terms of multiple or serial processing. For example, suppose a ring-set design calls for separate ring bands to be made up in two sizes: 6 and 9. If a ring enlarger (Fig. 322) is at hand, the craftsman should not waste time making the bands to the exact sizes required, but should cut band lengths to two standard sizes, each slightly below the required measurement, solder them, and then stretch them to the required sizes. This type of sizing is particularly useful if the band is patterned and cannot be cut down or enlarged without interfering with the pattern.

If a design employs a number of identical units, such as links in a chain or bracelet, labor time can be reduced by carrying out processes in sequence (**E.8**). If you have an order for three link bracelets, you can increase production efficiency by producing at least six, or even twelve, bracelets at one time, putting the excess number in inventory for future orders. A single jewelry item should seldom be reproduced one at a time.

A sketch or tracing of a particular design may not be sufficient for the rapid reproduction of a sheet-metal shape. If sheet shapes require duplication, it is useful to make accurate

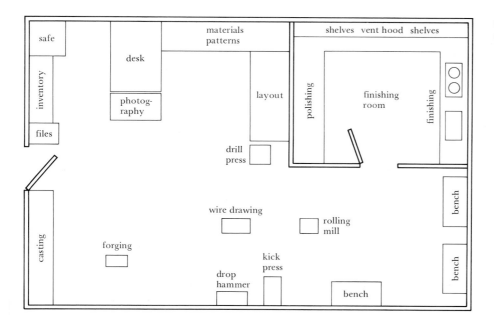

622. Plan of a medium-size producing workshop.

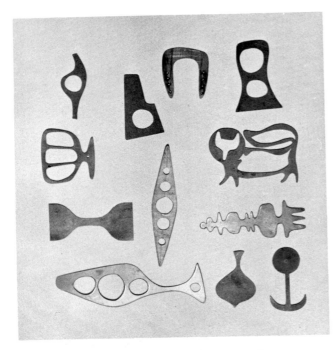

above: **623.** Brass templates for tracing sheet shapes.

below: **624.** A set of disk-cutting dies.

625–629. Sample production of a spiral-link bracelet.

625. Unit of hammered 14-gauge wire.

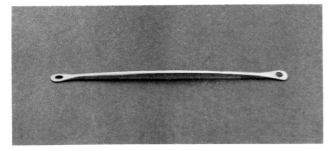

templates from 24-gauge brass sheet (Fig. 623). These templates allow quick tracing with a sharp scribe. They are identified by the code number of the design.

Greater speed and more accurate standardization can be achieved for sheet-metal shapes if they are sawed out after an impression of each shape has been die-stamped with a kick press or a drop hammer. This can be especially helpful for such small shapes as the claw setting made from sheet metal (Figs. 558–560). A number of dies are on the market, including disk-cutting dies (Fig. 624) that can replace the tedious sawing out of inside circles. Tool and die companies also make special cutting and forming dies, which are useful for stamping out whole shapes and for preforming repoussé patterns to be finished later by hand.

In the development of production designs, today's jeweler should not hesitate to try every kind of production aid available. Dies, drop hammers, kick presses, forming jigs, and other machines that can reduce production time must be considered in planning an item for production. The cost of such equipment, however, must be justified by the sales volume of the particular design. Initially a new design will probably be produced completely by hand. If it finds an especially good market and orders arrive in larger quantities, the cost of special dies will be justified by the saving of labor.

Another possibility worth studying is the use of repeated design units for more than one design. While this idea may be carried too far, it is especially fruitful in the development of matching sets of jewelry. Bracelets, necklaces, and earrings can all be based on identical design units. Cuff links, tie clips or tie tacks, and buckles may likewise be assembled from identical design units.

E.8 Sample Production Sequence As mentioned earlier, any design comprising a number of identical units can be produced most efficiently by taking each step at a time and preparing all of the repeated units simultaneously. For the sake of illustration, the procedure for producing a link bracelet like that in Figure 629 is outlined as follows:

1. Look up the code number in the *production record,* and record the information on a *job card.* It is found that each bracelet requires eight pieces of 14-gauge sterling wire, each $2\frac{1}{2}$ inches long; eight pieces of 18-gauge sterling wire, each $\frac{3}{4}$ inch long; two 18-gauge jump rings, $\frac{3}{16}$ inch in diameter; and one medium-size sister hook.
2. On a coil of 14-gauge sterling wire, measure off one $2\frac{1}{2}$-inch length of wire. Then, using this as a unit measure, cut off 47 more lengths for six bracelets.
3. Repeat the process for $\frac{3}{4}$-inch lengths from a coil of 18-gauge wire.
4. Take each length of 14-gauge wire and hammer each end flat. About twelve blows with a planishing hammer give the right, uniform flatness to the ends.
5. Flatten each of the 14-gauge wire units between the flattened ends, but in a plane perpendicular to them. In carrying out this process you should maintain a slight curvature in the unit (Fig. 625). Do not make the units too thin.
6. Smooth the hammered ends of the 14-gauge units with a fine file to remove any roughness. One stroke around each edge of each end will suffice.

7. Center-punch each end of each 14-gauge wire link.
8. Drill a No. 46 hole in each end of the links.
9. Polish each unit on both sides.
10. Mark the center of each 14-gauge unit with a pencil. For standardized production, this can be done by marking on a small board the length of the unit and a center mark. Each unit is centered on this marker and the center mark picked up quickly.
11. Take each link and center it in a pair of round-nose pliers jaws. Then twist the ends of the wire into a spiral around the pliers (Fig. 626).
12. Bend the ends of each link into position against the spiral, and adjust each link for size and shape until they are all identical (Fig. 627).
13. Now take the $\frac{3}{4}$-inch lengths of 18-gauge wire, and fuse a bead on one end of each unit. Immediately after fusing the bead, dip the unit into a cup of water to cool, and set it aside.
14. Fasten the spiral links together with the 18-gauge wire units, one at a time, fusing a bead on each free end. Be careful to keep the spiral links of each bracelet facing the same way (Fig. 628).
15. Attach and solder a sister hook to one end of each bracelet with a $\frac{3}{16}$-inch 18-gauge jump ring. Attach another jump ring to the other end of each bracelet, and solder the jump rings closed.
16. Oxidize each bracelet to a clear but not too heavy black, and polish the face and beads of each link.
17. Boil all the bracelets in soapy water, or place them in the ultrasonic cleaning machine (Fig. 450). Rinse them in alcohol, and dry (Fig. 629).
18. Price-tag each bracelet with price and code number, package each in a plastic envelope, and staple the envelopes closed.

From the foregoing description it can be seen that carrying a number of units through each stage of production will establish an efficient rhythm of activity. There is no doubt that this type of production leads to what may be viewed as a mechanical repetition of movements. It is just this kind of process that saves time and increases efficiency of movement.

An unfavorable reaction to the mechanical routine involved may be balanced by the consideration of two thoughts. First of all, any given sequence of craft operations depends on the subtlety of hand, eye, and mind that are required for every human bodily manipulation. What we mean in part by describing these activities as "mechanical" is that the various operations become so well mastered that they no longer require conscious deliberation and become habit patterns, leaving the mind free to make careful evaluations of the work in progress. Through repeated practice, the activities become so integrated into the craftsman's repertory of abilities that dexterity and skill reach higher levels of performance.

The second thought worthy of consideration is that only the repetition of a given pattern of movement will allow it to become continually refined and perfected. To be sure, inefficient, erroneous, or sloppy habit patterns may just as well be learned. But perfection of form in movement can emerge only from constant striving and an appreciation of the natural rhythms that lead to mastery.

above: 626. Forming a spiral by twisting the wire unit around round-nose pliers.

left: 627. Completed spiral link.

below: 628. Links fastened together with fused wires.

bottom: 629. Completed bracelet, with sister hook.

E.9 Operation Costs and Planning   The problem of thinking out in advance just what kind of capital investment is required to set up shop calls for some general figures on cost distribution to serve as a point of departure. While there is bound to be variation in the cost of operations from one jeweler to the next and one shop to another, certain percentage estimates for the allocation of expenses can be useful to the beginning jeweler as an initial guide.

Suppose you plan to set up a small shop for both the production and the retail sale of jewelry. For record-keeping and budgeting purposes, production or wholesale operations should be considered separately from those involved with retailing. Both operations must be maintained at profitable levels, so that one side will not erode the profits of the other. Furthermore, it is a good idea to "sell to yourself" at the same wholesale prices that you could reasonably charge another retailer in a location somewhat removed from your own store.

For the wholesale operations of small independent shop, costs will break down into something like the following percentages of gross wholesale sales:

materials	35%
overhead	35%
return	30%

Overhead includes rent, utilities, insurances, taxes, shop and office supplies, stamps, and everything else you have to buy except materials and supplies for jewelry making itself. "Return" includes wages paid to yourself and to assistants, as well as the final wholesale profit.

For retail operations, you should set a 100 percent markup on all items, just as you would for an outside retailer (**E.2**). In this area the following percentages of gross *retail* sales can serve as a guide:

wholesale cost of merchandise	50%
overhead	30%
net profit	20%

Here your overhead will include wages paid to sales clerks as well as the costs of rent, utilities, advertising, and so on. It is true that you are covering some items of overhead twice, but this will only make your estimates more conservative and help absorb costs that you have not anticipated.

Now let us apply some of these figures. Suppose that you set a goal for net earnings at $500 per month. Assuming that all your wholesale production goes to your own retail shop, you can figure that every $100 worth of wholesale production, yielding 30 percent or $30 profit, will be converted through markup into $200 in retail sales, yielding 20 percent or $40 profit. Thus every $100 worth of wholesale production will yield a total profit of $70 through wholesale and retail sales.

Simple division reveals that our hypothetical goal, $500 per month, is 7.1429 times greater than the $70 profit turned on $100 worth of production. Thus, in order to reach that goal, you must produce at wholesale $714.29 worth of jewelry per month, which will be converted into $1,428.58 in monthly retail sales. On a yearly basis, this amounts to $8,571.48 worth of wholesale production and $17,142.96 in retail sales, yielding a total annual profit of $6,000.

If the wholesale percentage figures are applied to this level of production, we find that the wholesale costs ($8,571) are distributed as follows:

materials	35%	$3,000
overhead	35%	$3,000
return	30%	$2,571
wholesale value		$8,571

Such percentages can serve as a rough estimate for the beginning shop, but the proportions will change as soon as operations expand. For example, if you manage to double your production from a shop that is already set up, your costs for materials will increase correspondingly, but overhead costs may rise only slightly. A doubling of the operation outlined above might produce a breakdown like the following:

materials	35%	$5,950
overhead	19%	$3,200
return	46%	$7,850
wholesale value		$17,000

Clearly, once a shop is established, the overhead remains relatively constant, so that any increase in volume results in an almost direct increase in return. (Similarly, volume can decline to a break-even point, below which no return will be realized.)

A final planning consideration is that you must carry a inventory of materials and supplies in sufficient quantity to support the necessary volume of production. As a general guide, figure that for every $100 of projected net income, you should carry a materials inventory of about $600. Thus, an income of $500 per month would require about $3000 worth of silver, gold, gems, findings, and the like.

Obviously, the figures presented here are neither final nor correct for all circumstances. They do reflect an approximate distribution of costs for a small shop, and they can provide a realistic basis for planning your own financial situation.

Terms printed in italics are themselves defined within the Glossary.

annealing The process of heating *work-hardened* metal in order to restore its malleability (**9.1**).

annealing booth An enclosed space that shields work from cooling drafts and room light during *annealing* (Fig. 273).

annealing pan A deep, circular, rotating tray filled with *pumice* pebbles in which metal to be *annealed* is heated (Fig. 273).

anode The positive terminal of an *electrolytic* cell. The negative is called a *cathode*.

anvil A heavy, steel-faced iron block on which metal is shaped (Fig. 581).

asphalt ground or **hard ground** In *etching*, an acid-resist coating of beeswax, *resin*, and asphaltum (or similar substance) painted on a metal plate. Once the ground has hardened, a design or image can be scratched through.

basse-taille A type of *enameling* in which transparent colors are fired over a textured metal surface (**18.15**).

bearing See *seat*.

bench pin or **file block** A wedge-shape block attached to the jeweler's workbench, used to hold work being filed (Fig. 520).

bevel The angle that one surface or line makes with another when they are not at right angles.

bezel A metal band that fits around a gemstone to attach it to the base jewelry (**21.1**).

binding wire Soft iron wire that holds parts of work together during such operations as *soldering* (**10.15**, Fig. 289).

bismuth block A block of soft, nonconducting material used to support work being subjected to heat, as in *soldering* (**10.14**). Bismuth often is preferred to *charcoal*, because it is clean and does not break apart.

brake A machine for bending sheet metal (Fig. 311).

buff A cover that is attached to the wheel of a *lathe* to cut, polish, or *burnish* a metal surface (**C.16**; see also **19.10**, Fig. 528).

buffing The process of cutting, polishing, or *burnishing* metal by applying it to a specially equipped *lathe* charged with a *compound;* also, the same process done by hand (**19.11**).

burnisher A tool with a polished, rounded tip for *burnishing* the surface of metal.

burnishing The traditional method of smoothing a metal surface by rubbing it with a *burnisher* (**19.12**).

bur A rotary bit attached to a power tool for drilling and grinding metal (Fig. 356).

C-clamp A C-shape device that holds two pieces of material together.

cabochon An unfaceted gem cut in a convex form and highly polished. The four types are low, normal, high, and double (**20.1**, Fig. 538).

cameo A low-relief sculpture cut on a stone of varicolored layers in such a way that figure and background are of contrasting colors.

carat A unit of weight for gemstones equal to 200 mg. (or 3.086 grains of troy or avoirdupois weight) (**C.22**). Compare *karat*.

Carborundum A grinding abrasive in the form of granules or a mounted stone.

casting The process of shaping a molten material by means of a mold that has been fashioned to a predetermined form. Methods include gravity, centrifugal, vacuum, and pressure casting (Chap. 14).

cathode The negative terminal of an electrolytic cell. The positive is an *anode*.

champlevé An *enameling* technique in which transparent or opaque colors are fired into *etched* or carved areas in a metal surface (**18.13**).

charcoal block A block of carvable, nonconducting material used to support work subjected to heat, as in *soldering* (**10.14**). Charcoal breaks apart more easily than *bismuth*.

charging The application of a *compound* to a *buff*; also, the application of *enamels* to a metal support.

chasing A technique for surface enrichment of metal that is accomplished by driving pointed tools into the metal with hammers; often used in connection with *repoussé* (**13.8**).

chasing plate A piece of soft iron approximately 1 inch thick to which metal is clamped for *chasing* (**13.8**).

cloisonné An *enameling* technique in which design areas are separated by thin wires (**18.11**, Figs. 505–511).

compounds Cutting or polishing materials mixed with grease or wax and applied to *buffs* for finishing metal surfaces (**C.16**; see also **19.11**, Fig. 530).

counterenamel A coating of *enamel* on the reverse side of a metal ground that prevents the enamels from cracking on the display side.

crocus cloth A type of *emery paper* coated with iron oxide for fine polishing.

cross-peen hammer A forging hammer with a wedge-shape face (**13.1**, Fig. 363).

crucible A graphite or ceramic container that holds molten metal during the *casting* process.

cuttlebone A traditional mold material made of the dried shell of a squidlike mollusk (**14.2**).

dapping A method of pushing out hollows in metal by punching it into a dapping block (Fig. 339) or *die*; also adaptable for making hollow beads (**11.19**).

dapping punch A steel tool with a round head used for *dapping* (Fig. 339).

die A form or mold used to shape metal (**E.7**). Dies generally serve when a number of identical pieces are to be shaped.

drawing The process of reducing the size of wire by passing it through a *drawplate* (**11.2**).

drawplate A piece of hardened steel with a series of round, half-round, square, and rectangular holes of graduated sizes (**11.2**, Fig. 305).

drop hammer A power hammer used in mass production to stamp out designs (**E.7**).

Egyptian paste A substance commonly found in Egyptian jewelry of the New Kingdom, thought to be made of silica, an alkali, an oxide of lead, and metallic oxides for color.

electrodeposition The transfer of metal ions from an *anode* to a *cathode* in an electrolytic solution; the basic chemical process of *electroforming* and *electroplating* (Chap. 16).

electroforming A metal-forming technique in which a layer of metal is deposited on a matrix of wax, polystyrene, or a similar material.

electrolyte A solution of water and metallic salts in which *electrodeposition* takes place (**C.17**).

electroplating The depositing of a thin coating of metal on another metal to create a new surface or to make a piece more durable (**16.2–3**).

embossing Raising a design in relief from a metal surface (**11.19**).

emery paper An abrasive sheet coated with powdered emery, *carborundum,* or garnet, used for finishing surfaces (**19.7**).

enameling The fusing of a glassy substance onto metal. Enamels are combinations of flux and metal oxides (for color) and can range from opaque to transparent (Chap. 18).

engraving The technique of cutting line images or designs into a durable material. In jewelry, gravers—sharp chisellike tools with different-shaped points—serve to cut away metal (**17.9–11**).

epoxy See *resin.*

etching The technique of creating designs on metal through the corrosive action of an acid solution on lines scratched through a resist (**17.12–14**).

eutectic A term for an alloy that has a melting point lower than any of its constituent metals. The principle of eutectics applies to *granulation,* because when small beads or granules are coated with copper, they will fuse to the mother metal before it begins to melt (**17.4**).

fibula From the Latin, a decorative fastener, often jeweled; the origin of the safety pin (Figs. 1, 47, 417).

file A tool made of steel with cutting ridges for forming and smoothing metal. The shape of a file varies according to its purpose; the types include round, half-round, ring, barrette, needle, and vixen-cut (**19.1**, Figs. 518, 519).

file block See *bench pin.*

File-Wax A hard, brittle wax that can be sawed or filed to make ring patterns for *casting* (**14.11**).

filigree A delicate design of fine wires soldered together in the frame of a heavier wire or onto a flat base (**11.23**, Fig. 347).

findings The trade name for standard catches, clasps, earring or cuff-link backs, and any commercially available fastenings (**B.3**, Chap. 15).

finishing The final treatment of a surface, usually by means of filing or polishing (Chap. 19).

fire scale or **firecoat** A dark film that appears on gold or silver when it is heated, causing the alloy to separate from the base metal. (For prevention of fire scale, see **C.12**).

flexible-shaft drill A high-speed, power tool with a variety of chucks to which drills, *burs,* grinding stones, and polishing buffs can be fastened. The fact that the shaft can bend facilitates work in hard-to-reach areas (**19.5**, Fig. 355).

flux A liquid or paste solution applied to surfaces to be joined in order to protect and free them from oxides, thus helping *solder* to flow easily (**C.10**; see also **10.10**).

forging Hammering metal on an *anvil* in order to form, thin, or stretch it (**13.1–4**).

fusing The liquefying of metal under a hot flame for joining or forming new shapes (**10.4–6**).

gallery wire Wire that is patterned or textured (**11.5**, **13.12**).

gauge plate A disk with slots of various sizes cut into the edge to measure the size of wire or sheet metal (**C.20**, Fig. 303).

granulation A type of surface treatment in which small beads or chips are fused onto metal to create a design or a rich texture (**17.3–8**, Fig. 472).

graver See *engraving.*

gum tragacanth A water-soluble gum that acts as an adhesive, especially for *enameling.*

hard ground See *asphalt ground.*

I.D. The inside diameter of a round object, especially a ring band (**C.19**, **15.10**).

ingot Metal cast into a shape convenient for storage or transportation; can be processed later into sheet or wire form.

inlay The technique of setting one material into an incised pattern or line in another material, usually for color contrast (**17.23–25**).

intaglio A technique in which a design is incised in stone (or metal) so that an impression yields an image in relief.

jig A device to maintain the desired relationship in position between a piece of work and a tool, or between parts of work during assembly.

jump ring The trade name for a small circle of wire.

karat A 24th part; a measure to express the fineness of gold, pure gold being 24 karats fine (**C.3**).

lathe A machine that rotates a tool on a horizontal axis while it shapes or polishes work that is hand-held (**19.10,** Fig. 527).

lemel Gold or silver filings or sawdust.

limoges enamel An *enameling* technique in which juxtaposed colors cover the entire surface of the metal (**18.14**).

liner A tool for cutting grooves in metal, used for *inlay* and *chasing* (Fig. 589).

liver of sulphur A substance made of potassium sulphate and water, used for coloring brass, copper, silver, and gold (**19.15**).

lost-wax process A casting method in which a wax model is burned away and replaced by molten metal (**14.14**).

mandrel A metal bar that serves as a core around which metal or other materials can be bent, *forged,* or otherwise shaped. A ring mandrel is a tapered rod divided by grooves to indicate ring sizes (Fig. 313).

Mohs' scale A scale that rates the hardness of minerals from talc, the softest (No. 1), through diamond, the hardest (No. 10) (**20.4**).

mokume An ancient Japanese technique for creating pattern on a metal surface that resembles moiré or "wood grain" (**17.26–27**).

mop A tangle of fine wire twisted into a pad and fixed to a handle for supporting work to be soldered (Fig. 288).

niello A mixture of alloys of sulphur with silver, copper, or lead, resulting in a deep black color; also, the technique of decorating metal with niello by filling incised lines or areas with the substance (Figs. 49, 99).

ochre See *yellow ochre.*

O.D. The outside diameter of a circle, especially a ring band (**C.19**).

opus interassile An ancient technique for creating a design in gold sheet by removing the background sections with a chisel (Fig. 31).

oxidizing flame A flame that is fed more compressed air than it can burn. The flame is blue in color, hotter than a *reducing flame,* and it leaves a dark film on metal surfaces (Fig. 278).

paillons Small pieces of *solder,* usually oblong, for joining seams in metal (**10.9**).

photoetching The registering on metal of textures and images derived from photographs (**17.19–21**).

pickle pan A lead pan for heating *pickle solution.*

pickle solution A solution of sulphuric acid and water that cleans stains from metal (**9.2**).

pickling A means of removing oxides, old *flux,* and other stains from metal through immersion in a solution of sulphuric acid and water (**9.2**).

piercing Sawing lines or designs into sheet metal.

pitch A mixture of burgundy pitch, plaster, and tallow; when mounded in a shallow bowl, it supports metal during the process of *repoussé* (**11.17, C.18**).

planishing A way of smoothing and evening metal by striking it with a *planishing hammer* (**13.5**).

planishing hammer A hammer with one flat face and one slightly crowned face, kept highly polished and used exclusively for smoothing metal (Fig. 363).

plate shapes Simple designs cut from sheet metal (Chap. 7).

pliers Small pincers with long jaws for holding, bending, cutting, or clipping metal. Types include square-nose, round-nose, flat-face, half-round, and snipe-nose.

plique-à-jour An *enameling* technique similar to *cloisonné,* except that there is no base metal. Transparent enamels are fused to an intricate framework of wires all touching one another. The effect resembles stained glass (**18.12**).

pumice A type of volcanic glass; in lump or stone form supports work being annealed; in powder form acts as a polishing agent.

punch A steel rod used with a hammer to stamp metal. Types include the tracer, which defines lines; the planisher, which smooths surfaces, and the background or matting punch, which provides texture. Dapping, hollow, and ring punches make spherical marks (**13.8**, Fig. 382).

pusher A tool with a polished, flat face for pressing metal, especially for pressing a *bezel* against stone (Fig. 552).

rasp A coarse file that cuts by means of raised points rather than intersecting rows of straight ridges.

reducing flame A yellow-tipped flame fed by an excess of gas that leaves metal with a mirrorlike surface (Fig. 278). Compare *oxidizing flame.*

repoussé A technique of pushing metal out from its reverse side with hammers and punches in order to create a low-relief design on the front (**11.16–17**).

resin An organic plastic substance. Rosin, a hard resin, is mixed with methyl alcohol to make a varnish for stopping out areas of work being *etched* (**17.12**).

resin, epoxy and polyester Thermoset plastics suitable for casting. Once set at room temperature, they can be heated with little distortion up to the burning point (**14.21–24**).

reticulation The fusing or melting of a metal surface to create texture (**17.2**).

ring-bending block A hardwood block with holes or V-cuts of decreasing sizes to close the ends of a ring together (**11.11**, Fig. 320).

ring clamp A wooden clamp that holds work steady during sawing operations without scratching it.

ring-size set A group of rings manufactured in standard sizes for fitting (Fig. 322).

ring stick A conical stick covered with an emery shell and placed on a buffing mandrel to polish the inside of a ring band (Fig. 526).

rivet A small pin inserted through holes in two sheets of metal to hold them together (**15.3–7**).

rolling mill A machine that presses metal sheet between two cylindrical rollers in order to reduce its thickness or press patterns into it (Fig. 309).

roll printing The process of texturing metal by rolling sheet metal and a patterned material through a rolling mill (**17.22**).

rouge A mineral compound whose flat particles have a burnishing or smoothing effect on metal, employed with a *buff* for polishing (**19.10, C.16**).

Scalex A commercial substance that prevents *fire scale* from forming on copper.

scorper A chisel-shape tool that is used to carve metal surfaces (**12.8**, Fig. 358).

scraper A tool with a long, flat blade for cutting away metal, cleaning out pits and imperfections, or removing lead build-up (**12.9**, Fig. 361).

scratch brush A wheel with bristles of fine brass or nickel-silver wire attached to a *buffing lathe* to give metal a burnished, mat finish (Fig. 528).

scribe A sharp, pointed tool for tracing lines and marking off metal to be cut.

seat or **bearing** A metal ring that fits inside a *bezel* to support a gemstone (**21.1**).

setting or **table** The form in which a gem is set (Chap. 21).

soft ground *Asphalt* (hard) *ground* to which grease or tallow has been added so that it does not harden; used for creating textured effects (**17.16**).

solder A metallic alloy used to join metals. Solder melts when heat is applied, then rehardens as it cools. Soft solder contains lead in an alloy with tin and melts at 400° F. Hard solder may be either silver alloyed with brass or gold alloyed with silver; its melting range is 1175°–1400° F. (**C.7–9**, **10.7–9**).

soldering pick A sharply pointed iron rod for picking up and accurately placing small pieces of *solder* (**10.20**).

stamping A method of texturing metal with *punches* (**13.12**).

stoning Grinding an object with a flat emery stone while holding it under running water, as for *enamels* (Fig. 509).

strip-plate form A three-dimensional design in which a forward plane is raised above a background plane by a length of bent strip metal (Fig. 230).

stripping Removing *fire scale* from silverwork by boiling it in a solution of nitric acid (**C.13**).

T-stake An *anvil* with a long, narrow surface for hammering (Fig. 379).

table See *setting*.

tree A tapered wax cone ("trunk") with wax patterns set circularly around it in two or more rows, for *casting* up to twelve pieces at one time (**14.15**, Fig. 418).

tripoli An abrasive compound applied to a cutting *buff* for coarse finishing (**C.16**).

upsetting Increasing the thickness and reducing the width of metal by hammering on its edges (**13.4**, **22.5**).

V-block A hardwood block with a V-shape cut that is attached to the jeweler's bench for supporting work being sawed (Fig. 352).

vermeil Gold-plated silver.

vise A tool with two jaws that screw closed for holding an object firmly in place. Types include the bench, pin, and hand vises (Figs. 304, 306).

welding Uniting metallic parts by heating and allowing the metals to flow together (**10.28–29**).

work hardening A brittle condition that occurs when metal is worked in hammering, bending, twisting, drawing, and so forth; results from the metal crystals becoming too closely packed. Work-hardened metal can be returned to a malleable state by *annealing* (**9.1**).

yellow ochre A powdered earth material mixed with a solution of boric acid to protect work from *fire scale* or to prevent *soldered* seams from running when a piece is reheated (**C.12**, **10.11**).

Bibliography

History

Aldred, Cyril. *Jewels of the Pharaohs: Egyptian Jewelry of the Dynastic Period.* New York: Praeger, 1971.

Anderson, Lawrence Leslie. *The Art of the Silversmith in Mexico: 1519–1936.* New York: Hacker, 1975.

Baerwald, Marcus, and Tom Mahoney. *Story of Jewelry.* New York: Abelard-Schuman, 1960.

Barsali, Isa Belli. *Medieval Goldsmith's Work.* London: Hamlyn, 1969.

Black, J. Anderson. *The Story of Jewelry.* New York: Morrow, 1974.

Boardman, John. *Greek Gems and Finger Rings: Early Bronze Age to Late Classical.* London, 1971.

Bradford, Ernle D. S. *Four Centuries of European Jewelry.* New York: Philosophical Library, 1953.

Carducci, Carlo. *Gold and Silver of Ancient Italy.* Greenwich, Conn.: New York Graphic, 1963.

Cellini, Benvenuto. *Treatises on Goldsmithing and Sculpture* (1568). Translated by C. R. Ashbee. London, 1898; reprinted New York: Dover, 1966.

Clifford, Anne. *Cut-Steel and Berlin Iron Jewellery.* Cranbury, N.J.: Barnes, 1971.

Emmerich, André. *Sweat of the Sun and Tears of the Moon: Gold and Silver in Pre-Columbian Art.* Seattle: University of Washington, 1965.

Evans, Joan. *A History of Jewellery, 1100–1870.* New York: Pitman, 1953.

Flower, Margaret. *Victorian Jewelry.* New York: Duell, Sloane, and Pearce, 1951.

Greek and Etruscan Jewelry. New York: Metropolitan Museum of Art, 1940.

Gregorietti, Guido. *Jewelry Through the Ages.* New York: Crescent, 1969.

Higgins, Reynold Alleyne. *Greek and Roman Jewellery.* New York: Methuen/Barnes & Noble, 1962.

Hood, Graham. *American Silver: A History of Style 1650–1900.* New York: Praeger, 1971.

Hughes, Graham. *Modern Jewelry: An International Survey, 1890–1963.* New York: Crown, 1963.

Jessup, Ronald. *Anglo-Saxon Jewellery.* New York: Praeger, 1953.

Muller, Priscilla. *Jewels in Spain, 1500–1800.* New York: Hispanic Society of America, 1972.

Rossi, Filippo. *Italian Jeweled Arts.* New York: Abrams, 1954.

Snowman, Kenneth. *The Art of Carl Fabergé.* Greenwich, Conn.: New York Graphic, 1974.

Steingräber, Erich. *Antique Jewelry.* New York: Praeger, 1957.

Design

General

Anderson, Donald M. *Elements of Design.* New York: Holt, Rinehart, and Winston, 1961.

Ballinger, Louise, and T. Vroman. *Design Sources and Resources.* New York: Reinhold, 1965.

Bevlin, Marjorie Elliott. *Design Through Discovery.* Second ed. New York: Holt, Rinehart, and Winston, 1970.

Collier, Graham. *Form, Space, and Vision.* Third ed. Englewood Cliffs, N.J.: Prentice-Hall, 1972.

Evans, Helen. *Man The Designer.* New York: Macmillan, 1973.

Hoffman, Armin. *Graphic Design Manual.* New York: Reinhold, 1965.

Getty, Nilda C. Fernandez. *Contemporary Crafts of the Americas: 1975.* Chicago: Regnery, 1975.

Nelson, George. *Problems of Design.* New York: Whitney, 1957.

Ocvirk, Otto G., Robert O. Bone, Robert E. Stinson, and Philip R. Wigg. *Art Fundamentals: Theory and Practice.* Second ed. Dubuque, Iowa: Brown, 1968.

Pye, David. *The Nature of Design.* New York: Reinhold, 1964.

Sausmarez, Maurice de. *Basic Design.* New York: Reinhold, 1964.

Sommer, Robert. *Design Awareness.* New York: Holt, Rinehart, and Winston, 1972.

Strache, Wolf. *Forms and Patterns in Nature.* New York: Pantheon, 1956.

Sutnar, Ladislov. *Visual Design in Action.* New York: Hastings, 1961.

The Craftsman's Art. London: Crafts Advisory Committee, 1973.

Wedd, J. *Patterns and Texture: Sources of Design.* New York: Studio Publications, 1956.

Jewelry

Adair, John. *The Navajo and Pueblo Silversmiths.* Norman, Okla.: University of Oklahoma, 1970.

Forms in Metal: 275 Years of Metalsmithing in America. New York: Museum of Contemporary Crafts and Finch College Museum of Art, 1975.

Hornung, Clarence. *A Source Book of Antiques and Jewelry Designs.* New York: Braziller, 1968.

Hughes, Graham. *The Art of Jewelry.* New York: Viking, 1972.

Jewelry and Hollowware Invitational: 1972. Ames, Iowa: Design Center Gallery, Iowa State University, 1972.

Jossic, Yvonne F. *1050 Jewelry Designs.* Philadelphia: Lample, 1946.

Lyon, Peter. *Design in Jewellery.* London: Owen, 1956.

Salvador Dali: A Study of His Art in Jewels. Greenwich, Conn.: New York Graphic, 1959.

Schoenfelt, Joseph. *Designing and Making Handwrought Jewelry.* New York: McGraw-Hill, 1960.

Seven Golden Years. London: Worshipful Company of Goldsmiths, 1974.

The Goldsmith. Saint Paul, Minn.: Minnesota Museum of Art, 1974.

Wedd, J. *Patterns and Texture: Sources of Design.* New York: Studio Publications, 1956.

Willcox, Donald J. *Body Jewelry: International Perspectives.* Chicago: Regnery, 1973.

Franke, Lois. *Handwrought Jewelry.* Bloomington, Ill.: McKnight, 1962.

Garrison, William E., and Merle E. Dowde. *Handcrafting Jewelry: Designs and Techniques.* Chicago: Regnery, 1972.

Hayes, Maggie. *Jewelry Book.* New York: Van Nostrand Reinhold, 1972.

Horth, A. C. *Repoussé Metalwork.* London: Methuen, 1905.

Kronquist, Emil F. *Metalwork for Craftsmen.* New York: Dover, 1972.

Martin, Charles J. *How to Make Modern Jewelry.* New York: Museum of Modern Art, 1949.

Meriel-Bussy. *Embossing of Metal: Repoussage.* New York: Sterling, 1970.

Pack, Greta. *Jewelry Making for the Beginning Craftsman.* New York: Van Nostrand Reinhold, 1957.

Rose, Augustus F., and Antonio Cirino. *Jewelry Making and Design.* Rev. ed. New York: Dover, 1967.

Sabroff, A. M., F. W. Boulger, and H. J. Henning. *Forging Materials and Practices.* New York: Van Nostrand Reinhold, 1968.

Shirley, A. J., and A. F. Shirley. *Handcraft in Metal: A Textbook for the Use of Teachers, Students, and Craftsmen.* Philadelphia: Lippincott, 1963.

Untracht, Oppi. *Metal Techniques for Craftsmen.* New York: Doubleday, 1968.

Von Neumann, Robert. *The Design and Creation of Jewelry.* Radnor, Pa.: Chilton, 1972.

Weiner, Louis. *Hand Made Jewelry.* New York: Van Nostrand, 1948.

Wilson, Henry. *Silverwork and Jewellery.* London: Pitman, 1902.

Winebrenner, Kenneth D. *Jewelry Making as an Art Expression.* Scranton, Pa.: International Textbook, 1955.

Zarchy, Harry. *Jewelry Making and Enameling.* New York: Knopf, 1959.

Technique

General

Abbey, Staton. *The Goldsmith's and Silversmith's Handbook.* New York: Heinman, 1968.

Allen, B. M. *Soldering Handbook.* New York: Drake, 1970.

Almeida, Oscar. *Metalwork and Its Decoration by Etching.* New York: Taplinger, 1964.

Baxter, William T. *Jewelry, Gem Cutting, and Metalcraft.* New York: McGraw-Hill, 1950.

Bovin, Murray. *Jewelry Making for Schools, Tradesmen, Craftsmen.* Forest Hills, N.Y.: Bovin, 1973.

Bowman, John J. *Jewelry Engraver's Manual.* New York: Van Nostrand, 1954.

Brynner, Irena. *Modern Jewelry: Design and Technique.* New York: Van Nostrand Reinhold, 1968.

Choate, Sharr. *Creative Gold- and Silversmithing.* New York: Crown, 1970.

Coyne, John, ed. *The Penland School of Crafts Book of Jewelry Making.* New York: Bobbs-Merrill, 1975.

Emerson, A. R. *Handmade Jewellery.* Leicester, Eng.: Dryad, 1955.

Fishlock, David. *Metal Coloring.* New York: International Publications, 1962.

Blacksmithing

Bealer, Alex W. *The Art of Blacksmithing.* New York: Funk and Wagnalls, 1969.

Holstrom, J. G. *Modern Blacksmithing.* New York: Drake, 1970.

Weygers, Alexander. *The Modern Blacksmith.* New York: Van Nostrand Reinhold, 1974.

Casting

Bovin, Murray. *Centrifugal or Lost-Wax Casting for Schools, Tradesmen, Craftsmen.* Forest Hills, N.Y.: Bovin, 1973.

Choate, Sharr. *Creative Casting: Jewelry, Silverware, Sculpture.* New York: Crown, 1966.

Clark, Carl D. *Molding and Casting: Its Technique and Application.* Butler, Md.: Standard Arts Press, 1972.

Heine, Richard W., et al. *Principles of Metal Casting.* New York: McGraw-Hill, 1967.

Pack, Greta. *Jewelry Making by the Lost-Wax Process.* New York: Van Nostrand Reinhold, 1968.

Story, Mickey. *Centrifugal Casting as a Jewelry Process.* Scranton, Pa.: International Textbook, 1963.

Electroplating and Electroforming

Blum, William, and George Hogaboom. *Principles of Electroplating and Electroforming.* New York: McGraw-Hill, 1949.

Gaida, B. *Electroplating Sciences.* New York: International Publications, 1971.

Lowenheim, Frederick. *Modern Electroplating.* New York: Wiley, 1963.

Ollard, Eric. *Introductory Electroplating.* New York: International Publications, 1971.

Spiro, Peter. *Electroforming.* New York: International Publications, 1971.

Yeates, R. L. *Electroplating: A Survey of Principles and Practice.* New York: International Publications, 1971.

Enameling

Ball, Fred. *Experimental Techniques in Enameling.* New York: Van Nostrand Reinhold, 1972.

Bates, Kenneth. *Enameling: Principles and Practice.* New York: World, 1951.

————. *The Enamelist.* New York: World, 1967.

Franklin, Geoffrey. *Simple Enameling.* New York: Watson-Guptill, 1971.

Neville, Kenneth. *The Craft of Enameling.* New York: Taplinger, 1966.

Seeler, Margaret. *The Art of Enameling.* New York: Van Nostrand Reinhold, 1969.

Taubes, Lili. *Basic Enameling.* New York: Pitman, 1970.

Thompson, Thomas E. *Enameling on Copper and Other Metals.* Highland Park, Ill.: Thompson, 1950.

Untract, Oppi. *Enameling on Metal.* Radnor, Pa.: Chilton, 1962.

Winter, Edward. *Enamel Art on Metals.* New York: Watson-Guptill, 1958.

Plastics

Cook, J. Gordon. *Your Guide to Plastics.* Watford, Herts. (Eng.): Merrow, 1968.

Hollander, Harry B. *Plastics for Artists and Craftsmen.* New York: Watson-Guptill, 1972.

————. *Plastics for Jewelry.* New York: Watson-Guptill, 1974.

Newman, Jay, and Lee Newman. *Plastics for the Craftsman: Basic Techniques for Working with Plastics.* New York: Crown, 1973.

Newman, Thelma. *Plastics as Design Form.* Philadelphia: Chilton, 1972.

Plastic as Plastic. New York: Museum of Contemporary Crafts, 1969.

Simmonds, Herbert R. *Source Book of the New Plastics.* New York: Reinhold, 1959.

Yarsley, V. E., and E. G. Couzens. *Plastics in the Modern World.* New York: Penguin, 1969.

Stones and Settings

Quick, Leland, and Hugh Leiper. *Gemcraft: How to Cut and Polish Gemstones.* Radnor, Pa.: Chilton, 1959.

Sanger, Arthur, and Lucille Sanger. *Cabochon Jewelry Making.* Peoria, Ill.: Bennett, 1951.

Sinkankas, A. *Gem Cutting: A Lapidary's Manual.* Princeton, N.J.: Van Nostrand, 1962.

Smith, G. F. H. *Gemstones.* London: Methuen, 1940.

Weinstein, Michael. *The World of Jewel Stones.* New York: Sheridan, 1958.

Periodicals

Artisan Crafts. Rte #4, Box 179F, Reed Springs, Mo. 65737. Quarterly.

Craft Horizons. American Crafts Council. 44 West 53 Street, New York, N.Y. 10019. Bimonthly.

Crafts. Crafts Advisory Committee. 12 Waterloo Place, London SW1Y 4AU, England. Bimonthly.

Design Quarterly. Walker Art Center. 1710 Lyndale Avenue South, Minneapolis, Minn. 55403. Quarterly.

The Journal of Contemporary Metalcraft, Casting, and Related Arts. Magic Circle Corp. 622 Western Avenue, Seattle, Wash. 98104. Quarterly.

The Working Craftsman (originally *Craft/Midwest*). Box 42, Northbrook, Ill. 60062. Quarterly.

Index

Photographic Sources

References are to Figure numbers unless indicated Pl. (plate).

Air-India, New York (43); Allcraft Tool and Supply Co., Hicksville, N.Y. (273, 277, 309, 322a); Carter Allen (216); American Crafts Council, New York (123, 131, 136–138, 140–141, 246); American Museum of Natural History, New York (75); Ib Andersen (160–162); Neil Anderson (469); L.F. Brown, Fort Collins, Colo. (120, 126, 209–210, 242, 332, 435–436); Ron Burton (Pl. 11); Caisse Nationale des Monuments Historiques, Paris (11); Craftool Co., Harbor City, Calif. (379); Bob Cramp (Pl. 4); Dreis and Krump, Chicago (311); Finelt Jewelry Casting Co., New York (407); Jan Fleischmann, Warsaw (186); Freer Gallery of Art, Smithsonian Institution, Washington, D.C. (5); George Gardner, Brooklyn, N.Y. (270, 274, 276, 286–287, 293, 329, 349, 353, 357, 363c–363d, 502, 505–509, 511, 518, 520–521, 527–534, 553); Gatto, J.A., Los Angeles (125); Paul H. Gesswein and Co., New York (322b, 355, 389, 450); Giraudon, Paris (515); Larry Gregory (Pl. 12); Hannibal, Athens (24); Bob Hanson, New York (69, 122, 127, 448, 504); Robert Harding Associates, London (13); Studio Hartland, Amsterdam (179); Hester and Associates, Dallas (143, 476); Hirmer Fotoarchiv, Munich (9, 22); Jelrus Technical Products Corp., New Hyde Park, N.Y. (406); Kennedy-Foster Co., Clifton, N.J. (579); Daniella Kerner (454–468); John King, New Canaan, Conn., and International Gem Corp., New York (Pl. 18); David Laplantz, Arcata, Calif. (129, 135, 234, 452); Lennart Larsen (15); K. Lindblom, Stockholm (167); Lisa Little, New York (72); Fotograf Ole Woldbye, Copenhagen (68); Metropolitan Museum of Art, New York (34); Günter Meyer, Pforzheim, W. Ger. (183); Minnesota Museum of Art, Saint Paul (110, 128, 132, 144–145); Museum of Modern Art, New York (89, 93–98); Ontario Research Foundation (272); Peck, Stow, and Wilcox Co., Southington, Conn. (350); Alexander Saunders Co., Cold Spring, N.Y. (405); Hank Simons (345–346, 474); Soprintendenza alle Antichità dell'Etruria, Florence (1); David Stormont (516); Sundahl, Trosa, Swed. (170, 198, 211, 213, 248, 252); Swest, Dallas (421, 449); Svend Thomsen, Hjørring, Den. (161); Charles Uht, New York (18, 70, 76); David Vine, New York (chapter openings); Wilkinson Co., Santa Monica, Calif. (422); Worshipful Company of Goldsmiths, London (154, 156).

Figures 574 and 575 have been redrawn from pictures supplied by Karlan and Fleicher, New York.

Cover photographs: Larry Gregory (*back, center*); Neil Hoffman (*back, left*); David Vine (title).